THE
WORLD ALMANAC
GUIDE TO

GOOD WORD
USAGE

THE
WORLD ALMANAC®
GUIDE TO

GOOD WORD
USAGE

EDITED BY

Martin H. Manser

with Jeffrey McQuain

INTRODUCTION BY

Edwin Newman

CONSULTANT EDITORS

Jonathon Green • Betty Kirkpatrick • John Silverlight

COMPILERS

Rosalind Fergusson • Jenny Roberts

WORLD ALMANAC
AN IMPRINT OF PHAROS BOOKS • A SCRIPPS HOWARD COMPANY
NEW YORK

Acknowledgments
The editor expresses his thanks to the following: Sarah
Peasley for help in compiling the text, Rosalind Desmond for
her careful checking, Margaret McPhee for advice on
Australian English, and Kathy Rooney, of Bloomsbury for
encouragement at every stage of the book's production.

First American edition.

First published in Great Britain in 1988 as *The Bloomsbury Good Word Guide.*

Library of Congress Cataloging-in-Publication Data:
The World almanac guide to good word usage / edited by Martin H.
Manser with Jeffrey McQuain; consultant editors, Jonathon Green,
Betty Kirkpatrick, John Silverlight; compilers, Rosalind Fergusson,
Jenny Roberts.—1st American ed.
    p. cm
  Orginally published: The Bloomsbury good word guide. England:
Bloomsbury Publishing, 1988.
  ISBN 0-88687-570-6: $19.95
  1. English language—Usage—Dictionaries. I. Manser, Martin H.
II. McQuain , Jeff, 1955- . III. Title: Bloomsbury good word
guide.
PE1460.W675 1989   89-33731
428' .003—dc20   CIP

Printed in the United States of America.

World Almanac
A Scripps Howard Company
200 Park Avenue
New York, NY 10166

10   9   8   7   6   5   4   3   2   1

INTRODUCTION

*We would like to share some important safety infor-
mation with you.*

The last time I heard that, from a flight attendant aboard an airliner about to take off from Los Angeles for New York, I had to
fight down the urge to abandon the flight. The urge became even
stronger when the pilot went on the intercom to announce that
weather conditions were unsettled, but "hopefully it won't be
too turbulent." Still I stayed in my seat, wondering whether, after
all these years, it was worth the trouble to wince at the pilot's
hopefully and trying to drive the misuse of *share* out of my mind.
Why do they want to *share* the information? Why not just give it
to us? Or simply say, "Here is some information about safety"?
Share used—or misused—in this way is becoming almost un-
avoidable. People are forever sharing their experiences with us, or
their observations, their wisdom, their thoughts. *Share,* in these
contexts, is a soppy word, carrying with it a phony and patronizing benevolence. Is it, however, wrong? Is it, as I have suggested,
not good usage?

These may not be the world's most pressing problems, but
good usage does matter. It helps us through life because it helps
us to be clear and specific in what we say, and to avoid misunder-
standings. It may well help to advance us in our occupations, and
perhaps most important (not important*ly*), it makes life more
pleasant and satisfying. Life is more rewarding when we frame
our thoughts in interesting ways—and more rewarding for others,
as well.

How do we decide what good word usage is? Why this usage
and not that? There is no central authority to which to appeal.
Even if there were, it is safe to say that it would have little effect.
The United States is not that kind of country, and American English is not that kind of language.

Decisions about usage are made by experts—grammarians and
dictionary editors—but not by them alone. Anyone who wants to
sound off about language is free to do so, and may even find himself being listened to. Actual practice itself is influential; that is,
what the generality of people write and say. The language is not
static. If what had immemorially been considered a mistake—
comprised of in place of *composed of* is an example—becomes sufficiently widespread, it may also become accepted. "Sufficiently
widespread" is, of course, vague. Just how widespread is suffi-

ciently widespread? Again, there is no formal or official way to decide such matters. A usage takes hold and that is that.

Consider an instance of how the language changes. Is *chair* acceptable in place of *chairman, chairwoman, chairperson*? Is *chair* permissible as a verb? If a dinner can be hosted, why cannot a meeting be chaired, and gaveled to order by the chair?

Or there is *charisma*. Is it possible for someone to have a small amount of charisma, or does that deny the very meaning of the word? And (see paragraph one) wasn't it the women's movement that made *flight attendants* of stewardesses?

This does not mean that whatever happens to be popular should never be resisted. I, for example, dislike and deplore the increasingly frequent use of *protest* in place of *protest against*. You will read, "The union protested the new work rules." You will hear, "Five hundred demonstrators lay down in the street to protest abortion." As I see it, that usage is wrong. Think of "She protested her innocence" and "Methinks he protesteth too much." Besides, what is wrong with complain, dislike, oppose, object to, regret, condemn, take exception to, reject, disagree, dissent, come out against? How long, however, do you hold out? That is the question, and it is the sort of question this book answers.

The book does much more than that. It spots the buzzwords (*share*, in the usage to which I objected earlier, is one of them) and it spots the jargon that makes so much American speech and writing turgid and overblown. Why, it may be asked, pay so much attention to buzzwords and jargon? Are they so objectionable? In my opinion, emphatically yes. Jargon is not necessarily bad in itself. Any occupation will develop a jargon; it serves as a form of shorthand for those in the know. It may, however, also be used to pump up what is being said, to give it the ring of importance and of technical knowledge, to suggest that some special qualifications are needed to understand what is being said. As for buzzwords, they are often used where they do not belong and are, at best, tiresome.

We all need a guide through the language. Some light their own way, but they are few and even they do not go entirely on their own. Martin Manser and Jeffrey McQuain are excellent guides. They are students of English and they are practical men, aware of what is going on in our language inside the halls of academe and outside. They offer sensible and immediately applicable advice. How should you pronounce *dissect*? Is it all right to say *enthuse*? Is the correct spelling *acknowledgment* or *acknowledgement*? What is the difference between a *calendar* and a *calender* and, for that matter, a *colander*? When is *can* called for, and when is *may*? What is the difference between *classic* and *classical*, *historical* and *historic*? Is it acceptable to use a singular verb with *media*, as in "The media is altogether too powerful"? When may *none* be used with a plural verb?

It is impossible to open *The World Almanac Guide to Good Word Usage* at any page without learning something useful and without being reminded of how marvelously interesting and entertaining our language is. That is a very considerable achievement.

Where there is ambiguity—between *could* and *might*, for example—Manser and McQuain are mentors or, if you like, ushers, not taskmasters. Is there a distinction to be drawn between *whatever* and *what ever*? As Casey Stengel used to say, "You could look it up." If Casey were still with us, he might have added, "in this book."

A personal crotchet: There is much talk these days about the twenty-first century and whether we will be ready for it, whether our institutions, our industry, our science, our agriculture will measure up to its demands. It is as though the world will be more exacting because the century has a different number. Manser and McQuain earn my gratitude by pointing out that the first century began January 1 of the year 1 A.D. It follows that the twentieth century will not end until December 31, 2000, and that the twenty-first century will begin on January 1, 2001. Not, repeat not, January 1, 2000, as the common assumption has it. Can those who can hardly wait to meet the challenges of the twenty-first century be restrained? This book may help to restrain them. If it does, it will be worth it for that alone.

—EDWIN NEWMAN

Guide to pronunciation

a as in bad
à as in arrest
ah as in father
air as in dare
ar as in carpet
àr as in burglar
aw as in saw
ay as in may
b as in bed
ch as in cheese
d as in dig
dh as in these
e as in get
ĕ as in open
ee as in see
eer as in here
er as in bird
ĕr as in butcher
ew as in few
ewr as in pure
f as in fit
g as in go
h as in hat
i as in it
ĭ as in pencil
ī as in try
j as in jam
k as in keep
kh as in loch
ks as in mix
kw as in quiz
l as in lie

m as in mad
n as in nod
ng as in sing
n(g) as in restaurant
o as in hot
ŏ as in cannon
ō as in no
oi as in boy
oo as in zoo
oor as in cure
or as in tore
ŏr as in doctor
ow as in now
p as in pat
r as in rim
rr as in marry
s as in sat
sh as in ship
t as in take
th as in thin
u as in up
ŭ as in crocus
uu as in push
v as in van
w as in water
y as in yes
yoo as in unite
yoor as in Europe
yr as in tire
z as in zoo
zh as in treasure

Stressed syllables are shown in italics: [*sis*tĕr].

How to use this book

Entries, listed in a single alphabetical ordering, cover five main areas of the English language:

spelling

> **accommodation** The word *accommodation* is often misspelled. Note the double *c* and double *m*.

pronunciation

> **controversy** In the traditional pronunciation of this word, the stress falls on the first syllable [*kont*rŏversee]. The variant pronunciation, with stress on the second syllable [kŏn*trov*ĕrsi], is heard but is disliked by many users. See also STRESS.

grammar and punctuation

> **participles** All verbs have *present participles*, which are formed with *-ing*: □ *seeing* □ *walking*, and *past participles*, formed with *-d* or *-ed* for regular verbs and in other ways for irregular verbs: □ *loved* □ *finished* □ *given* □ *gone* □ *thought*.
> • Participles are often used as adjectives: □ *broken promises* □ *a leaking tap*. They are also used, with an inversion of the usual sentence construction, to introduce a sentence such as: □ *Sitting in the corner was an old man.* □ *Attached to his wrist was a luggage label.* Care should be taken with such introductory participles, because they are sometimes used to link items that are quite unrelated: see DANGLING PARTICIPLES.

> **period** The principal use of the period as a punctuation mark is to end a sentence that is neither a direct question nor an exclamation.
> • See also EXCLAMATION POINT; QUESTION MARK; SENTENCES.
> In creative writing, reference books, etc., the period may also mark the end of a group of words not conforming to the conventional description of a sentence: □ *He had four drinks. Four very large drinks.*
> A period is also used in decimals: □ *3.6 yards of silk.* Periods are also used in many ABBREVIATIONS.
> A period is sometimes called a *stop*, a *point*, or (in British English) a *full stop.*
> See also BRACKETS; QUOTATION MARKS; SEMICOLONS.

usage

> **complement or supplement?** *Complement* and *supplement* have a distinct difference in meaning. Both as noun and as verb, *complement* suggests the addition of something necessary to make something whole or complete: □ *The closings were forced by the hospital's inability to recruit 92 nurses out of its full complement of nearly 800* (Daily Telegraph, June 3, 1987). □ *The music complemented the mime aptly.* *Supplement* suggests an addition to something that is already complete: □ *Her fees for private tuition supplemented her teacher's salary.* □ *Most Sunday newspapers publish a color supplement.*

buzzwords—vogue expressions, often originally from specialist subjects

> **interface** In science, computing, etc., the noun *interface* denotes a surface forming a common boundary or a point of communication. Its extended use as a synonym for "interaction," "liaison," "link," "(point of) contact," etc., is disliked by many people: □ *the interface between professionals and lay people in the caring professions* □ *the interface of history and literature* □ *at the interface between design and technology.*
> • The verb *interface* is also best restricted to technical contexts: □ *The office microcomputers will interface with the main computer.*

Most entries are divided into two parts. The first part gives a concise statement of the main points of the word's usage, pronunciation, spelling, etc. The second part, printed on a new line after a •, gives additional explanatory information.

> **fraction** Some people dislike the use of a fraction to mean "a small part" or "a little": □ *We flew there in a fraction of the time it takes to go by sea.* □ *Could you turn the volume down a fraction, please?*
> • A fraction is not necessarily a small part of the whole: nine-tenths is a fraction.
>   To avoid possible ambiguity or misunderstanding, express a small fraction clearly as such: □ *Why dine out when you can eat at home for a small fraction of the cost?* □ *Only a small fraction of the work has been completed.*

Examples of the use of words are preceded by □ . Many of the examples are drawn from actual quotations of contemporary usage.

> **flagship** The noun *flagship*, which denotes the ship that carries the commander of a fleet, is increasingly used in figurative contexts with reference to the most important of a group of products, projects, services, etc.: □ *Whenever they've got some morning grocery shopping to do, they head off to one of Randall's flagship stores in Houston* (*Newsweek*, June 27, 1988). □ *The [Laura Ashley] company has recently opened a furnishing store in Madison Avenue, New York* (*The Bookseller*, June 19, 1987).

Indications of incorrect usages are sometimes shown to contrast with the correct forms.

> **your** or **you're?** These two words may be confused. *Your* means "belonging to you": □ *your house* □ *your rights.* *You're* is an abbreviation of *you are:* □ *Hurry up, you're going to be late!*
> • Note also the spelling of *yours:* □ *That's mine, not yours;* the spelling with an apostrophe, *your's,* is wrong.

A distinction is made between the use of many words in informal and formal contexts.

> **affect** or **effect?** The noun *effect* means "result"; the verb *affect* means "influence" or "have an effect on," hence its frequent

confusion with the verb *effect*, which means "bring about" or "accomplish": □ *The new legislation may have an effect on small businesses.* □ *The new legislation may affect small businesses.* □ *We have effected a number of improvements.*

> • The verb *effect* is largely restricted to formal contexts. The verb *affect* is also used in the sense of "assume," "pretend," or "feign": □ *I affected an air of indifference.* □ *She affected to despise them.* □ *He affected ignorance.*

incredible or incredulous? *Incredible* means "unbelievable"; *incredulous* means "disbelieving": □ *He told her an incredible story.* □ *She looked at him with an incredulous expression.*
> • The use of the adjective *incredible* in the sense of "wonderful" or "amazing" should be restricted to informal contexts: □ *We had an incredible holiday.* See also CREDIBLE, CREDITABLE, OR CREDULOUS?

Differences between American English and British English spelling, usage, etc., are highlighted.

fulfill Note the spelling of this word and the derived noun *fulfillment*, with the second *l* doubled.
> • In British English neither *l* is doubled in *fulfil* or *fulfilment*, however, the final *l* of the verb is doubled in British English before a suffix beginning with a vowel, as in *fulfilled* and *fulfilling* (see also SPELLING 1).

At many entries, advice is given to avoid overusing a particular word or expression.

aggravate The use of the verb *aggravate* and its derivatives in the sense of "annoy," "irritate," or "exasperate" dates back to the early 17th century but is still disliked by some people. It is therefore best restricted to informal contexts and the offending word replaced by one of its synonyms: □ *I was aggravated by the noise.* □ *She has a number of aggravating habits.* □ *His lackadaisical attitude is a constant source of aggravation.*

Cross-references are used to show where an entry may be found or where there is additional information.

compliment see COMPLEMENT OR COMPLIMENT?

government In the sense of the "group of people who govern a country, state, etc.," *government* is usually a singular noun: □ *The government is blamed for the rise in unemployment.* It is considered plural in British English: □ *The government have rejected the proposal.*
> • See also COLLECTIVE NOUNS; SINGULAR OR PLURAL?

xi

THE
WORLD ALMANAC
GUIDE TO

GOOD WORD
USAGE

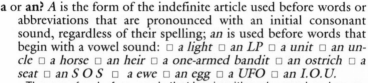

a or an? *A* is the form of the indefinite article used before words or abbreviations that are pronounced with an initial consonant sound, regardless of their spelling; *an* is used before words that begin with a vowel sound: □ *a light* □ *an LP* □ *a unit* □ *an uncle* □ *a horse* □ *an heir* □ *a one-armed bandit* □ *an ostrich* □ *a seat* □ *an S O S* □ *a ewe* □ *an egg* □ *a UFO* □ *an I.O.U.*

• The use of *an* before words that begin with an *h* sound and an unstressed first syllable, such as *hotel, historic, hereditary, habitual,* etc., is optional. Nowadays, the preference is increasingly to use *a* followed by *hotel,* etc., with the *h* sounded, rather than *an* followed by *hotel,* etc., with the *h* not pronounced.

A and *an* are usually unstressed, pronounced [ă] and [an]. The pronunciation [ay] is used only for emphasis: □ *He told you to take a biscuit, not the whole plateful!* In this example *a* would be pronounced [ay].

abbreviations Abbreviations are useful space-saving devices. They are used heavily both in informal writing and in technical or specialized writing, but less in formal writing. Some abbreviations stand for more than one thing, and it is better to spell these out unless the context makes the meaning clear. □ *He was a C.O. in the war* is confusing, as the abbreviation means "commanding officer" and "conscientious objector."

• The main problems with abbreviations concern punctuation. The modern tendency is to omit periods whenever possible: □ *NBC* □ *NATO,* and so on. Periods are rarely omitted from capitalized abbreviations: □ *U.S.A.* □ *E.E.C.,* but they are often omitted from acronyms: □ *NATO* □ *UNESCO.* When an abbreviation is a contraction (i.e., the final letter of the abbreviation corresponds with the final letter of the word), there is usually a period: □ *Mr.* □ *Dr.* □ *Rd.* There is also a period when the abbreviation is just the first part of the word: □ *Rev.* □ *Feb.,* although here the British trend is to leave out the period. Abbreviated names take periods: □ *C.S. Lewis* □ *J.F.K.* There should be no period if a capital letter does not stand for a whole word: one should not write *T.V.* (television) as *tele-* is not a complete word. There are usually periods in the abbreviations of weights and measures: □ *lb.* □ *in.* but never for chemical symbols: □ *Fe* □ *Cu.*

Apostrophes are no longer used for shortened forms that are in general use: □ *bus* □ *flu* □ *phone* □ *photo* □ *vet.*

Most abbreviations form their plurals with *'s:* □ *M.D.'s* □ *Ph.D.'s.* A few abbreviations form their plurals by doubling: □ *pp.* (pages) □ *ll.* (lines).

1

Most abbreviations (except for acronyms) are pronounced by spelling out the letters. When preceded by the indefinite article, those abbreviations that begin with a vowel sound take *an:* □ *an I.R.S. audit* □ *an E.S.P. test* and those beginning with a consonant sound take *a:* □ *a B.A.* □ *a U.S.S.R. study.*
See also **ACRONYMS.**

aberration This word, meaning "deviation from the norm": □ *a temporary mental aberration,* is sometimes misspelled. Note the spelling: a single *b* and a double *r.*

ability see **CAPABILITY, CAPACITY, OR ABILITY?**

-able or **-ible?** Both forms of this suffix are added to words to form adjectives, *-able* being the suffix that is productive and the more frequently used: □ *washable* □ *comfortable* □ *collapsible.*
• The form *-able* is always used for words composed of other English words: □ *drinkable; -ible* is used for some words of Latin origin: □ *credible* □ *defensible.*
On whether to retain the silent final *-e* in words such as *lik(e)able,* see **SPELLING 3.**

about see **AROUND OR ABOUT?**

above or **over?** The preposition *above* means "at a higher level than"; *over* means "vertically or directly above," "on top of," or "across": □ *He raised his hand above his head.* □ *She held the umbrella over her head.* □ *There's a mark on the wall above the radiator.* □ *I've put my towel over the radiator.* □ *The airplane flew above the clouds.* □ *The airplane flew over Southampton.*
• In many contexts the two words are interchangeable: □ *Hang the picture above/over the mantelpiece.* □ *Our bedroom is above/over the kitchen.*
The use of *above* as a noun or adjective, with reference to something previously mentioned, is disliked by some users but acceptable to most: □ *You will need several items in addition to the above.* □ *Please quote the above reference number on all correspondence.*

abridgment or **abridgement?** This word, meaning "a shortened version of a work such as a book," may be spelled *abridgment* or *abridgement.* Either spelling is acceptable, but *abridgment* is preferred.

abscess This word, meaning "a collection of pus surrounded by inflamed tissue," is often misspelled. Note the *sc* at the beginning of the second syllable.

abuse or **misuse?** The noun *abuse* denotes wrong, improper, or bad use or treatment; the noun *misuse,* denoting incorrect or unorthodox use, is more neutral: □ *the abuse of power* □ *child abuse* □ *the misuse of words* □ *misuse of the club's funds.*
• The same distinction applies to the verbs *abuse* and *misuse:* □ *to abuse a privilege* □ *to misuse one's time.*
In some contexts the two words are interchangeable: □ *Mr. Douglas Hogg, the Home Office minister who chairs the ministerial group on the misuse of drugs . . . Miss Mary Tracey, of the Standing Conference on Drug Abuse (Daily Telegraph, September 30, 1987).* □ *He predicted that it would not lead to an upsurge in alcohol misuse. . . . But Action on Alcohol Abuse attacked the move at a time of increased medical concern about excessive drinking (Daily Telegraph, Aug. 5, 1987).*

The word *abuse* also refers to insulting language: □ *The president was abused by the crowd.* □ *The pickets shouted abuse at the strikebreakers.*

As in the word *use,* the final [s] sound of the nouns *abuse* [ăbews] and *misuse* [misews] changes to [z] in the verbs.

abysmal This word, meaning "very bad; dreadful": □ *abysmal weather,* is sometimes misspelled. The word comes from *abyss,* hence the *y* in the spelling.

academic The adjective *academic* is widely used in the sense of "theoretical": □ *an academic question* □ *of academic interest only,* but some people object to its frequent use in place of *irrelevant:* □ *Whether he wins this race or not is academic, because he is already several points ahead of his nearest rival.*

accelerate The word *accelerate,* meaning "speed up," is sometimes misspelled. Note the double *c* but a single *l.*

accents Accents are sometimes used on words that are now accepted into English, though the tendency is increasingly to omit them.

• Accents are generally used when they show the pronunciation of the word: the cedilla in *façade* shows that the *c* is soft; the acute accent on *cliché* shows that the word is pronounced [klee*shay*] not [kleesh]. A circumflex accent on the *o* of *role* is unnecessary and is usually omitted.

access The use of the word *access* as a verb is best restricted to the field of computing, where it means "gain access to (stored information or a computer memory)": □ *Booksellers can already access teleordering computer to computer or through Prestel viewdata* (*The Bookseller,* May 15, 1987).

• The extended use of the verb in general contexts is disliked by many users: □ *We often receive requests to "access" our membership lists and these are almost always refused* (*Club Lotus News,* 1987, Issue No. 3).

accessory or **accessary?** The spelling of this word in the sense "supplementary attachment" is *accessory:* □ *car accessories.*

• In the legal sense of "a person who incites another to commit a crime," the spelling is also *accessory, accessary* being an older variant: □ *an accessory before the fact.*

accommodation The word *accommodation* is often misspelled. Note the double *c* and double *m.*

accountable The adjective *accountable,* meaning "answerable," should be applied only to people: □ *Union leaders are accountable to the rank-and-file members.* □ *We were accountable for their welfare.*

• In other contexts the adjective is often better replaced by its synonym *responsible:* □ *An unexpected fall in demand was responsible* [not *accountable*] *for the company's financial problems.*

The noun *accountability* is best avoided where *responsibility* would be adequate or more appropriate: □ *the individual responsibilities* [not *accountabilities*] *of the directors.*

acetic or **ascetic?** These words are sometimes confused. *Acetic* acid is the main substance in vinegar. A person who practices self-denial is known as an *ascetic.*

acknowledgment or **acknowledgement?** This word may be spelled with or without the *e* after the *g;* either spelling is acceptable, but *acknowledgment* is preferred.

A

acoustics The word *acoustics* is often misspelled, the most frequent error being the doubling of the first *c*.
• For the use of *acoustics* as a singular or plural noun, see -ICS.

acquaint The verb *acquaint* is best avoided where *tell* would be adequate or more appropriate: □ *He acquainted me with his plans,* for example, may be more simply expressed as *He told me his plans.*
• The passive form *be acquainted with* can often be replaced by *know:* □ *I am not acquainted with the rules.*
Note the spelling of *acquaint* and its derivatives, particularly the presence and position of the letter *c*.

acquirement or **acquisition?** In the sense of "something acquired," the rare *acquirement* is largely restricted to abilities or skills and *acquisition,* the more frequent word, to material things or people: □ *Fluency in spoken and written Japanese is one of her many acquirements.* □ *He showed me his latest acquisition.*
• Either noun may be used to denote the act of acquiring: □ *the acquirement/acquisition of knowledge* □ *the acquisition/acquirement of wealth,* but *acquisition* is preferred.

acronyms An acronym is a word formed from the initial letters or syllables of other words: □ *OPEC* (Organization of Petroleum Exporting Countries) □ *radar* (radio detecting and ranging).
• The punctuation of acronyms varies. The usual style is capitals without periods: □ *WHO* □ *SEATO,* although some of the better-known acronyms are sometimes seen with only an initial capital: □ *NATO/Nato* □ *AIDS/Aids.* Acronyms that refer to some piece of technical equipment, rather than an organization: □ *sonar* (sound navigation and ranging) □ *radar* □ *laser* (light amplification by stimulated emission of radiation) □ *scuba* (self-contained underwater breathing apparatus), become so accepted that they are written in lowercase letters like ordinary words, and many people do not even realize that these are acronyms. Other acronyms have become so popular that it is rare to hear their full names: □ *MASH* □ *AWOL.*
Recently there has been a tendency to make acronyms correspond with actual English words: □ *SALT* (Strategic Arms Limitation Talks) □ *WASP* (White Anglo-Saxon Protestant). The more appropriate the word to the subject, the better: □ *MADD* (Mothers Against Drunk Driving) □ *NOW* (National Organization for Women). It sometimes seems almost as though organizations and systems are made to fit the acronyms, rather than vice versa: □ *SPELL* (Society for the Preservation of English Language and Literature) □ *In 1984, Holmes, the Home Office Large Major Enquiry System was set up. In spite of its name, Holmes is not an electronic version of the master detective, but a means of investigating crimes through computers* (The Times of London, Sept. 7, 1987).

acrylic This word is sometimes misspelled. Note particularly the *yl,* not *il,* in the middle of the word.

act or **action?** Each of these nouns means "something done," but *action* tends to emphasize the process of doing whereas *act* denotes the deed itself: □ *Terrorist action has increased.* □ *It was an act of terrorism.*
• The British use of the word action as a verb, meaning "take action on" or "put into action," is disliked by many people, including

Fritz Spiegl (*Daily Telegraph,* Aug. 19, 1987), who criticized "the many new verbs spawned by the Caring Industry. They no longer do things. They 'action' them."

actualize The verb *actualize,* meaning "make actual," is disliked by some users as an example of the increasing tendency to coin new verbs by adding the suffix *-ize* to nouns and adjectives: □ *They have actualized their plans.*

• See also -IZE OR -ISE?

actually Many people object to the frequent use of the adverb *actually* where it adds nothing to the meaning of the sentence: □ *Actually, I prefer coffee to tea.* □ *We weren't actually very impressed by his performance.* □ *She doesn't live here, actually.*

• In some contexts, however, *actually* may serve the useful purpose of contrasting what is actual or real with what is theoretical or apparent: □ *I know how to make a soufflé, but I've never actually made one.* □ *It sounds difficult, but it's actually quite easy.*

See also IN FACT.

acumen In the traditional pronunciation of this word, which means "the ability to make good judgments": □ *sound business acumen,* the stress falls on the second syllable [ăkyoomĕn]. The pronunciation with the stress on the first syllable [akyoomĕn] is, however, more frequently heard.

A.D. and **B.C.** The abbreviation *A.D.,* which stands for *Anno Domini,* is traditionally placed before the year number; *B.C.,* which stands for *before Christ,* always follows the year number: □ *The custom dates back to A.D. 1462.* □ *The city was destroyed in 48 B.C.*

• In modern usage *A.D.* sometimes follows the year number: □ *The battle took place in 1127 A.D.*

It is strictly tautological to precede *A.D.* with *in,* since *Anno Domini* literally means "in the year of the Lord," but the omission of *in* is generally considered to be unidiomatic: □ *He died in A.D. 1042.*

B.C. and *A.D.* are also applied to centuries, although the use of *A.D.* for this purpose is disliked by some people and is often unnecessary: □ *since the fourth century B.C.* □ *until the ninth century A.D.*

The abbreviations are always written in capital letters (small capitals are sometimes used in printed texts), with or without periods (see also ABBREVIATIONS).

adjectives An adjective is a word that provides information about a noun: □ *fat* □ *blue* □ *happy* □ *intelligent* □ *dirty.* The main division of adjectives corresponds to the position that they take. Attributive adjectives come before a noun: □ *a stupid boy.* Predicative adjectives follow a verb: □ *The sky is gray.* Postpositive adjectives follow a noun: □ *the chairman elect.*

• Of course, some adjectives can be used in all three positions: □ *a long walk* □ *the sides are long* □ *two yards long.* Most can be used attributively and predicatively: □ *sweet tea* □ *The tea is sweet.* Some adjectives can only be attributive: one says: □ *the principal reason,* not *The reason is principal.* Some can only be predicative: one says: □ *The baby is awake,* but not *the awake baby.* Some are used only in the postpositive position: □ *There were drinks galore.*

Nouns can sometimes be used attributively as adjectives: □ *a glass bowl* □ *a Meissen plate* □ *cotton shirts,* and adjectives can be used as nouns: □ *the poor* □ *the blind* □ *the quick and the dead.* Adjectives are occasionally used in the place of adverbs: □ *They sell their goods dear.* Such words as: □ *fast* □ *late* □ *early* function as both adjectives and adverbs.

Such adjectives as: □ *entire* □ *extreme* □ *total* □ *unique,* cannot be used in the comparative or superlative, and cannot be modified by words like *very, utterly,* or *totally.* Some can, however, be modified by *almost* or *nearly:* □ *an almost total disaster* □ *a nearly perfect round.* Other adjectives are generally not to be modified in any way: □ *a postgraduate student* □ *a deciduous tree* □ *the pregnant woman,* but it is occasionally possible to modify such an adjective for effect: □ *He looked very dead.*

The overuse of adjectives should be avoided, particularly when they are tautologous: □ *true facts* □ *wet liquid* (see **TAUTOLOGY**). Care should be taken with choice of adjectives, and the less informative ones should be avoided. *He's a nice man* tells one very little about a man; he might be *good-natured, sympathetic, witty, attractive, respectable,* or none of these. Long strings of adjectives should also be avoided in ordinary speech or writing unless they are needed for a precise description: □ *a small brown one-eyed mongrel.* In poetry several adjectives can be used to good effect: □ *A poor, weak, palsy-stricken, churchyard thing* (Keats).

See also **COMPARATIVE AND SUPERLATIVE; NOUNS.**

adjourn This word, which means "stop for a short time" and "go," is sometimes misspelled. Note the *d* and the *jour,* as in *journey.*

administer or **administrate?** Either verb may be used in the sense of "manage," "supervise," "control," or "direct," with reference to the work of an administrator: □ *She has administered/administrated the company since the death of her father.*

• *Administer* also means "give," "apply," or "dispense": □ *to administer first aid* □ *to administer justice. Administrate* is not used in such contexts.

admission or **admittance?** Each of these nouns means "permission or right to enter." *Admission* is the more frequent, *admittance* being largely restricted to formal or official contexts: □ *Admission is by ticket only.* □ *No admittance.* □ *He presents the picture of a boy for whom an early admission could well be advantageous. . . . Education officials say they blocked his admittance because class sizes at the school were too large (Sunday Times,* Aug. 23, 1987).

• Of the two words, only *admission* may be used to denote the price charged or a fee paid for entrance.

The noun *admission* also means "confession" or "acknowledgment": □ *an admission of guilt* □ *by her own admission.*

admit In the sense of "confess" or "acknowledge," *admit* is generally used as a transitive verb: □ *He admitted his mistake.* □ *I admitted that I had lied.* □ *Do you admit writing this letter?*

• The insertion of the preposition *to* in such contexts is disliked by some users: □ *He admitted to his mistake.* □ *Do you admit to writing this letter?*

Admit is followed by *to* in the sense of "allow to enter" or "give access": □ *We were not admitted to the club.* □ *This gate admits to the garden.* In the formal sense of "be open to" or "leave room for," *admit* is followed by *of:* □ *The phrase does not admit of a different interpretation.*

admittance see ADMISSION OR ADMITTANCE?

adolescence This word is sometimes misspelled. Note particularly the *sc* and the *nc.*

adopted or **adoptive?** The adjective *adopted* is applied to children who have been adopted; *adoptive* relates to adults who adopt another person's child: □ *their adopted daughter* □ *her adoptive parents.*
• Careful users maintain the distinction between the two words.

adult The noun *adult* is usually stressed on the second syllable, but the pronunciation [adŭlt] is heard more frequently than [ădult] in British English.

• The adjective *adult,* which principally means "mature" or "of or for adults": □ *an adult approach* □ *adult education,* is often used as a euphemism for "pornographic": □ *adult videos* □ *an adult film.* □ *Adult Theaters* (film listing, *The Washington Post,* Jan. 6, 1989).

adverbs Adverbs modify other parts of speech and answer questions such as how? (adverbs of manner): □ *quietly* □ *greedily,* when? (adverbs of time): □ *then* □ *tomorrow,* where? (adverbs of place): □ *there* □ *outside.*
• They can modify verbs: □ *She wrote neatly,* adjectives: □ *extremely hot,* other adverbs: □ *fairly well,* whole clauses or sentences: □ *Anyway, it doesn't matter now,* or can be used to link clauses: □ *I dislike him; nevertheless, I feel responsible for him.* Adverbs are frequently formed by adding -*ly* to an adjective: □ *darkly* □ *wisely,* but this does not apply to all adverbs: □ *therefore* □ *quite* □ *upstairs* □ *not.*

It is usually acceptable to place an adverb between parts of a verb: □ *I have often spoken about the matter,* but adverbs should not come between a verb and its direct object. Whether the adverb is positioned after the object or before the verb depends on the length of the object clause: □ *They tortured the prisoners cruelly.* □ *They cruelly tortured the political prisoners who had been arrested for demonstrating against the regime.* Careful positioning of the adverb is sometimes necessary in order to avoid ambiguity in a sentence: □ *She disliked intensely sentimental films.* If *intensely* goes with *disliked,* it should be placed before the verb.
See also ADJECTIVES; SPLIT INFINITIVE.

adversary The pronunciation of this word with stress on the second syllable [ădversăree] is disliked by many users, who prefer the traditional pronunciation with stress on the first syllable [advĕrsăree]. See also STRESS.

adverse or **averse?** *Adverse,* meaning "unfavorable," "antagonistic," or "hostile," usually precedes an abstract noun; *averse,* meaning "disinclined," "unwilling," or "having a strong dislike," usually relates to people and is never placed before the noun it qualifies: □ *adverse criticism* □ *an adverse effect* □ *These working conditions are adverse to efficiency.* □ *The committee was not averse to the proposal.* □ *Her father is not averse to using violence.* □ *They are averse to all publicity.*
• The two adjectives are sometimes confused in the sense of "opposed."

Averse is often preceded by *not* and may be followed by *to* or, more rarely, *from, to* being preferred in modern usage.

Adverse may be stressed on either syllable, but the pronunciation [adˈvers] is less frequent than [ˈădvers]. *Averse* is always stressed on the second syllable [ăˈvers].

advertise This word, meaning "promote or publicize": □ *a brochure advertising vacations*, is sometimes misspelled. This is one of the words ending -*ise* that cannot be spelled -*ize*; see also -IZE OR -ISE?

advise The use of the verb *advise* as a synonym for "tell," "inform," "notify," etc., is best avoided in general usage: □ *Please advise us of your new address.* □ *I told* [not *advised*] *him that the meeting had been canceled.*
• The *s* of *advise* should not be replaced by *z* in American or British English. See also COUNSEL OR ADVISE?; -IZE OR -ISE?

adviser or **advisor?** This word, meaning "person who gives advice," may be spelled either *adviser* or *advisor*. Either spelling is acceptable, but *adviser* is preferred.

aerial This word, meaning "of the air; from an aircraft" and "device that receives or sends out broadcast signals," is sometimes misspelled. Note particularly the *ae*- at the beginning of this word.

aero see AIR OR AERO?

affect or **effect?** The noun *effect* means "result"; the verb *affect* means "influence" or "have an effect on," hence its frequent confusion with the verb *effect*, which means "bring about" or "accomplish": □ *The new legislation may have an effect on small businesses.* □ *The new legislation may affect small businesses.* □ *We have effected a number of improvements.*
• The verb *effect* is largely restricted to formal contexts. The verb *affect* is also used in the sense of "assume," "pretend," or "feign": □ *I affected an air of indifference.* □ *She affected to despise them.* □ *He affected ignorance.*

affinity The use of the preposition *for* with the noun *affinity*, in the sense of "liking" or "attraction," is disliked by some users but acceptable to most: □ *He has a natural affinity for young children.*
• Those who object to this usage restrict the noun to the meaning "reciprocal relationship or similarity," in which sense it is followed by *between* or *with*: □ *the affinity between the two friends* □ *her affinity with her brother.*

afflict or **inflict?** To *afflict* is to distress or trouble; to *inflict* is to impose: □ *He afflicted the prisoners with cruel torture.* □ *He inflicted cruel torture on the prisoners.* □ *Egypt was afflicted with a plague of locusts.* □ *A plague of locusts was inflicted on Egypt.*
• The direct object of *afflict* is the sufferer; the direct object of *inflict* is the suffering. The two verbs should not be confused.

afterward or **afterwards?** *Afterward* is the usual form of the adverb meaning "subsequently," the variant *afterwards* being more frequently used in British English: □ *I'll do the cleanup afterward.* □ *His foot was sore for days afterward.*
• See also -WARD OR -WARDS?

again This word may be pronounced either [ăˈgen] or [ăˈgayn]. The first of these is the more frequently used.

aged This word is pronounced [ˈayjid] in the sense "very old": □ *his aged uncle* □ *looking after the aged.* When the word is used with a specific age: □ *She was aged twenty,* it is pronounced [ayjd].

ageing see AGING OR AGEING?

agenda The word *agenda* is now used as a singular noun, with the plural form *agendas:* □ The agenda for tomorrow's meeting has been changed. □ *This item has appeared on a number of previous agendas.*
• Originally the plural form of the singular noun *agendum, agenda* literally means "things to be done." The singular form *agendum* remains in occasional very formal use in the sense of "item on the agenda."

aggravate The use of the verb *aggravate* and its derivatives in the sense of "annoy," "irritate," or "exasperate" dates back to the early 17th century but is still disliked by some people. It is therefore best restricted to informal contexts and the offending word replaced by one of its synonyms: □ *I was aggravated by the noise.* □ *She has a number of aggravating habits.* □ *His lackadaisical attitude is a constant source of aggravation.*
• The principal meaning of *aggravate* is "make worse": □ *Your resignation will aggravate our problem.* □ *The child's suffering was aggravated by the intense heat.*

aggressive The use of the adjective *aggressive* in the sense of "assertive" or "forceful" is best avoided where there is a risk of confusion with its principal meaning of "belligerent" or "hostile": □ *an aggressive salesman* □ *an aggressive approach.*
• The derived noun *aggressiveness* may be used for both senses of the adjective, but *aggression,* with its connotations of hostility, should be restricted to the principal meaning: □ *the aggressiveness of the salesman's approach* □ *an act of aggression.*

aging or **ageing?** The preferred spelling of this word, meaning "(the process of) becoming old," is *aging.*

ago or **since?** It is wrong to place *ago* and *since* side by side: □ *It was a week ago that* [not *since*] *I posted the letter.* □ *It is a week* [not *a week ago*] *since I posted the letter.*
• Note that *ago* is preceded by the past tense and *since* by the present tense in sentences of this type. The first example could be more simply expressed as: □ *I posted the letter a week ago.* The adverbial use of *since* for this purpose: □ *I posted the letter a week since,* is regarded as very old-fashioned.
    The word *since* is also used as a preposition: □ *We have lived here since 1984.* If a period of time rather than a specific time is mentioned, the preposition *for* should be substituted for *since:* □ *We have lived here for three years.*

agoraphobia This word, describing a fear of open spaces, is sometimes misspelled. Note the *o* after the *ag-.*
• The word originates from the Greek word *agora,* "marketplace."

aid The noun *aid* is specifically used to denote a tangible source of help, assistance, or support, such as a device: □ *hearing aid* □ *teaching aids* □ *audiovisual aids,* or money, supplies, equipment, etc., given to those in need: □ *overseas aid.*
• In the second sense the word has been used in a series of fundraising campaigns inspired by the rock musicians of *Band Aid* (1984) and the immensely successful rock concert *Live Aid* (1985): □ *Prince Charles has shelved plans to raise millions for Britain's poorest areas . . . Inner City Aid, the charity he helped launch last*

A

year as "Band Aid for the inner cities," has stopped campaigning (*Sunday Times*, Oct. 4, 1987).

The noun *aid* also occurs in certain fixed expressions, such as *legal aid, first aid*, and *in aid of*, but its use as a general synonym for "help," "assistance," or "support" is disliked and avoided by many users.

ain't As a contraction of *are not, is not, have not*, or *has not, ain't* is wrong. It is, however, widely used in speech and in such jocular expressions as: □ *Things ain't what they used to be.* □ *You ain't heard nothing yet.*

• As a contraction of *am not*, ain't is regarded by some users as slightly more acceptable, especially in informal English in the interrogative form *ain't I*, which is replaced in British English by the grammatically irregular *aren't I* and in formal contexts by the full form *am I not*.

air or **aero?** Either of these words may be used adjectivally or as prefixes in the sense of "relating to airplanes or aircraft": □ *aerodynamics* □ *airliner* □ *aerodrome* □ *airport* □ *aeronautics* □ *the air force* □ *aerospace* □ *airspace*.

• In some British words the prefix *air-* is replaced by *aero-*: the noun *airplane*, for example, is rendered as *aeroplane* in British English.

aisle This word is sometimes misspelled, the most frequent mistake being the omission of the silent *s*.

alibi The use of the noun *alibi* as a synonym for "excuse" or "pretext" is disliked by many people and is best restricted to informal contexts: □ *He used the power failure as an alibi for not finishing his essay.* □ *Her illness provided her with an alibi to leave early.*

• The word *alibi*, which literally means "elsewhere," is principally used in law to denote a defendant's plea (or evidence) that he or she was somewhere other than the scene of a crime: □ *I have an alibi for the afternoon of the robbery—I was at a conference in Birmingham.*

align This word, meaning "bring or come into line; support," is sometimes misspelled. Note the single *l* and also the silent *g*.

all The use of the preposition *of* between *all* and *the, this, that, these, those*, or a possessive adjective is optional, *all of* being preferred in American English and *all* in British English: □ *All (of) the birds have flown away.* □ *I can't carry all (of) that.* □ *Do all (of) these books belong to you?* □ *All (of) her children are right-handed.* □ *They spent all (of) their leave in France.*

• *All* is used alone before nouns that are not preceded by *the, these, my, their*, etc.: □ *All birds have wings.* □ *All leaves have been canceled. All of* is always used before personal pronouns: □ *all of us* □ *all of it*. See also **ALL RIGHT** OR **ALRIGHT?**; **ALTOGETHER** OR **ALL TOGETHER?**; **NOT**.

all right or **alright?** The spelling *all right* is correct; the spelling *alright* is wrong.

• Some users defend the spelling *alright*, arguing that *altogether* and *already* are analogous spellings. Such users want to distinguish *alright*, "satisfactory or acceptable": □ *The play was alright for children*, and *all right*: □ *The answers were all right*, i.e., all the answers were right.

all together see **ALTOGETHER** OR **ALL TOGETHER?**

allude The verb *allude* means "refer indirectly"; it should not be

A

used in place of the verb *refer* itself: □ *He was alluding to the death of his father when he spoke of the loss of a lifelong friend.* □ *She referred* [not *alluded*] *to "the specter of layoffs" in her speech on unemployment.*
• *Allude* should not be confused with *elude* (see AVOID, EVADE, OR ELUDE?) See also ALLUSION, ILLUSION, OR DELUSION?; ALLUSIVE, ELUSIVE, OR ILLUSIVE?

allusion, illusion, or **delusion?** An *allusion* is an indirect reference (see ALLUDE); an *illusion* is a false or misleading impression or perception; a *delusion* is a false or mistaken idea or belief: □ *an allusion to his schooldays* □ *an optical illusion* □ *to destroy one's illusions* □ *delusions of grandeur* □ *to labor under a delusion.*
• The nouns *allusion* and *illusion* are confused because of their similarity in pronunciation, *illusion* and *delusion* because of their similarity in meaning.

Illusion and *delusion* are virtually interchangeable in some contexts, but careful users maintain the distinction between these words where necessary. An *illusion* is often pleasant and harmless; a *delusion* may be a sign of mental disorder: □ *the illusions of childhood* □ *the delusion that she is Marilyn Monroe.* An *illusion* temporarily deceives the senses and is sometimes known to be false; a *delusion* is a strongly held opinion that is not easily eradicated.
See also ALLUSIVE, ELUSIVE, OR ILLUSIVE?

allusive, elusive, or **illusive?** The adjectives *allusive* and *illusive* relate to the nouns *allusion* and *illusion,* respectively (see ALLUSION, ILLUSION, OR DELUSION?); *elusive* means "difficult to catch, find, achieve, describe, define, remember," etc.: □ *an allusive style* □ *an illusive hope* □ *an elusive quality.*
• These words differ only in the pronunciation of the first syllable: *allusive* [a*loo*siv], *elusive* [ee*loo*siv], and *illusive* [i*loo*siv].
Of the three adjectives *elusive* is the most frequent. *Allusive* is rarely used, and *illusive* is usually replaced by its synonym *illusory.*

alright see ALL RIGHT OR ALRIGHT?

also The use of the adverb *also* in place of the conjunction *and* is disliked and avoided by many users, especially in formal writing: □ *Please send me a copy of your new catalogue and a list of local dealers* [not . . . *a copy of your new catalogue, also a list* . . .].
• The combination *and also,* however, is generally acceptable: □ *Please send me a copy of your new catalogue and also a list of local dealers.*
In some sentences *also* must be carefully positioned in order to convey the intended meaning: □ *She also* [as well as someone else] *was carrying an umbrella.* □ *She was carrying an umbrella also* [as well as something else]. □ *She was wearing a raincoat, and she was also carrying an umbrella.*
See also NOT ONLY . . . BUT ALSO.

altar or **alter?** These words are sometimes confused. An *altar* is a place where sacrifices are offered to a god and also the table on which the bread and wine are blessed in Communion services: □ *The priest approached the altar.* *Alter* with an *e* means "change": □ *a scheme for radically altering the whole tax system.*
• The different words both have the same pronunciation [*aw*/těr].

alternate or **alternative?** The adjective *alternate* means "every other" or "occurring by turns"; the adjective *alternative* means "offering a choice" or "being an alternative": □ *on alternate Saturdays* □ *alternate layers* □ *alternative routes* □ *an alternative suggestion.*

• The use of *alternate* in place of *alternative* is acknowledged by most dictionaries but disliked by many users. *Alternative* should not be used in place of *alternate.*

Note the difference in pronunciation between the adjective *alternate* [aw/lternăt] and the verb *alternate* [aw/těrnayt].

The adjective *alternative* is used with increasing frequency in the specific sense of "not conventional" or "not traditional": □ *alternative medicine* □ *alternative lifestyle* □ *alternative technology* □ *alternative energy.* This usage is best avoided where there is a risk of ambiguity: *I decided to buy an alternative newspaper.*

The noun *alternative* traditionally denotes either of two possibilities, or the opportunity of choosing between them, but is widely used with reference to three or more options or choices: □ *Are the current alternatives to welfare effective?* (*Daily Telegraph*, Oct. 6, 1987). □ *If Owen had been picked as late as spring this year, so that the Alliance campaign could have presented him as the alternative to Thatcher and Kinnock* (*Daily Mail*, June 30, 1987). Criticism of this usage on etymological grounds (*alternative* is derived from the Latin word *alter*, meaning "other (of two)" is dismissed by most authorities as pedantry.

although or **though?** As conjunctions, meaning "despite the fact that," *although* and *though* are interchangeable in most contexts: □ *We bought the table, although/though it was damaged.*

• *Though* is slightly less formal but more versatile than *although:* it may be used in combination with *even* for extra emphasis; in the phrase *as though* (see AS IF OR AS THOUGH?); after an adjective; and as an informal substitute for the adverb *however:* □ *We bought the table, even though it was damaged.* □ *We bought the table, damaged though it was.* □ *Ground coffee tastes better than instant coffee; it's more expensive, though.*

Though and (less frequently) *although* are also used in the sense of "but" or "and yet": □ *They applauded, though not enthusiastically.* □ *It's possible, though unlikely.*

The shortened forms *altho', altho, tho',* and *tho* are best avoided in formal writing.

See also IF.

altogether or **all together?** The adverb *altogether* means "in all" or "completely"; *all together* means "at the same time" or "in the same place": □ *She has nine pets altogether.* □ *Your system is altogether different from ours.* □ *He disappeared altogether.* □ *They arrived all together.* □ *We keep our reference books all together on a separate shelf.*

A.M. and **P.M.** Periods are often retained in the abbreviations *A.M.* (for ante meridiem, meaning "before noon") and *P.M.* (for post meridiem, meaning "after noon") to distinguish *A.M.* from the verb *am.*

• The use of lowercase letters is also acceptable. See also ABBREVIATIONS.

The abbreviation *A.M.* refers to the hours from midnight to noon;

P.M. refers to the hours from noon to midnight: □ *12:05 A.M.* is five minutes after midnight. □ *12:05 P.M.* is five minutes after noon. Such phrases as *8:15 A.M. in the morning* and *11:45 P.M. at night* are tautological; either *A.M.* or *in the morning* and either *P.M.* or *at night* should be omitted.

amateur This word, meaning "person who follows an activity as a pastime rather than as a profession": □ *an amateur golfer*, has several pronunciations, the most frequent being [amăchĕ], as well as [amătewr], [amătĕ], and [amă*ter*].

ambience Some people object to the frequent use of the noun *ambience* as a pretentious synonym for "atmosphere": □ *the ambience of the restaurant.*
• The French spelling *ambiance* and an Anglicized form of the French pronunciation are sometimes used in English. The English pronunciation of *ambience* is [ambiĕns].

ambiguous or **ambivalent?** *Ambiguous* means "having two or more possible interpretations or meanings" or "obscure"; *ambivalent* means "having conflicting emotions or attitudes" or "indecisive": □ *The phrase "a French horn player" is ambiguous.* □ *Many people are ambivalent about the issue of disarmament: they recognize the importance of the nuclear deterrent but feel that the money spent on nuclear weapons could be put to better use.*
• Careful users maintain the distinction between the two adjectives, avoiding the temptation to use *ambivalent* in place of *ambiguous*. In some contexts, including the above example, *be ambivalent* may be better replaced by *have mixed feelings* or *be of two minds*.

amend or **emend?** Of these two verbs *amend*, meaning "correct," "improve," or "alter," is the more general, *emend* being restricted to the correction of errors in a printed or written text: □ *The ambiguous wording of the opening paragraph has been amended.* □ *They have amended the rules.* □ *The manuscript was emended by an eminent scholar.*
• The pronunciation of *amend* [ămend] is very similar to that of *emend* [imend]. Their derived nouns, however, are quite different: □ *an amendment* □ *an emendation*.

amenity The noun *amenity* is ultimately derived from the Latin word for "pleasant." A few users prefer to restrict the term, which is generally used in the plural form *amenities*, to what is conducive to comfort or pleasure, objecting to its extended application to what is merely useful or convenient: □ *The amenities of the hotel include a sauna, swimming pool, restaurant, bar, and 24-hour room service.* □ *The town lacks some of the basic amenities, such as public toilets and a trash dump.*
• *Amenity* is usually pronounced [ameniti], with a short *e*.

America The word *America* is most frequently used with reference to the United States of America, although it strictly denotes the whole landmass comprising Canada, the U.S.A., Central America, and South America.
• *The United States of America* may be shortened to *the United States, the U.S.A., the U.S.,* or (in informal contexts) *the States:* □ *I often go to the States on business. U.S.A.* and *U.S.* are sometimes written or printed without periods (see also **ABBREVIATIONS**).

Like *America,* the adjective *American* is largely restricted in general usage to the meaning "of the U.S.A." The abbreviation *U.S.* may be used adjectivally to avoid ambiguity: □ *a U.S. actor.* There is no single noun that specifically denotes a native or citizen of the U.S.A., but *American* is generally used for this purpose: □ *The book was written by an American.*

Americanisms For many years American English has been a significant influence on British English. Although many British purists dislike American English, in some respects its differences arise from greater conservatism than British English. Such words as: □ *gotten* □ *fall* (autumn) as well as many American spellings, were originally the British forms and have changed in Britain but not in the United States. American English is also a fertile ground for innovative words and idioms, and British English often borrows the more striking ones. Such American words as: □ *truck* □ *commuter* □ *teen-ager* have become part of British vocabulary.
• The most noticeable differences between American and British English are those of vocabulary. Many American are familiar with the better-known British equivalents: □ *pavement* (sidewalk) □ *lift* (elevator) □ *biscuit* (cookie) □ *holiday* (vacation). It is when the same word or phrase is used with different meanings that confusion arises. If an American says: □ *I put on my vest and pants and washed up,* an English person might think of him washing the dishes in his underwear.

There are various differences between American and British spellings: □ *tire—tyre* □ *center—centre* □ *color—colour* □ *mold—mould.* British English has in most cases resisted American spellings, although the American tendency to drop the *o* or *a* in such words as *foetus* or *encyclopaedia* is beginning to be adopted in British spelling.

The significant differences in grammar include a few past tenses such as the American *strove* (strived) or *gotten* and the American tendency to say: □ *Do you have . . . ?* where the British would say: □ *Have you . . . ?* or: □ *Have you got . . . ?* See also **QUOTATION MARKS; SHALL OR WILL?; SUBJUNCTIVE; TENSE.**

Much as many British people deplore the adoption of such innovative American words and phrases as □ *laid-back* □ *no way* □ *hype,* it can be assumed that such words will continue to cross the Atlantic and that they will continue to be absorbed into British English.

amiable or **amicable?** *Amiable* means "friendly," "pleasant," "agreeable," or "congenial"; *amicable* means "characterized by friendliness or goodwill": □ *an amiable man* □ *an amicable agreement* □ *She smiled at me in an amiable manner.* □ *The dispute was settled in an amicable manner.*
• The two adjectives should not be confused.

amok or **amuck?** The work *amok,* pronounced [ămŭk] or [ămŏk] and used especially in the phrase *run amok,* "behave in a violent manner; go berserk," has the rarer variant spelling *amuck,* pronounced [ămŭk].
• The word derives from Malay *amoq,* "frenzied attack."

among or **amongst?** The words *among* and *amongst* are inter-

A

changeable in all contexts, *among* being the more frequent in modern usage: □ *They hid among/amongst the bushes.*

● Some users prefer *among* before a consonant sound and *amongst* before a vowel sound: □ *among strangers* □ *amongst ourselves.*

See also BETWEEN OR AMONG?

amoral or **immoral?** *Amoral* means "not concerned with morality" or "having no moral standards"; *immoral* means "not conforming to morality" or "infringing upon accepted moral standards": □ *an amoral judgment* □ *an amoral politician* □ *immoral behavior* □ *an immoral young man* □ *Some people consider vivisection to be immoral; others have an amoral attitude toward the issue.*

● Careful users maintain the distinction between the two adjectives, either of which can be used in a derogatory manner.

The first syllable of *amoral* may be pronounced as *a* long *a* [aymorrăl] or a short *a* [amorrăl]; *immoral* is pronounced [imorrăl]. Note the spellings of the two words, particularly the single *m* of *amoral* and the double *m* of *immoral*.

amuck see AMOK OR AMUCK?

an see A OR AN?

anesthetic This word, meaning "a substance that produces a loss of pain," is spelled *anaesthetic*, with a second *a*, in British English.

analogous The adjective *analogous* is best avoided where *similar, equivalent, comparable, corresponding, like,* etc., would be adequate or more appropriate: □ *The new system is analogous to that used in the electronics industry.*

● The usual pronunciation of *analogous* is [ănalŏgŭs], with the hard *g* of *goat* and *analogue,* not the soft *g* of *gem* and *analogy.*

analyze The *z* of *analyze* should not be replaced with *s* in American English, *analyse* being the British spelling of the word.

●   See also -IZE OR ISE?

Some people object to the use of the verb *analyze* in place of *discuss, examine,* etc.: □ *Your proposal will be analyzed at the next committee meeting.* The frequent use of the noun *analysis* in general contexts is also disliked, especially the phrases *in the last analysis, in the final analysis,* and *in the ultimate analysis,* which can usually be replaced by *in the end, at last, finally, ultimately,* etc.

analysis see ANALYZE.

ancillary This word, meaning "supplementary or subsidiary": □ *ancillary services,* is sometimes misspelled. Note particularly the *c,* the double *l,* and the ending *-ary,* not *-iary.*

and The use of *and* at the beginning of a sentence is disliked by some users but acceptable to most. And it can sometimes be an effective way of drawing attention to what follows.

● Two or more subjects joined with *and* are used with a plural verb unless they represent a single concept. See also SINGULAR OR PLURAL?

For the use of a comma before *and* in a series of three or more items, see COMMA 1. *And* may also be preceded by a comma in other contexts, especially in complex sentences or where there is a risk of ambiguity: □ *Jenny owns the red car, and the black car belongs to her brother.* □ *He unlocked the door with the key that he had found inside the stolen purse, and went in.* □ *She has been to Spain, Portugal, and Italy, and hopes to visit Greece next year.* The omission of the first *and* in the last example and in similar sentences is a frequent error.

The use of *and* in place of *to* is best avoided in formal contexts: □ *We'd better try and find it.* □ *I'll come and see you tomorrow.*

See also **AND/OR; I OR ME?**

and/or The phrase *and/or* should be used only where three possibilities are envisaged: □ *cotton and/or nylon socks*, for example, means "cotton socks, nylon socks, and socks made from a mixture of cotton and nylon."

• The phrase should not be used where *and* or *or* would be adequate: □ *This food is suitable for hamsters and* [not *and/or*] *gerbils.* □ *The bank is not open on Saturdays or* [not *and/or*] *Sundays.*

And/or is best restricted to official, legal, or commercial contexts and replaced elsewhere by a slightly longer phrase: □ *The casserole may be served with potatoes or carrots or both* [not *potatoes and/or carrots*].

angle Some people object to the frequent use of the noun *angle* in place of *point of view, standpoint*, etc.: □ *The report has been written from the wrong angle.*

• The verb *angle* implies a lack of objectivity: □ *The play was angled to make the audience sympathize with the criminal.*

anonymous This word, meaning "of unknown origin or identity": □ *an anonymous donor*, is sometimes misspelled, the most frequent error being to replace the *y* with an *i*.

ante- or **anti-?** These two prefixes are sometimes confused. *Ante-*, from Latin, means "before": □ *antenatal* □ *anteroom* □ *antecedent. Anti-*, from Greek, means "against; opposite to": □ *antiapartheid* □ *anti-aircraft* □ *anti-American* □ *antiseptic*.

• In American English *anti-* is pronounced [antī] or [anti], *ante-* [anti]; in British English, either prefix is pronounced [anti].

In informal spoken English, *anti* is sometimes used as a preposition, meaning "opposed to": □ *He's very anti politics*.

anticipate The verb *anticipate* is widely used as a synonym for "expect": □ *We do not anticipate that there will be any problems.*

□ *Oil prices showed their expected leap yesterday ... But the rally was not as strong as some traders anticipated* (*Daily Telegraph*, June 30, 1987). This usage is disliked by some people, who restrict the verb to its accepted more formal senses of "forestall," "act in advance of," etc.: □ *Preventative medicine anticipates disease.* □ *They anticipated the attack by boarding up their doors and windows.* □ *You must learn to anticipate his needs.*

• The verb is best avoided altogether where there is a risk of ambiguity, as in such sentences as *I anticipated her resignation* and *The driver anticipated the accident.*

any The use of a singular or plural verb with the pronoun *any* de-

pends on the sense and context in which it is used: □ *Is any of the furniture damaged?* □ *Ask him whether any of his children watch/watches the program.*
• In the first example *any*, like *furniture*, must be used with a singular verb. In examples of the second type, a singular verb is preferred if *any* is used in the sense of "any one" and a plural verb if *any* implies "some." See also SINGULAR OR PLURAL?
The use of *any* in place of *at all* is used in American English but is avoided in British English: □ *Her manners haven't improved any.* See also ANYBODY OR ANYONE?

anybody or **anyone?** The pronoun *anybody* and its synonym *anyone* are interchangeable in all contexts.
• Each is used with a singular verb but may sometimes be informally followed by a plural personal pronoun or possessive pronoun (see THEY): □ *Has anybody/anyone finished their work?*
Note the difference between the one-word compound *anyone* and the more specific two-word form *any one*, each of which may be applied to people: □ *Anyone could have started the fire.* □ *Any one of the tenants could have started the fire.* Only the two-word compound is used of things: □ *These tables are not reserved, so you can sit at any one you like.*

apartheid The name of the South African political system *apartheid* may be pronounced in several different ways. Some users prefer the pronunciation [ăpart̄hayt] following the Afrikaans original. Other frequently used pronunciations are [ăparthīt] and [ăparthīd] as well as pronunciations in which the *h* is not sounded: [ăpartīt] and [ăpartīd].

apostrophe The apostrophe is used mainly to denote possession and other relationships: □ *Angela's house* □ *the Church of England's doctrines* □ *the birds' nests,* and to indicate omitted letters in contractions: □ *can't* □ *you're* □ *there's.*
• Difficulties with the possessive use of the apostrophe center on its presence or absence and its position before or after the *s* (for the basic rules see 'S OR S'?). Advertisers are particularly guilty of sins of omission: □ *mens clothes* □ *last years prices* □ *special childrens menu,* and marketplaces are particularly prone to forming plurals with apostrophes: □ *potato's* □ *apricot's.* Units of measure often have their apostrophes omitted; it should be: □ *50 years' service* □ *a six months' stay in America.* With well-known organizations and products the tendency is now to drop the apostrophe: □ *Barclays Bank* □ *Macmillans* □ *Veterans Administration.*
Possessive personal pronouns do not take apostrophes: □ *his book* □ *its name* □ *it is ours,* but indefinite pronouns do: □ *anybody's guess* □ *no one's fault.* Purists have maintained that as *else* is not a noun or pronoun it cannot take an apostrophe, and have used the form: □ *someone's else,* but *someone else's* is now generally acceptable.
There are a few exceptions to the rule that apostrophes cannot be used for plurals. They can be used to indicate the plurals of individual letters, words, and numbers in such expressions as: □ *It takes two I's in the past tense.* □ *She often begins sentences with and's and but's.* □ *His 1's look like lowercase L's.* The apostrophe

may also be used for the plural of abbreviations: □ *C.P.A.'s* □ *M.D.'s.*

Apart from the use of the apostrophe to indicate contractions such as *shouldn't, I'm, 'n'* (for *and:* □ *salt 'n' vinegar flavored chips* □ *rock 'n' roll*), it is used to indicate missing letters in poetic forms such as *e'er, o'er,* in terms such as *o'clock, will-o'-the-wisp,* and in names such as *O'Connor.* It might also be used in writing dialogue to indicate Cockney or dialect speech: □ *'E was goin' to 'Ackney.* □ *. . . 'tis said 'a was a poor parish 'prentice* (Hardy, *The Mayor of Casterbridge*). Apostrophes are also sometimes used to indicate missing numbers: □ *the generation who were young in '60.*

Apostrophes are no longer used for shortened forms that are in general use: □ *flu* □ *phone* □ *photo* □ *plane.*

See also CONTRACTIONS; DATES; -ING FORMS; ITS OR IT'S?; POSSESSIVES.

apparatus This word is usually pronounced [apăratŭs] though the pronunciation [apăraytŭs] is also sometimes heard.

appendixes or **appendices?** The noun *appendix* has two accepted plural forms, *appendixes* and *appendices.*

• The plural form *appendixes* is preferred for the anatomical sense of the word: □ *During her early years as a surgeon, she removed countless tonsils, adenoids, and appendixes,* and the sense of "supplement (to a book, document, etc.)." The plural form *appendices,* pronounced [ăpendiseez], is preferred by some users: □ *One of the appendices lists foreign words and phrases in general usage.*

applicable In the more traditional pronunciation of this word, the first syllable is stressed [aplikăbl]. The pronunciation with the second syllable stressed [ăplicăbl] is probably more frequently heard, however. See also STRESS.

appreciate The frequent use of the verb *appreciate* in place of *realize* or *understand* is disliked by a few users: □ *I appreciate that the child's parents were unaware of the risk.* □ *Do you appreciate our problem?*

• The principal senses of *appreciate* are "be grateful for," "recognize the worth of," and "increase in value": □ *He would appreciate some assistance.* □ *She does not appreciate good wine.* □ *Their house has appreciated considerably during the past six months.*

a priori The Latin phrase *a priori,* which literally means "from the previous," is applied adjectivally to deductive reasoning, arguments, statements, etc.

• The phrase is usually pronounced [ay prīorī], the pronunciations [ay prīoree] and [ah preeoree] being accepted variants.

apt see LIABLE OR LIKELY?

Arab, Arabian, or **Arabic?** The adjective *Arab* relates to the people of Arabia and their descendants, *Arabian* to Arabia itself, and *Arabic* to the language of Arabia and other Arab countries: □ *an Arab sheik* □ *the Arab nations* □ *The Arabian Nights* □ *the Arabian Sea* □ *an Arabic numeral* □ *Arabic literature.*

• Each of the three words may be used as a noun, *Arabian* being a rare variant of *Arab*: □ *His sister married an Arab.* □ *Arabic is the official language of Egypt.*

The word *Arab* is also applied to a breed of horse that is used for riding; the *Arabian Desert* is in East Egypt and is popularly used for the desert of Arabia; and *gum arabic* (note the lowercase *a*) is a gum obtained from certain acacia trees.

arbiter or **arbitrator?** An *arbiter* is a person who has the power to judge or who has absolute control; an *arbitrator* is a person who is appointed to settle a dispute: □ *an arbiter of style* □ *an arbiter of human destiny* □ *The arbitrator's decision proved acceptable to both parties.*

• The general term *arbiter* may be used in place of the more specific *arbitrator*, but the two nouns are not fully interchangeable.

arbitrarily The adverb *arbitrarily* should be stressed on the first syllable [arbitrărĕlee].

• The pronunciation [arbitrerrĕlee], in which the primary stress shifts to the third syllable, is unacceptable to some people.

arbitrator see ARBITER OR ARBITRATOR?

archeology This word, describing the study of the material remains of ancient cultures, is spelled *archeology*; it is spelled *archaeology* with the vowels *-aeo-* in the middle of the word in British English.

archetypal The adjective *archetypal* is best avoided where *typical, characteristic, classic, original,* etc., would be adequate or more appropriate: □ *an archetypal English village.*

Argentine or **Argentinian?** Either word may be used as an adjective, meaning "of Argentina," or as a noun, denoting a native or inhabitant of Argentina. *Argentine* is preferred, but *Argentinian* is also frequent in both senses: □ *the Argentine/Argentinian flag* □ *an Argentine/Argentinian ship* □ *Her stepfather is an Argentine/Argentinian.*

• The word *Argentine* may be pronounced [arjĕnteen], or [arjĕntīn], rhyming with *mean* or *mine.*

The republic of Argentina is sometimes called in British English the *Argentine*: □ *They lived in the Argentine for several years.*

arise or **rise?** *Arise* means "come into being," "originate," or "result"; *rise* means "stand up," move upwards," or "increase": □ *A problem has arisen.* □ *The quarrel arose from a misunderstanding.* □ *He rose to greet her.* □ *The water level is rising.*

• *Arise* may be substituted for *rise* in some senses of the latter, but this usage is largely restricted to formal or poetic contexts and is generally regarded as old-fashioned.

See also RAISE OR RISE?

aristocrat This word is usually stressed on the second syllable [ăristŏkrat].

• British speakers usually stress the first syllable [aristŏkrat].

around or **about?** Some prefer *about* to *around* in the sense of "approximately": □ *We have about/around 200 employees.* □ *He left at about/around eleven o'clock.*

In the sense of "here and there," around and about are interchangeable in most contexts: □ *to run around/about* □ *sitting around/about all day* □ *toys scattered around/about the room.*

In the sense of "surrounding," *about* is less frequent than *around*.

• See also **AROUND** OR **ROUND?**

around or **round?** *Around* and *round* are synonymous in most of their adverbial and prepositional senses, *around* being preferred in American English and *round* in British English: □ *I turned around/round.* □ *The wheels went around/round.* □ *They sat around/round the table.* □ *She wore a gold chain around/round her ankle.*

• See also **AROUND** OR **ABOUT?**

arouse or **rouse?** *Arouse* means "stimulate" or "excite"; *rouse* means "wake" or "stir": □ *Their curiosity was aroused.* □ *The ban on smoking has aroused widespread opposition.* □ *The noise of the airplanes roused the child.* □ *I was roused to anger by his accusations.*

• The direct object of *arouse* is usually an abstract noun; the direct object of *rouse* is usually a person or an animal. The substitution of *arouse* for *rouse* in the sense of "wake" is acceptable but rare.

artist or **artiste?** An *artist* is a person who is skilled in one or more of the fine arts, such as painting or sculpture; an *artiste* is a professional entertainer, such as a singer or dancer: □ *the Dutch artist Vincent Van Gogh* □ *We watched the artiste perform.*

• In its extended sense of "skilled person," the noun *artist* may be substituted for *artiste,* which is becoming less frequent. Each noun may be applied to a person of either sex.

as The *as . . . as* construction may be followed by a subject pronoun or an object pronoun: □ *She loves the child as much as he* [as much as he does]. □ *She loves the child as much as him* [as much as she loves him].

• In informal contexts the subject pronoun is sometimes replaced by the object pronoun, especially in simple comparisons: □ *as tall as me* □ *as old as them.* This usage, which is unacceptable to many people, should be avoided in formal contexts.

The *as . . . as* construction is sometimes ambiguous: □ *She loves the child as much as her husband,* for example, may mean "She loves the child as much as her husband does" or "She loves the child as much as she loves her husband." In such cases the missing verb may be inserted for clarity.

The substitution of *so . . . as* for *as . . . as* in negative constructions is optional: □ *He is not so/as clever as his sister.* When the construction is followed by an infinitive with *to,* however, *so . . . as* is preferred: □ *I would not be so careless as to leave my car unlocked.*

When the *as . . . as* construction is followed by a comparative adjective or adverb, the second *as* is sometimes omitted in informal contexts but is retained by careful users in formal contexts: □ *Her car is as old (as) or older than mine.* □ *He dances as badly (as) or worse than you.*

The use of the *as . . . as* construction when *as* alone is required, in the sense of "though," is disliked in British English: □ *Tired as he was* [not *As tired as he was*], *he finished the race.*

See also **AS FROM; AS IF** OR **AS THOUGH?; AS PER; AS TO; AS WELL AS; AS YET; BECAUSE, AS, FOR,** OR **SINCE?; COMPARATIVE AND SUPERLATIVE; LIKE; SUCH AS** OR **LIKE?**

as for see AS TO.

as from The phrase *as from* is best avoided where *from, on, at,* etc., would be adequate or more appropriate: □ *From* [not *as from*] *next Monday on, I shall be available for work.* □ *Sunday deliveries will cease on* [not *as from*] *Nov. 1.* □ *The increase will come into effect at* [not *as from*] *midnight.*

• As from may serve a useful purpose in the context of retrospective payments, agreements, etc.: □ The reduced interest will be payable as from last July.

Asian or **Asiatic?** Either word may be used as an adjective, meaning "of Asia," or as a noun, denoting a native or inhabitant of Asia. *Asian* is preferred in both senses, the use of *Asiatic* with reference to people being considered by some to be racially offensive: □ *an Asian/Asiatic country* □ *an Asian* [not *Asiatic*] *doctor* □ *an Asian* [not *Asiatic*] *living in Europe.* See also INDIAN.

• The word Asian may be pronounced [ayzhăn] or [ayshăn].

as if or **as though?** *As if* and *as though* are interchangeable in most contexts: □ *The car looked as if/though it had been repainted.* □ *She trembled, as if/though aware of our presence.* □ *He opened his mouth as if/though to speak.*

• As if is preferred in emphatic exclamations: □ As if it mattered! □ As if I needed their advice! See also SUBJUNCTIVE; WERE OR WAS?

as per The use of the phrase *as per* in place of *according to* is widely regarded as COMMERCIALESE: □ *as per instructions* □ *as per the specifications.*

• The use of the jocular expression as per usual in place of as usual is best restricted to informal contexts: □ The train was ten minutes late, as (per) usual.

asphalt This word, used to describe a material used in road surfacing, is often misspelled. Note particularly the *sph.*

asphyxiate This word, meaning "suffocate," is sometimes misspelled. Note particularly the *phy,* as in *physics.*

assassinate This word, meaning "murder an important person": □ *The president was assassinated,* is often misspelled. Remember the two double *s*'s.

• The nouns assassin and assassination follow the same spelling pattern.

assent or **consent?** Either word may be used as a verb, meaning "agree," or as a noun, meaning "agreement." The verb *consent* sometimes implies greater reluctance than *assent:* □ *They readily assented to our plan.* □ *After hours of persuasion, they consented to end the strike.*

• The noun assent has connotations of acceptance or acquiescence, whereas the noun consent denotes approval or permission: □ with the assent of my colleagues □ without her parents' consent.

assignation or **assignment?** Each of these nouns may be used to denote the act of assigning: □ *the assignment/assignation of household chores,* but *assignment* is more frequently used.

• Assignation has the additional meaning of "secret meeting"; assignment also means "task": □ an assignation with her lover □ having completed his first assignment. The two words are not interchangeable in either of these senses.

assimilate This word, meaning "absorb or integrate" or "become alike," is often misspelled. The only double consonants are the *-ss.*

assume or **presume?** In the sense of "suppose" or "take for granted," the verbs *assume* and *presume* are usually interchangeable: □ *I assume/presume you will accept their offer.*

• In some contexts *assume* may suggest a hypothesis postulated without proof and *presume* a conclusion based on evidence: □ *He assumed that she was an experienced player and did not offer her any advice.* □ *From her performance in the opening game, he presumed that she was an experienced player.*

Each verb has a number of additional senses. *Assume* means "undertake," "feign," or "adopt": □ *to assume responsibility* □ *to assume a reaction of astonishment* □ *to assume a new name. Presume* means "dare" or "take advantage of": □ *I did not presume to contradict him.* □ *They presumed on our hospitality.*

assurance or **insurance?** *Insurance* is used to denote financial protection against a certainty, such as the death of the policyholder: □ *life insurance.* British English uses *assurance* as a synonym: □ *life assurance.*

• Of the two nouns only *insurance* is used with reference to financial protection against a possibility, such as fire, accidental damage, theft, medical expenses, etc.: □ *car insurance* □ *fire insurance* □ *travel insurance* □ *health insurance.*

The noun *assurance* has a number of other meanings derived from the verb *assure,* such as "guarantee," "confidence," etc.: □ *an assurance of help* □ *an air of assurance.*

See also ASSURE, ENSURE, OR INSURE?

assure, ensure, or **insure?** To *assure* is to convince; to *ensure* is to make certain; to *insure* is to protect financially: □ *He assured me that the carpet would not be damaged.* □ *Please ensure that you do not damage the carpet.* □ *I insured the carpet against accidental damage.*

• The word *insure* is sometimes used in place of *ensure.*

See also ASSURANCE OR INSURANCE?

asthma This word, which describes the disorder that makes breathing difficult, is sometimes misspelled, the most frequent error being in the combination of the consonants *sthm.*

as though see AS IF OR AS THOUGH?

as to Many people object to the unnecessary use of *as to* before *whether, what, why,* etc.: □ *There is some doubt (as to) whether she is suitably qualified.* □ *He offered no explanation (as to) why he was late.*

• *As to* is also best avoided where *of, about, on,* etc., would be adequate or more appropriate: □ *Please give me your opinion as to the efficiency of the system.* □ *They received no warning as to the risks involved.*

The phrase *as to* (or *as for*) may serve a useful purpose at the beginning of a sentence, in the sense of "with regard to" or "concerning": □ *As to/for the results of the survey, they will be published in next month's magazine.* □ *As for his sister, she survived the accident.*

as well as When two or more verbs are linked by the phrase *as well as,* in the sense of "in addition to," the verb that follows *as well as* is usually an *-ing* form: □ *The burglar broke a valuable vase, as*

well as stealing all my jewelry. □ *As well as weeding the flower bed, the gardener pruned the roses and mowed the lawn.*
• For the use of a singular or plural verb after nouns linked by *as well as,* see SINGULAR OR PLURAL?
  As well as is best avoided where there is a risk of confusion with the literal sense of the phrase: □ *Mark plays golf as well as Peter,* for example, may mean "Both Mark and Peter play golf" or "Mark and Peter are equally good at golf."

as yet The phrase *as yet,* meaning "up to now" or "so far," is best avoided where *yet* would be adequate: □ *Have you sold any tickets yet* [not *as yet*]? □ *I haven't sold any tickets (as) yet.* □ *No tickets have been sold (as) yet.* □ *Only a few tickets have been sold (as yet).*

at or **in?** *In* is used before the name of a town, city, country, etc.: □ *She works in New York.* □ *We have a house in Florida.*
• When the speaker or writer is referring to his or her own place of residence, work, etc., *at* generally indicates a more exact or specific position than *in*: □ *He lives in our neighborhood.* □ *He lives at 27 North Street.* □ *She works in a bank.* □ *She works at the library.*

ate This word, which is the past tense of the verb, is pronounced [ayt]. The pronunciation [et] is considered nonstandard.

attach This word, meaning "join or fasten," is sometimes misspelled. Note the double *t* and the *ch.* There is no *t* before the *ch.*

at this moment in time Many people object to the frequent use of the cliché *at this moment in time* in place of *now:* □ *I am not in a position to comment on the situation at this moment in time.* Also objected to is *at that point in time* for *then.*

attribute The verb *attribute,* meaning "ascribe," is generally used with the preposition *to:* □ *They attributed the accident to careless driving.* □ *To what do you attribute your success?* □ *The idea was attributed to his colleague.*
• The passive use of *attributed* with the preposition *with,* in the sense of "given credit," is wrong: *His colleague was credited* [not *attributed*] *with the idea.*
  Note the difference in pronunciation between the verb *attribute* [ătribewt] and the noun *attribute* [atribewt]. See also STRESS.

aural or **oral?** These two words are sometimes confused, partly because they often have the same pronunciation [awrăl]. *Aural* means "of the ear or the sense of hearing"; *oral* means "of the mouth; expressed in speech." *Aural comprehension* involves a person's ability to understand a spoken language; an *oral examination* is one in which the questions and answers are spoken, not written.
• The preferred pronunciation [oral] for *oral.*

Australianisms There are fewer differences between Australian and British English than between American and British English, probably because until comparatively recently nearly all settlers in Australia were British or Irish. The words that were adopted by the early settlers from the Aboriginal languages: □ *koala* □ *boomerang,* are now in general use, and many people are familiar with those Australian words that were coined in the context of the early days of European settlement: □ *outback* □ *bushranger* □ *swagman* □ *digger* □ *walkabout.*
• Although the speech of many Australians is not markedly differ-

ent from British forms, Australian English is associated with the pronunciation known as *Broad Australian* or *Strine*. In the amusing book *Let Stalk Strine,* published in 1965, examples are given of this characteristic pronunciation: □ *egg nishner* (air conditioner) □ *garbler mince* (couple of minutes) □ *chee semmitch* (cheese sandwich).

Australian English seems particularly adapted to informal use (the very formal British *good day* becomes the informal Australian greeting *g'day*), and it abounds in colorful slang. The word best known in Britain: □ *cobber* is out of date, although □ *dinkum* and □ *pommy* or *pom* (a British person) are still used. The words □ *chunder* (vomit) □ *crook* (ill) □ *rubbish* (as a verb; see **NOUNS**) are becoming familiar in Britain. Slang words are often formed by adding *-ie* or *-o* to an abbreviated word: □ *arvo* (afternoon) □ *garbo* (refuse collector) □ *sickie* (day taken off work for real or invented illness).

Australian spelling has traditionally been identical to British. In recent years, however, Australian spelling, as well as pronunciation and vocabulary, has been influenced by American English.

author The use of the word *author* as a verb, in place of *write*, is disliked and avoided by careful users in all contexts: *She has written* [not *authored*] *a number of books on the subject.*
• On the use of *authoress*, see -**ESS**.

authoritarian or **authoritative?** The adjective *authoritarian* means "favoring obedience to authority as opposed to individual freedom"; *authoritative* means "having authority" or "official": □ *an authoritarian father* □ *an authoritarian regime* □ *an authoritarian policy* □ *an authoritative voice* □ *an authoritative article* □ *an authoritative source.*
• The word *authoritarian,* which is also used as a noun, usually has derogatory connotations, whereas *authoritative* is generally used in a complimentary manner.
   Authoritative is often misspelled, the most frequent error being the omission of the fourth syllable.

avenge see **REVENGE OR AVENGE?**

averse see **ADVERSE OR AVERSE?**

avoid, evade, or **elude?** *Avoid* means "keep away from"; *evade* and *elude* mean "avoid by cunning or deception": □ *He avoided the police by turning down a side street.* □ *He evaded the police by hiding in the basement.* □ *He eluded the police by using a series of false names.*
• Each of the three verbs has other senses and uses: □ *She managed to avoid damaging the car.* □ *He is trying to evade his responsibilities.* □ *Your name eludes me.*
   In British English the difference between the terms tax *avoidance* and tax *evasion,* both of which relate to methods of reducing or minimizing tax liability, is that tax *avoidance* is legal and tax *evasion* is not.

avoidance see **AVOID, EVADE, OR ELUDE?**

await or **wait?** *Await* is principally used as a transitive verb, meaning "wait for" or "be in store for"; *wait* is chiefly used intransitively, often followed by *for*, in the sense of "remain in readiness or expectation": □ *They awaited the verdict of the jury with trepidation.* □ *I wonder what adventures await you in your new ca-*

reer. □ *She asked us to wait outside.* □ *He waited for the rain to stop.*

• In the sense of "wait for," *await* is largely restricted to formal contexts, where its direct object is usually an abstract noun. In other contexts *wait for* is preferred: *We're waiting for* [not *awaiting*] *a taxi.*

Wait is used as a transitive verb in the phrase *wait one's turn* and similar expressions. The phrasal verb *wait on* means "serve"; its use in place of *wait for* or *await* is disliked by many people: □ *They're waiting on the results.*

awake, awaken, wake, or **waken?** All these verbs may be used transitively or intransitively in the literal senses of "rouse or emerge from sleep" and the figurative senses of "make or become aware": □ *Please waken me at six o'clock.* □ *He wakes earlier during the summer.* □ *Her sister's plight awakened her to the problems faced by single parents.* □ *They awoke to the dangers of drug abuse.* *Wake* and *waken* are preferred in literal contexts and *awake* and *awaken* in figurative contexts.

• The verb *wake*, which is more frequently used than *waken*, is often followed by *up:* □ *Don't wake the baby up.* □ *I woke up in the middle of the night.* *Woke* and *waked*, respectively, are the usual forms of the past tense and past participle of *wake*, although the past tense *waked* and the past participle *woken* are also used from time to time. *Waken* is a regular verb.

Awaken and (less frequently) *awake* are also used in the sense of "arouse": □ *His absence from work may awaken/awake her suspicions.* The usual forms of the past tense and past participle of the verb *awake* are *awoke* and *awaked*, respectively, *awoken* being an accepted variant. Like *waken*, *awaken* is a regular verb.

The word *awake* is also used as an adjective, meaning "not asleep" or "alert": □ *Did the children manage to stay awake?* □ *The police are awake to the situation.*

award-winning The adjective *award-winning*, which is frequently used in advertising, is meaningless unless the nature of the award is specified: □ *an award-winning design* □ *an award-winning writer.*

• It is therefore best avoided or replaced with a more precise synonym, such as *excellent* or *remarkable.*

aware The use of the adjective *aware* before the noun it qualifies, in the sense of "knowledgeable" or "alert," is disliked by many users: □ *one of our more aware students* □ *financially aware individuals.*

• *Aware* is usually placed after a noun or pronoun and is often followed by *of:* □ *I am aware of the need for secrecy.*

awful see **AWFULLY.**

awfully The use of the adverb *awfully* as an intensifier is best restricted to informal contexts: □ *I'm awfully sorry.* □ *It's awfully difficult to decide which to buy.*

• The substitution of *awful* for *awfully* in this sense is wrong.

Ultimately derived from the noun *awe, awful* and *awfully* are rarely used in their literal senses ("being inspired or filled with awe") today. Their principal meanings in modern usage are "bad" or "badly": □ *The weather is awful.* □ *They played awfully in yesterday's game.*

ax In journalese, the verb *ax* is frequently used in the sense of "dismiss," "terminate," "remove," etc.: □ *Britain's biggest teaching union, the National Union of Teachers, is to ax a third of its head office staff* (*Sunday Times*, Aug. 23, 1987). □ *Coloroll, the wallpaper and furnishing company, is to ax 120 jobs* (*Daily Telegraph*, June 16, 1987). □ *The Burbank Starlight Bowl will be looking for management as city officials have axed [its] operator* (*Variety*, Dec. 28, 1988-Jan. 3, 1989).
• This usage is best avoided in general contexts.

A

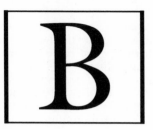

bachelor This word, meaning "unmarried man": □ *a confirmed bachelor,* is sometimes misspelled. The most frequent error is to insert a *t* before the *ch.*

back-formation Back-formation is a way of creating new words, usually verbs, by removing an affix from an existing word: □ *donate* (from donation) □ *extradite* (from extradition). Many such words have been used for so long that they are no longer recognized as back-formations: □ *edit* (from *editor*) □ *laze* (from *lazy*) □ *burgle* (from *burglar*) □ *enthuse* (from *enthusiasm*).

• Back-formations often arise as a result of false assumptions about the composition of a word. People hearing the word *scavenger* might assume incorrectly that the noun comes from a verb *scavenge* and so come to use this verb. Sometimes, however, the removed affix is not a genuine affix at all. The 19th-century writer on obesity and slimming, William Banting, invented a system of diet that became known as *the banting system,* which in turn gave rise to the verb *to bant.*

New verbs are regularly being formed in this way: □ *televise* □ *automate.* Many, such as *liaise* (from liaison) are disliked when newly coined, but when such verbs are created from a genuine need for them in the language, they tend to be retained.

background Some people object to the use of the word *background* to mean "the circumstances that relate to, lead up to, or explain an event or experience," preferring to use such words as *circumstances, conditions, context,* or *setting* instead.

• Recently *background* has also been used for a person's work or professional experience and training: □ *The successful applicant will probably have a construction background* (*Executive Post,* May 21, 1987).

backlash *Backlash* is used metaphorically to describe a strong adverse reaction to a recent event or political/social development or tendency: □ *the backlash against the radical new changes in education policy.*

• The metaphor suggests a sudden reaction, but in fact the word is often used in describing a gradual reaction, perhaps over years: □ *The philosophy of the New Right can be seen as a backlash against the pacifism and permissiveness of the 1960's.*

backward or **backwards?** *Backward* is preferred both as an adjective and as the usual form of the adverb meaning "toward the back" or "in reverse": □ *a backward step* □ *a backward child* □ *walking backward* □ *written backward.*

• The adverb *backwards* is more frequently used in British English. See also -**WARDS** OR **WARDS**?

bacteria The term *bacteria* refers to all microorganisms exhibiting certain characteristics. They are thought of as disease-bearing, but in fact many are harmless and some essential to human life, although others do cause disease.

• *Bacteria* is a plural noun so expressions such as: □ *I think it's caused by a bacteria* are incorrect; the singular term is *bacterium*.

bade *Bade* is a form of the past tense of the verb *bid:* □ *He bade them farewell.* Its traditional pronunciation is [bad], but [bayd] is also acceptable. The past tense *bid* is an acceptable variant.

bail or **bale?** The spellings of these words are often confused. The primary senses of these words are as follows. *Bail* is the security deposited as a guarantee of the appearance of an arrested person; a *bale* is a large quantity of hay, old newspapers, etc. The associated verbs also follow these spellings: □ *Davies was released on $10,000 bail.* □ *His friends bailed him out for $10,000.* □ *bales of old papers* □ *to bale hay.*

• In the senses of scooping water out of a boat, helping someone out of a difficult situation, and escaping from an aircraft in an emergency by using a parachute, *bail out* is preferred.

In British English the *bails* are the two crosspieces over the stumps in cricket.

baited or **bated?** These two words are occasionally confused. *Baited* means "provoked or teased" or "hooked or trapped with food to attract a fish or animal." *Bated* is used mainly in the expression *with bated breath*, meaning "tense with anxiety or excitement": □ *They waited with bated breath for news of the missing child.*

bale see BAIL OR BALE?

balk or **baulk?** Either spelling may be used for this word: □ *He balked* [or *baulked*] *at paying such a high price.* □ *The horse balked* [or *baulked*] *at the fence.* □ *As usual she was balked* [or *baulked*] *in her ambitions by a man.* The spelling *balk*, however, is preferred.

balmy or **barmy?** These words are sometimes confused. *Balmy* means "mild and pleasant": □ *a balmy evening. Barmy,* an informal word in British English, means "foolish": □ *I've never heard of such a barmy idea!*

• *Balmy* derives from *balm,* a plant with fragrant leaves that is used for flavoring foods and for scenting perfumes. The word is derived from the Latin *balsamum,* "balsam." *Barmy* comes from the Old English *beorma,* "the yeasty froth of fermenting beer."

In American English, and sometimes in British English, *balmy* is the spelling used for the slang *barmy.*

banister A *banister,* a handrail supported by posts that is fixed alongside a staircase, has the less common variant spelling *bannister.*

baptismal name see FIRST NAME, CHRISTIAN NAME, FORENAME, GIVEN NAME, OR BAPTISMAL NAME?

barbarian, barbaric, or **barbarous?** *Barbaric* means "crude, primitive, uncivilized": □ *They discovered a barbaric tribe living in the bush;* or sometimes merely "uncultured, unsophisticated": □ *Most teen-agers have barbaric tastes in music. Barbarian* as a noun means "someone living barbarically" and as an adjective is synonymous with *barbaric*. *Barbarous* means "cruel, harsh, or inhuman": □ *Torture is condemned as a barbarous practice.*

• *Barbaric* is often used with the same condemnatory meaning as *barbarous,* although it can be used approvingly: □ *The dance had a barbaric vitality.*

barely see HARDLY.

barmy see BALMY OR BARMY?

base or **basis?** Both *base* and *basis* mean "a foundation, substructure, or support." *Base* is usually used to refer to the bottom support of a tangible object: □ *the base of a wall*, while *basis* is used for abstract or theoretical foundations: □ *on the basis of all the evidence received* □ *The new pay scale provides a sound basis for the new contract.*

• *Base* is also used to mean "a principal ingredient": □ *The cocktail has a whiskey base,* and "a center," as in: □ *We used the apartment as our New York base. Base* can be used as a verb: □ *The company is based in Chicago,* and an adjective: *base price.*

  The plural of both *base* and *basis* is *bases,* but the plural of *base* is pronounced [baysiz] and the plural of *basis* [bayseez].

basically The literal sense of *basically* is "concerning a base or basis, fundamentally": □ *His argument has a superficial persuasiveness, but it is basically flawed.* □ *I believe she is basically a good person.*

• It is often used to mean no more than "importantly": □ *It is basically the case that fats can cause heart disease,* and it has recently become fashionable to put it at the beginning of a sentence, where its presence is often superfluous. This usage is disliked by some: □ *Basically, I don't think he should have been offered the job.*

basis see BASE OR BASIS?

bated see BAITED OR BATED?

bath or **bathe?** *Bath* is the noun, *bathe* the verb. In British English *bath* is a verb meaning "have a bath (in a bathroom)," or "wash someone else in a bath": □ *bath the baby,* as well as *bathe* for "swim, usually in the sea, for pleasure": □ *Who's coming for a bathe?*

• *Bath* is pronounced [bath] and *bathe* [baydh]. The past tense of both verbs is *bathed* and the present participle *bathing.*

bathroom see TOILET, LAVATORY, LOO, OR BATHROOM?

baulk see BALK OR BAULK?

B.C. see A.D. AND B.C.

be The infinitive *be* is used in some dialects in place of other parts of the verb: □ *It be a fine day.* In standard speech it is used mainly in imperatives: □ *Be quiet!,* after *to:* □ *You ought to be careful,* and after an auxiliary verb: □ *He should be home soon.*

• Two common uses after an auxiliary verb concern age and money: □ *She'll be 40 tomorrow.* □ *That'll be $10 exactly. Be* is often used to mean "become": □ *What do you want to be when you grow up?*

beautiful This word, meaning "delightful to the senses": □ *a beautiful woman* □ *a beautiful sunset,* is sometimes misspelled. Note particularly the first letters *beau-.*

• The word derives from the Old French word *biau* and comes ultimately from the Latin *bellus,* meaning "pretty."

B

because The conjunction because means "for the reason that":
□ *You're cold because you need warmer clothes.*
• It is often used incorrectly in such constructions as: □ *The reason her accent is so good is because her mother is French,* which should be: *Her accent is so good because her mother is French,* or: *The reason for her accent being so good is that her mother is French.* A somewhat informal use of *because* is to mean "the fact that": □ *Because he's deaf doesn't mean he's crazy.* See also NOT; REASON.

because, as, for, or **since?** Each of these words is used to introduce clauses that give the reason for whatever has been said in the main clause.
• *As* and *since* are similar in use, although *since* to some means only "after the time that." They are used more often at the beginning of a sentence than *because,* and tend to be used when the reason is already well known or when the reason is considered not as important as the main statement: □ *As you're only staying a little while, we'd better have coffee now.* □ *He refrained from smoking between courses, since he knew that was generally thought to be impolite.* □ *As/Since we went there in the summer, the weather was gloriously hot. Because* tends to put the emphasis on the cause: □ *He married her because she was rich. Because* is also sometimes used to introduce a reason for stating a fact: □ *You must have forgotten to invite him, because he didn't turn up. For* would be acceptable here although it would have a more formal sound. *For* almost always comes between the elements it joins and places equal emphasis on the main statement and the reason: □ *She never saw him again, for he returned to Greece soon afterward.*
Ambiguity in the use of *as* should be avoided, since it can mean both "while" and "because": □ *As Hugh went out to do the shopping, Sandra looked after the baby.*

because of see DUE TO, OWING TO, OR BECAUSE OF?

beggar This word, describing a person who begs, is sometimes misspelled. Note the ending *-ar,* not *-er.*
• This spelling is different from that of other "doer" words such as *hunter, miner,* and *writer.*

beg the question To *beg the question* is sometimes used as if it meant "evade the question skillfully" or even "raise the question." In fact it means "base an argument on an assumption whose truth is the very thing that is being disputed."
• For example, to argue that God must exist because one can see evidence of His creation in the natural beauties that surround us is *begging the question,* for the premise that these natural beauties are evidence of God's creation is unproved, and dependent on the truth of God's existence, which is supposed to be the conclusion of the argument.

behalf To speak or act *on behalf of* someone else is to act as the representative of that person or those people: □ *I am speaking on behalf of my union.* In (or on) *behalf of* is "in the interest of": □ *The warden interceded in behalf of the prisoner.* A frequent mistake is to use *on behalf* instead of *on the part:* □ *That was a serious error on behalf of those governments.*

beige This word, describing a very pale brown color, is sometimes misspelled. Note the *ei* and the soft *g*. See also SPELLING 5.

beloved This word, meaning "dearly love," may be pronounced [bi-*luv*id] or [bi*luvd*]. Either is acceptable, with the latter becoming more frequent.

below, beneath, under, or **underneath?** These words all mean "lower than," and the distinctions between them are subtle.

• *Below* and *under* are often synonymous; *below* is contrasted with *above,* and *under* with *over.* Below alone is used to refer to written material following: □ *See Chapter 5 below,* and is more often used in comparison of levels: □ *She lives in the apartment below.* □ *He was below me in rank. Under* is used in reference to being subject to authority: □ *He served under Eisenhower. Underneath* is used mainly for physical situations, and often suggests close proximity: □ *She kept her savings underneath her mattress. Beneath* can be synonymous with *underneath* but sounds either old-fashioned or poetic; it is now used mainly to mean "unworthy of": □ *beneath contempt.*

beneficent, beneficial see BENEVOLENT, BENIGN, BENEFICENT, OR BENEFICIAL?

benefit Note the single *-t-* in the spelling of the past tense: *benefited* and the present participle: *benefiting.*

benevolent, benign, beneficent, or **beneficial?** These are all adjectives suggestive of doing or intending good. *Benevolent* means "disposed to do good; charitable": □ *a donation from a benevolent well-wisher. Benign* means "kind, mild, and well-disposed," and can be used of things as well as people: □ *a benign climate;* it is also used as a medical term meaning "noncancerous": □ *a benign tumor. Beneficent* means "doing good; promoting good" and is used of people: □ *the help of a beneficent stranger,* whereas *beneficial* means "promoting good or well-being" and is more often used of things: □ *The waters are said to be beneficial to one's health.*

bereft *Bereft* was formerly synonymous with *bereaved* but is now used mainly to suggest, not just loss from death, but deprivation of any nonmaterial thing: □ *He was now bereft of all hope.*

• When used of death, *bereft* may suggest the desolation of loss more forcefully than does *bereaved:* □ *A year after his death she still wandered bereft through the silent house.* It should not be used merely as a synonym for "without," with no sense of loss, as in: □ *I was unable to help, being bereft of any mechanical skill.*

beside or **besides?** Beside means literally "by the side of": □ *Come and sit beside me,* and is also used in the expression *beside oneself,* meaning "extremely agitated": □ *He was beside himself with grief. Besides* can mean "moreover": □ *I won't be able to go; besides, I don't want to,* "as well as": □ *Besides the usual egg dishes, the restaurant offers some unusual breakfast specialties,* and "except for; other than": □ *He's interested in nothing besides baseball.*

• This last use is always inclusive, not exclusive as with *except: Besides Ben, my colleagues are all Jewish* implies that Ben is Jewish; while *Except for Ben . . .* implies that he is not.

best-selling *Best-selling* is the adjective derived from *best seller,* which is applied to anything that has sold very well, but particu-

B

larly a book which has sold a great number of copies: □ *Stephen King, author of the best-selling horror novels.*
• The term *best-selling* is applied to the author as well as the books: □ *best-selling novelist, Tom Clancy.*

between The preposition *between* is used either before a plural noun: □ *the interval between the acts* or in conjunction with *and;* it should not be used with *or:* □ *You must choose between your family life and* [not *or*] *your work.*
• Between should not be used with *each* or *every* followed by a singular noun: □ *There is a distance of one foot between the markers* [not *between each marker*].
See also I OR ME?

between or among? *Between* is generally used when speaking of the relationship of two things, and *among* of three or more: □ *There was a clear hostility between George and Henry.* □ *There was dissent among the committee members.*
• However, in current usage, between is becoming acceptable as a substitute for *among:* □ *agreement between the NATO countries,* although *among* is still only used for several elements. *Between* is also used when discussing the joint activities of a group: □ *The street musicians collected $50 between them,* and in the expression *between ourselves,* meaning "in confidence": □ *Just between ourselves, I think he's heading for a nervous breakdown.*
See also AMONG OR AMONGST?

bi- The prefix *bi-* always refers to the idea "two" but sometimes in the sense of doubling: □ *bicycle;* □ *bilingual,* and sometimes halving: □ *bisection.* This is particularly confusing with expressions like *biweekly,* which sometimes means "every two weeks" and sometimes "twice a week." It is probably best to avoid *biweekly* and *bimonthly* and express in a fuller form what is intended.
• *Biannual* means "twice a year," while *biennial* means "every two years." *Bicentennial* means "every two hundred years."

bias The doubling of the final *s* of the word *bias* before a suffix beginning with a vowel is optional. Most dictionaries give *biased,* with *biassed* as an acceptable alternative.
See also SPELLING 1.

bid The noun *bid,* normally meaning "an offer," takes on a new meaning in popular journalism, where it is used, particularly in headlines, to mean "an attempt or effort": □ *Athlete's bid for title* □ *Rescue bid fails* □ *Candidate's bid to win votes.*

big bang The *big-bang theory* is a cosmological theory suggesting that the universe originated in an explosion of a mass of material.
• In British English, the *Big Bang* is also a vogue expression to describe the radical reorganization of the London Stock Exchange in 1986: □ *The glamour and high rewards generated by Big Bang are filtering beyond the city dealers and into the traditionally sober world of the chartered accountant* (The Times of London, Sept. 21, 1987). □ *British Rail is to set up a new region for East Anglia, the first since nationalization in 1948, to cope with growth in the area caused largely by the effects of the Big Bang in the city of London* (The Guardian, Sept. 22, 1987).

billion *Billion* means "one thousand million," and this usage has been increasingly adopted in Britain and internationally. (*Billion* has traditionally meant "one million million" in Britain.)

• With specific figures, the word *of* is not used: □ *Five billion dollars,* not *five billions of dollars.* When used to mean "a great number," *billions of* is sometimes used: □ *Billions of people are living in poverty.*

bio- The prefix *bio-* comes from the Greek word bios, meaning "life," and words beginning with it have a connection with life or living organisms: □ *biology* □ *biography* □ *biopsy.*

• There are several recently coined words having the *bio-* prefix: □ *bionic* "the application of knowledge about living systems to the development of artificial systems" □ *biodegradable* "able to decompose organically without harming the environment" □ *biorhythms* "supposed regular cycles in human physiological processes that affect emotions and behavior" □ *bioethics* "study of moral problems connected with such issues as euthanasia, surrogate motherhood, genetic engineering, etc."

bizarre Note the spelling of this word, meaning "eccentric or odd." There is a single *z* and a double *r*.

• Do not confuse *bizarre* with *bazaar,* "a type of market."

black *Black* is the word now usually applied to dark-skinned people of Afro-Caribbean origins and is the term most black people themselves prefer: □ *black power* □ *black consciousness.* In Britain it is sometimes extended to include other nonwhite races. *Colored* (as opposed to *people of color*) is considered offensive; in South Africa it is a technical term used to refer to South Africans of mixed descent. The terms *Negro* and *Negress* are also considered offensive.

• *Black* is used in many words and phrases, usually having negative connotations: □ *black magic* □ *a black day* □ *black market.* Some black people resent the association of the color black with evil and unpleasantness and, while it is difficult to find synonyms for established words such as *blackmail,* it is desirable to avoid such possibly offensive terms as: □ *a black look* □ *black spot* □ *blacken someone's name.*

blame *Blame,* as a verb, means "hold responsible; place responsibility on": *He's to blame for all this confusion.* The expression *blame (it) on:* □ *They all blame it on me* is disliked by some careful users, who would substitute: □ *They blame me for it* or: □ *They put the blame on me.* However, the usage is well-established and is acceptable in all but very formal contexts.

blatant or **flagrant?** *Blatant* and *flagrant* are each concerned with overtly offensive behavior, but their usage is not identical. *Blatant* means "crassly and conspicuously obvious": □ *She was dressed in a blatantly seductive manner;* and "offensively noisy." *Flagrant* means "conspicuously shocking or outrageous": □ *The European parliament sees the tougher measures as a "flagrant violation of human rights and justice"* (*Sunday Times,* July 19, 1987).

• *Blatant* may be used of a person: □ *a blatant liar,* but *flagrant* is used only of abstract things and carries a stronger suggestion of moral disapproval.

blessed This word sometimes causes problems with pronunciation. The word *blessed,* the past tense of the verb *bless:* □ *He blessed the child,* is pronounced [blest]. The noun or adjective *blessed:*

B

□ *the blessed event* □ *the Blessed Sacrament,* is usually pronounced [*bles*id] but is occasionally pronounced [blest].

blond or **blonde?** These two spellings of the word meaning "light in color," are sometimes confused. *Blond* is used when the subject is masculine: □ *He has blond hair; blonde* is used when the subject is feminine: □ *She is a blonde.*

blue-chip *Blue-chip* is a stock-market term referring to a share issue that is considered to be both reliable and profitable: □ *a blue-chip investment.*

• It is extended to companies and any extremely worthwhile asset or property: □ *one of the world's most successful manufacturers . . . with a blue-chip reputation* (*Sunday Times,* June 7, 1987). The meaning now seems to have become further extended, to something like "classy" or "fashionable and exclusive": □ *polo, the blue-chip sport* (*Daily Telegraph,* July 23, 1987), although many people dislike the use of the term in this way.

blueprint A *blueprint* is literally a print used for mechanical drawing, engineering, and architectural designs. It is used metaphorically to mean any plan, scheme, or prototype: □ *a blueprint for a successful life* □ *A Blueprint for Government Ethics* (editorial headline, *The New York Times,* Jan. 3, 1989). Although a literal blueprint is a finished plan, the metaphorical use, very popular as a jargon and journalistic term, is just as often applied to preliminary schemes. Care should be taken, however, not to overuse this word.

boat or **ship?** The use of *boat* or *ship* is mainly a matter of size. *Boat* is usually applied to smaller vessels, especially those that stay in shallow or sheltered waters: □ *a rowboat* □ *lifeboat,* and *ship* to larger vessels that travel the open seas: □ *steamship* □ *warship.*

• Most sailing expressions refer to ships even when applied to boats: □ *amidships* □ *aboard ship* □ *The fishing boat was shipwrecked.*

bona fide Bona fide is an adjective meaning "of good faith; genuine or sincere": □ *I will accept any bona fide offer. Bona fides* is a singular noun meaning "good faith, sincerity, honest intention": □ *He had no documentary proof, but we did not doubt his bona fides.*

• *Bona fide* is also sometimes used to mean "authentic," as in: □ *It's not a reproduction; it''s a bona fide Matisse.*

Bona fide is pronounced [*bōnă fīd*], in Britain [*bōnă fīdi*]. Bona fides is pronounced [*bōnă fīdeez*].

born or **borne?** These two spellings are sometimes confused. *Borne* is the past participle of the verb *bear:* □ *They had borne enough pain.* □ *The following points should be borne in mind.* □ *His account is simply not borne out by the facts.* □ *It was borne upon him that the decision was irrevocable.* □ *airborne supplies.* In the sense of "giving birth," *borne* is used in phrases where the female who bears is the subject: *She has borne six children,* and also in the passive with *by:* □ *borne by her. Born* is used for all other passive constructions when the verb is not followed with *by:* □ *He was born in Italy.* □ *Twins were born to her.* □ *a born leader* □ *his foreign-born wife.*

born-again The term *born-again* was originally confined to the con-

text of evangelical Christianity, to mean "converted": □ *a born-
again believer.*
• The term is now often used generally to refer to a conversion to
any cause or belief, particularly when accompanied by extreme enthusiasm or fervor: □ *a born-again conservationist* □ *In their
"born-again" zeal, some former opponents of the E.E.C. may develop dangerous illusions on the possibilities of . . . reform of
E.E.C. institutions* (*The Guardian,* May 10, 1987). Occasionally,
born-again is also used to mean "renewed; fresh, new, or resur-
gent": □ *a born-again car* □ *born-again post offices with remod-
eled buildings* □ *Born-again Baker Street* (London Transport advertisement, 1987). The origin of the term *born again* is John 3:3 in
the Bible.

borne see BORN OR BORNE?

borrow Besides its literal meaning of "take something for a limited
period with intention of returning it": □ *I borrowed this book
from the library, borrow* can also be used metaphorically to refer
to words, ideas, etc., taken from other sources: □ *Wagner borrowed this theme from Norse mythology.* □ *Some American
slang is borrowed from Yiddish.*
• One borrows *from,* not *off* someone: □ *I borrowed it off my friend*
is generally considered wrong. See also LEND OR LOAN?

both *Both* is used as a determiner, a pronoun, and a conjunction:
□ *Both legs were amputated.* □ *I like both.* □ *He is both an artist
and a writer.* It should not be used where more than two things
are involved, as in: □ *She's both selfish, mean, and malicious.*
• The constructions □ *Both his parents are teachers* and □ *Both
of his parents are teachers* are equally acceptable. However, in
possessive constructions, it is usually necessary to use *of:* □ *the
opinion of both of them,* not *both of their opinion.*
    When two things are being considered separately, it is often bet-
ter to use *each* to avoid ambiguity. □ *We were both given a box of
chocolates* might involve two boxes or one shared box. In general,
one should be careful about placing the word *both* in order to avoid
ambiguity: □ *He has acted in both films and theater* might suggest *two films.*
    Both as a conjunction goes with *and,* and as with all such pairs
of conjunctions must link grammatically similar things. One can
say: □ *She is both charming and intelligent,* but not *She is both
charming and an intellectual.*
    Both is often used redundantly, when some other phrase in the
sentence conveys the same sense: □ *They are both identical.*
□ *Both of them are equally to blame.*

bottleneck A *bottleneck* is a term originally applied only to narrow
stretches of road that cause traffic jams. It is now extended to anything that holds up free movement or progress: □ *A bottleneck at
City Hall is resulting in long waits for licenses.*
• As a vogue word, it is sometimes overworked and its literal meaning forgotten. The original metaphor is referring to the narrowness
of the neck of a bottle, which makes such phrases as: □ *an enormous bottleneck* □ *an increasing bottleneck* □ *reducing the bottleneck* absurd.

bottom line *Bottom line* is a vogue expression, taken from financial

B

reports where the final line registers the net profit or loss. It can mean "the most important or primary point of consideration": □ *The bottom line is that we have no more resources for the project;* or "the final result": □ *The bottom line was their divorce.* Care should be taken not to overuse this phrase.

• It is also sometimes used as a hyphenated adjective to mean "having a pragmatic concern for cost and profit": □ *He has a bottom-line approach to running the company.*

bottom out To *bottom out* was formerly used to describe a leveling out of something that has reached its lowest point: *Industrial output is now bottoming out.* It is more recently being used to suggest that the low point is prior to an upsurge: □ *The market has now bottomed out and is expected to improve by the spring.*

bouquet Many users prefer to pronounce the first syllable of this word [boo-] rather than [bō-], and to stress the second syllable [boo*kay*].

bourgeois This word, meaning "middle-class": □ *a bourgeois mentality,* is sometimes misspelled. Note the first syllable *bour* and the *e* that softens the *g* in the second syllable.

• The word comes from the Old French word *borjois,* meaning "burgher or merchant."

boy A *boy* is a male child or adolescent. The use of the noun as a synonym for "man" is largely restricted to informal contexts: □ *one of the boys* □ *a local boy* □ *the new boy* □ *a night out with the boys.*

boycott This word, meaning "refuse to deal with": □ *boycott the Olympic games,* is sometimes misspelled. Note the double *t* at the end of the word.

• The term is an eponym; it originates from the name of Charles Cunningham *Boycott* (1832-97), an Irish land agent who was ostracized for refusing to grant reductions in rent.

brackets Brackets, or square brackets, are used for brackets within parentheses: □ *Browning's wife (the poet Elizabeth Barrett Browning [1806–61]) was an invalid.* They are also used to indicate editorial comment or explanation in quoted matter: □ *The Young Visiters [sic]* □ *"who would fardels [burdens] bear."* To use parentheses implies that the words inside them were part of the original quotation. See also **PARENTHESES**.

brake or **break?** These words are sometimes confused. A *brake* is a device to slow something down: □ *the brakes on a car. Break* has many meanings including "(cause to) full into pieces," "stop," and "transgress": □ *break a vase* □ *break for lunch* □ *break the law.*

breach or **breech?** The word *breach* means "the breaking or violating of a rule or arrangement": □ *a breach of promise. Breach* should not be confused with *breech,* "the rear part of the body" and "the part of a gun behind the barrel": □ *a breech birth.*

break see **BRAKE OR BREAK?**

breakthrough *Breakthrough* as a metaphor to mean "a sudden advance in (particularly scientific or technological) knowledge" has become something of a journalistic cliché. One reads, for example, of: □ *a major breakthrough in cancer research* so frequently that it has lost all impact.

• *Breakthrough* is also sometimes used to mean "success."

□ *Oscar breakthrough for film actress* or "new idea": □ *The big difference is the brightness, a major Magnavox breakthrough* (advertisement, *TV Guide*, Jan. 7-13, 1989).

breech see BREACH OR BREECH?

Britain The expression *Britain* is often used vaguely, sometimes as a substitute for *Great Britain*, sometimes for the *United Kingdom* or the *British Isles*. Assuming that it is an abbreviation of *Great Britain*, one uses it to mean England, Scotland, and Wales.
• The *United Kingdom* includes Northern Ireland as well as England, Scotland, and Wales. The *British Isles* includes all the United Kingdom, together with the Republic of Ireland, the Isle of Man, and the Channel Islands.

Briticisms British English is the basis on which the English of America, Australia, New Zealand, South Africa, the West Indies, and the rest of the English-speaking world was built. To greater or lesser degrees, the English of each of these countries has gone its own way, producing distinct varieties of English, while the English spoken in Britain has its own characteristics, known as Briticisms.
• Specifically British, usually in contrast to American, usage of grammar, spelling, and so forth, is discussed under various headings in this book. It is vocabulary and idiom that mark the speaker or writer of British English. A sentence such as: □ *I rang you from a call box, but the line was engaged* marks the speaker as British; in other English-speaking countries it would have been: *I called you from a phone booth, but the line was busy.* Such familiar words or phrases as: □ *bank holiday* □ *fortnight* □ *white coffee* □ *spring onion* □ *Father Christmas* □ *roundabout* (both in the senses of merry-go-round and traffic circle) are peculiarly British uses.

Of course, there is no one standard form of English spoken throughout Britain; marked differences in pronunciation, vocabulary, grammar, and usage are found in the different countries and regions of Britain. See also DIALECT.

brochure This word is usually pronounced [brōshoor].
• Note also the *ch*, not *sh*, in the spelling.

buffet In the senses "a counter where food is served" and "food set out on tables": □ *a buffet car* □ *a buffet lunch*, *buffet* is pronounced [bufay]. In the sense "strike sharply": □ *buffeted by the wind*, the pronunciation is [bufit].

bulk *Bulk* means "thickness, volume, or size; a heavy mass": □ *the vast bulk of the stone walls.* It is also used in the expression *in bulk* to mean "in large quantities": □ *We buy rice in bulk.*
• *Bulk* is frequently used to mean "the greater part of, the majority": □ *the bulk of her fortune* □ *the bulk of the population.* Some people object to the application of *bulk* to anything other than mass or volume, but this usage is established and generally acceptable.

bulletin This word, meaning "statement of news": *No further bulletin will be issued this evening,* is sometimes misspelled. Note the double *l* and single *t.*

buoyant This word, meaning "able to float": *a buoyant raft,* is sometimes misspelled. The most frequent mistake is to place the *u* and the *o* in the wrong order.

B

bureaucracy Note the spelling of this word: the first *u*, the vowels *eau*, and the suffix *-cracy* (not *-crasy*).

burglarize, burgle, rob, or **steal?** *Burglarize* is more frequent than *burgle*, a back-formation from burglar, and means "break into a building in order to steal": □ *Their house was burglarized/burgled when they were on vacation. Burglary* is one instance of *theft*, which is the general term for acts of stealing, and always involves unlawful entry. *Robbery* often involves violence, and one speaks of robbing a person or place: □ *rob a bank* □ *rob an old lady*, while one *steals* other people's possessions: □ *He stole her jewelry.*

burned or **burnt?** Either word may be used as the past tense and past participle of the verb *burn*. In transitive contexts *burned* is preferred (*burnt* in British English); in intransitive contexts *burned* is the preferred form: □ We *burned the letters.* □ *He has burned his hand.* □ *She burned with anger.* □ *The fire had burned all night.*
• See also **-ED** OR **-T?**
Burnt is also used as an adjective: □ *burnt toast* □ *a burnt offering.*
Burned is pronounced [bernd] or sometimes [bernt]; *burnt* is always pronounced [bernt].

bus Although the noun *bus* was originally short for *omnibus*, it is now never spelled with an apostrophe.
• The word was rarely used as a verb until the 1960's when the controversy over the practice of sending schoolchildren by bus to different districts in order to achieve a racial balance in the schools gave rise to the need for such a verb. The preferred spellings of the verb's forms are *buses, bused,* and *busing.*

business This word is sometimes misspelled. The most frequent mistake is the omission of the letter *i*, which is silent in the pronunciation.

but There are various problems with the usage of the word *but*. As a conjunction, it is used to link two opposing ideas: □ *He lives in New Jersey but works in New York.* It should not be used to link two harmonious ideas: □ *She is not American-born, but originates from Kenya*, and should not be used in a sentence with *however*, which conveys the same meaning: □ *But their suggestions for improvement, however, were ignored.*
• The problem with *but* used to mean "except" is whether it should be followed by an object or a subject; is it *all but he or all but him?* There is no absolute rule here, but a rough guide to natural usage is to use the object when it falls at the end of a clause and the subject when it comes in the middle: □ *They had all escaped but her.* □ *All but she had escaped.*
The expressions *can but* and *cannot but* are slightly formal and old-fashioned but still used: □ *setting a standard others can but hope to follow* (advertisement, *Sunday Times*, May 28, 1987). The oddity is that the expressions mean much the same thing, for the *not* of *cannot* combines with the *but* to form a double negative. When used with *help* in *can't help but,* a triple negative is formed, but in fact the expression is used positively: □ *I can't help but regard your attitude as hostile.* The phrase is clumsy and should be avoided. The combination *cannot help but* is awkward and should

be avoided; the expressions *can but* and *cannot but* can also be rephrased: □ *I can only regard your attitude as hostile.* □ *I can't help regarding your attitude as hostile.* See also CONJUNCTIONS; HELP; NOTHING BUT; NOT ONLY ... BUT ALSO.

buyout A *buyout* is the purchase of a company, often by a group of managers or employees: □ *Buyout Incentives of '86 Legislation* (headline, *The New York Times*, Jan. 2, 1989). □ *And* ... *certainly in the U.K.* ... *management buyouts are currently a very popular flavor* (*The Bookseller*, Oct. 9, 1987).

by or bye? These spellings are sometimes confused. Note the spelling of the following compounds and expressions: □ *bylaw* □ *bypass* □ *byproduct* □ *by and by* ("later") □ *by and large* ("generally"), □ *by the by* "incidentally" □ *a bye* in sports, and □ *bye-bye* (informal for *goodbye*).

by the same token *By the same token* is a fashionable expression meaning "for the same reason; in a similar way": □ *Middle-aged men should avoid overworking because of the effects of stress on the heart and, by the same token, should avoid fatty foods.* Care should be taken to avoid overusing this phrase.

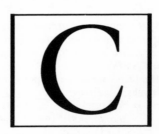

Caesarean This word, meaning "of or relating to any of the Caesars," is used particularly in the expression *Caesarean section,* "the surgical operation for the delivery of a baby by cutting through the wall of the mother's abdomen and into the womb." The variant spellings *Caesarian, Cesarean,* and *Cesarian* are also used. Note, too, that any of these spellings may be written with a lowercase *c: She had a caesarean.*
  • The word derives from Julius *Caesar,* who, it is traditionally thought, was born by this method.

calendar, calender, or **colander?** These words are often confused. A *calendar* tells the date, a *calender* is a machine used to smooth paper or cloth, and a *colander* is a perforated bowl used for draining food.
  • The first two words are pronounced in the same way [kalindĕ]. *Colander* is pronounced [kulĕndĕ] or [kolăndĕ].

calorie Note the spelling of this word, which is a unit for measuring the energy value of food and also a measurement of heat.

Calvary see CAVALRY OR CALVARY?

camouflage This word, meaning "disguise": □ *The trees provided excellent camouflage,* is sometimes misspelled. Note the *ou* and the soft *g.*

can or **may?** The verb *can* means "be permitted" or "be able"; the verb *may* means "be permitted" or "be likely." In the sense of "be permitted," *may* is preferred in formal contexts, and *can* is best restricted to informal contexts: □ *Can I come to your party?* □ *May I borrow your pen, please?*
  • The negative contraction *mayn't* is disliked by many people and is usually replaced with *can't: Can't* [not *Mayn't*] *she stay?*
    These verbs can be ambiguous: □ *He can go* may mean "He is permitted to go" or "He is able to go"; □ *He may go* may mean "He is permitted to go" or "He is likely to go." *Could* and *might,* the past tenses of *can* and *may,* respectively, are equally ambiguous: □ *She said he could go.* □ *She said he might go.*
    Could and *might* are also used in polite requests: *Could/Might I have another cup of coffee, please?*
    See also BUT; CANNOT AND CAN'T; HELP; MAY OR MIGHT?

candelabra The word *candelabra,* meaning "a branched candlestick or lamp," is in the original Latin word a plural noun, from the singular *candelabrum.* Careful speakers therefore consider it incorrect to speak of: □ *a valuable candelabra* or to say: □ *There were candelabras in every room,* although such usage is widespread.

• *Candelabra* are often confused with *chandeliers,* which hang from the ceiling, whereas *candelabra* stand on surfaces.

cannon or **canon?** These two words are sometimes confused. A *cannon* is a large gun; a *canon,* with a single *n,* is a ruling laid down by the church, a title given to a clergyman, or the complete work of one author: □ *Shakespeare's canon.*

cannot and **can't** *Can not* is sometimes written as two words, but *cannot* is standard. It may be necessary to write *can not* when the *not* is stressed: □ *No, I can* not *lend you any more money,* or in sentences such as: □ *It can* not *only chop vegetables but also grind coffee beans,* where the *not* goes with *only,* rather than *can.*

• Care should be taken when using *cannot* in such constructions as: □ *Her work cannot be too highly praised.* □ *You cannot put too much pepper in,* where ambiguity may arise. Was her work excellent or poor? Should a large or small amount of pepper be put in?

The contraction *can't* is normally used in speech and often in writing.

See also **BUT; CAN OR MAY?; HELP**

canon see **CANNON OR CANON?**

can't see **CANNOT AND CAN'T.**

canvas or **canvass?** *Canvas* is a certain type of woven cloth: □ *a canvas bag* □ *a painting on canvas. Canvass,* with a double *s,* means "solicit votes": □ *He canvassed the neighborhood for his party.*

capability, capacity, or **ability?** Each of these words refers to the power to do something. *Capability* suggests having the qualities needed to do something: □ *She has the capability to handle the work. Capacity* suggests being able to absorb or receive: □ *Children are born with the capacity to acquire language. Ability* may sometimes suggest above-average skills: □ *He has considerable mathematical ability.*

• *Capacity* has several other meanings: "volume." □ *The pot has a capacity of two quarts,* "(maximum) output": □ *The factory is working at full capacity,* "a particular role": □ *I am speaking in my capacity as treasurer.* It is also used as an adjective in the journalistic phrase: □ *a capacity crowd at the stadium.*

capital letters Capital letters are used to draw attention to a particular word. There are some generally accepted rules for their use, but some areas where it is a matter of choice.

• Capitals are used to mark the first word of a sentence, a direct quotation, or a direct question within a sentence (see also **QUESTION MARK; QUOTATION MARKS; SENTENCES**). They are sometimes used after a colon (see **COLON**). They are used for the first word of each line of poetry: □ *Forewarned of madness/In three days time at dusk/The fit masters him* (Robert Graves), and for the major words of titles of literary, musical, or artistic works: *The Mill on the Floss* □ *Peter and the Wolf.*

Capitals are used for proper nouns and most adjectives derived from them: □ *John Brown* □ *New York* □ *Texaco* □ *Wall Street-* □ *French* □ *Jewish* □ *Freudian.* If an adjective is not closely connected with its original proper noun, it does not usually take a capital: □ *brussels sprouts* □ *french doors,* and capitals are sometimes not used for verbs derived from proper nouns:

□ *Anglicize* □ *boycott* (see also **EPONYMS; TRADE NAMES**). Titles of people or places are capitalized when part of a proper name but not when used alone: □ *my aunt* □ *Aunt Jane* □ *universities* □ *Harvard University* □ *a professor of history* □ *Professor Thompson*. For institutions the rule is that capitals are used in specific references but not in general ones: □ *many world governments* □ *the Government has agreed* □ *he goes to a Baptist church* □ *St. Mark's Church* □ *the Church of England*. The pronoun *I* always takes a capital, but no other pronouns apart from those referring to God, where some people choose to capitalize *He, Him, His.*

Capitals are used for days of the week, months, holidays, and religious holidays: □ *Monday* □ *February* □ *Easter* □ *Yom Kippur,* but not for seasons. They are used for historical, cultural, and geological periods: □ *the Restoration* □ *the Enlightenment* □ *the Spanish Civil War* □ *the Stone Age.* Capitalize Capitol (the building), not capital (a city).

Capitals should never be used for emphasis; italics should be used for this purpose: an *enormous* [not *ENORMOUS*] bear!

See also **ABBREVIATIONS; HYPHEN; COLON; EAST, EAST,** OR **EASTERN?; NORTH, NORTH,** OR **NORTHERN?; SOUTH, SOUTH,** OR **SOUTHERN?; WEST, WEST,** OR **WESTERN?**

carat, karat or **caret?** These words are sometimes confused. A *carat* is a unit for measuring the weight of precious stones; a *karat* is a unit for measuring the purity of gold. A *caret,* spelled with an *e,* is a character used in written or printed matter to indicate that an insertion should be made.

carburetor Note the spelling of this word, particularly the *u* and the single *t.*
• The spelling in British English is *carburettor.*

carcass This word, which describes the body of a dead animal: □ *a chicken carcass,* is spelled *carcass* (also *carcase* in British English).

caret see **CARAT, KARAT,** OR **CARET?**

case *Case* is very often loosely used to mean "state of affairs, the truth," in sentences where it is either redundant or could be replaced by simpler or more specific wording: □ *Is it the case that you are his aunt?* could be changed to: *Are you his aunt?* □ *Teenage pregnancies are now less common than was the case five years ago* could be changed to: *. . . than they were five years ago.* The expression is acceptable in sentences such as: □ *This rule does not apply in your case.*
• *In case* is used as a conjunction: □ *in case it rains.* The use of *just in case,* with no clause: □ *Take your raincoat, just in case,* is acceptable only in informal contexts.

caster or **castor?** For the senses "a swiveling wheel on furniture" and "a container from which sugar may be shaken," the spelling *caster.* The medicinal or lubricating oil, *castor oil,* is, however, always spelled with an *o.*

catalyst *Catalyst* is a scientific term applying to a substance that speeds up a chemical reaction though itself remaining chemically unchanged. It is also used as a metaphor to apply to a person or an event that, by its action, provokes significant change: □ *The shooting of Archduke Ferdinand acted as the catalyst for the out-*

break of World War I. Overuse of the word *catalyst* is disliked by some.

catarrh This word, which describes an inflammation of the throat and nasal passages, is sometimes misspelled. Note particularly the single *t* and the *rrh*.

catastrophic The adjective *catastrophic* comes from *catastrophe,* which was originally used in Greek drama to describe the denouement of a tragedy. The word should be applied to extremely severe disasters and tragic events: □ *the catastrophic earthquake in Mexico City.*

• It is often used informally for quite minor disasters: □ *Do you remember that catastrophic dinner party when I burned the casserole?*

Catch-22 In Joseph Heller's novel *Catch-22,* published in 1961, the catch in question was that airmen could be excused from flying missions only if they were of unsound mind, but a request to be excused from flying missions was a sign of a concern for personal safety in the face of danger and therefore evidence of a rational mind, so it was impossible to escape flying missions. A *Catch-22 situation* is any such circular dilemma or predicament from which there is no escape, and is often extended to any situation or problem where the victim feels that it is impossible to gain a personal benefit or make the right decision.

Catholic or **catholic?** *Catholic* with a small *c* is an adjective meaning "general, wide-ranging, or comprehensive": □ *It is a catholic anthology, which includes poems by Shelley, Auden, and Allen Ginsberg. Catholic,* with a capital, as a noun or adjective, usually refers to the Roman Catholic Church: □ *He's a good Catholic.* □ *They go to a Catholic school.*

• It is advisable to use the term *Roman Catholic,* not *Catholic* alone, when speaking in a specifically theological context.

cavalry or **Calvary:** These words are sometimes confused. *Cavalry* is used to refer to soldiers trained to fight on horseback and the branch of the army that uses armored vehicles. *Calvary* is the hill near Jerusalem where Christ was crucified.

caviar or **carviare?** Each of these spellings is acceptable for the word that describes the salted roe of the sturgeon, with *caviar* more frequent.

ceiling *Ceiling* is frequently used, particularly in economic jargon, to mean "an upper limit": *The organization is urging the government to put a ceiling on rent increases.* As the word *ceiling,* in its literal meaning, is in constant use, it can sound odd to speak of *increasing* or *reducing a ceiling,* an *unworkable ceiling,* and so on: □ *Sir Gordon Borrie . . . said, "If money and manpower ceilings were to become too tight in relation to the demands put upon my office, then the taxpayer . . . would be likely to pay the price in other ways" (The Guardian,* July 1, 1987).

celibate *Celibacy* means "the state of being unmarried, often because of a religious vow." *Celibate* is used as a noun to describe a person living in a state of celibacy and, by implication, chastity: □ *As celibates, priests find it difficult to give advice on marital problems,* and as an adjective: □ *She never married but chose a celibate life.*

• The word is sometimes used to mean "abstaining from sexual intercourse": □ *After 20 years of marriage, they decided to live a celibate life together.* Careful users consider this usage to be incorrect.

Celsius see CENTIGRADE, CELSIUS OR FAHRENHEIT?

censure, censor, or **censer?** The verbs *censure* and *censor* are often confused. *Censure* means "to blame, criticize strongly, or condemn": □ *The judge censured them for the brutality of the attack. Censor* means "examine letters, publications, films, etc., and remove any material that is considered obscene, libelous, or contrary to government or official policy": □ *All prisoners' mail is censored.* The person who examines letters, etc., in this way is also known as a *censor.*

• The adjective from *censor* is *censorial* and from *censure, censorious.*

Care should be taken not to confuse the spelling of *censor* with that of *censer,* a word meaning "a container used for burning incense."

centenary or **centennial?** *Centenary* and *centennial* are each used to mean a 100-year anniversary: □ *1982, the centenary of Joyce's birth. Centennial* is used more frequently, however, and can also be used as an adjective: □ *a centennial celebration.*

• The recommended pronunciation of *centenary* is [sentenăree], although some people pronounce it [sentenăree]. *Centennial* is pronounced [senteniăl].

centigrade, Celsius, Fahrenheit? All these terms denote scales of temperature. The centigrade and *Celsius* scales are identical; the degree Celsius is now the principal unit of temperature in scientific contexts.

• The Fahrenheit scale, on which water freezes at 32° and boils at 212°, refers mainly to the weather: □ *The temperature reached 80° today.* The centigrade scale, on which water freezes at 0° and boils at 100° at sea level, is also known as the Celsius scale.

Celsius and *Fahrenheit* should always begin with a capital letter, being the surnames of the scientists who devised the scales.

center or **middle?** *Center* and *middle* are sometimes used virtually synonymously: □ *Put it in the center/middle of the table. Center* is used as a precise geometrical term: □ *the center of the circle,* whereas *middle* is more often used generally in situations where the geometric center is not obvious or measurable: *the middle of the sea.* For *center,* the British spelling is *centre.*

• *Center* is also used to mean a place where activity is concentrated: □ *shopping center. Middle* is used to mean the point equally distant from extremes, either literally: □ *middle name,* or figuratively: □ *middle-of-the-road politics.*

center on or **center around?** The verb *to center* can be used with *on* or *upon:* □ *His argument centers on* (or *upon*) *Marxist theory.*

• The expression *center around:* □ *The film centers around the Vietnam War.* □ *Her hobbies centered around the arts* is frequently used, although it is disliked by many careful users, as being illogical, as, it is argued, a center cannot be *around* anything.

Because this usage is so widely objected to, it is best avoided.

centrifugal There are two pronunciations for this word. The traditional pronunciation stresses the second syllable [sen*tri*fyoogăl], but the alternative pronunciation [sen*tri*fyoogăl] is widely used in contemporary English.

centuries People often become confused about when centuries start and end and how one should refer to them. As there was no year A.D. 0, we calculate in hundred-year periods from the year A.D. 1. This means that the 20th century began on Jan. 1, 1901 (not 1900), and will end on Dec. 31, 2000.
• Although the expressions *the 1800's* and *the 19th century* are almost synonymous, in fact the 1800's means 1800–1899 inclusive and the 19th century 1801-1900 inclusive.

cereal or **serial?** These two words are sometimes confused. A *cereal* is a plant that produces grain for food: □ *breakfast cereals.* This word must not be confused with *serial,* which describes a novel or play produced in several parts and at regular intervals: □ *a television serial.*

ceremonial or **ceremonious?** The adjectives *ceremonial* and *ceremonious* are sometimes confused. *Ceremonial* means "marked by ceremony or ritual": □ *The Inauguration is the first ceremonial occasion for a new President. Ceremonious* means "devoted to formality and ceremony" and usually carries a slightly pejorative suggestion of overpunctiliousness or pomposity: □ *She presided over the dinner table with a ceremonious air.*

chain reaction *Chain reaction* is an expression from scientific terminology referring to a chemical or nuclear reaction that creates energy or products that cause further reaction. It is now more often used to mean any series of events where each one sets off the next one, though this usage is disliked by some: □ *The shooting started a chain reaction, which eventually set off the street riots.*

chair The noun *chair* is sometimes used to denote a person presiding over a meeting, committee, etc., to avoid the potentially sexist terms *chairman* and *chairwoman* and the controversial *chairperson:* □ *The new chair will be elected next week.*
• This usage is disliked by many. See also **PERSON.**
 The verb *chair,* meaning "preside over," is acceptable to most users: □ *The leader of the union chaired the conference.*

challenge *Challenge* is often used in a sense that is considerably removed from its usual meanings, to mean "stimulate" or, as a noun, "something that is stimulating or demanding": □ *Gifted children need challenging work.* □ *The job presents a challenge.*
• *Challenged* sometimes means little more than "interested or excited": □ *The film challenged us visually and musically.*

chamois This word may cause problems with pronunciation and spelling. The antelope *chamois* is pronounced [*sham*ee], sometimes [*sham*wah]. The leather *chamois* made from the skin of this animal or a sheep is also usually pronounced [*sham*ee].

changeable This word, meaning "liable to change": □ *changeable weather,* is sometimes misspelled. Note the *e* of change, which is retained before the suffix *-able.*
• See also **SPELLING 3.**

chaperon or **chaperone?** An older woman who accompanies a young unmarried woman on social occasions is known as a *chaperon* or a *chaperone.* The noun, and its derived verb, may be spelled with or without the final *e*, *chaperone* being more frequent.

• The usual pronunciation for both spellings is [shapĕrōn].

character The word *character* can be used legitimately for the distinguishing qualities that make up individual people or things, of people with unusual traits, of people portrayed in works of fiction, and of moral firmness and integrity: □ *Such behavior did not seem consistent with what I knew of her character.* □ *It is a lively town with a great deal of character.* □ *Everyone knows him—he's a real character.* □ *Mrs. Gamp is a minor character in* Martin Chuzzlewit. □ *Anyone who takes this job on will need character and determination.* □ *The character issue is important in the next election.*

• *Character* is often used vaguely in such phrases as: □ *the strange character of this declaration* □ *programs of an intellectual character* □ *the intimate character of our conversation.* Where it is used to mean no more than "type" or "quality," *character* would be better replaced or omitted.

charisma The word *charisma* was originally used only in theological contexts to refer to supernatural spiritual gifts of healing, speaking in tongues, etc. A *charismatic church* is one where emphasis is placed on the exercise of these gifts. *Charisma* and *charismatic* are now often used to describe a person with unusual qualities of leadership, personal appeal, and magnetism, though care should be taken to avoid overusing these expressions: □ *Lange is planning to run a presidential-style election campaign, based on his own charisma* (*Sunday Times,* July 5, 1987).

• The word *charismatic* is sometimes used more loosely to mean "charming or showing a confident efficiency": □ *Our client . . . is looking for two charismatic sales managers* (advertisement, *Daily Telegraph,* June 10, 1987).

chauvinism The word *chauvinism* means "excessive or fanatical patriotism" and comes from Nicholas *Chauvin,* a soldier of Napoleon's army who was noted for his overzealous patriotism. It is used more loosely to describe any prejudiced belief in the superiority of a group or cause, particularly in the term *male chauvinism,* which is often applied by feminists to male supremacists: □ *"The media . . . fanned the flames of male chauvinism, stereotyping all women who took a serious interest in the issues as bra-burners"* (Elaine Storkey, *What's Right with Feminism*).

• Some people, encountering the word for the first time in the context of male chauvinism, have taken *chauvinist* to be synonymous with *sexist:* Her husband's an awful *chauvinist.* The word should not be used in this sense unless preceded by *male.*

chilblain A sore that is caused by exposure to the cold is known as a *chilblain.* The word is sometimes misspelled, the most common error being to retain the second *l* of *chill,* which has been lost in the formation of this noun.

childish or **childlike?** *Childish* is almost always used in a pejorative sense to indicate immaturity and the less endearing characteristics of childhood: □ *She refused to tolerate his selfish behavior and childish outbreaks of temper.* □ *The drawings looked like childish scribbles. Childlike* is usually applied to the attractive qualities of childhood, such as enthusiasm and innocence: □ *At 85, she retains a childlike curiosity about her environment.*

Chinese *Chinese* as an adjective means "coming from China": □ *Chinese writing;* it is also used as a singular or plural noun for a person or people of Chinese nationality: □ *I saw a group of Chinese touring around Washington.* □ *There is a Chinese studying at my college.*

• The singular expression a *Chinese* sounds odd to most people, who prefer to say a *Chinese man/woman.* The term *Chinaman* is out-of-date, derogatory, and offensive.

chiropodist This word, describing a person who treats and looks after people's feet, may be pronounced [ki*ro*prop*ŏ*dist] or [shi*ro*pŏdist], although the first of these is preferred by many users.

cholesterol This word is sometimes misspelled. Notice the two *o's* and two *e's.*

• Remember also that the first syllable is *chol-* and not *chlo-* as in *chlorine.*

chord or **cord?** These spellings are sometimes confused. In the musical or mathematical senses, the spelling is *chord. Chord* is also used when describing an emotional reaction: □ *He struck the right chord.* In the anatomical sense: □ *umbilical cord* □ *vocal cords* □ *spinal cord,* the word is spelled without the *h.* The word that describes any type of string is spelled *cord:* □ *nylon cord.*

Christian name see FIRST NAME, CHRISTIAN NAME, FORENAME, GIVEN NAME, OR BAPTISMAL NAME?

chronic *Chronic* means "long-standing; permanently present": □ *She has suffered from chronic asthma all her life.* □ *Malnutrition is a chronic problem in the Third World.*

• It is often confused, in its medical context, with *acute,* which means "intense and of sudden onset": □ *I suddenly got a chronic pain in my shoulder.* Because *chronic* is so often used of pains and illnesses to mean "very bad," it is also sometimes used in nonstandard British English to mean "bad or dreadful": □ *"Drink! my word! Something chronic"* (Shaw, *Pygmalion*).

chutzpah *Chutzpah* or *chutzpa* is a Yiddish expression now in general use that, in one word, conveys "nerve, gall, effrontery, audacity, brazen self-confidence, arrogance."

• In *The Joys of Yiddish,* Leo Rosten writes, "Chutzpa is that quality enshrined in a man who, having killed his mother and father, throws himself on the mercy of the court because he is an orphan." It is pronounced [*khuut*spă].

circumstances *Under the circumstances* suggests a connection between circumstances and an action: □ *He was starving and, under the circumstances, cannot be blamed for stealing food.*

• *Under* is also used in a negative context: □ *Under no circumstances will I allow it.*

cirrhosis This word is sometimes misspelled. Note particularly the *-rrh-* combination.

city or **town?** In general a *city* is a place that is larger and more important than a town: □ *She had only lived in small towns before and was apprehensive about moving to the city.*

civic, civil, or **civilian?** These words all refer to citizenship but have different meanings. *Civic* means 'of a city': □ *civic affairs*, or is used of the attitudes of citizens to their city: □ *a sense of civic pride. Civil* relates to citizens of a state, rather than a city: □ *civil rights*, or is used as distinct from criminal, religious, or military: □ *civil law* □ *civil marriage* □ *civil defense. Civilian* means anyone not a member of the armed forces, police, or other official uniformed state organization: □ *The major had been a bank manager in civilian life.*

• *Civil* is also used to mean "polite or courteous": □ *The proprietor was very civil to us.*

clad or **clothed?** *Clad* means the same as *clothed* but, except in such expressions as *thinly clad* or *ill-clad*, is considered archaic or poetic. It can be used of things other than clothes: □ *rose-clad trellises* □ *snow-clad* □ *ironclad*, or of clothes where the note of archaism is appropriate: □ *clad in armor*, but for ordinary dress, clothed is used: □ *She was clothed completely in black.*

• *Clad* cannot be used as opposed to *naked*, as can *clothed*: □ *With that paunch, he looks sexier clothed these days.*

claim The verb *claim* means "demand something as a right": □ *The dismissed workers are claiming unemployment pay;* "take something one rightfully owns or that is one's due": □ *He claimed his father's estate.* □ *She claimed the prize*, and "assert forcefully, especially when faced with possible contradiction": □ *He claims that there have been no composers of genius since Beethoven.*

• This last use was at one time disliked, as having no connection with the recognition of rights, but it is now widely used and accepted. It should, however, be avoided when the assertion is not particularly forceful or controversial, when *maintain, allege, contend,* or sometimes just *say,* is often better.

clandestine This word, meaning "secret," is generally stressed on the second syllable [klandĕstin], although it is possible to stress the word on the first syllable [*klan*dĕstin].

classic or **classical?** There is some overlap in the meanings of *classic* and *classical*, but they have distinct separate meanings. *Classic* means "typical of, or unusually fine in its class": □ *classic symptoms of diabetes* □ *a classic example of 1960's pop art. Classical* essentially means "of the classics, i.e., the literature, history, and philosophy of ancient Greece and Rome": □ *a classical education* □ *classical drama.*

• Classic is also used to mean "elegant and unlikely to become dated": □ *a classic dress* □ *a classic design*, and "definitive, absolute": □ *The court, however, refused . . . an injunction halting further distribution of "Rear Window," . . . identifying a possible "public injury by denying the public the opportunity to view a classic film for many years to come"* (Variety, Jan. 4-10, 1989). While *the classics* are the works of ancient Greece and Rome, *a classic* is any work of the highest standard and enduring quality, whatever its date: □ *the jazz classic "St. Louis Blues."*

Classical, too, can suggest elegance, but there is a definite link with the standards and forms of ancient Greece and Rome. *Classical music* is, therefore, the music of about 1750–1830, which is characterized by its formal beauty. The term is, however, widely applied to all serious music, as distinct from jazz, folk, and popular music.

claustrophobia The fear of being in confined spaces is known as *claustrophobia*. Note the *claustro-* in the spelling.

clean or **cleanse?** Whereas *clean* functions as adjective, noun, adverb, and verb, *cleanse* is used only as a verb. The two words are almost synonymous, but *cleanse* has more of a suggestion of very thorough cleaning that also purifies: □ *I'll just clean the apartment quickly.* □ *The wound must be cleansed before a dressing is applied.*

• *Cleanse* has a more formal sound than *clean* and is sometimes used figuratively to mean "purify," as it is in the older translations of the Bible: □ *Wash me thoroughly from mine iniquity, and cleanse me from my sin* (Psalm 51:2).

clichés The word cliché, referring to a phrase or idiom that has become stale through overuse, is almost always used pejoratively. Examples of clichés are: □ *from time immemorial* □ *as old as the hills* □ *last but not least.*

• Not all fixed phrases are necessarily bad. Some clichés were quite apt when first used but have become hackneyed over the years. One can hardly avoid using the occasional cliché, but clichés that are inefficient in conveying their meaning or are inappropriate to the occasion should be avoided.

There are various categories of cliché. There are overworked metaphors and similes: □ *leave no stone unturned* □ *as good as gold,* overused idioms: □ *to add insult to injury* □ *a blessing in disguise,* the clichés of public speakers: □ *someone who needs no introduction* □ *in no uncertain terms* □ *without fear or favor,* and the quotation (or usually misquotation) from the Bible or Shakespeare: □ *to gild the lily* □ *All that glitters is not gold.* Journalists are perhaps the worst offenders. To them all countries in armed conflict are *war-torn,* all negative forecasts *dire,* and all denials *categorical.*

Many clichés have become such through many years of use. But it can take a very short time for a newly coined phrase to become a cliché. Some modern examples are: □ *at the end of the day* □ *at that point in time* □ *keep a low profile.*

client or **customer?** A *client* is someone who receives the services of a professional person or organization, while a *customer* is someone who buys goods from a shop or other trading organization: □ *The attorney had several Asian clients.* □ *She was a regular customer at the fish market.*

• A collective noun for regular clients is *clientele,* and this plural is also sometimes used for customers, particularly if there is a suggestion of superiority in the shop or its customers: □ *The customers at the mall have less exacting tastes than the clientele of Beverly Hills boutiques.* The rather formal word *patron* is also sometimes used of customers, when there is a sense of them bestowing the favor of their custom on an establishment.

clientele The preferred pronunciation of this word, which means "collective body of clients": □ *an exclusive clientele,* is [klīon*tel*].

climactic or **climatic?** These two words have completely different meanings. *Climactic* is the adjective from *climax:* □ *This aria marks the climactic point of the opera. Climatic* is the adjective from climate: □ *The climatic conditions are unsuitable for outdoor activities.*

- Both words should be distinguished from the noun *climacteric,* which means "a crucial stage in life; the menopause or corresponding male equivalent."

climate The word *climate* has been extended in meaning to embrace not just the atmosphere in terms of the weather, but atmosphere in general: □ *a climate of hope.* It is used rather more specifically of the prevailing state of affairs or the attitudes and opinions of people at a particular time: □ *the economic climate* □ *the change in the moral climate of America* (Franklin D. Roosevelt).

climatic see CLIMACTIC OR CLIMATIC?

clone *Clone* is a word taken from genetic science, in which it means "the asexually, and often artificially, produced offspring of a parent, which are genetically identical to the parent and to each other." Despite the dislike of some people, the word is now used popularly to suggest anything very similar to something else: □ *Marketing the Arts* is a new magazine, tabloid size, a clone of *Campaign* (*Daily Telegraph,* Aug. 5, 1987). It is also used synonymously with *lookalike:* □ *a dozen Elvis Presley clones.*

close proximity *Proximity* means "being close or near in space or time": □ *Its proximity to the station made the house particularly convenient.* As "close" is part of the meaning of the word, it is never necessary to add *close* before *proximity:* □ *His close proximity made me feel uneasy.*

- See also TAUTOLOGY.

clothed see CLAD OR CLOTHED?

coarse or **course?** These words are sometimes confused. *Coarse* means "rough or crude": □ *coarse behavior* □ *coarse cloth.* The noun *course* means "progression of events": □ *in the course of time,* or "route": □ *The ship steered a difficult course.* The verb *course* means "hunt or pursue"; *coursing* is the sport in which game is hunted with dogs.

cocoon This word, which means "protective covering": □ *The butterfly emerged from its cocoon,* is sometimes misspelled. Note the repetition of *co.*

coherent or **cohesive?** *Coherent* and *cohesive* have the same roots in the verb *to cohere,* but they are used differently. *Coherent* means "logically consistent; comprehensible": □ *a coherent argument* □ *coherent speech.* *Cohesive* means "clinging or sticking together": □ *the cohesive properties of the mortar,* and is used figuratively of anything that holds together or has unity: □ *Union members should think of themselves as a cohesive group.*

coiffure This word, meaning "hairstyle," is usually pronounced [kwah*fewr*]. This should be clearly distinguished from the pronunciation of *coiffeur* meaning "hairstylist" [kwah*fer*].

- Note the different endings of these nouns and also the double *f* in the spelling.

colander see CALENDAR, CALENDER, OR COLANDER?

collaborate or **cooperate?** Both *collaborate* and *cooperate* mean "work together for a common purpose": □ *The two scientists have collaborated/cooperated for years on various projects.* *Collaborate* has the extra sense of working with or assisting an enemy, particularly an enemy occupying one's country: □ *The French politicians who had collaborated with the Nazis were discredited after the war.*

- *Collaborate* is more likely to be used of a cooperative enterprise of an intellectual or artistic nature; people might *collaborate* in writing a book but *cooperate* in organizing a party.

collective nouns The term collective noun applies to such nouns as: □ *flock* □ *gang* □ *troop,* which are usually followed by *of* and another noun: □ *a flock of sheep,* to other nouns which apply to groups, such as: □ *audience* □ *orchestra* □ *crowd,* and to "class" collectives, which include various things of a certain kind: □ *furniture* □ *underwear* □ *aircraft.*

- Some collective nouns have very restricted uses. A *pride* can only be of lions; a *school* only of fish and other aquatic animals. Others, such as *herd* or *heap* have a more general use.

The main problem with collective nouns is whether to treat them as singular or plural. With some nouns there is no choice. Class collectives always take a singular verb: □ *My luggage is missing.* Words for people in general or a particular class of person: □ *folk* □ *the police,* take a plural verb: □ *The police are investigating the cave.* It is with group nouns such as: □ *audience* □ *jury* □ *committee* that problems arise. American English tends to treat such words as singular when thought of as a whole: □ *The Government is undecided,* whereas British English treats them as plural: □ *The Government are undecided.* See also SINGULAR OR PLURAL?

colon A colon introduces a clause or word that amplifies, interprets, explains, or reveals what has gone before it: □ *He was beginning to be anxious: they had been gone for five hours.* □ *Only one month has fewer than 30 days: February.* Its other main uses are to introduce lists: □ *She's lived in three cities: Boston, Chicago, and Dallas,* and to introduce lengthier quotations, often when quotation marks are not used and the quoted material is indented.

- The clause preceding a colon should usually be able to stand on its own grammatically.

Capitals should only be used after colons if the word following is a proper noun; if the first word of a quotation is capitalized; if the colon follows a formal salutation or brief instruction: □ *To whom it may concern:* □ *Note:* □ *Warning:* or sometimes if the material following the colon is a whole sentence or sentences expressing a complete thought.

Colons are also used to introduce speech in plays: □ *Cecily: Are you called Algernon? Algernon: I cannot deny it.* They are used between titles and subtitles: □ *Men Who Play God: The Story of the Hydrogen Bomb;* in biblical references between chapter and verse: *James 2:14–17;* in business correspondence: □ *To:* □ *Reference:* and to show the relationship of one number to another: □ *The ratio was 2:1.* Colons are also used in books such as this to introduce examples.

The use of the dash following a colon is restricted to lists, usually where each item starts on a new line and is indented. Even then the practice is old-fashioned and not recommended. See also DASH.

colored see BLACK.

comic or **comical?** *Comic* and *comical* are not quite synonyms. *Comic* means "of comedy, intended to cause laughter or amuse-

ment": *a comic actor* □ *a comic strip. Comical* means "having the effect of causing laughter or amusement": □ *a comical sight.*
• Something can be *comic,* in that it is intended to be funny, even if it fails actually to arouse mirth: □ *His comic songs did not raise a smile. Comical* is often used in cases where the humor is unintentional: □ *It was comical to see their attempts to appear sophisticated.*

comma Of all the punctuation marks, the comma is the most likely to cause confusion or ambiguity through its misuse, overuse, or omission. Some of the conventions that formerly governed its use are now regarded as optional; it is important, however, to be consistent within a single piece of writing. Excessively long sentences containing many clauses separated by commas are best divided into shorter units; short sentences that require many commas for clarity should be reworded if possible. The principal uses of the comma are listed below.

• **1** The individual items of a series of three or more are separated by commas; the final comma preceding *and* or *or* is optional (purists, however, insist on the final comma): □ *We have invited Paul, Michael, Peter, and Mark.* □ *She plays tennis, hockey and volleyball.* □ *He doesn't like cabbage, carrots, or beans.*

The same conventions apply to series of longer units: □ *I closed the window, drew the curtains, and went to bed.* Omission of the final comma may cause confusion if the last or penultimate item contains *and:* □ *The desserts include cake, pie and ice cream, and pudding.*

2 The use of a comma between adjectives that precede the noun they qualify is optional in most cases: □ *a large, red, juicy tomato* □ *a small round black button.*

When the final adjective has a closer relationship with the noun, it should not be preceded by a comma: □ *a picturesque French village* □ *a rude little boy* □ *an eccentric old woman.*

In the following examples, omission of the comma could cause ambiguity or confusion: □ *light, yellow cake* □ *a freshly ironed, neatly folded shirt.*

3 Commas separate nonessential or parenthetical clauses from the rest of the sentence: □ *The mayor, who is very fond of gardening, presented the ribbons at the flower show.* □ *My diamond necklace, a valuable family heirloom, has been stolen.*

It is important to make certain that both commas are present (unless the clause falls at the end of the sentence) and that they enclose the appropriate information: it should be possible to remove the words between the commas without affecting the basic message of the sentence. As a general rule, the subject of a sentence should not be separated from its verb by a single comma. Commas are not used around essential or defining clauses or phrases: □ *The classical guitarist Andrés Segovia has died.* □ *The jacket that I bought last week has a broken zipper.*

In some cases, the removal or insertion of parenthetical commas can alter the meaning of a sentence: □ *My daughter Elizabeth is a doctor* implies that the speaker has two or more daughters, one of whom is named Elizabeth; □ *My daughter, Elizabeth, is a doctor* implies that the speaker has only one daughter.

See also **PARENTHESES; BRACKETS; DASH; THAT OR WHICH?**

4 The use of the comma or commas to separate such words and phrases as *however, therefore, nevertheless, of course, for example,* and *on the other hand* from the rest of the sentence is optional: □ *I wondered, however, whether he was right.* □ *The vacation will include visits to some of the local attractions—for example, the caves.* □ *We could go by train or of course we could use the car.*

5 Commas are always used to separate terms of address, interjections, and brief clauses that end questions from the rest of the sentence: □ *I'm sorry to have troubled you, madam.* □ *Please sit down, Mr. Smith, and tell me what happened.* □ *Oh, what a beautiful garden! It's cold today, isn't it?*

6 The main clause of the sentence may be separated from a preceding subordinate clause by a comma (the comma is sometimes omitted after a short subordinate clause): □ *After loading all their luggage into the car and locking up the house and garage, they set off on their vacations.* □ *When it stops raining, we will go out.*

See also **DANGLING PARTICIPLES.**

7 Two or more main clauses linked by a coordinating conjunction (*and, or, but,* etc.) should be separated with a comma before the conjunction. The comma is sometimes omitted if the clauses have the same subject or object: □ *Tom washed the dishes and Sarah dried them.* □ *Take a walk or ride your bicycle.* If the clauses are fairly short, the comma is optional: □ *The truck crashed but the driver was uninjured.* □ *The hotel is very comfortable, and the food is excellent.*

Between longer or more complex main clauses, a comma is often necessary to avoid ambiguity or confusion. (Where such clauses are not linked by a coordinating conjunction, they should be separated by a **SEMICOLON** rather than a comma.)

8 A comma may be used in place of a repeated verb in the second of two related clauses: □ *She speaks French and German; her husband, Spanish and Italian.* See also **DATES; LETTER WRITING; NUMBERS; QUOTATION MARKS.**

commemorate This word, meaning "remember with a ceremony": □ *They commemorated the 200th anniversary of the constitution* is sometimes misspelled. Note particularly the double *m* followed by a single *m.*

commence *Commence* means the same as *begin* or *start* but should be used only in formal contexts, in which its opposite is *conclude,* rather than *end:* □ *The meeting will commence at 9:30 A.M. and conclude at noon.*

• It sounds affected or pompous if one uses *commence* in contexts in which *begin* or *start* is appropriate: □ *I shall commence my new job tomorrow.* □ *The car commenced to make a rattling noise. Commencement* is the noun from *commence* and should be used in similar contexts: □ *the commencement of the fiscal year. Commencement* is also the ceremony at which students receive degrees.

commensurate Commensurate means "equal in measure or extent, proportionate": □ *The rent charged is commensurate with the apartment's current value.* It is a word very often used in connection with salaries: □ *Remuneration will be commensurate with the importance of this key role (Executive Post,* July 16, 1987).

Commissioner means "an important official of a government, etc.: □ *the police commissioner* □ *the commissioner of the bureau.* Do not confuse this word with the British English *commissionaire*, meaning "attendant in uniform."

commitment The sense of *commitment* that means "loyalty to a cause or ideology" is an increasingly popular one: □ *a genuine Christian commitment* □ *his commitment to the animal-rights movement* □ *As my commitment to the struggle for racial justice intensified, I wanted to go further in my relationship with the black community* (Jim Wallis, *The New Radical*). Many users dislike this word's overuse.
• Note the double *m* and single *t* of *commit*. Neither t is doubled in *commitment*.

committee The noun *committee* may be singular or plural: □ *The committee meets on Thursdays.* □ *The committee were unable to reach a unanimous decision.* When thought of as a whole, *committee* is considered singular.
• See also COLLECTIVE NOUNS: SINGULAR OR PLURAL?
Note the spelling of *committee*, particularly the double *m*, double *t*, and double *e*.

common see MUTUAL, COMMON, OR RECIPROCAL?

communal This word, meaning "of a community": □ *communal living*, has different pronunciations. Both [*kom*yoonăl] and [komyoonăl] are accepted, the latter being more frequent.

community *Community* has become a vogue word in two different ways. The application of the word to a recognizable group within a larger society: □ *the Jewish community* □ *the black community*, has given the word an association with minority groups.
• The *community* is also used in a much vaguer sense to mean "society in general." When psychiatric patients are discharged from a hospital and are to be *cared for in the community*, it usually means no more than that they are to live in society.

comparable The traditional pronunciation of this word is [*kom*părăbl]. The variant [kom*par*ăbl] is avoided by careful speakers. See also STRESS.

comparative and superlative The comparative form of an adjective or adverb is used when two things are compared: □ *Anne is smaller than her sister*, while the superlative is used as the extreme degree of comparison for three or more things: □ *Anne is the smallest girl in her class.*
• The two main ways to form comparatives and superlatives are by adding the suffixes *-er* and *-est*, or preceding the word with *more* or *most*: □ *sad—sadder—saddest* □ *eager—more eager—most eager*. One-syllable words always take *-er* and *-est*, as do two-syllable words ending in *-y*: □ *big—bigger* □ *pretty—prettiest*. Two-syllable words ending in *-le*, *-ow*, *-er* sometimes also take *-er* and *-est*: □ *little—littler* □ *shallow—shallower* □ *clever—cleverer*.
Other two-syllable words and all words of three or more syllables take *more* and *most*: □ *more abject* □ *most horrific* □ *most interesting*. Most compound adjectives can use either form: □ *fairer-minded* □ *more fair-minded*. There are two well-known words with irregularly formed comparatives and superlatives: □ *good/well—better—best* □ *bad/badly—worse—worst*.
More is used instead of *-er*, even with one-syllable words, in cer-

tain contexts: when two adjectives are being compared with each other: □ *He's really more shy than aloof;* and when the aptness of an adjective is being challenged: □ *She's no more short than a giraffe!*

Some adjectives (see **ADJECTIVES**) cannot be used with the comparative or superlative forms. One cannot say *more total* or *most unique*. It is, however, possible to use comparative forms w hen suggesting a closer approximation to perfection: □ *A fuller description will be given tomorrow.*

Mistakes concerning comparatives and superlatives include the use of the comparative in phrases such as: □ *three times wider,* □ *five times more expensive,* instead of: □ *three times as wide* □ *five times as expensive,* although when an actual measure is specified it is appropriate to say: □ *three feet wider* □ *five dollars more expensive.* Another mistake is the use of *more* in phrases such as: *one of the more promising of the new novelists,* when it is clear that more than two people are being compared. A (possibly deliberate) mistake much used by advertisers is the use of the comparative when it is unclear what is being compared: □ *X washes whiter and cleaner!* □ *Y gives you a better, closer shave!,* and the unbridled use of superlatives: □ *The most luxurious vacation ever!*

Finally, a frequent mistake is the misspelling of *comparative* as *comparitive,* probably based on *comparison.*

comparatively Comparatively means "relatively, as compared with a standard": □ *It was comparatively inexpensive for vintage champagne.*

• It is often used as a synonym for "rather, fairly, or somewhat," with no question of comparison: *It is a comparatively small resort,* but many people dislike this usage.

compare to or **compare with?** *Compare to* and *compare with* are not interchangeable. *Compare to* is used when things are being likened to each other: □ *He compared her skin to ivory.* *Compare with* is used when things are being considered from the point of view of both similarities and differences: □ *Tourists find London hotels expensive compared with those of other European capitals.* When *compare* is used intransitively, *with* should be used: □ *His direction compares with early Hitchcock.*

• *Compared to* and *comparable to* are frequently used where *with* is appropriate: □ *Compared to my brother, I'm poor.* □ *It's not comparable to the homemade version.*

competition or **contest?** *Competition* and *contest* involve rivalry against an opponent or opponents and can be synonymous: □ *At 18 she won a contest/competition for young musicians.* However, *contest* is restricted to the sense of organized competitive events or exertions to achieve victory over opponents: □ *the contest for nomination as a party's candidate.* *Competition* is used more generally of rivalry: □ *There will be keen competition for tickets,* and is also used of the people or organization against which one is competing: □ *We must assess the strengths and weaknesses of the competition.*

complement or **compliment?** These two words are often confused. Both as a noun and as a verb, *complement* suggests the addition of something necessary to make something whole or complete: □ *a ship's complement* □ *The flowers complemented the room's decor perfectly.* Compliment is used as a noun and a verb to refer to an expression of praise, respect, or admiration: □ *She complimented her host on the excellent meal.* □ *The compliment embarrassed him.* To avoid mistakes remember the *e* of complement is also in *complete.*

complement or supplement? *Complement* and *supplement* have a distinct difference in meaning. Both as noun and as verb, *complement* suggests the addition of something necessary to make something whole or complete: □ *The closings were forced by the hospital's inability to recruit 92 nurses out of its full complement of nearly 800 (Daily Telegraph, June 3, 1987).* □ *The music complemented the mime aptly.* Supplement suggests an addition to something that is already complete: □ *Her fees for private tuition supplemented her teacher's salary.* □ *Most Sunday newspapers publish a color supplement.*

complete When used to mean "total," *complete* is an *adjective* (see ADJECTIVES) that should not be modified. □ *We were in almost complete darkness.* However, *complete* also has the meaning of "thorough": □ *a complete overhaul,* and in that sense can be modified with *more* or *most*: □ *This is the most complete study of the period yet published.*

complex The noun *complex* is taken from psychoanalysis, where it means "a set of subconscious repressed ideas and emotions that can cause an abnormal mental condition": □ *an Oedipus complex* □ *an inferiority complex.* The term has been taken up and used popularly to mean any behavioral problem or obsession, even if it is completely conscious. This usage is disliked by some. □ *She's got a complex about spiders.* □ *"You're crazy," Clevinger shouted . . . "You've got a Jehovah complex"* (Joseph Heller, *Catch-22*).

• *Complex* is also used to mean "something made up of interrelated parts" and is now often applied to a group of buildings as in: □ *shopping complex* □ *housing complex.*

complex or complicated? *Complex* and *complicated* are very similar in meaning, and the differences in usage are subtle ones. Both mean "consisting of many parts that are intimately combined": □ *This is a complex/complicated problem.*

• *Complicated* emphasizes the fact that the multifaceted nature of a thing makes it difficult to solve or understand, and there is sometimes a negative connotation to it—a suggestion that it could possibly be simpler: □ *Our tax forms are unnecessarily complicated.* *Complex* is more neutral and emphasizes the intricacy of the combination of parts rather than the resulting difficulties: □ *The blood-clotting system is a complex mechanism.*

compliment see COMPLEMENT OR COMPLIMENT?

compose, comprise, or **constitute?** Each of these verbs is concerned with parts making up a whole. Either *compose* or *constitute* is used to mean "come together to make (a whole)," but *compose* is usually used in the passive and *constitute* in the active: □ *The team is composed of several experts.* □ *the foods that constitute the average diet.* Comprise can be used to mean only "consist of": □ *The house comprises three bedrooms, a living room, a kitchen, and a bathroom.* The use: □ *Eleven players com-*

prise a team is incorrect; the use of *comprised of: The team is comprised of eleven players* is considered wrong by some.
- See also CONSIST OF OR CONSIST IN?

concept The precise meaning of *concept* is "an idea of a category or thing that is formed by generalization from particular instances." The meaning has widened to embrace ideas in general, and is often now used to mean "an accepted idea of a particular thing": □ *the concept of adult education.* It is frequently used very loosely to mean little more than "an idea or notion," particularly in advertising. Many people dislike this usage: □ *a new concept in slimming.*
- *Conceptualize* means "form a concept" or "interpret conceptually": □ *The Greeks conceptualized all their experiences in terms of the gods.* It should not be used to mean "think," "imagine," or "visualize."

concerning *Concerning* means "relating to, on the subject of, or about": □ *The principal is available to talk to students concerning their career choices.* It is more formal than *about.*

condition or **precondition?** A *condition* is a requirement or stipulation on which an agreement or contract depends: □ *I will let you go on condition that you are back before midnight.* While a condition can be fulfilled either before or after the agreement is made, *precondition* is a requirement that must be satisfied in advance of an agreement being made: □ *Assent to the manifesto was a precondition of membership.*
- *Condition* can be used, not just of agreements, but also of situations and states of being: □ *the condition of the world* □ *in good/ poor condition,* and the words are used synonymously to mean anything that has to be true or occur before something else can happen: □ *The establishment of a just society is an essential condition/precondition for peace.*

conduit This word, which describes a pipe or channel conveying liquid, has various pronunciations. The most widely used pronunciation is [*kon*dooit], but [*kon*dit], [*kon*dyooit], and [*kon*dwit] are also heard.

confidant or **confident?** A *confidant,* feminine *confidante,* is someone in whom one can confide. Each word is pronounced either [*kon*fidant] or [konfi*dahnt*]. These words should not be confused with *confident,* which means "assured or certain": □ *a confident young man.*

confrontation A *confrontation* is a face-to-face meeting, especially in the context of opposition, challenge, or defiance: □ *the confrontation with enemy forces.* Popular journalism has now weakened the meaning so that any disagreement or conflict of ideas is now inevitably referred to as a *confrontation.*
- Similarly, any person or group with a tendency to argumentativeness is described as *confrontational:* □ *indications of a much less confrontational Soviet stance in Afghanistan, in Eastern Europe, in Africa and elsewhere* (*The New York Times,* Dec. 25, 1988).

conjunctions *Conjunctions* are words that link two or more words, clauses, or sentences: □ *and* □ *but* □ *or* □ *because* □ *when.*
- *And, but, yet, nor, for, so,* and *or* are known as coordinating conjunctions. They connect words and clauses of the same grammatical type: □ *Martha and Mary* □ *I love Mozart, but I detest Mahler.*

They often connect clauses that share a common verb, which does not need to be repeated: □ *She is young yet surprisingly wise.* Some coordinating conjunctions, such as *but* and *yet,* can be used only to link two sentence elements, but *and* and *or* can link more than two: □ *I'm tired and cold and hungry and miserable.*

Conjunctions such as *because, when, if, though, unless* are known as subordinating conjunctions, as they connect a subordinate clause to its main clause: □ *He's tired because he works too much.* □ *It won't work unless everyone cooperates.*

Correlative conjunctions are the pairs *either . . . or* and *neither . . . nor* that are used together: □ *Neither Williams nor Jenkins is present.* □ *He's either wicked or mad.*

Some people still have objections to sentences starting with the conjunctions *and, but,* and *or,* a device that can be effective if used sparingly.

See also SINGULAR OR PLURAL?

conjurer or **conjuror:** Either spelling is perfectly acceptable, *conjurer* perhaps being more frequent.

connection or **connexion?** This word, meaning "a relationship between two things; joint": □ *His death must have had some connection with the stormy weather.* □ *faulty electrical connections,* is spelled connection. Connexion is a rarer variant spelling found occasionally in British English.

connoisseur A person who is an expert with discriminatory taste in a certain field is called a *connoisseur.* Note the double *n,* double *s,* and the *oi* vowels between them.

conscientious This word, meaning "diligent and careful": □ *She was a conscientious worker,* is sometimes misspelled. Note in particular the *t.*

consensus *Consensus* means "opinion shared unanimously, a view generally held or accepted": □ *He had broken the pro-nuclear consensus shared by all postwar leaders* (*Sunday Times,* May 31, 1987).

• As the meaning contains the idea of a generally held opinion, the frequently used expressions *general consensus* and *consensus of opinion* are tautologies, and are avoided by careful users.

Consensus is frequently misspelled as *concensus,* perhaps from a mistaken belief that it is connected with the word *census.* Instead, it derives from the same root as *consent.*

consent see ASSENT OR CONSENT?

consequent or **consequential?** *Consequent* means "following as a direct result": □ *She was hit by a truck, and the consequent injuries left her a permanent invalid. Consequential* can also be used to mean "following as a direct result": □ *his conviction for the crime and consequential prison term. Consequential* also means "important": □ *Their decisions were becoming increasingly consequential in determining the direction of the company.* It is also used in legal expressions such as *consequential loss* to mean "an indirect result" and has the additional meaning of "self-important; pompous": □ *His manner was pretentious and consequential.*

consequent or **subsequent?** *Consequent* and *subsequent* are sometimes confused. Whereas *consequent* means "following as a direct result," *subsequent* means only "occurring after": □ *her ac-*

cident and consequent pain □ *her accident and subsequent recovery.* Consequent takes the preposition *on* (or *upon*), whereas subsequent takes *to:* □ *increase in salaries consequent on the pay review* □ *his behavior subsequent to his arrival.*

consequential see CONSEQUENT OR CONSEQUENTIAL?

conservative or **Conservative?** *Conservative* with a lowercase *c* means "tending to support tradition and established institutions, opposed to change, moderate, cautious, conventional": □ *The college has a reputation for being conservative and still refuses to admit women students.* □ *He has conservative tastes and dresses in somber colors.* A *Conservative* is someone who supports or is a member of the Conservative Party in Britain or elsewhere; it is also used as an adjective: □ *a Conservative leader.*

• A *conservative estimate* is one that is cautious and moderate, but the term is often used to mean "a low estimate": □ *It's worth a million dollars at the most conservative estimate.*

consider *Consider* means "regard as being": □ *I consider him a nonentity, "think about carefully":* □ *I have considered all aspects of the problem,* and "regard sympathetically": □ *We will not fail to consider your feelings on the matter.*

• In the first sense given above, *consider* is more or less synonymous with *regard . . . as,* and this usage leads some people to add *as* to *consider:* □ *He considered their work as vitally important.* This construction is wrong. There is, however, nothing wrong with using *as* when *consider* is used in the sense of "think about, give consideration to": □ *The songs are tuneful, but considered as an opera, the work lacks unity.*

considerable *Considerable* means "worth consideration; significant": □ *She has made a considerable contribution to biochemical research.* It has been extended to mean "large in amount": □ *They have saved a considerable amount of money,* although some people dislike the imprecise nature of this use.

• *Considerable* is usually attached to abstract nouns: □ *a considerable quantity* □ *considerable numbers of,* but it can be used with concrete nouns: □ *They have mined considerable gold.* (This use is not yet acceptable in British English.) When the meaning is "significant," one can also attach *considerable* to a concrete noun: □ *a considerable pianist.*

consist of or **consist in?** *Consist of* means "comprise, be made up of": □ *Breakfast consists of eggs, toast, and coffee.* Consist *in* means "have its essence in": □ *The appeal of the writing consists in its use of language rather than its content.*

• *Consist of* usually precedes a list of concrete nouns, whereas *consist in* is usually applied to abstract nouns.

constable In British English, a police officer of the lowest rank is known as a *constable.* The word has two pronunciations: the British [*kun*stăbĕl] or the American [*kon*stăbĕl].

constitute see COMPOSE, COMPRISE, OR CONSTITUTE?

contact The meanings of *contact* as a noun include "the state of touching": □ *He avoided all physical contact with dogs,* "link or relationship": □ *The two towns have commercial contacts,* and "communication": □ *I am in regular contact with her.* A modern use is "a person one knows who may be useful to one": □ *I have a good contact in the police department.*

• The use of the verb *contact* to mean "communicate with": *I will contact you next week* is still disliked by some people. It is, however, particularly useful in cases in which one wishes to avoid specifying whether communication will be made by letter, telephone, message, or personal visit.

contagious or **infectious?** *Contagious* and *infectious* are used of diseases that can be passed on to others. *Contagious* diseases are those that are easily passed on usually by physical contact, such as influenza; *infectious* diseases are those passed on through a specific kind of contact, such as venereal disease.

• In figurative use the words are synonymous: □ *His optimistic mood was infectious/contagious.*

containerize *Containerize* is a verb formed from the noun *container* in its sense of a large packing case in which goods are transported by road and sea, being handled mechanically throughout. To *containerize* means both "pack into containers for transport and transport in this method": □ *The beans must be containerized before the end of the week,* and "change over to the use of containers": □ *We are containerizing our shipping procedures.*

C

contemporary The primary meaning of *contemporary* is "happening or living at the same time as": □ *the contemporary writers Joyce and Beckett.* It has more recently been used to mean "happening at the present time; current": □ *Contemporary values are materialistic and selfish.*

• A development of this meaning has been the use of *contemporary* to mean "modern, up-to-date," sometimes qualified with *very, extremely,* etc.: □ *They sell the most contemporary fashions in town.* This use is disliked by many people and is best avoided. One should beware of ambiguities between the first and second meanings of *contemporary:* □ *a contemporary biography of Shelley* may mean one written when Shelley was alive or one written recently.

contemptible or **contemptuous?** *Contemptible* and *contemptuous* are concerned with *contempt,* but they have distinctly different meanings. *Contemptible* means "despicable; deserving scorn or contempt": □ *His meanness was contemptible. Contemptuous* means "scornful, feeling or showing contempt": □ *She observed his feeble efforts with a contemptuous smile.*

contest see COMPETITION OR CONTEST?

contingency A *contingency* is "something that happens by chance; something unforeseen that might possibly occur in the future": □ *We must prepare ourselves for every contingency.*

• In modern use the word almost always appears in the phrase *contingency plans* and is usually applied, not to unforeseen future events, but to those that are predictable, although not inevitable: □ *The town made contingency plans in case of a severe winter.*

continual or **continuous?** *Continual* means "frequently repeated"; *continuous* means "without break or interruption": □ *Our neighbor's continual complaints forced us to move.* □ *The continuous noise from the generator kept him awake all night.*

• The fundamental difference in sense, which also applies to the adverbs *continually* and *continuously,* is that something *continual* stops from time to time, whereas something *continuous* does not stop until it reaches its natural end. It is acceptable in certain contexts to interchange the two words, but this practice may lead to ambiguity and is therefore best avoided if possible. *Continual* is not used of physical objects, such as a *continuous roll of paper,* nor may *continuous* be substituted for continual in such phrases as: □ *continual interruptions.*

contractions The most common contractions in English involve the verbs *am, are, is, have, has, had, will, shall,* and *would* and the word *not:* □ *I'm* □ *you're* □ *she's* □ *we've* □ *he'll* □ *they'd* □ *can't* □ *shouldn't.*

• An apostrophe indicates the missing letter(s), although in the contraction *shan't,* in which there is more than one set of missing letters, only the missing *o* is indicated. The contracted form *'d* can stand for either *had* or *would,* and *'s* can be either *is* or *has*—or *us* when used in the word *let's;* it should always be clear from the context which word is intended. Two irregular contractions are *won't* (will not) and *aren't* (are not), which can also mean *am not,* as in: □ *Aren't I right?* □ *Aren't I clever!*

Contractions are almost always used in speech. They may be used in written passages of dialogue, and they are generally acceptable in all but the most formal writing. Some contractions are more likely to be written than others. □ *He's late* and □ *Jill's late* are more acceptable in writing than: □ *Dinner's late* □ *The train's late,* and the *'ll* contraction (except when used with personal pronouns): □ *you'll* □ *Tim'll be there.* □ *The bus'll be on time* is not usually used in writing.

Care should be taken with the placing of the apostrophe. A frequent mistake is placing it where the syllables break, rather than where the letter is missing: *wouldn't* [not *would'nt*].

See also AIN'T; 'S OR S?

contrary This word, meaning "opposed in position": □ *On the contrary, I would like to go for a walk,* is stressed on the first syllable [*kon*trăiree]. Only in the sense "perverse or stubborn": □ *such a contrary girl,* is it stressed on the second syllable [kŏn*trai*ree].

contribute In the traditional pronunciation of this word, the stress is on the second syllable [kŏn*trib*yoot]; some British users stress the first syllable [*kŏn*tribyoot].

controversy In the traditional pronunciation of this word, the stress falls on the first syllable [*kon*trŏversee]. The variant pronunciation, with stress on the second syllable [kŏn*tro*versee], is heard but is disliked by many users. See also STRESS.

convalescence This word, meaning "recovery after an illness," is sometimes misspelled. Note the combinations *sc* and *nc.*

converse The *converse* of a statement or proposition is one that reverses the elements of the proposition: □ *You say that your mother dislikes you, but in fact the converse is true—you dislike your mother.* The word is now usually used much more loosely to mean "opposite": □ *The previous speaker claimed that nuclear weapons help to preserve peace, but I maintain the converse.*

• The adverb *conversely,* similarly, is now used to mean just "in an opposite way": □ *In such an emergency one can stop the car or, conversely, one can accelerate out of danger.*

convertible This word, meaning "capable of being changed":

□ *The car is a convertible,* is sometimes misspelled. The ending is *-ible,* not *-able.*

cooperate see COLLABORATE OR COOPERATE?

cord see CHORD OR CORD?

co-respondent see CORRESPONDENT OR CO-RESPONDENT?

correspond There are two main meanings of *correspond.* One is "communicate with someone by exchange of letters": □ *He met his Italian penpal after they had corresponded for years.* The other meaning is "match or be equivalent or comparable in some respect": □ *Your account corresponds exactly with the description of the other witnesses.*

• In this second meaning *correspond to* is considered correct by many careful users, although *correspond with* is often used.

correspondent or **co-respondent?** A *correspondent* is someone who communicates by letter: □ *She has correspondents in three countries,* or someone who contributes news reports to a newspaper or magazine or to radio or television programs: □ *And now a report from our Middle East correspondent.* A *co-respondent* is the person cited in divorce proceedings as the lover of the husband or wife who has been accused of adultery: □ *Divorced couples hobnobbed with each other and with each other's co-respondents* (Noel Coward, *Present Indicative*).

cosmetic Some people dislike the use of *cosmetic* as an adjective to apply to anything that improves the outward appearance of something: □ *One supplier of decaffeinated coffee . . . plans to switch from the chemical process . . . although a spokesman insisted this was necessary for "cosmetic" reasons only* (Sunday Times, June 7, 1987).

• It is extended further to anything that makes a superficial improvement, but does not make any fundamental change: □ *Charges that the planned changes would have only a cosmetic effect were hotly denied.*

cost or **price?** *Cost* and *price* are often used synonymously as nouns to mean "the amount paid or charged for something": □ *We were afraid the cost/price would be more than we could afford.*

• *Price* is more often used when preceded by an adjective: □ *an exorbitant price* □ *bargain prices,* and when speaking of the amount needed in order to bribe someone: □ *"All those men have their price"* (Sir Robert Walpole). *Cost* is used in the plural for the expenses of a law suit: □ *The court awarded him costs,* and either *cost* or *price* is used to describe the expenditure in terms of effort and sacrifice made in order to achieve an end: □ *"To give and not to count the cost"* (St. Ignatius Loyola). □ *This was indeed a high price to pay for success.*

could see CAN OR MAY?

council or **counsel?** The noun *council* means "a body of people meeting for discussion and consultation": □ *the town council.* The noun *counsel* means "advice": □ *She always gave wise counsel,* and has the corresponding verb *to counsel,* meaning "give advice to (someone)": □ *She was counseled about her future career.* □ *He was counseled against acting rashly.* □ *psychiatric counseling.*

• A *councilor* (in British English, *councillor*) is a person who belongs to a *council,* just as a *counselor* (in British English, *counsel-*

C

lor) is a person who *counsels:* □ *marriage-guidance counselors.*
A *counsel* is a lawyer or group of lawyers: □ *the counsel for the defense.*

counsel or **advise?** In many instances *counsel* and *advise* are synonymous, although *counsel* is rather more formal: □ *I would advise/counsel you not to drink if you're driving home. Advise* is more likely to be used in informal contexts and when the advice is not of great importance: □ *He advised me to come early. Counsel* is more appropriate when the advice is serious and when it is given by trained or professional counselors: □ *He has been counseled by social workers, doctors, and clergy, but he still can't sort out his problems.*

country or **nation?** These words are often used interchangeably: □ *the poorer countries/nations of the world. Country* should be used when the context is one *of geographical characteristics:* □ *Wales is a mountainous country,* and *nation* when speaking of the people or of social and political characteristics: □ *Wales is a nation of musicians and orators.*

• *Nation* carries a suggestion of a people with a common culture, language, and traditions, and is often best replaced with the more general *people* when describing a multicultural society such as modern Britain.

course see COARSE OR COURSE?

credibility gap *Credibility gap* is a fashionable expression used to describe the lack of trust created by a discrepancy between what is said officially and what is actually seen to happen: □ *The public cynically accepts the credibility gap between election promises and subsequent policies.*

credible, creditable, or **credulous?** The three adjectives *credible, creditable,* and *credulous,* and their corresponding nouns *credibility, credit,* and *credulity* are sometimes confused. *Credible* means "believable": □ *My story may not sound credible, but I assure you it's true. Creditable* means "deserving praise": □ *Her readiness to forgive her attacker is creditable. Credulous* means "gullible; too ready to believe": □ *Only the most credulous person could believe such nonsense.*

• There is a further, fashionable use of *credible* to mean "authentic; convincing": □ *They serve a credible paella,* and a corresponding use of *credibility* to mean "convincingness, soundness": □ *You will also be a self-starter with both initiative and the ability to establish rapidly your credibility with other planners* (*Sunday Times,* Aug. 23, 1987). The British vogue term *street credibility* or *street cred* means "good standing in terms of popular youth culture": □ *Youth workers need authority as well as street cred.*

crescendo *Crescendo* is a musical term that is frequently misused both in its technical and figurative sense. In music it describes a gradual increase in volume: □ *The brass sections take up the theme as the crescendo builds.* It can be used of other sounds or to describe any buildup of intensity: □ *The baby's whimpering increased in a crescendo to a howl.* □ *Public interest in the matter has risen in a crescendo.*

• Because people sometimes mistakenly talk of *building up/rising to a crescendo,* the word is often interpreted to mean the loud climax that is actually the culmination of a crescendo, and it is used to mean both "loud noise" and, in figurative contexts, "peak, climax, or milestone": □ *The drum solo ended in a deafening crescendo.* □ *She reached the crescendo of her career before she was 30.*

crisis *Crisis* literally means "turning point," and it should be used for situations that have reached a turning point for better or worse, for decisive moments in dramas, for crucial states of affairs where significant changes are likely: □ *The illness had passed its crisis, and it was clear that she would live.* □ *The worsening economic crisis* □ *It is feared that the crisis that resulted in the military coup may lead to civil war.*

• To the dislike of some people, *crisis* is now often applied to situations that are worrying or serious but without any definite implication of imminent change: □ *Independent television is facing a crisis through declining audiences* (*Daily Telegraph*, May 25, 1987), or for quite trivial problems: □ *I've got a crisis here—my zipper's broken.*

Note the spelling of the plural of *crisis*, which is *crises*, pronounced [*krīseez*].

criterion or **criteria?** The word *criterion*, meaning "a standard by which to judge or evaluate something," is a singular noun: □ *Exam results were the only criterion for deciding whether candidates should be interviewed.* The plural of *criterion* is *criteria*: □ *on the condition that the basic criteria of the code are accepted and met* (*The Bookseller*, May 15, 1987).

• Many people take *criteria* to be a singular noun and speak of a *criteria*, with sometimes the plural *criterias*. This usage is wrong.

critic or **critique?** A *critic* is someone who criticizes. The word is sometimes used in the sense of someone who finds fault or expresses disapproval: □ *Acupuncture has many critics in the medical profession.* It is also used of someone who is employed to evaluate works of art, music, or literature: □ *The public loved the play, but the critics did not have a good word to say for it.* A *critique* is a work of criticism, usually applied to an academic work that analyses and discusses ideas in depth: □ *This is a thoughtful critique of logical positivism.*

critical *Critical* means "inclined to judge severely": □ *My mother is so critical of the way I bring up the children;* "involving careful or scholarly evaluation": □ *a critical account of Jung's work;* "involving a turning point; crucial": □ *We are at a critical point in our negotiations.*

• This last use is often applied to serious or dangerous stages of illnesses and has in its turn led to such uses as: □ *A woman was later described as "critical" in the hospital, with one wrist almost severed* (*Daily Telegraph*, June 2, 1987).

critique see CRITIC OR CRITIQUE?

cross section A *cross section* is a piece of something that has been cut off at right angles or a drawing of the dimensions revealed by such a cutting: □ *The diagram shows an artery in cross section.* The expression is more often used popularly to mean "a typical or representative sample": □ *Five thousand people were interviewed as a cross section of the general public.*

crucial The use of *crucial* as a synonym for *important* is best avoided in formal speech and writing, in which it should be restricted to the sense of "decisive" or "critical": □ *constituencies where the self-employed vote could be crucial to the outcome of the election* (*Daily Telegraph*, June 1, 1987).

• *Crucial* is widely used in informal contexts, and increasingly by journalists, broadcasters, advertisers, and others, to emphasize the importance of events or issues that are by no means decisive or critical. The word has the same derivation as *crux*, meaning "a decisive point," which is most frequently encountered in the expression the *crux of the matter.*

cuisine The word *cuisine* is used to describe a style of cooking food, particularly one that is typical of a particular country or region: □ *Peppers and tomatoes are characteristic of Basque cuisine;* for the food itself: □ *Their cuisine is excellent;* and in various phrases that convey a particular style of cooking: □ *nouvelle cuisine* □ *cuisine minceur.*

• *Cuisine* carries a suggestion of good food skillfully cooked so its use in such a sentence as: □ *It was typical fast-food cuisine—everything cooked in grease is either inappropriate or jocular.*

culminate *Culminate* means "form a summit; reach the highest or most crucial point": □ *The church culminates in a steeple.* □ *Their friendship culminated in marriage.*

• The word is very often used as though it were merely a synonym for *result* or *conclude:* □ *The growing unrest culminated in industrial action being taken.* This use is so widespread as to be generally accepted, although some careful users object to it.

cultured or **cultivated?** *Cultured* and *cultivated* are almost synonymous in that they are both used to mean "educated, refined." The more frequent *cultured* is particularly applied to education in terms of an understanding and appreciation of the arts: □ *They were cultured people who attended concerts and art galleries,* whereas *cultivated* is applied to behavior and speech: □ *He gradually dropped his irritating twang and spoke in a soft, cultivated accent.*

• *Cultured* and *cultivated* also have connections with things that are produced artificially: □ *cultured pearls* □ *cultivated plants.*

curb *Curb* means "check or control": □ *He curbed his anger,* or the edge of a pavement; in British English, the latter sense is indicated by the spelling *kerb.*

currant or **current?** A *currant* is a raisin of a small seedless grape used in cooking: □ *She always put lots of currants in her cakes,* or any of several different soft fruits: □ *red currant jam* □ *black currant juice.* A *current* is a steady flow: □ *They did not swim, because the current was very strong.* □ *electric current.*

current The adjective *current* means "occurring in or belonging to the present time; presently existing or in progress": □ *Current techniques for treating the disease are acknowledged to be inadequate;* and "accepted or prevalent at this time": □ *The current opinions of some Roman Catholics are in conflict with those of the Vatican.*

• *Current* and *currently* are often used where there is no need to emphasize that one is talking about the present as contrasted with the past or future: □ *The company currently employs more than 2,000 people.*

curriculum This word, meaning "program of available courses in a school or college": □ *a wide-ranging curriculum,* is sometimes misspelled. Note that the only double letter is *r,* as in *current.*
• A *curriculum vitae,* often abbreviated to *C.V.,* is a summary of a person's career and qualifications that may be required when applying for a job. Vitae may be pronounced [*veetī*] or [*vītee*].

curtsy or **curtsey?** A *curtsy* is a formal greeting made by a woman in which the head and shoulders are lowered, the knees are bent, and the skirt is held outward with both hands: □ *She curtsied to the Queen.* The alternative spelling *curtsey* is also perfectly acceptable.

customer see CLIENT OR CUSTOMER?

cynical or **skeptical?** A *cynical* person is one who has a distrust of human nature and sincerity, believing others to be motivated by self-interest: □ *He had a cynical belief that nobody chose a career in law or medicine for any reason except the money.* Skeptical (British English, *sceptical*) means "doubtful, unwilling to believe without rational proof": □ *They are skeptical about the possibility of a miracle.*

czar see TSAR OR CZAR?

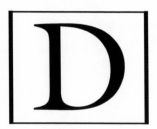

dais This word, meaning a "raised platform," is usually pronounced [*day*is]. It was formerly pronounced as only one syllable [days], now rarely heard, but is now frequently pronounced [*dñ*s].

dangling participles Participles (and other modifiers) are often used to introduce a phrase that is attached to a later-mentioned subject: □ *Startled by the noise, she dropped her book.* □ *Being by now very hungry, we stopped at a restaurant.* There is a tendency, though, for such introductory participles to become apparently attached to the wrong noun: □ *Startled by the noise, her book fell to the floor.* □ *Being by now very hungry, a restaurant was a welcome sight.* It was not the book that was startled or the restaurant that was hungry. (These examples indicate *misplaced participles*). Then there is the sentence in which the participle appears to have no subject at all, which is the thought behind the term dangling participle □ *Lying in the sun, the heat felt good.* Who, or what, was lying in the sun?

• Some participles are habitually used in a manner where they might be thought to dangle, but they are usually being used as prepositions or conjunctions, and such use is informally acceptable: □ *Speaking of fruit, does anyone want an apple?* □ *Considering the odds against them, they did well.* Also, the increasingly popular use of *having said that:* □ *Having said that, it's time to leave* is considered unacceptable by many people.

dare The verb *dare* can be used in two ways. It can be used as an ordinary verb, followed by an infinitive with *to:* □ *I dare you to jump.* □ *We'll see if she dares to contradict him;* or it can be an auxiliary verb, followed by an infinitive without *to:* □ *He dared not go there at night.* □ *How dare you say that?*

• As an auxiliary, the verb is used only in the forms *dare* and *dared*, in negative and interrogative constructions.

The expression *dare say* means "suppose, expect, or think likely": □ *I dare say we'll go there again.* It is used only in the present tense and in the first person, and is sometimes written as one word: □ *I daresay.*

dash *Dashes* can be used both singly and in pairs. Although the dash is useful, most of its functions may be performed by other punctuation marks, and excessive use of the dash is sometimes considered to be the mark of a careless writer. A sentence should never contain more than one dash or pair of dashes.

• Two dashes are is used to mark a break in a sentence, very much in the same way as parentheses □ *My mother—a Southerner by birth—had little time for Yankees.* As with parentheses, the material between the dashes should be able to be removed, leaving the sentence grammatically complete. Commas should not be used with a pair of dashes.

Single dashes are used to introduce a statement summarizing what has gone before: □ *Beer, sweets, and cigarettes—these are the main threats to the nation's health.* They are used to introduce an afterthought or a sharp change in subject or continuity: □ *I'm surprised to see Joe here—he's usually late.* □ *You take two eggs—but perhaps you don't even like omelettes?* □ *I don't believe it—caviar!*

Dashes are also used to indicate an unfinished sentence or hesitant speech: □ *I think he's—* □ *I—um—er—I don't—er—know.* They are often used to precede the attribution of a quotation: □ *"No man is an island"—Donne.* They are, occasionally, used to indicate an omission of part of a name, and to replace all or part of an *obscenity:* □ *I traveled to the small mountain town of L—.* □ *It's none of your d— business.* They are also used between points in space, where they are equivalent to *to:* □ *London–Paris.*

A dash may be thought of as a less formal punctuation mark than a colon, indicating an afterthought: □ *Sagittarius is "the Archer"–"Sagitta" means "arrow" in Latin.* For dashes with colons, see **COLON.**

data *Data* means "facts, information that can be used as a basis for analysis": □ *We have data on traffic accidents during the past three years.*

• *Data* is actually a plural, with the singular *datum,* but this singular is rarely used and *data* has come to be regarded as a collective noun, which is appropriate to its use for a body or aggregate of information. There is still considerable controversy over whether it should take a singular or plural verb, but the singular verb is now usual: □ *This data is essential.* Some careful users, however, still insist on using the noun as a plural: □ *These data are essential.*

The pronunciation [*dah*tă] is preferred, although [*day*tă] is sometimes used.

dates It is usual to write dates in figures, rather than words, except in some very formal contexts, such as legal documents. There are various ways of expressing dates: the standard form is Oct. 5, 1987 (in Britain *5 October 1987*).

• The abbreviated form 5/10/87 is acceptable in informal use, but it should be used with caution as this abbreviation would mean May 10 in Britain where the fifth of October would be abbreviated *5.10.87 (5/10/87* in Canada).

Centuries may be written as numbers or written out in full: □ *the 19th century* or □ *the second century,* and the abbreviation A.D. usually precedes the date, whereas B.C. follows it: □ *A.D. 527* □ *1000 B.C.* See also **A.D.** AND **B.C.**

The apostrophe in a series of years: □ *1980's* □ *the 1800's* is sometimes omitted.

de- The prefix *de-* is used to signify "the opposite or reverse": □ *declassify,* "removal": □ *demystify* or "reduction": □ *demote.*

• As a productive prefix, *de-* is constantly being used to create new words: □ *decriminalize* (to reduce the criminal status of an offense), □ *desegregate* (to reverse a practice or law involving racial segregation), □ *de-escalate* (to decrease in scope or extent), □ *deinstitutionalize* (to release patients from an institution), □ *de-*

,*bug* (to remove errors from or to remove electronic listening devices from). Some users object to the coining of such forms.

debris This word, meaning "rubble or remains": □ *They removed the debris from the building site,* is stressed on the second syllable [de*bree*]. The variant pronunciation [*day*bree] is sometimes used, and this pronunciation should be used when the word is written with an acute accent: □ *débris.*

debut *Debut,* meaning "first appearance": □ *He made his debut in a James Bond film,* may be pronounced [day*byoo*] or [de*byoo*]. If the word is spelled with an acute accent: □ *début,* the first pronunciation should be used.
  • The use of *debut* as a verb: □ *She debuted last month,* is disliked by many users.

deceitful or **deceptive?** *Deceitful* and *deceptive* imply misleading appearances or cheating. *Deceitful,* however, may suggest an intention to deceive or mislead, even if not successful, and therefore carries negative moral overtones: □ *It was deceitful of you to pretend to be an orphan. Deceptive* applies to a misleading effect or result rather than dishonest motivation, and something might be unintentionally deceptive: □ *The ring's dull appearance was deceptive, for on closer inspection it turned out to be gold.*

deceptively The adverb *deceptively* suggests misleading appearances and is used to indicate that something is not as it seems. A *deceptively healthy man* is actually a sick man; a *deceptively dietetic meal* is, in fact, fattening.
  • The word is frequently misused to mean "surprisingly" or "contrary to appearances": □ *a semi-detached house offering deceptively spacious accommodation* (advertisement, *Chichester Observer,* July 16, 1987).

decidedly or **decisively?** *Decidedly* usually means "definitely; unquestionably": □ *It was a decidedly welcome suggestion.* It is also sometimes used to mean "firmly; resolutely," and decisively is used in the same way: □ *"I'm going ahead with it," she said decidedly/decisively. Decisively* is also used to imply decision-making that is marked by firmness, confidence, and lack of wavering: □ *He studied the options briefly before decisively choosing the second one.*
  • *Decisive* can be applied to anything that makes a particular outcome inevitable: □ *decisive evidence may settle a dispute;* and *decisively* is also used in this sense: □ *Her conduct at the interview influenced the board decisively.*

decimate *Decimate* literally means "destroy one in ten," from the Roman practice of killing every tenth soldier as a punishment for mutiny. The word is now used popularly to mean "inflict considerable damage; destroy a large part of": □ *The weather decimated today's sports program* (BBC-TV, Jan. 17, 1987). This use probably arises from the mistaken belief that the word means "to destroy all but a tenth," and although the usage is very widespread, many careful users still dislike it. *Decimate* should not be used to mean "annihilate totally," or in such constructions as: □ *badly decimated* □ *utterly decimated* □ *The majority of the cattle were decimated by the disease.*

decisively see DECIDEDLY OR DECISIVELY?

defective or **deficient?** *Defective* means "having a fault; not working properly": □ *The washing machine I bought yesterday turned out to be defective.* Deficient means "lacking": □ *She sings well, but her voice is deficient in power.*

• Although *deficient* may be applied to concrete as well as abstract nouns: □ *Your diet is deficient in calcium,* it is not usually applied to manufactured objects. *Defective* is usually applied to concrete nouns, including manufactured objects, but can be applied to some abstract nouns, particularly those denoting some physical quality: □ *His sense of hearing is defective.*

defense The noun *defense:* □ *the importance of the country's defense,* is spelled *defence* (with a *c*) in British English; the adjective *defensive* is spelled with an *s:* □ *The players adopted a defensive strategy,* in American and British English.

deficient see DEFECTIVE OR DEFICIENT?

definite or **definitive?** These two words are sometimes confused, although their meanings are different. *Definite* means "precise, exact, or unambiguous": □ *The rules draw a definite distinction between professionals and amateurs. Definitive* means "final; conclusive": □ *This is the definitive game in the tournament,* and is frequently used in criticism in the sense of "authoritative" to describe a work or performance that is unlikely to be improved upon: □ *Painter has written the definitive biography of Proust.*

• Careful users avoid the vague use of *definite* for emphasis: □ *He has a definite resemblance to Winston Churchill.*

definitely This word, meaning "certainly": □ *He was definitely going to win,* is sometimes misspelled, the most frequent error being the replacement of the second *i* with an *a.*

definitive see DEFINITE OR DEFINITIVE?

deity The pronunciation of *deity* is either [*day*itee] or [*dee*itee]. Although the former is widely used, the latter is the more traditional pronunciation.

delusion see ALLUSION, ILLUSION, OR DELUSION?

demise The original meaning of *demise* was "the transfer of an estate or of sovereignty," and because such a transfer was frequently the result of death, the word came to mean "death": □ *We were sad to hear of the demise of your husband.* This usage is formal and somewhat outdated.

• *Demise* may be used figuratively to mean "the ending of existence or activity": □ *The demise of the steel industry there caused massive unemployment in the area.* Its use to mean merely "failure" or "decline": □ *the demise of the cinema should be avoided.*

demonstrable This word may cause problems with pronunciation. The most widely used pronunciation is [di*mon*străbl], which is stressed on the second syllable. Some careful speakers prefer the traditional [*dem*ŏnstrăbl], which is stressed on the first syllable.

denationalization see PRIVATIZATION OR DENATIONALIZATION?

denouement This word, meaning "final outcome": □ *the stunning denouement of the novel,* may be spelled *denouement* or *dénouement,* the former being more frequent. Note the *oue* vowels in the middle of the word.

• The word may be stressed on the first or third syllables, and is usually pronounced [day*noomon*].

deny see REFUTE OR DENY?

depend *Depend* means "be contingent": □ *It depends on the weather*, or "be reliant on": □ *They depend on Social Security*. It is normally used with *on* or *upon*, except sometimes in certain constructions in which *it* is the subject: □ *It depends whether I'm well enough*. □ *It depends what you mean by socialism*.
• This usage is widespread but disliked by some careful users, who insist on the word *on* or *upon* following *depend* in all cases. The expression: □ *It all depends*, as a complete utterance, is acceptable only in informal speech.

dependent or **dependant?** The adjective, meaning "reliant," is spelled *dependent*: □ *industries that are dependent on oil* □ *He is completely dependent on other people's help*. The noun *dependent*, "someone who relies on another person for financial support": □ *Apart from your children, do you have any dependents?*, is sometimes spelled *dependant*, with an *a*. The two are often confused, as in a pamphlet for *Exmoor Area Tourist Attractions*, 1987: □ *But this freedom will remain largely dependant upon visitors respecting the life of the countryside*.

deploy *Deploy* is a military term meaning "organize troops or equipment so that they are in the most effective position": □ *the decision to deploy missiles*. The word is used fashionably of any utilization or organization of resources, although careful users object to its frequent use in this sense: □ *It will be up to you to set ambitious revenue targets and then train, develop, and deploy your team-members to ensure that those targets are met and surpassed* (*Daily Telegraph*, June 10, 1987).

deprecate or **depreciate?** *Deprecate* means "express disapproval of": □ *She deprecated the Government's record on equal opportunities*. *Depreciate* means "reduce in value," often used intransitively: □ *It depreciates by about $100 every year*, and "belittle or disparage": □ *He depreciated their attempts to talk English*.
• *Deprecate* is often used instead of *depreciate* in the sense of "disparage" and is also extended to mean "play down; show modesty." This usage of *deprecate* is disliked by some people, although it is acceptable in the well-established use of *self-deprecating*: □ *Jewish humor tends to be ironic and self-deprecating*.

deprived *Deprived* means "having something taken away or withheld": □ *Brain damage can occur if a baby is deprived of oxygen during labor*. It should properly be applied to things that were once possessed or would be possessed in normal circumstances, but the modern tendency is to connect it with basic necessities and rights. As an adjective, it has become a vogue word often meaning little more than "poor": □ *It is always the most deprived women, usually with housing problems or of low intelligence, who are involved* (*The Times of London*, Sept. 29, 1987).

derisive or **derisory?** *Derisive* means "expressing derision; mocking or scornful": □ *His speech was received with derisive mirth*. *Derisory* or *derisive* means "deserving derision": □ *It was a derisory/derisive performance*.
• *Derisory* is used particularly in the sense of "ridiculously inadequate; contemptibly small": □ *He was retired with a derisory pension* (BBC Radio, August 5, 1987).

desert or **dessert?** These words are sometimes confused. The only time that *dessert* is used is for a description of the last course of a meal: □ *a deliciously sweet dessert. Desert* is used for all other senses: □ *the Gobi Desert* □ *She got her just deserts.* □ *a deserted city.*

desiccated This word, meaning "dried": □ *desiccated coconut,* is sometimes misspelled. Note the single *s* and double *c*.
• It is worth remembering the Latin *dé* and *siccare,* meaning "to dry," from which the word originates.

designer *Designer* has recently become a vogue adjective that is applied to clothes and other manufactured goods that are produced by any well-known company with a reputation for fashionable design: □ *designer jeans* □ *designer watches* □ *He won't wear anything without a designer label.*
• The use has been extended to mean "chic or trendy" and is applied, sometimes jocularly, to anything that is in fashion: □ *designer stubble* (a fashionably unshaved appearance) □ *The R.S.P.C.A. condemns designer pets* (*Daily Mail,* June 18, 1987).

despatch see DISPATCH OR DESPATCH?

desperate This word, meaning "having no hope": □ *a desperate man* □ *a desperate situation,* is sometimes misspelled. The middle part of the word is spelled *per,* not *par* as in *separate.*

despicable *Despicable,* meaning "contemptible": □ *It was a despicable act,* is usually stressed on the second syllable [dispikăbl]. Careful users, however, prefer the traditional pronunciation with the stress on the first syllable [despikabl].

despite or **in spite of?** *Despite* and *in spite of* are interchangeable: □ *Despite/In spite of his injury, his playing was superb.* In spite of is used more frequently, although *despite* has the advantage of brevity.
• *Despite* needs no preposition; *despite of* is incorrect, and it is never necessary to precede either *despite* or *in spite of* with *but.*

dessert see DESERT OR DESSERT?

destined *Destined* means "being determined or intended in advance; directed toward, or having, a particular purpose or end": □ *She believed her son was destined to be the messiah.* □ *The ship was destined for Australia.*
• Some people object to the use of *destined* as a synonym for *intended,* with no suggestion of *destiny*; another use that is disliked is *was destined to be* to mean "later became": □ *He was destined to be prime minister.* These uses, however, are well-established and generally acceptable.

desultory This word should be stressed on the first syllable [desŭltree].

detract or **distract?** *Detract* means "to take away from; diminish" and is usually used figuratively to describe the diminishing of some desirable quality: □ *The new hotels can only detract from the resort's charm. Distract* means "to take one's mind off something; divert attention": □ *I tried to concentrate, but I was distracted by the noise outside.*

development Since third-world countries have been referred to as *underdeveloped countries,* and then *developing countries,* the word *development* has come to have a specialized meaning in terms of the economic growth and improvements in living conditions of third-world countries: □ *the World Development Movement* □ *The rich world need provide only $5 billion a year in de-*

velopment assistance (Ronald Sider, *Rich Christians in an Age of Hunger*).

• Note the spelling: there is no e after the *p*.

device or **devise?** These words are sometimes confused. *Device* is a noun meaning "contrivance or gadget": □ *a device for opening bottles*, or "scheme or ploy": □ *It was a cunning device to get his own way. Devise* is a verb meaning "plan": □ *They devised a new method for classifying the books.*

• Note that *devise* is one of the few verbs that cannot be spelled *-ize*: see also **-IZE OR -ISE?**

dexterous or **dextrous?** This word, meaning "skillful or nimble": □ *a dexterous artisan*, may be spelled *dexterous* or *dextrous* although the former is the much more frequently used spelling.

• Note that *ambidextrous* is always spelled without the extra e.

diagnosis or **prognosis?** *Diagnosis* and *prognosis* are most often used in medical contexts. A *diagnosis* is the identification of a disease, from studying the symptoms: □ *The doctor took one look at her spots and diagnosed chickenpox.* A *prognosis* is a forecast of the likely course of an illness and the prospect of recovery: □ *The doctor's prognosis is that he will never fully regain his eyesight.*

• *Diagnosis* and *prognosis* can be used of problems in general, with the meanings, respectively, of "an analysis of the cause of the problem" and "a forecast of the course and outcome of a problem": □ *They diagnosed a major fault in the writing.* □ *His prognosis indicated that the business was heading for bankruptcy.*

dialect *Dialect* usually refers to an established variety of a language, confined either to a region or to a social group or class.

• The *dialect* used by educated middle- or upper-class people is often regarded as the standard form of a language and other dialects as nonstandard (see **PRONUNCIATION**). At one time nonstandard regional dialects were a handicap to acceptance in "civilized" society; now a number of television and radio announcers have regional accents, although nonstandard grammar or vocabulary would still be considered unacceptable.

Dialect involves variations in pronunciation, vocabulary, and grammar. Southern speakers, for instance, may not pronounce the *g* of the words ending in *-ing.* Easterners seem to prefer *drought* to the Midwestern *drouth.* Also, New Yorkers tend to stand *on line,* while the rest of the country stands *in line.* Such differences in dialect, however, help to add depth and color to the language.

dialogue *Dialogue* is now rarely used for an ordinary conversation between two or more people, but is usually applied to exchanges of opinion and high-level negotiation between organizations and individuals who are usually ideologically opposed or have a conflict of interest: □ *We must bring about meaningful dialogue between management and unions.* □ *Mr. Gorbachev said, "The meeting . . . might start a peaceful chain-reaction in the sphere of strategic offensive arms . . . and many other items on a possible agenda of international dialogue"* (*The Times of London*, Oct. 2, 1987).

• *Dialogue* is sometimes used as a verb. □ *We must dialogue with each other.*

diaphragm A *diaphragm* is a separating membrane and especially refers to the partition that separates the chest from the abdomen. The word also refers to a contraceptive device. In spelling, note the *ph* and the silent *g*.

diarrhea This word is often misspelled. Note particularly the *rrh* and also the *-ea* ending.
• In British English, an *o* is usually inserted: *diarrhoea*.

dice *Dice* was originally the plural form of a singular noun *die*, but this singular form is now almost never used except in the expression: □ *The die is cast*. *Dice* is used now either as a singular or as a plural: □ *He made a dice out of a sugar cube*. □ *You need two dice for that game*.
• The word is also used for a gambling game played with dice: □ *"I cannot believe that God plays dice with the cosmos"* (Albert Einstein).

dichotomy A *dichotomy* is a division of two things that are sharply contrasted, especially if they are mutually exclusive, contradictory, or irreconcilably different: □ *the dichotomy between Christianity and atheism*. It has become a vogue word used generally to mean "conflict, split, schism, or difference": □ *A new dichotomy is developing in the organization*. This usage is disliked by some people, both for its lack of precision and its pretentiousness.

dietitian or **dietician?** A person who studies the principles of nutrition is known as a *dietitian*, with the rarely used variant *dietician*.
• Note that the science itself is called *dietetics*.

different from, different to or **different than?** It is possible to follow *different* with *from*, *to*, or *than*. *Different from* is the most frequently used form and the most acceptable: □ *Your life is different from mine*. *Different to* is often used in informal British English: □ *The happy situation he finds himself in is very different to the experiences of graduates in the early 1980's* (*Sunday Times*, June 14, 1987). It is, however, disliked by some people and not formally used in American English. *Different than* is disliked by many users of English and generally should be avoided.
• *Different than* is considered most acceptable when followed by a clause: □ *My values now are different than they were when I was a teen-ager,* because it removes the need for clumsy phrases such as: □ *from those that I had*.

differential *Differential*, as adjective and noun, is a term in mathematics and has the nontechnical meanings of "based on a difference; a difference between comparable things." It is now most frequently used in reference to differences in pay rates for various jobs in the same industry, based on differences in skills, work conditions, etc.: □ *Pay differentials between nursing and administrative staff have widened*.
• It is sometimes used to mean only "a difference": □ *a differential of $20 a week,* but this application is inappropriate, as a *differential* is a discrepancy based on related *differences,* not the difference itself.

different than, different to see DIFFERENT FROM, DIFFERENT TO, OR DIFFERENT THAN?

dilapidated This word, meaning "falling into ruin": □ *a dilapidated cottage,* is sometimes misspelled, the most frequent mistake being to begin the word with *de-*, rather than the correct *di-*.

dilemma A *dilemma* is a situation in which one is faced with two equally unsatisfactory alternatives: □ *It was an impossible dilemma—she could stay with her husband and be miserable, or she could leave him and lose the children.*

• It is considered acceptable informally to speak of a *dilemma* when more than two choices are involved, provided they are equally unattractive, but one should not use *dilemma* for desirable things: □ *His mouth watered as he pondered the dilemma of whether to choose the chocolate cake or the pistachio ice cream.* *Dilemma* is often used to mean just "a problem," where there is open choice or no element of choice at all: □ *the dilemma of what to wear* □ *the dilemma of how to attract new members.* Careful users dislike this imprecise use of the word.

dimension The literal uses of *dimension* are concerned with measurement, *dimensions* being also used figuratively to mean "scope or extent": □ *They were now in a position to assess the dimensions of the tragedy.* The word is also fashionably used as a synonym for *aspect* or *factor:* □ *The fact that one of the applicants was black and one a woman added a new dimension to their decision.*

• Some people dislike the overuse of the nonliteral senses of this word.

diminution This word means "decrease in size, intensity, etc.": □ *the possible diminution in readers.* Note the spelling and the pronunciation [dimi*noo*shĕn].

dinghy or **dingy?** These words are sometimes confused. A *dinghy* is a small boat; *dingy* is an adjective meaning "gloomy or shabby": □ *a dingy basement apartment.*

• *Dinghy* is pronounced with a hard *g* [*ding*gee]. The pronunciation of *dingy* is [*din*jee].

dining room see LOUNGE

diphtheria This word causes problems with spelling and pronunciation. Note the *phth* in the spelling. The *ph* sound is pronounced *f* by careful users [dif*theeri*ă] or *p* [dip*theeri*ă].

diphthong Note the *phth* in the spelling. The *ph* sound is pronounced *f* by careful users [*dif*thong] or *p* [*dip*thong].

disadvantaged Like *underprivileged* and *deprived, disadvantaged* has become a fashionable euphemism for "poor," with particular emphasis on the lack of a reasonable standard of housing, living conditions, and opportunities for gaining employment: □ *Racism and disadvantage are real, she tells her students . . .* (*The Washington Post,* Jan. 8, 1989).

disassociate see DISSOCIATE OR DISASSOCIATE?

disastrous This word is sometimes misspelled. Note that the *e* of *disaster* is dropped before the suffix *-ous* is added.

• In pronunciation careful users avoid sounding the *e* of *disaster:* [di*zas*trĕs] rather than [di*zas*tĕrĕs].

The overuse of this word, to describe something very bad in its performance or results, is disliked by many.

disc or **disk?** The preferred spelling is *disk* for a flat, round, or circular shape: □ *a slipped disk.* In British English this word is usually spelled *disc. Disk* or *disc* is used in computer science, to describe a thin plate on which data is stored: □ *a floppy disk,* or in spelling *compact disc.*

discipline Note the *c* following the *s* in the spelling of this word.

discomfit or **discomfort?** There is some overlap between these words and often confusion as to the distinction between them. *Discomfit* means "defeat or thwart": □ *He discomfited his opponent,* and "disconcert, confuse, or embarrass": □ *They were discomfited by his strange manner. Discomfort,* as a verb, means "make uncomfortable or uneasy." This condition might be one of physical distress: □ *The hard seats discomforted her,* or mental uneasiness, in which case the distinction between *discomfort* and *discomfit* often becomes blurred: □ *His ominous tone discomforted them.*

• *Discomfort* is both a verb and a noun, but the noun from *discomfit* is *discomfiture.*

discreet or **discrete?** These two words are sometimes confused. *Discreet* means "judicious or prudent": □ *You can confide in him; he is very discreet; discrete* means "separate or distinct": □ *discrete elements in the composition.*

discriminating or **discriminatory?** These adjectives are derived from *discrimination* and are connected with "distinguishing, making distinctions," but they are used in very different ways. *Discriminating* is applied to someone who is discerning in matters of taste and able to tell the difference between good and poor quality: □ *We'd better serve the Bordeaux because Paul is discriminating when it comes to wine. Discriminatory* is now almost always applied to discrimination that is unjust and based on prejudice: □ *Feminists are organizing a boycott of the bank because of its discriminatory practices.*

disinterested or **uninterested?** *Disinterested* means "impartial; having no self-interest": □ *As a disinterested party, he felt free to intervene in the dispute. Uninterested* means "having no interest; indifferent; bored": □ *I was quite uninterested in their home movies.*

• Perhaps because *uninterested* is not in frequent use, *disinterested* is now often used in its place to mean "lacking interest," which was, in fact, the original meaning of *disinterested.* However, its use in this sense is objected to by many people: □ *"It was nothing but copying documents and tedious things like that, canceled checks and invoices. . . . I've never been so disinterested."* Macon stirred and said, *"Don't you mean uninterested?"* (Anne Tyler, *The Accidental Tourist*).

disk see DISC OR DISK?

disorient or **disorientate?** *Disorient* and *disorientate* are interchangeable and mean "cause to lose bearings or sense of identity; confuse": □ *They had redesigned the roads since his last visit, and he was completely disoriented/disorientated.* □ *After years of being institutionalized, she was disoriented/disorientated after her discharge. Disorient* is preferred by some users as the shorter and simpler alternative; it is also the standard form in American English, while *disorientate* is more frequently used in British English.

• See also ORIENT OR ORIENTATE?

dispatch or **despatch?** The preferred spelling is *dispatch* for the verb meaning "to send quickly" or the noun meaning "message or report": □ *The letter was immediately dispatched.* □ *The dispatch arrived that afternoon.*

dispel or **disperse?** *Dispel* means "scatter; drive away" and is often used for abstract things: □ *He allowed them to see the original document so as to dispel their doubts about its authenticity. Disperse* means "break up": □ *The family were dispersed over Europe,* "spread over a wide area": □ *The gas dispersed over half the town,* and "dissipate, evaporate, or vanish": □ *The mist had now dispersed, and visibility was normal.*

dissect This word, meaning "separate or cut up for analysis," is spelled with a double and not a single *s*. Do not model it on *bisect.*
• Although *dissect* is often pronounced to rhyme with *bisect* [dī-sekt], careful users prefer [disekt].

dissociate or **disassociate?** *Dissociate* and *disassociate* are interchangeable opposites of *associate*: □ *One of the committee members told me after the meeting that she wished to dissociate/disassociate herself from what the chairman had said.*
• Many users prefer the form *dissociate*, although *disassociate* is older.

distinct or **distinctive?** These two adjectives are frequently confused although they are not interchangeable. Distinct means "definite; clearly perceivable or distinguishable": □ *There's a distinct taste of garlic in this stew. Distinctive* means "characteristic, peculiar to, distinguishing": □ *He had the distinctive accent of a Southerner.*

distract see DETRACT OR DISTRACT?

distrust or **mistrust?** *Distrust* and *mistrust* are often used interchangeably: □ *Somehow I distrust/mistrust the whole business. Distrust* is more frequently used and has a far more emphatic suggestion of suspicion and lack of trust: □ *I have known him to be deceitful in the past, and I have come to distrust everything he says. Mistrust* is rather more tentative and is used for a less positive lack of trust or when the doubt is directed against oneself: □ *There was something about her manner that made me uneasy, and I found myself beginning to mistrust her.* □ *I mistrust my critical judgment when it comes to my own writing.*

disturb or **perturb?** *Disturb* can mean "interrupt; inconvenience": □ *His sleep was disturbed by the doorbell.* □ *I hope I'm not disturbing you by phoning so late,* "throw into disorder": □ *The maid had disturbed all her papers,* and "upset; destroy the mental composure of": □ *I was deeply disturbed by this revelation.* In this last use, *disturb* is virtually synonymous with the less frequently used word *perturb,* which means "cause disquiet to; cause mental disturbance": □ *His violent language and abrupt departure had perturbed her.*

dived or **dove?** The preferred past tense of *dive* is dived: □ *They all dived for cover.* However, the past tense *dove* is used in several regions of the United States and Canada: □ *She dove beautifully, and a moment later she was swimming back to the side of the pool* (Philip Roth, *Goodbye, Columbus*).
• The use of *dove* is now generally considered acceptable in all but the most formal writing.

divorcé(e) A divorced man is called a *divorcé* [divorsay], and a divorced woman is called a *divorcée.* (pronounced the same).

do *Do* is used as an informal replacement for various verbs, such as "visit": □ *We're doing the museums tomorrow,* "perform": □ *The local theater is doing The Cherry Orchard,* "move": □ *The car was doing 80 miles an hour.*

• There are also the slang meanings of "cheat": □ *You've been done!* "serve (a prison sentence)": □ *He's done time,* "take, use": □ *They do drugs.* Primarily in British English *do* is also used informally as a noun to mean "a party or social event": □ *I'm going to the company's Christmas do,* or as a slang shortening of "hairdo": □ *I like your do.*

The addition of *do* in constructions when a previously mentioned verb is omitted: □ *They behaved just as I wanted them to do* is best reserved for informal use.

document *Document* is used as a verb to mean "provide documentary evidence, or information to act as factual support": □ *His essay was well documented with authoritative references.* It is also used in reference to the production of a written, filmed, or broadcast work that has detailed factual information: □ *The program documents life in a women's prison.*

dominate or **domineer?** To *dominate* means "rule, exert power or control over": □ *Her charm and energy were such that she came to dominate the whole company.* It can also mean "occupy a preeminent position": □ *Our products dominate the pet-food market,* and "overlook from a superior height": □ *The church is built on a hill and dominates the town. Dominate* is often used in a negative way that would be better reserved for *domineer,* which means "tyrannize, exert power in an arbitrary or overbearing manner." It is most frequently used as a present participle that functions as an adjective: □ *his cruel domineering manner.*

do's and don'ts In the phrase *do's and don'ts,* note that the apostrophe in *don'ts* comes after the *n* and not after the *t.* The apostrophe in *do's* is sometimes omitted.

double negative The double negative, as in: □ *I didn't do nothing.* □ *He hasn't had no trouble,* is always avoided by careful users. The objection to such constructions is that the negatives cancel each other out and reverse the meaning of the sentence.

• When two negatives are intended to cancel each other: □ *She is not without talent.* □ *It is not impossible,* they are, however, acceptable. Another generally acceptable, if colloquial, use is in such sentences as: □ *I shouldn't be surprised if it doesn't snow.*

The cruder double negative is not difficult to avoid. It is more likely to occur with the semi-negative adverbs *hardly, scarcely, barely:* □ *They were left for hours without hardly any food,* or in complex sentences where the various negative phrases might get muddled: □ *Despite his injury, he denied that it was unlikely that he would not play again this season.*

The word *neither* should not be used in sentences that are already negative: □ *I'm not hungry and I'm not thirsty neither.* □ *I didn't neither.*

doubling of consonants On the rule of doubling consonants in such words as: □ *drop—dropped* □ *refer—referred,* see **SPELLING 1.**

doubt The main problem with *doubt* is what preposition or conjunction to use with it. When *doubt* is used as a noun, it is most often followed by *about:* □ *I have my doubts about it,* but it can

D

be followed by *that* in a negative construction: □ *There is no doubt that he is telling the truth.* When *doubt* is used as a verb, it can be followed only by *that* in negative constructions: □ *I don't doubt that you are right,* and in most other constructions it is followed by whether: □ *They doubted whether she would be welcome.*

• *If* is a possible alternative to *whether,* but it is suitable for more informal use: □ *I doubt if I can make it.*

doubtful or **dubious?** *Doubtful* and *dubious* mean "giving rise to doubt, uncertain, questionable," and they are often more or less interchangeable: □ *They were doubtful/dubious about whether the car was safe. Doubtful* is more neutral and is more likely to be used when expressing uncertainty: □ *The eventual result remains doubtful. Dubious* carries more negative overtones and is often used to suggest a suspicion that a person or practice is underhanded or dishonest in some way: □ *He was involved with some dubious export company.*

doubtless see UNDOUBTEDLY.

dove see DIVED OR DOVE?

downward or **downwards?** *Downward* is used as an adjective, or an adverb meaning "to a lower level": □ *a downward slope* □ *to look downward.*

• The adverb *downwards* is more frequently used in British English. See also -WARD OR -WARDS?

draft or **draught?** The preferred spelling is *draft.* A *draft* is a preliminary outline: □ *a rough draft of the essay.* A *draft* is also a money order or a group of soldiers. *Draught* is the British spelling for *draft.*

• A person who draws up a rough version of a document is a *draftsman*; an artist or someone who prepares detailed drawings of buildings, machinery, etc., is also a *draftsman.*

The board game of *checkers* called *draughts* in British English.

dramatist or **playwright?** *Dramatist* and *playwright* are synonymous words, each dating from the late 17th century and meaning "a person who writes plays": □ *He is a poet as well as a dramatist/playwright.*

• There may be a slight tendency to apply *dramatist* to those who write more serious plays or plays that conform to the traditional categories of drama: □ *Racine was a dramatist writing in the classical tradition,* and *playwright* to modern writers and those whose work is less serious: □ *playwrights like Neil Simon who are popular on both sides of the Atlantic.*

Note the spelling of the final syllable of *playwright: -wright,* not *write.*

draught see DRAFT OR DRAUGHT?

drawing room see LOUNGE.

dreamed or **dreamt?** Either word may be used as the past tense and past participle of the verb *dream* : □ *I dreamed/dreamt I was in Australia,* but *dreamed* is somewhat preferred.

• See also -ED OR -T?

Dreamed may be pronounced [dreemd] or [dremt]; *dreamt* is always pronounced [dremt].

drunk or **drunken?** *Drunk* and *drunken* are adjectives applied to alcoholic intoxication, but *drunk* is normally used after the

verb: □ *She got drunk on cheap wine,* whereas *drunken* is normally used before a noun: □ *We were just sipping sherry—it was hardly a drunken orgy.* □ *the campaign against drunken driving.*
• *Drunk* implies temporary intoxication, whereas *drunken* suggests a habitual state of being *drunk.*

dubious see DOUBTFUL OR DUBIOUS?

due to, owing to, or **because of?** Although these phrases have roughly the same meanings, they are not used in the same way. *Due to* should only be used adjectivally: □ *His shakiness is due to Parkinson's disease,* whereas *owing to* and *because of* can be used either adjectivally or as prepositions: □ *The delay was owing to a power failure.* □ *Because of poor health, he took early retirement.* □ *She was now rich, owing to her successful venture.*
• Although the use of *due to* as a preposition is objected to by careful users, this usage is becoming increasingly widespread: □ *Due to the sheer size of the operation, we now need additional people to join our . . .* Membership Recruitment and Corporate Marketing Departments (*Sunday Times,* May 28, 1987).

dwelled or **dwelt?** Either word may be used as the past tense and past participle of the verb *dwell. Dwelt* is the preferred form: □ *He dwelt on her infidelity.*
• See also -ED OR -T?

dying or **dyeing?** These spellings are sometimes confused. *Dying* is the present participle of the verb *die:* □ *looking after dying patients* □ *his dying words. Dyeing* is the present participle of the verb *dye,* meaning "change the color of: □ *She was dyeing her hair blond.*

dynamic *Dynamic* is a very much overworked vogue word meaning "lively, forceful, or energetic": □ *The Party needs young, dynamic leadership.*
• Its frequent use, particularly in employment advertising, has considerably weakened its impact: □ *a dynamic statewide health organization based in Richmond . . . is searching for a senior management official* (advertisement, *The Wall Street Journal,* Dec. 27, 1988).

each When *each* is used as a determiner or as a pronoun that is the subject of a sentence, the rule is that subsequent verbs and pronouns should be singular: □ *Each man has his price.* □ *Each of the operas was sung in English.*
• The rule is frequently broken, partly because those who are sensitive to sexism in language prefer: □ *Each student had papers handed to them* [rather than *to him*]. Of course, one can avoid both sexism and grammatical error by rephrasing such sentences: □ *All the students had papers handed to them.* When *each* follows a plural noun or pronoun that is the subject of the sentence, the verb following is plural: □ *The cakes each have cherries on top.*

each and every *Each and every* is used for emphasis in phrases such as: □ *Each and every person has a vital part to play.* □ *I am deeply grateful to each and every one of you.* It is disliked by most careful users as a cliché and as an unnecessarily wordy construction where *each, everyone,* or *all* could be substituted.

each other or **one another?** The traditional rule is that *each other* is used when two elements are involved and *one another* when more than two are involved: □ *Helen and Charles love each other deeply.* □ *All the people at the party already knew one another.* This rule, however, is often ignored.
• There is a slight difference in the two phrases in that *each other* tends to emphasize each individual element whereas *one another* sounds more general. It would be preferable to say: □ *They were throwing one another into the swimming pool* rather than *throwing each other;* the former gives a general impression of horseplay and allows for the odd person who was neither thrown nor throwing, whereas the latter suggests something much more systematic.

east, East, or **eastern?** As an adjective, *east* is always written with a capital *E* when it forms part of a place name: □ *East River* □ *the East End.* The noun *east* is usually written with a capital *E* when it denotes a specific region, such as the East Coast or the countries of Asia: □ *She has traveled extensively in the East.* □ *East-West relations.*
• In other contexts, and as an adverb, *east* is usually written with a lowercase *e:* □ *They sailed east in search of land.* □ *The east wind chilled him to the marrow.* □ *The sun rises in the east.*
The adjective *eastern* is more frequent and usually less specific than the adjective *east:* □ *along its eastern shore* □ *in eastern Massachusetts.*
Like *east, eastern* is written with a capital *E* when it forms part of a proper name, such as: □ *the Eastern Orthodox Church.* With or

without a capital *E*, it also means "of the East": □ *eastern/Eastern philosophy*; with the capital *E* preferred.

eatable or **edible?** Some users define *eatable* as "palatable," but with the suggestion of "tasting not unpleasant" rather than "delicious": □ *He had managed to get together a reasonably eatable meal.* *Edible* or *eatable* means "suitable for eating as food": □ *Common sorrel is edible/eatable but wood sorrel is poisonous.*

• If something is not *edible*, it would be either impossible or dangerous to eat it, but some users suggest that a substance can be *edible* without being *eatable*—for example, raw potatoes. Despite these differences the two words are often used interchangeably in informal contexts: □ *The cabbage was overcooked but just about eatable/edible.*

echelon *Echelon* is a military expression applying to the formation of units or to a division of a supply organization. It is now often used as a fashionable synonym for *grade, rank, level of power,* or to describe the people at that level: □ *the management echelon* □ *the upper echelons of the civil service.*

• Note the spelling: *ch*, not *sh*, and although the word comes from the French *échelon*, there is no acute accent on the English word. The usual pronunciation is [esh*ă*lon]; [aysh*ă*lon] is rarely heard.

eco- The growing popularity of the science of *ecology*, the study of living things in their relation to the environment, has given rise to several words with the prefix *eco-*, some legitimate terms in ecology: □ *ecospecies* □ *ecotype* □ *ecosystem*, and some more modern coinages: □ *ecocatastrophe* □ *eco-freak.* □ *ecocide*

• New *eco-* words are being spawned all the time: □ *a new magazine . . . described as the journal of eco-politics (The Guardian,* Feb. 11, 1982) □ *the eco-warriors of Greenpeace (Sunday Times,* May 31, 1987) □ *His exciting accounts of the eco-guerrillas' attacks on . . . whaling ships (The Bookseller,* May 8,1987).

economic or **economical?** *Economic* is the adjective from *economics* or *the economy* and is concerned with the production, distribution, and structure of wealth: □ *economic theories* □ *the Government's economic policies. Economical* is the adjective from *economy* and is concerned with thrift and the avoidance of waste: □ *an economical car* □ *a large economical pack.*

• *Economic* tends to be used when a producer or seller is being considered and *economical* when the consumer is in question: an *economic price* is one that benefits the seller, but an *economical price* benefits the buyer. Although careful users keep the distinction between the two words, each is frequently used with the meaning belonging to the other: □ *Labor gave fewer details of their economical brief* (BBC Radio, May 20, 1987). □ *Buying a whole chicken makes economic sense* (advertisement, *Bejam* magazine, Autumn 1987).

economics see -ICS.

ecstasy This word, meaning "intense emotion," especially of happiness, is sometimes misspelled. Note particularly the *-cs-* and the *-asy* ending, as in *fantasy.*

-ed or **-t?** The past tense and past participle of the verbs *burn, dream, dwell, kneel, leap, spill,* and *spoil* may end in *-ed* or *-t.*

• In most cases the *-ed* form is preferred; the *-t* form is slightly more frequent in British English. (The past of *mean,* however, is always *meant.*) For further discussion and specific information on pronunciation and adjectival use, see the entries at the individual words.

edible see EATABLE OR EDIBLE?

-ee or **-er?** In general, the suffix *-ee* can be applied to the recipient of an action denoted by the verb to which the suffix is attached, and the suffix *-er* is applied to the thing or person who performs the action: □ *employer–employee* □ *trainer–trainee;* however, this rule does not apply in all cases. The suffix *-ee* can sometimes indicate someone who behaves in a particular way: □ *absentee* □ *parolee* □ *retiree* □ *escapee,* and the suffix *-er* can be applied to something that is a suitable object for an action: □ *prisoner* □ *a real looker.*

• The suffix *-ee* is also found as a substitute for *-ie* or *-y,* suggesting smallness, in the word *bootee,* and is sometimes applied to people or things associated with a particular noun: □ *goatee* □ *bargee* □ *refugee* although *-er* is more often used in this way: □ *villager* □ *docker* □ *islander.*

effect see AFFECT OR EFFECT?

effective, effectual, efficacious, or **efficient?** The distinction between these words is subtle. *Effective* means "having or producing the desired effect": □ *The talks were effective in settling the dispute. Effectual,* a formal word, means "capable of achieving the desired effect": □ *All plans to reduce the trade deficit have not so far proved effectual. Efficacious,* also a formal word, means "having the power to achieve the desired effect" and is usually applied to medical treatment: □ *an efficacious remedy. Efficient* is applied to people or things producing results through a good and economical use of resources: □ *an efficient machine* □ *an efficient secretary.*

• *Effective* is used in various other ways. It can mean "impressive": □ *an effective performance,* "operative; in force": □ *The law is effective as of today,* and "actual; in practice if not theory": □ *He had become the effective leader.*

e.g. and **i.e.** The abbreviation *e.g.* stands for the Latin *exempli gratia* and means "for example." It is used before examples of what has previously been mentioned: □ *We could show you some of the sights—e.g., Buckingham Palace and the Tower of London.* The abbreviation *i.e.* is often used in error for *e.g.,* but it stands for the Latin *id est* and means "that is." It is used before amplifications of what has previously been mentioned: □ *They were vegans— i.e., vegetarians who also avoid eggs and dairy products.*

• The abbreviations *e.g.* and *i.e.* are best confined to official writing or very informal writing; instead, *for example* and *that is* should be used, as they should in speech.

egoism or **egotism?** The words *egoism* and *egotism* are frequently used interchangeably, but there are differences between them. *Egoism* is applied to the ethical theory that all actions and motivation are based on self-interest. An *egoist* is a believer in this theory or, much more often, a person who is selfish and self-seeking: □ *His conduct was characterized by ruthless egoism. Egotism* means "being self-obsessed; self-centered." The typical *egotist* is vain, boastful, and uses the word *I* constantly: □ *Her egotism makes her oblivious to other people's concerns.*

• The conspicuous self-obsession of *egotists* often makes them absurd or pathetic figures, whereas *egoists* may pursue their own interests in a covert but calculating manner.

eighth Note that in the spelling of this word the letter *h* occurs twice: *eight* and *h*.

either As an adjective or pronoun, *either* is used with a singular verb: □ *Is either child left-handed?* □ *Is either of your children left-handed?*

• In the *either* . . . *or* construction, a singular verb is used if each subject is singular and a plural verb is used if each subject is plural: □ *Either David or Peter is responsible.* □ *Either their parents or their teachers are responsible.* The use of a plural verb with the pronoun *either* or with singular subjects in an *either* . . . *or* construction is avoided by careful users, especially in formal contexts.

When a combination of singular and plural subjects occurs in an *either* . . . *or construction,* the verb traditionally agrees with the subject that is nearer to it: □ *Either David or his parents are responsible.* □ *Either his friends or his brother is responsible.* The same principle is applied to singular subjects that are used with different forms of the verb: □ *Either you or I am* [not *are*] *responsible.* If the resulting sentence sounds awkward or unidiomatic, it may be reordered or rephrased.

The alternatives presented in an *either* . . . *or* construction should be grammatically balanced: □ *Dilute the soup either with milk or water* may be changed to: *Dilute the soup either with milk or with water* or: *Dilute the soup with either milk or water.*

As a pronoun, *either* should be used only of two alternatives: □ *I haven't seen either of my parents since June.* □ *Any* [not *Either*] *of the four knives may be used to cut vegetables.* However, the use of the *either* . . . *or* construction with three or more subjects is acceptable to some: □ *Either Sarah, Jane, or Pauline will be there.*

The first syllable of *either* may be pronounced to rhyme with *tree* or *try.* The pronunciation [eedhĕr] is more frequent.

See also NEITHER; OR.

eke out The original meaning of *eke out* is "make something more adequate by adding to it": □ *She eked out the meal with extra rice.* It is frequently used in two other senses: "make something last longer by using it economically": □ *They eked out the supplies over two weeks,* and "make (a living) with laborious effort": □ *The children eked out a living by selling wildflowers to tourists.*

• These newer uses, particularly the latter, are disliked by some careful users, but they are well established and generally acceptable.

elder, eldest, older, or **oldest?** *Elder* and *eldest* are applied only to people, and usually within the context of family relationships: □ *my eldest brother* □ *She is the elder of my two daughters.* One cannot say: *Rachel is elder than Sarah* or: *He is elder/eldest* without adding *the.* *Older* and *oldest* can be used of things as well as people and in a far wider range of constructions: □ *I am older than David.* □ *He is oldest.* □ *It is the oldest church in New York.*

• *Elder* is also used in such expressions as: □ *I am his elder by eight years,* although: □ *I am older than him by eight years* sounds

less formal. *Elder* is also used for people noted for age and experience: □ *an elder statesman* □ *village elders* □ *one's elders and betters;* and for an officer in some Protestant churches.
See also COMPARATIVE AND SUPERLATIVE.

electric or **electrical?** *Electric* and *electrical* mean "worked by electricity," although *electric* tends to be applied more to specific, and *electrical* to general things: □ *electric lighting* □ *an electric motor* □ *electrical appliances* □ *electrical equipment.*
• *Electric* is also applied to things that produce or carry electricity: □ *electric current* □ *an electric shock,* and is used figuratively to describe something stimulating or thrilling: □ *The atmosphere was electric. Electrical* is also used to mean "connected with electricity": □ *electrical engineering.*

elemental or **elementary?** *Elemental* means "of or like the elements or forces of nature": □ *This evoked a flood of elemental passion.* It is also sometimes used to mean "fundamental or essential": □ *an elemental truth of Christianity.* It should not be confused with elementary, which means "very simple; introductory": □ *I know nothing about computers, so I need an elementary manual.* □ *elementary school.*
• A further possible mistake is the confusion of *elementary* with *alimentary,* which means "having to do with the provision of nourishment": □ *the alimentary canal.*

elicit see ILLICIT OR ELICIT?

ellipsis There are two meanings of the term *ellipsis* in grammar: one is for the punctuation marks . . . , usually indicating omission; the other is for the omission of words in a sentence, in order to shorten the sentence or to avoid repetition: □ *See you Friday.* □ *I ought to write some letters and make some phone calls.*
• The *ellipsis* . . . is used mainly to indicate an omission from a quoted passage: □ *"There's rosemary, that's for remembrance . . . and there is pansies, that's for thoughts."* If the quotation does not start at the beginning of a sentence, the ellipsis precedes it: □ *". . . a good fellow of infinite jest,"* and when the end of a sentence is omitted, the three dots of the ellipsis are followed by a fourth, to indicate a period: □ *"Cudgel thy brains no more. . . .";* if a whole sentence is left out the sentence before the omitted one takes a period and the ellipsis follows. An ellipsis is always three dots, or four if a period is included, except when a whole line of poetry is omitted, when a row of dots may be used to fill the length of the line.
The ellipsis is also used in the same manner as the dash, to indicate halting speech, an unfinished sentence, or an omitted obscenity (see DASH). When used for an unfinished sentence, a dash suggests a more abrupt break, while an ellipsis gives an impression of speech trailing off: □ *"I suppose I had hoped that you might . . . ."* An ellipsis should not be used at the end of a passage to suggest that the rest of an episode can be left to the reader's imagination.
When using the ellipsis in sentences to avoid repetition, one should note the danger that the omitted word(s) might not correspond with the word(s) repeated, as in the following two examples. In: □ *I know him as well or even better than you do,* a second *as,* after *as well,* is omitted, but this word is not repeated. In: □ *No one*

has ever or will ever solve the mystery, the omitted word is *solved,* not *solve.* The only case in which such a false ellipsis is acceptable occurs when the omitted word is part of the verb *to be:* □ *I'm going to London and Sarah to Rome.*

else *Else* is often followed by either *than* or *but:* □ *Nothing else than revolution is possible.* □ *Anybody else but him would be preferable.* Some careful users object to following *else* with *than* or *but,* and difficulties can be avoided by substituting phrases such as *nothing but* or *anyone other than.*

• The use of *else* as a conjunction: □ *Stop, else you'll have an accident* is also disliked by many people. Unless it is used in very informal speech, *or else* should be substituted.

For possessive forms see APOSTROPHE.

elude see AVOID, EVADE, OR ELUDE?

elusive see ALLUSIVE, ELUSIVE, OR ILLUSIVE?

embarrass This word, meaning "cause to feel shy, ashamed, or self-conscious": □ *She was embarrassed by her brother's behavior,* is often misspelled. Note the double *r,* the double *s,* and the last vowel, which is an *a,* not an *e.*

emend see AMEND OR EMEND?

emigrant or **immigrant?** An *emigrant* is someone who is migrating from his or her country: □ *Thousands of emigrants left Britain for America and Australia.* An *immigrant* is someone who is migrating into another country: □ *Some of the immigrants had only been in the country for a week.*

• The word *émigré* is applied to someone who was forced to leave a country, usually because of a repressive political regime or a repressive intellectual atmosphere. The reasons for leaving are generally less pressing than for those described as *refugees,* and *émigré* carries a suggestion of refined class and intellect that *refugee* lacks: □ *Nabokov is the most famous of Russian émigré writers.*

eminent, imminent, or **immanent?** *Eminent* means "outstanding, notable, or distinguished," and is particularly applied to people who have achieved some distinction or fame in their profession, or in the arts or sciences: □ *an eminent judge* □ *an eminent poet. Imminent* means "impending; about to happen; threatening": □ *It then seemed that war was imminent.*

• *Imminent* should not be confused with the far less frequently used word *immanent,* which means "inherent, dwelling within," and has the theological meaning of "pervading all things throughout the universe."

emotional or **emotive?** *Emotional* or *emotive* mean "causing or arousing emotion, especially as opposed to reason": □ *Capital punishment is an emotional/emotive subject. Emotional* also means "expressing emotion, showing excessive emotion": □ *an emotional person* □ *an emotional meeting.*

empathy *Empathy* means "an imaginative identification with another's feelings or ideas": □ *He read all he could about the king, and meditated on his character, so by the time he came to play the part he felt a real empathy with Henry.* It has recently become a fashionable word, and its frequent use as a mere synonym for sympathy is disliked by some: □ *Essential attributes are . . . an empathy for the ideals within a voluntary organization (Daily Telegraph, June 11, 1987).*

emulate *Emulate* means "attempt to equal or do better than, especially by close imitation": □ *Since the company's success, all our competitors are trying to emulate our products.*

• The word is often used in the sense of "imitate closely" without the idea of rivalry: □ *As a teen-ager, he had admired John Lennon devotedly and had tried to emulate him in his dress and speech.*

encyclopedia or **encyclopaedia?** Either spelling of this word is acceptable. *Encyclopedia* is the more frequent spelling.

end product and **end result** *End product* usually means the "final product of a process, or series of processes": □ *We use the best materials so that the end product is a quality item.* □ *These young men are the end products of expensive private schools and the most exclusive colleges.*

• It is now sometimes used to mean simply "the eventual outcome," as is the phrase *end result:* □ *The agreement is the end product/end result of many years of negotiation.* Many careful users dislike both these phrases, because the *end* is clearly redundant.

enervate *Enervate* means "weaken, to lessen vitality or strength": □ *It was an enervating climate, and they felt listless most of the time.*

• It is sometimes incorrectly used as though it meant the opposite, as a synonym for *invigorate* or *energize,* and is also sometimes used as though it meant "irritate" or "get on someone's nerves." *Enervate* is most often used in the forms *enervated* or *enervating.*

England see BRITAIN.

enhance *Enhance* means "improve, increase the value or attractiveness of": □ *The new windows have enhanced the value of the house.* □ *This week's running debacle over Labor's defense policies has hardly enhanced Mr. Kinnock's appeal to any Tories who might be wavering* (*Sunday Times,* May 31, 1987).

• It has become a fashionable word, particularly used by employers in connection with extra benefits offered to employees: □ *Excellent salaries are enhanced by a wide range of benefits including relocation assistance* (*Daily Telegraph,* May 28, 1987).

enormity or **enormousness?** *Enormity* means "the quality of being outrageous or wicked, a very wicked act": □ *Those experiences alerted him to the enormity of what was being done to the Jews* (*The Guardian,* May 25, 1987). *Enormousness* means "the quality of being extremely large": □ *They were daunted by the enormousness of the task.*

• *Enormity* is frequently used as though it meant *enormousness,* but many careful users of English still dislike it.

enquiry see INQUIRY OR ENQUIRY?

ensure see ASSURE, ENSURE, OR INSURE?

enthuse The verb *enthuse* is a back-formation from *enthusiasm* and means "show enthusiasm": □ *The critics rarely enthuse about new plays,* or "make enthusiastic": □ *Mr. Neil Kinnock's achievement has been to mobilize and enthuse the traditional Labor vote* (*Sunday Times,* May 31, 1987).

• Although it has been in use for more than 160 years, it is still disliked by many people and is perhaps best avoided in formal use.

envelop or **envelope?** The verb *envelop* means "enclose, surround, or enfold," and is used both literally and figuratively: □ *He was* *enveloped in a blanket and barely visible.* □ *She spent a happy childhood, enveloped in love and security.* The noun *envelope* means "something that envelops, a wrapper (particularly for a letter)"': □ *It arrived in a plain brown envelope.*

• *Envelop* is pronounced [envelŏp]. The preferred pronunciation of *envelope* is [envălōp], although [onvălōp] is also heard.

environment *Environment* can be applied to the surrounding conditions of people and other organisms and might include physical and social influences, though many people are careful not to overuse this word.

• Although *environment* has been in use for almost 400 years, it has taken on a new emphasis in recent years and has become a fashionable word in the context of ecology and the protection of the world's physical environment from pollution: □ *the World Wildlife Fund's plan to trade Third World debt for tropical rain forest preservation . . . will be an important step toward using market incentives to better the environment* (The Wall Street Journal, Dec. 30, 1988).

envision or **envisage** *Envision* or *envisage* mean "have a mental image of, especially something hoped for in the future": □ *They envisioned/envisaged a world in which war and poverty no longer existed. Envision* is more often used in American English and *envisage* in British English.

• The words should not be used as mere synonyms for "expect": □ *A further downward trend in stock prices is envisioned.* Careful users avoid using these words with *that:* □ *We envision* [not *envision that*] *the situation will improve.*

envy or **jealousy?** *Envy* involves the awareness of an advantage possessed by someone else, together with a desire to have that advantage for one's own: □ *I envy your ability to relax. Jealousy* involves a concern to avoid the loss of something that one regards as one's own, and includes the tendency to be suspicious of rivalry and infidelity in relation to a person one is close to: □ *Her husband's jealousy forced her to conceal even the most innocent encounters with other men,* as well as vigilance in preserving a possession: □ *They guarded their professional reputation jealously.*

ephemeral This word, meaning "lasting only a short time": □ *the ephemeral pleasures of life,* is sometimes misspelled. Note particularly the *ph*, pronounced [f], and the sequence of vowels.

epic *Epic* originally applied to long narrative poems on a grand, heroic scale, such as Homer's *Iliad* and *Odyssey* or the Finnish *Kalevala.* It was extended to other works with some of these qualities or to series of events or episodes that might be fit subjects for an epic: □ *an epic novel* □ *the epic battle between Greenpeace and the whaling ships.*

• It is also sometimes used of anything more than usually large and impressive: □ *an epic gathering,* but it is preferable not to use the word so that it entirely loses its connection with its heroic origins.

epitome This word, meaning "typical example": □ *He is the epitome of the absent-minded professor,* is sometimes mispronounced. Note that there are four syllables [eepitŏmee].

eponyms An *eponym* is a word derived from the name of a person: □ *sandwich* □ *quisling* □ *cardigan* □ *ampere.* There are eponymous nouns: □ *martinet* □ *watt,* adjectives: □ *quixotic* □ *herculean,* and verbs: □ *bowdlerize* □ *guillotine.*

• The main problem with the use of eponyms is whether or not they are written with a capital letter. The rough rule is that the closer the connection between the word and the name, the more likely it is that a capital should be used. When one calls a young man given to amorous adventures a *Romeo*, one is making a definite allusion to the Shakespearean character and would use capitals. One would use a capital when referring to *Platonic forms* but not when referring to *platonic love*, a concept further removed from Plato. There are no firm rules with things named after their inventor, or someone associated with the invention. Generally such words are more likely to be capitalized when used adjectivally than when used as nouns: □ *Wellington boots* □ *wellingtons,* but this usage is very much a matter of custom. *Pullman cars* and *Bunsen burners* are nearly always capitalized, while *diesel engine* hardly ever is. Eponymous verbs such as: □ *boycott* □ *pasteurize* never have capital letters, unless, of course, they begin sentences.

equable or **equitable?** *Equable* means "regular, moderate, not given to extremes," and is frequently applied both to climates that are consistently mild and not subject to sudden changes, and to people who are placid and even-tempered. *Equitable* means "fair, reasonable, impartial": □ *It was an equitable agreement, which both parties found satisfactory.*

equal to or **equal with?** When briefly indicating identity, equivalence, or similarity, *equal* is used as a verb with no preposition: □ *x = 5.* In longer constructions, using *equal* as an adjective, it is preferable to use *equal with*, rather than *equal to:* □ *The team has gained five points and is now equal with the opposing team.* *Equal to* has the specific meaning of "capable of meeting the requirements of": □ *He seemed too young and inexperienced to be equal to the task.*

equitable see EQUABLE OR EQUITABLE?

-er see -EE OR -ER?

-er or **-or?** The suffix *-er* is used, among other things, to form nouns to indicate occupations: □ *lawyer* □ *bricklayer,* and those who perform certain actions: □ *player* □ *messenger.* The suffix *-or* is used in the same way with other words, normally those formed from Latin roots. Often these are words with no English verb base: □ *sponsor* □ *doctor* □ *author* □ *mentor,* but that is not always the case: □ *actor* □ *investigator* □ *sailor.*

• It is not always possible to guess which ending should be used and sometimes either may be acceptable: □ *adviser/advisor* □ *vendor/vender.* The *-er* ending is more usual and can be assumed with most recently coined nouns and those that do not have Latin roots.

erogenous *Erogenous* zones are the parts of the body that are sensitive to sexual stimulation. Note the spelling of the word *erogenous:* a single *r* and *-gen-,* not *-gyn-* as in *misogynist.*

escalate *Escalate* is a back-formation from *escalator,* and as a vogue word meaning "expand, rise, intensify," tends to be overused. It is best confined to the description of an upward movement that increases step by step: □ *Rents have escalated over the last five years.* □ *escalating pitch is hurting their voices and distorting music* (*The New York Times,* Jan. 1, 1989).

especially or **specially?** These adverbs are often used interchange-

E

ably, but there is a difference in their meanings. *Especially* means "more than usual, in particular, above all": □ *He was especially hungry.* □ *I hate dogs, especially big ones.* Specially means "specifically, on purpose, in this particular way": □ *The car is specially designed for handicapped people.* □ *I made it specially for you.*

• *Specially* is often used where *especially* is intended, and sometimes, as in the last example, this usage might lead to confusion as *specially for you* might mean "for you above all" or "specifically for you."

-ess The use of the feminine suffix *-ess* is frequently regarded as patronizing or sexist and is often unnecessary.

• Such nouns as *author, poet, sculptor, editor, manager*, etc., can be applied to people of either sex, making *authoress, poetess, sculptress, editress*, and *manageress* redundant. *Actress* and *hostess* are retained in some contexts, although *actor* and *host* are generally considered to be of neutral gender. Certain occupational titles, such as *waiter* and *steward*, tend to be used as masculine nouns, *waitress* and *stewardess* being their feminine equivalents. The suffix *-ess* is obligatory in such words as *princess, duchess, countess*, and *marchioness*.

See also SEXISM.

essentially *Essentially* should be used primarily to mean "basically, inherently, or most importantly": □ *The play is essentially a tragedy, although there is some comic relief.*

• It tends sometimes also to be used with a weaker meaning of "in general terms": □ *It was essentially a good match,* or "importantly": □ *Your view isn't essentially different from mine.*

establishment *The Establishment* refers to the powerful figures in government (especially the civil service), the legal system, the established church, the armed forces, etc., who are thought to control a nation □ *At the London meeting, the Prime Minister, the Archbishop of Canterbury, and the Lord Chief Justice were among the Establishment figures present. The Establishment* (sometimes with a lowercase *e*) is thought to have a conservative outlook, generally opposing changes to the existing order, and as such is often used as a derogatory term.

• A further meaning of *establishment* is "a controlling or influential group": □ *the modern-art establishment.*

et al. *Et al.* is an abbreviation of *et alii* and means "and other people." It is used particularly in writings of a formal or technical nature to indicate the omission of other names: □ *Similar findings have been recorded by Jones, Bernstein, et al.*

• It should not be used in ordinary writing or in speech, and should be used only when a list is specific and does not start with *for example* or *such as.*

etc. The abbreviation *etc.* stands for *et cetera*, which means "and other things, and so forth": □ *Students must take several courses: English, history, chemistry, etc.*

• It is used in technical or informal writing, but in formal writing *and so on* or *and so forth* is preferred. One should not write *and etc.* or use it in a list preceded by *for example* or *such as.* There is never any point in writing *etc. etc.*, and its use in speech is always unacceptable.

ethics see -ICS.

ethnic The original meaning of *ethnic* is "having to do with groups of people classed by common race, traits, or customs": □ *There are many different ethnic groups in the U.S.S.R.* As a vogue word, ethnic is now used to mean "having to do with race": □ *Fresh ethnic violence scarred Pakistan yesterday* (*Daily Telegraph*, Aug. 28, 1987), "foreign" (particularly Asian or Caribbean): □ *A great deal of ethnic food is not hot, but spiced, with pronounced flavors* (*Sunday Times*, June 28, 1987), and "nonwhite": □ *Labor now has three other ethnic Members of Parliament* (*Sunday Times*, June 14, 1987).

euphemisms A *euphemism* is the use of an inoffensive term as a substitute for one that might give offense. Such terms tend to be used particularly when referring to sexual and bodily functions: □ *private parts* (genitals) □ *restroom* (toilet), and to death: □ *She passed away.* □ *I lost my husband two years ago.*

• Some euphemisms have arisen out of genuine feelings of sensitivity, but many are attempts to cover up something reprehensible: □ *the Nazi final solution* (mass extermination of the Jews) □ *being economical with the truth* (lying).

The invention of new euphemisms in the business and professional worlds is becoming almost an art form: □ *At one international computer company the accepted wording for falling behind is "achieving schedule overrun"* (*Sunday Times*, June 7, 1987). □ *[An American] hospital recently announced the relapse of an important patient by saying he "did not fully achieve his wellness potential." He later experienced a "terminal episode"* . . . previously known as death (*The Times of London*, Sept. 3, 1987).

Euro- Although the United Kingdom is part of Europe, British people have traditionally spoken of *Europe* to mean all the continent apart from the United Kingdom. When United Kingdom membership of the European Economic Community was debated, it was often referred to in British English as *going into Europe*, and *Europe* is now often used as a synonym for the E.E.C.

• The prefix *Euro-* is sometimes used in words that are connected with Europe in general: □ *Eurocommunism* □ *Eurobond* but more often with those having connections with the *E.E.C.*: □ *Euromart* □ *Eurocurrency* □ *Eurocrat.*

evade, evasion see AVOID, EVADE, OR ELUDE?

even The position of the word *even* in a sentence can influence its meaning. Compare the following sentences and their implications: □ *Even I like opera on television* (other people like it more). □ *I like even opera on television* (presumably I would prefer things other than opera). □ *I like opera even on television* (though it is inferior on television). In formal writing it is best always to put *even* before the word it modifies, in order to make the meaning unambiguous, although in speech it is often more natural to put even before the verb: □ *He doesn't even stop working on vacation.*

eventuate *Eventuate* is used, usually in formal contexts, to mean "result": □ *If the proposed merger takes place, this might eventuate in the new company having a monopoly of the market.* It is disliked by many people as pompous and affected, and conveying nothing that is not conveyed by simpler and more usual words.

ever The use of *ever* with superlatives in such constructions as: □ *the largest pie ever* □ *his fastest speed ever*, is disliked by some people because they feel that *ever* includes the future, as well as the past. The usage is well established, but the criticism can be met by changing the constructions slightly: □ *the largest pie ever baked* □ *his fastest speed to date/the fastest he has ever run.*
• The expressions *ever so* and *ever such* as intensives: □ *He's ever so clever.* □ *It's ever such a nice house* should be confined to informal contexts, and *ever so* without an adjective or adverb following: □ *Thanks ever so* is better avoided.
On whether to write *whatever* or *what ever*, *wherever* or *where ever*, etc., in such sentences as: □ *What ever did he say next?* □ *Wherever you travel, you'll find businesses that accept our credit card*, see **WHATEVER OR WHAT EVER?**

every *Every* is used with singular nouns and all related words should be in the singular form: □ *Every machine is equipped with a safety device.* The temptation to use plurals arises when one wishes to avoid such gender-specific constructions as: □ *I hope every committee member has remembered to bring his agenda.* Rather than use the ungrammatical *their agendas* or the rather clumsy *his or her agenda*, it is better to rephrase the sentence: □ *I hope all committee members have remembered to bring their agendas.*

everybody or **everyone?** The pronoun *everybody* and its synonym *everyone* are interchangeable in all contexts.
• Each is used with a singular verb but is sometimes informally followed by a plural personal pronoun or possessive adjective (see **THEY**): □ *Everybody/Everyone has paid their fare.*
Note the difference between the one-word compound *everyone* and the more specific two-word form *every one*, either of which may be applied to people: □ *Everyone knew the answer.* □ *Every one of the contestants knew the answer.* Only the two-word compound is used of things: □ *I bought six glasses, and every one was cracked.*

evince *Evince* is a formal verb meaning "show clearly; make apparent": □ *Her writing evinces keen perception and skills of observation.* Some careful users believe it should be applied only to qualities, not to attitudes or emotions, although it is generally acceptable in such applications.

exaggerate This word, meaning "represent as greater than is true," is sometimes misspelled. Note that there is only one *x* as in *exact*, but a double *g* as in *dagger*.

except It is usually better to use *except* rather than *except for:* □ *We all went for a walk except Flora.* The exceptions are at the beginning of a sentence: □ *Except for Stuart, we are all under 40*, and when a whole statement is being qualified and *except for* means "if it were not for": □ *The room was silent except for the occasional squeak of a pen.*
• *Except for* is also used with the meaning "without; but for": □ *I wouldn't have got this far except for your support*, but this usage is informal, and some careful users dislike it.
Except as a preposition should be followed by the object form: □ *except me* [not *I*] □ *except him* [not *he*].

exceptional or **exceptionable?** *Exceptional* means "out of the ordinary; uncommon": □ *It's been an exceptional day*, and "unusually good": □ *This is an exceptional wine.* *Exceptional* is applied to children of either below- or above-average ability, and is now applied particularly to physically or educationally handicapped children. *Exceptional* should not be confused with *exceptionable*, which means "objectionable; something to which exception might be taken": □ *His words were not offensive in themselves, but there was something in his manner that they found exceptionable.*

exclamation point Exclamation points or exclamation marks are used to indicate strong feeling or urgency: □ *Hurray!* □ *Go away!* □ *Help!* Exclamation marks may come at the end of a sentence, as a substitute for a period, or at the end of a quotation, within quotation marks: □ *"Ouch!" he cried.* Occasionally, they may occur in the middle of a sentence.

• Exclamation ponts are used after interjections, oaths, and words representing loud noises: □ *Oh!* □ *Ow!* □ *Crash!* □ *Damn!* □ *Gracious!*, after alarms and commands: □ *Look out!* □ *Quiet!* □ *Fire!*, and after insults and curses: □ *You bastard!* □ *Rot in hell!* They are used after various exclamations expressing surprise, indignation, pleasure, or displeasure, often starting with how or what, and some that have the form of questions: □ *How beautiful!* □ *What fun!* □ *What a disgusting mess!* □ *How we laughed!* □ *Aren't you silly!* They are also used after longer sentences when strong emotion is being expressed: □ *I'm absolutely sick to death of all of you!*

There are no words or utterances that always need an exclamation point. The presence or absence of one indicates the intonation required when reading a word or sentence. □ *You can't be serious!* would be read with a different intonation from: *You can't be serious?* or: *You can't be serious.*

Exclamation points should be used sparingly, and never doubled or tripled. The excessive use of exclamation points in writing, particularly when used in an attempt to create an atmosphere of excitement, fun, or humor, generally has a negative effect on the reader.

exercise This word, with various meanings, including "a set of energetic movements," "a short piece of school work," and "make use of," is sometimes misspelled. There is no *c* after the *x;* note also the final two consonants: *c* and *s.*

• This word may not end *-ize: see also* -IZE OR -ISE?

exhausting or **exhaustive?** *Exhausting* means "extremely tiring": □ *I find Christmas shopping very exhausting.* It should not be confused with *exhaustive*, which means "thorough; comprehensive; considering all possibilities": □ *They made exhaustive inquiries, but to no avail.* □ *This is an exhaustive study, covering every aspect of the subject.*

exhilarate This word, meaning "thrill or excite": □ *an exhilarating experience*, is sometimes misspelled, the most frequent error being the omission of the *h.*

existential *Existential* usually means "relating to existence, particularly human existence": □ *an existential problem*, or "grounded in human existence; empirical": □ *an existential argument for* *the existence of God.* It is also sometimes used to mean "existentialist, based on existentialist philosophy": □ *existential angst* □ *Sartre's existential theories.*

• It is also sometimes used as a vogue word to mean "referring to a subjective intellectual viewpoint," but such use is generally considered pretentious.

exorbitant This word, meaning "excessive": □ *an exorbitant price to pay,* is sometimes misspelled. There is no *h* in the spelling, unlike *exhilarate.*

exotic The original meaning of *exotic* is "from another country, not native to the place it is found": □ *exotic flowers.* By this definition rice would be an exotic food in the United States, but it is never spoken of as such, because *exotic* is now almost always used with the meaning of "unusual, excitingly different, interestingly foreign": □ *exotic perfume* □ *exotic dances* □ *travel to distant exotic lands.*

expatriate The word *expatriate,* meaning "a person who is living in a country that is not his or her native country," is sometimes misspelled. Note the spelling of the ending of this word: *-iate,* not *-iot* as in *patriot.*

expeditious or **expedient?** *Expeditious* and *expedient* come from the same root, but have quite different meanings. *Expeditious* means "speedy; efficient": □ *Our courier service is the most expeditious method of sending packages. Expedient* means "convenient for a particular situation or aim": □ *It would not be expedient to change the law at the present time.*

• *Expedient* is associated with practical action and often also a concern for self-interest rather than moral considerations: □ *You can't learn too soon that the most useful thing about a principle is that it can always be sacrificed to expediency* (W. Somerset Maugham, *The Circle*).

explicable In the traditional pronunciation of this word, which means "able to be explained": □ *no explicable reason for their behavior,* the stress was on the first syllable [*eks*plikăbl]. It is no more usual and perfectly acceptable to stress the second syllable [ek*splik*ăbl]. See also STRESS.

explicate *Explicate* means "explain in detail; analyze and explore the implications of": □ *This series of lectures aims to explicate Kant's critical philosophy and explore its influence on German idealism.* It is a formal word, usually confined to intellectual contexts, and it is pretentious to use it merely as a synonym for *explain.*

explicit or **implicit?** *Explicit* means "clear; unambiguous, stated or shown in a direct manner": □ *He gave them explicit instructions so there was no possibility of their making a mistake. Implicit* means "implied; understood although not directly expressed": □ *He detected an implicit criticism in her words,* and "without reservation; unquestioning": □ *I have implicit faith in your organizational abilities.*

• Because *explicit* is often used in such phrases as: □ *explicit scenes of sex and violence,* some people now use the word to mean "frankly portraying (usually sexual) *material*": □ *It is very explicit and is not suitable for family viewing.* It would be preferable to say *explicitly sexual* or *sexually explicit,* if that is what is meant.

exquisite *Exquisite,* meaning "very delicate and beautiful": □ *exquisite carvings,* may be pronounced in two ways. Some users prefer the stress to fall on the first syllable [*eks*kwizit]. More users find this pronunciation slightly affected and prefer to stress the second syllable [eks*kwi*zit].
• Overuse of this word is disliked by many users.

extempore or **impromptu?** These two words have similar meanings but are not quite interchangeable. Each is applied to speeches and performances that are not rehearsed in advance. *Extempore,* however, suggests that nothing has been memorized or written down beforehand, although the speaker or performer may have thought about the content in advance: □ *He never wrote his sermons down but preached extempore. Impromptu* suggests something improvised on the spur of the moment, with no prior notice: □ *She was surprised to be asked to address them but managed a splendid impromptu speech.*

exterior, external, or **extraneous?** *Exterior* means "on the outside; relating to the outside": □ *The house needs some minor exterior repairs.* □ *Beneath his charming exterior, he has a cold and selfish nature. External* means "outwardly visible; suitable for the outside." □ *He has a few external injuries.* □ *This lotion is for external use only. Extraneous* usually means "not essential or relevant to the issue": □ *extraneous details* □ *Let's concentrate on the main issue and ignore those extraneous points.*

extraordinary This word, meaning "unusual or exceptional": □ *an extraordinary memory for details,* is sometimes misspelled, the most frequent mistake being the omission of the first *a.* Remember *extra* and *ordinary.*

extrapolate Apart from specialized mathematical uses, *extrapolate* is usually applied to the estimation or prediction of unknown factors by the examination, analysis, and extension of known data and past experience: □ *We can extrapolate from the existing figures and our knowledge of the previous trends in mobility and birth control to produce an estimate of the populations of major cities in 20 years' time.* Careful users, however, are aware that this word is in danger of overuse.

extrinsic see INTRINSIC OR EXTRINSIC?

extrovert or **introvert?** *Extrovert* and *introvert* are terms coined by the psychologist Carl Jung, but are now in general use. *Extroverts* are people who are more concerned with their environments than with their own inner selves; they are generally sociable, outgoing, and confident: □ *He is an extrovert and enjoys nothing better than a noisy, crowded party. Introverts* are primarily concerned with their own mental and emotional lives. They are withdrawn and quiet, and prefer reflection to activity: □ *She tends to be an introvert and is happiest in her own company.*
• The original spelling was *extravert.* The spelling *extrovert* was formed by analogy with *introvert* and is now standard.

façade This word, which means "front," as in: □ *the palace's ornate façade*, is usually spelled with a cedilla under the *c*.
● The spelling is sometimes Anglicized by dropping the cedilla, but the French pronunciation [fasahd] is retained.

face or **face up to?** Some users object to *face up to* as an unnecessary extension of the verb *face*, meaning "confront" or "accept," but there is a slight difference in sense and usage between the two: *to face up to one's punishment* suggests a greater degree of effort and courage than *to face one's punishment*.
● The verb face often requires qualification: □ *He faced death with equanimity.* □ *They face the future with hope/fear. Face up to,* on the other hand, conveys the subject's feelings of resignation, determination, etc., by implication: □ *I will just have to face up to the prospect of unemployment.*

facetious This word, which means "jocular" or "flippant," as in: □ *a facetious remark*, is sometimes misspelled.
● It is worth remembering that *facetious* is one of the few words in the English language in which each vowel appears only once and in alphabetical order.

facile In the sense of "easily achieved" or "superficial," the adjective *facile* is often used in a derogatory manner: *facile prose* is produced with little effort and lacks substance; a *facile argument* is glib and lacks sound reasoning.
● The usual pronunciation of facile is [fasil], rhyming with *mill*.

facilitate The verb *facilitate* means "make easier"; it should not be used as a synonym for "help" or "assist": □ *His cooperation facilitated our task.* □ *We were helped* [not *facilitated*] *in our task by the information he gave us.*
● *Facilitate* is largely restricted to formal contexts.

facility or **faculty?** These two words are sometimes confused in the sense of "ability." *Facility* is ease or skill that often is gained from familiarity; *faculty* is more likely to denote a natural power or aptitude: □ *a facility for public speaking* □ *a faculty for understanding complex scientific concepts.*
● Each word has additional meanings. A *faculty* is a division of a college or university: □ *faculty meeting.*

A *facility* provides the means for doing something; with this sense, referring to buildings or equipment, the word is usually found in the plural: □ *meeting facilities* □ *sports facilities* □ *facilities for the blind.*

The extended use of *facility* or *facilities* as synonyms for "premises," "factory," or "shop" (or, euphemistically, for "toilet," as in: □ *"May I use your facilities?"*) is avoided by careful users.

faction This word, a blend of *fact* and *fiction*, was coined in the mid-1960's and is used especially by critics to denote a book, play, film, etc., that describes historically true events, using the techniques of fiction.

• John Silverlight (*Words*) notes that the term has "a dismissive quality." The word is best avoided where there is a risk of confusion with the more generally known sense of *faction*, a minority group within a larger party: □ *the growing faction within the party.*

factor A *factor* is a contributory element, condition, or cause; many people object to its frequent use as a synonym for "point," "thing," "fact," "event," "constituent," etc.: □ *A rise in the cost of raw materials and a fall in demand were important factors in the company's collapse.* □ *We must discuss all the relevant points* [not *factors*].

faculty see FACILITY OR FACULTY?

Fahrenheit Note the spelling of this word, which should always begin with a capital letter.

• See also CENTIGRADE, CELSIUS, OR FAHRENHEIT?

faint or **feint**? *Faint* means "not clear" or "not strong"; it is also a noun or verb referring to a brief loss of consciousness. *Feint*, derived from the verb *feign*, refers to an action or a movement intended to distract or mislead: □ *On hearing the news, she fell to the floor in a faint.* □ *The boxer made a feint with his left fist and then struck with his right.*

fantastic The use of *fantastic* as a synonym for "excellent" or "very great" is best restricted to informal contexts: □ *a fantastic trip* □ *fanastic wealth.*

• *Fantastic*, related to the noun *fantasy*, originally meant "fanciful" or "unreal": □ *a fantastic tale.* The word should be used with care, however, even in these senses, to avoid misinterpretation through association with its informal usage.

farther, farthest, further, or **furthest**? In the senses of "more (or most) distant" and "more (or most) advanced," as the COMPARATIVE and SUPERLATIVE of *far*, *farther* is not fully interchangeable with *further*, nor is *farthest* with *furthest.*

• Restrict *farther* and *farthest* to physical distance, using *further* and *furthest* for more figurative senses: □ *the farthest country* □ *further from the truth.*

In the sense of "additional," *further* is more acceptable than *farther*: □ *further supplies* □ *further questions. Further* is also preferred in certain set phrases, such as: □ *further education* □ *until further notice.*

Farther is not interchangeable with *further* when the latter is used as a verb, meaning "advance" or "promote": □ *to further one's career.*

fascinate This word, meaning "attract and capture the interest of," as in *fascinating tales about her experiences in China*, is sometimes misspelled. The most frequent error is the confusion or omission of the *-sc-.*

• The term originates from the Latin *fascinare*, "to bewitch."

fast-moving This expression is sometimes used in commerce and advertising to describe products that sell quickly: □ *one of the world's most successful manufacturers and marketers of fast-moving consumer goods* (*Sunday Times*, June 7, 1987).

F

• *Fast-moving* is also used in similar contexts to create the impression of an enterprising, up-to-date company: □ *one of America's most innovative and fast-moving corporations.* Although these usages are widely accepted in the business world, they may not be understood by lay people and are best avoided in more general contexts.

fatal or **fateful?** *Fatal* means "causing death or ruin"; *fateful* means "decisively important": □ *a fatal illness* □ *a fatal mistake* □ *their fateful meeting* □ *that fateful night.*

• Each word is related to *fate*: *fatal* originally meant "decreed by fate"; *fateful* means "controlled by fate."

In its extended sense of "having momentous and disastrous effects," *fatal* is sometimes interchangeable with *fateful*: □ *a fatal/fateful decision. Fatal* should not be used in this sense if there is a possibility of misinterpretation: □ *a fateful journey* may change one's life; *a fatal journey* may end in death.

It is also worth remembering that the consequences of something *fateful* can be good, although the word is very rarely used in this sense.

Fateful may not be substituted for *fatal* in such phrases as: □ *fatal wounds.*

feasible The use of *feasible* to mean "probable," "likely," or "plausible" is avoided by many careful users, especially in formal contexts, where the word is restricted to its original sense of "practicable" or "capable of being done": □ *The committee decided that the project was feasible.*

• In informal usage, *feasible* now shares the double meaning of *possible*, describing something that can be done or something that might happen, and is therefore equally ambiguous: □ *Raising prices is a feasible solution to the problem.*

Note the spelling of the word: *feasible* ends in *-ible*, not *-able.*

feature The verb *feature* is best avoided where *have, include, display, appear,* etc., may be more appropriate; to *feature* is principally used in the entertainment world: □ *The concert features such stars as George Harrison and Eric Clapton* □ *a new leisure center, featuring volleyball and tennis courts and an indoor swimming pool.*

• As a noun and verb, *feature* should be reserved for what is prominent, distinctive, characteristic, or important: □ *The spiral staircase is a feature of the house, which also has* [not features] *central heating and wall-to-wall carpeting.*

February This month name causes problems of spelling and pronunciation, the most frequent being the omission of the first *r.*
• The full pronunciation of the word is [febrooări].

feedback The use of *feedback* as a synonym for "response" or "reaction" is disliked by some people, who prefer to restrict the term to its scientific or technical usage.
• In science and technology, *feedback* is the return of part of the output of a system, device, or process to its input, the most familiar example being the high-pitched whistle heard when the output from a loudspeaker returns to the microphone.

In scientific contexts as well as in general usage, *feedback* often leads to modification: □ *We must try to get as much feedback as possible from the public to see if our ideas are successful.*

□ *Feedback from customers helped us choose the most practical design.*

feel Some people dislike the use of the noun *feel* in the sense of "impression" or "quality," as in the phrases *a nice feel to it, a different feel,* etc.: □ *The car has a strange feel to it.*

• Such expressions may be more succinctly worded by using the verb *feel:* □ *The car feels strange.*

feet see **FOOT OR FEET?**

feint see **FAINT OR FEINT?**

female or **feminine?** The adjective *female* refers to the sex of a person, animal, or plant; it is the opposite of **MALE**: □ *a female giraffe* □ *female reproductive cells. Feminine* is applied only to people (or their attributes) or to words (see **GENDER**); it is the opposite of **MASCULINE**: □ *feminine charms.*

• With reference to people, *female* is used only of the childbearing sex; it is used to distinguish women or girls from men or boys but has no further connotations: □ *There are more female students than male students at the college.* See also **WOMAN**.

Feminine, on the other hand, may be used of both sexes; it refers to characteristics, qualities, etc., that are considered typical of women or are traditionally associated with women: □ *a feminine hairstyle* □ *a feminine voice.*

Feminine is occasionally confused with *feminist,* which refers to the movement or belief (*feminism*) that women should have the same rights, opportunities, etc., as men, particularly in economic, political, and social fields. A *feminist* is a person who supports feminism, especially someone who is actively trying to bring about change: □ *She regards herself as a staunch feminist.*

ferment or **foment?** These two verbs are virtually interchangeable in the sense of "to stir up": □ *to foment/ferment trouble.*

• This figurative sense is now the most frequent use of *foment;* in medical contexts it retains its original meaning of "to bathe or apply warmth to."

The principal meaning of *ferment,* however, is "to undergo fermentation," referring to the chemical reaction involved in the formation of alcohol. Its figurative usage is an extension of this sense.

fête This word, used as a noun or verb, may be spelled with a circumflex accent over the first *e,* but *fete* is more frequent.

• The word may be pronounced to rhyme with *gate* or *get,* the first of these being the more frequent.

fetus or **foetus?** There are two possible spellings for this word. The first is more frequent in American English, and the second in British English.

few The difference between *few* and *a few* is one of expectation or attitude rather than number; each expression means "some, but not many": □ *They brought few books.* □ *They brought a few books.*

• The first of these sentences suggests that more books were expected; the second, that no books were expected. The actual number of books may be the same in both cases.

Few has negative force, contrasting with many; *a few* has positive force, contrasting with none: □ *I have many acquaintances but few friends.* □ *There are no pears left, but there are a few apples.*

The same principles may be applied to *little* and *a little:* □ *I added little salt to the soup.* □ *I added a little salt to the soup.*

For the distinction between *(a) few* and *(a) little,* see FEWER OR LESS.

fewer or less? *Fewer,* the comparative of *few,* means "a smaller number of"; *less,* the comparative of *little,* means "a smaller amount or quantity of": □ *fewer cars* □ *less unemployment.* The general rule is that *fewer* (or *few*) is used with plural nouns and *less* (or *little*) with singular nouns, whether the nouns are concrete or abstract: □ *fewer pleasures* □ *few chairs* □ *less wood* □ *little hope* □ *fewer noises* □ *less noise.*

• The use of *less* in place of *fewer* occurs widely in informal speech and also, occasionally, in more formal contexts: □ *Please remember, on Tuesdays and Thursdays there are less lines in the afternoon* (Post Office advertisement, *The Guardian,* Nov. 13, 1984). Many people find this usage ungrammatical and therefore unacceptable in formal speech and writing.

The same principles apply to the phrases *fewer than* and *less than:* □ *fewer than four people* □ *less than a pint of milk;* however, plural units of measurement, time, money, etc., are regarded as singular in such cases: □ *It took less than five seconds.* □ *He earned less than $50 last week.*

financé or fiancée? An engaged woman's future husband is her *fiancé;* an engaged man's future wife is his *fiancée.*

• The feminine form is sometimes misspelled, the second *e* being dropped in error.

Unlike some other words of French origin, *fiancé* and *fiancée* are always written with an acute accent over the (first) *e.*

The pronunciation of both words is identical [feeonsay].

fictional or fictitious? *Fictional* means "of fiction" or "not factual"; *fictitious* means "false" or "not genuine": □ *a fictional detective* □ *his fictional works* □ *a fictitious address* □ *her fictitious companion.*

F

• The two words are largely interchangeable in the sense of "imaginary," "invented," or "not real": □ *This novel is a work of fiction. Names, characters, places and incidents are either the product of the author's imagination or are used fictitiously* (disclaimer on the copyright page, Barbara Michaels, *Shattered Silk*).

Fictional, however, is more frequently used with direct reference to stories, novels, plays, etc.; *fictitious* is preferred for deliberate justification that is intended to deceive: □ *Fagin, Scrooge, and other fictional characters* □ *this fictitious character you claim to have met in the park.*

fifth The second *f* in this word is sometimes not sounded in speech.

• The pronunciations [fifth] and [fith] are both acceptable, but some people object to the omission of the second *f.*

fill out? or **fill in?** Application forms and other official documents are usually *filled out* rather than *filled in:* □ *Fill out this form and give it to the receptionist.*

• *Fill in* is the more frequent verb in British English.

finalize The verb *finalize* is best avoided where *complete, finish, conclude, settle,* etc., would be adequate or more appropriate: □ *The preparatory work must be finished* [not *finalized*] *as soon as possible.*

- The word does, however, serve a useful purpose in some official contexts, combining the senses of "to reach agreement on" and "to put into final form": □ *The committee met to finalize arrangements for the prime minister's visit.*

fiord or **fjord?** Either spelling of this word is acceptable.

- Derived from the Old Norse *fjörthr*, the word is usually applied to the narrow inlets of the sea along the Scandinavian coastline. *Fjord*, the Norwegian spelling of the word, is preferred by some users.

first or **firstly?** *Firstly* may be used in place of the adverb *first* when enumerating a list: □ *There are three good reasons for not buying the house: firstly, it is outside our price range; secondly, it is too close to the highway; thirdly, the garden is too small.*

- The use of *first . . . secondly . . . thirdly*, in accordance with a former convention that rejected the word *firstly*, remains acceptable and is still favored by some users. Others, however, find this usage inconsistent, preferring *first . . . second . . . third* or *firstly . . . secondly . . . thirdly*, according to the context.

Firstly should not be substituted for *first* in any of its other adverbial uses: □ *When he first* [not *firstly*] *came to this country, he could hardly speak any English.* □ *Janet came in first* [not *firstly*], *followed by the others.*

first name, Christian name, forename, given name, or **baptismal name?** All these expressions are used to denote the name or names one has in addition to one's surname; *first name* is the most frequent choice: □ *a dictionary of first names.*

- The principal objection to *Christian name* is that it is inapplicable, and possibly offensive to non-Christians. For this reason the expression is generally avoided on official forms. It remains in regular use, however, in informal contexts: □ *We never address our teachers by their Christian names.*

The term *first name* may lead to confusion among people who bear more than one such name: □ *My first name is Leonard, but I prefer to be called by my middle name, Mark.*

Forename is sometimes used on official forms but is rarely heard in informal speech. It is not, however, the ideal solution, being inappropriate for people whose surname precedes their other names (Hungarians or the Chinese, for example). The same problem may occur with the use of *first name.*

Less frequently used are *given name* and *baptismal name.* Like *Christian name* the latter is inapplicable to non-Christians.

fish or **fishes?** The plural of *fish* is *fish* or *fishes; fish* is used in a wider range of contexts than the alternative form: □ *Fish live in water and breathe through their gills.* □ *There are five fish in the pond* □ *the various fishes in the aquarium.*

- Considered as a food item, *fish* usually remains in the singular: □ *Fish is more expensive than some cuts of meat.*

The plural form *fishes* is most frequently found in technical contexts, often with reference to individual groups or species: □ *The major division in this group is between jawless and jawed fishes* (*Longman Illustrated Animal Encyclopedia*).

fix or **repair?** These verbs are used in the sense of "mend," *repair* being more formal than *fix:* □ *Have you fixed the radio yet?* □ *He was ordered to repair the damaged boat.*

F

• The verb *fix* has a number of other meanings, principally "make firm" or "fasten."

fjord see FIORD OR FJORD?

flagrant see BLATANT OR FLAGRANT?

flagship The noun *flagship*, which denotes the ship that carries the commander of a fleet, is increasingly used in figurative contexts with reference to the most important of a group of products, projects, services, etc.: □ *Whenever they've got some morning grocery shopping to do, they head off to one of Randall's flagship stores in Houston* (*Newsweek*, June 27, 1988). □ *The [Laura Ashley] company has recently opened a furnishing flagship store in Madison Avenue, New York* (*The Bookseller*, June 19, 1987).

flair or **flare?** The noun *flair* means "a natural aptitude or instinct"; *flare* is a noun or verb referring to a sudden burst of flame: □ *a flair for cookery* □ *the flare of the torch.*

• The two words are sometimes confused, though not always with the humorous effect of an advertisement from the *Gloucestershire Echo* quoted by "Peterborough" in the *Daily Telegraph* (June 3, 1987): □ *Chef/Cook. Really talented person with flare required at Burlington Court Hotel, experience essential.*

Each word has additional senses: *flair* is an informal synonym for "stylishness"; a *flare* is a light signal used especially at sea. To *flare* may also mean "to become wider": □ *a flared skirt.*

flak The use of *flak* in the sense of "heavy adverse criticism or opposition" is best restricted to informal contexts: □ *Government bureaucrats come in for a lot of flak from the general public.*

• The principal meaning of *flak* is "antiaircraft fire"; of German origin, the word is an acronym for *Flieger* (flyer) *Abwehr* (defense) *Kanonen* (guns).

The spelling *flack,* an Anglicized variant, is also occasionally used.

flammable see INFLAMMABLE.

flare see FLAIR OR FLARE?

flaunt or **flout?** *Flaunt* means "show off" or "display ostentatiously"; *flout* means "treat with contempt" or "disregard": □ *to flaunt one's wealth* □ *to flout the rules.*

• The use of *flaunt* in place of *flout* is avoided by careful users in all contexts, but the confusion occurs with some frequency: □ *If Christians are to campaign against total deregulation [of the laws on Sunday trading] . . . they must be seen to obey, and not flaunt, the present law* (Jubilee Center leaflet, 1987). This confusion may be due to the sense of openness that is conveyed by both verbs: the open disregard shown by one who *flouts* a law may be seen as an open display, or *flaunting,* of contempt.

floor or **story?** Each of these nouns denotes a particular level of a building or the rooms on this level. The word *floor* is more frequently used with reference to the interior of the building, *story* with reference to the exterior or structure. □ *He lives on the fourth floor.* □ *The new office block will be nine stories high.*

• The *first floor* of a building is at ground level. In British English this is known as the *ground floor,* the *first floor* being the floor above (called the *second floor* in American English). This difference in usage does not apply to the word *story,* spelled *storey* by the British.

See also CEILING; STORY OR STOREY?

flounder or **founder?** To *flounder* is to struggle, move with diffi-culty, or act clumsily; to *founder* is to fail, break down, collapse, or sink. Each verb can be used literally or figuratively: □ *They floundered in the mud.* □ *She floundered on to the end of the speech.* □ *The project foundered through lack of support.* □ *The ship foundered at the harbor entrance.*

• The two verbs are often confused, especially in figurative con-texts, *flounder* being used in place of *founder:* □ [of the Stoke Mandeville Wheelchair Games] *future Games could flounder un-less $2.5 million pounds is raised* (Bucks Advertiser, Aug. 8, 1986).

The two words are not unrelated: *flounder* is probably a blend of *founder* and *blunder. Founder* itself is ultimately derived from the Latin *fundus,* "bottom."

fout see FLAUNT OR FLOUT?

flu The word *flu*—the shortened form of *influenza*—is more frequent in general and some technical contexts than *influenza:* □ *She's home with (the) flu.*

• *Influenza* tends to be restricted to very formal contexts. See also ABBREVIATIONS; APOSTROPHE.

Flu should not be confused with the noun *flue,* which denotes a shaft or pipe in a chimney or organ. (*Flue* was once a variant spell-ing of *flu,* but is no longer used for this purpose.)

fluorescent This word, which is usually applied to light fittings, col-ors, paint, etc., may cause spelling problems.

• Note the order of the vowels in the first syllable (as in *fluoride),* the -*sc*- combination, and the -*ent* ending.

focus The doubling of the final *s* of the verb *focus* before a suffix be-ginning with a vowel is optional. Most dictionaries give *focused* and *focusing* as the preferred spellings, with *focussed* and *focus-sing* as acceptable variants.

• The noun *focus* has two plural forms, *focuses* and *foci* [*fōsī*], the latter being largely restricted to technical contexts. The final *s* of the noun *focus* is never doubled before the plural ending. See also SPELLING 1.

The noun *focus* is often used in the figurative sense of "center of attention or activity": □ *The proposed route for the new bypass is the focus of today's meeting.* It is better avoided, however, where *emphasis, object, point,* etc., would be more appropriate: □ *the emphasis* [not *focus*] *on unemployment in the party's platform.*

foetus see FETUS OR FOETUS?

folk The use of the noun *folk* as a synonym for "people" is generally considered to have slightly old-fashioned and sentimental asso-ciations: □ *country folk* □ *old folk* □ *a name that will be famil-iar to many folk.*

• The word is chiefly used adjectivally, in the sense of "traditional": □ *folk music* □ *folk dance* □ *folklore.*

Like *people,* the noun *folk* is used with a plural verb: □ *Poor folk often dream of a life of luxury. Folks,* the plural form of the word, is largely restricted to informal contexts, in the sense of "relatives": □ *My folks are coming here tomorrow* or "people in general": □ *That's all, folks!*

following The preposition *following* may be confused with the pre-sent participle; it is best avoided where *after* or *because of* is less ambiguous: □ *They went home after* [not *following*] *the party.*

F

• *Following* may serve a useful prepositional purpose in the dual sense of "after and as a result of": □ *Following the burglary, we added several locks to the doors and windows.*

Following is also used as an adjective meaning "next" or "about to be mentioned": □ *I left the following morning.* □ *The following tools will be required . . . .*

foment see FERMENT OR FOMENT?

foot or **feet?** The plural of *foot*, as a unit of measurement, may be *foot* or *feet:* □ *a six-foot fence* □ *five feet tall* □ *nine feet nine inches long* □ *a pane of glass measuring two foot six by four foot three.*

• In compound adjectives that precede the noun, the singular form *foot* is always used: □ *a three-foot rod.* The same convention applies not only to other units of measurement but also to such expressions as *a two-car family.*

For measurements in feet and inches, *feet* is preferred in more formal and precise contexts: □ *seven feet four inches*, without hyphens or a comma. In informal usage the word *inches* is omitted and the plural form *foot* is more frequent: □ *seven foot four.*

In such expressions as *three feet high* or *ten foot wide*, the same distinctions of formality and precision may be applied: □ *The wall must be exactly three feet high.* □ *The room is about nine foot wide.* For large measurements, such as the height of a mountain, *feet* is preferred in all contexts.

for see BECAUSE, AS, FOR, OR SINCE?

for- or **fore-?** The prefix *for-* usually indicates prohibition (*forbid*), abstention (*forbear*), or neglect (*forsake*). The prefix *fore-* means "before": □ *foreboding* □ *forecast* □ *forefather.*

• Confusion of these two prefixes may lead to spelling mistakes. See also FORBEAR OR FOREBEAR?; FORGO OR FOREGO?

forbade *Forbade*, the past tense of the verb *forbid*, may be pronounced [fŏrbad] or [fŏrbayd].

• The first of these pronunciations, rhyming with *mad* rather than with *made*, is the more frequent.

Forbad, an alternative spelling of *forbade*, is always pronounced [fŏrbad].

forbear or **forebear?** *Forbear* is the only accepted spelling of the verb, which means "to refrain": □ *I shall forbear from criticizing her appearance.* The noun, meaning "ancestor," may be written *forebear* or *forbear*, the spelling *forebear* being the more frequent: □ *His forebears were wealthy landowners.*

• See also FOR- OR FORE-?

The two words are not identical in pronunciation: the verb is stressed on the second syllable [forbair]; the noun, whichever spelling is used, is stressed on the first syllable [forbair].

forbid or **prohibit?** Each of these verbs is used in the sense of "refuse to allow," *prohibit* being more authoritative than *forbid:* □ *I forbid you to visit her.* □ *The rules prohibit us from visiting her.*

• Note the difference in construction: *forbid* is followed by an infinitive with *to*; *prohibit* is followed by an *-ing* form with *from*.

See also FORBADE.

forceful or **forcible?** *Forceful* means "having great force"; *forcible* means "using force": □ *a forceful personality* □ *forcible expulsion.*

• Something that is *forceful* may be contrasted with something that has little force; something that is *forcible* may be contrasted with something that uses no force.

In many contexts, in the sense of "powerful" or "effective," the two words are virtually interchangeable: □ *a forceful/forcible reminder*. (Some people may interpret a *forceful* reminder as one that is powerfully presented, a *forcible* reminder as one that has a powerful effect.)

Forcible should not be replaced by *forceful* where physical force or violence is involved or implied: □ *forcible entry*.

fore- see FOR- OR FORE-?

forebear see FORBEAR OR FOREBEAR?

forego see FORGO OR FOREGO?

forename see FIRST NAME, CHRISTIAN NAME, FORENAME, GIVEN NAME, OR BAPTISMAL NAME?

forever or **for ever?** The adverb *forever* should be written as a single word in all contexts, such as the principal sense of "eternally": □ *We shall remember her forever.* □ *It will stay there forever.*

• In the sense of "continually" or "incessantly," *forever* is also preferred. □ *He is forever changing his mind.*

For ever may occur when *for* is used as a conjunction.

The use of *forever* to mean "a very long time" is best restricted to informal contexts: □ *It will take forever to get this carpet clean.*

foreword or **preface?** These nouns are used to denote the statement or remarks that often precede or replace the introduction to a book.

• *Preface* is the older of the two words and the more frequent; some authorities suggest that a *foreword* is usually written by a person other than the author of the book: □ *The foreword will be written by a distinguished historian.* □ *Have you read the author's preface?*

forgo or **forego?** *Forgo* is the usual spelling of the verb that means "do without" or "give up," *forego* being a rare variant spelling of this verb: □ *The union will not forgo the right to strike.*

• The verb *forego*, meaning "go before" or "precede," is most frequently found in the adjectival forms *foregoing* or *foregone*, which have no alternative spellings: □ *the foregoing instructions* □ *a foregone conclusion.* See also FOR- OR FORE-?

former or **latter?** Of two previously mentioned items or people, *the former* denotes the first and *the latter* the second: □ *On Monday evening there will be a lecture on local history and a meeting of the chess club: the former will be held in the main hall, the latter in the lounge.*

• *The former* or *the latter* should not be used to refer to a single previously mentioned item; a simple pronoun, such as *it* or *this*, is usually adequate in such cases: □ *The killer left the scene of the crime in a stolen car; this* [not *the latter*] *was later found abandoned.*

Of three or more items or people, the first-mentioned should be referred to as *the first, the first-named*, or *the first-mentioned* (not *the former*) and the last-mentioned should be referred to as *the last, the last-named*, etc. (not *the latter*): □ *The secretary, the treasurer, and the chairman had a meeting at the house of the first-mentioned* [not *the former*] *yesterday evening.*

F

For the sake of simplicity or clarity, *the former, the latter, the first-named, the last-mentioned*, etc., should be avoided if possible by restructuring the sentence or by repeating the names of the items or people concerned.

formidable This word may be stressed on the first syllable [*formid-ăbl*] or the second syllable [*fŏrmidăbl*].

• The first of these pronunciations is the more widely accepted. See also **STRESS**.

formulae or **formulas?** The noun *formula* has two accepted plural forms: *formulae* and *formulas*.

• *Formulae*, usually pronounced to rhyme with *tree*, is less frequent and largely restricted to scientific contexts: □ *chemical formulae*.

For all senses of *formula*, the plural form *formulas* is preferred by most users: □ *no easy peace formulas that will resolve the dispute* □ *There are many different formulas for success.*

forte The noun *forte*, denoting a person's strong point, may be pronounced as two syllables [*fortay*] or as a single syllable [*fort*].

• The second of these pronunciations is the more frequent of the two and is closer to the French original (*forte* is the feminine form of the French adjective *fort*, meaning "strong").

The two-syllable pronunciation may have been influenced by the musical term *forte*, meaning "loud" or "loudly." Pronounced [*fortay*], this word is of Italian origin.

fortuitous or **fortunate?** *Fortuitous* means "happening by chance" or "accidental"; *fortunate* means "having or happening by good fortune" or "lucky": □ *a fortuitous meeting* □ *a fortunate child*.

• A *fortuitous* occurrence is not necessarily good, but the similarity between the two words, and their frequent confusion, has led to the increasing acceptance of "fortunate" as a secondary meaning of *fortuitous*. Many people object to this usage, which can result in ambiguity: □ *a fortuitous discovery* may be accidental, or lucky, or both.

Unlike *fortunate*, the adjective *fortuitous* is not applied to people: □ *You were fortunate to find another job so quickly.*

forward or **forwards?** As an adjective, *forward* is never written with a final *s*: □ *forward motion* □ *a forward remark* □ *forward planning*. In some of its adverbial senses, the word may be written *forward* or *forwards*: □ *He ran forward/forwards to greet his father.*

• Some users restrict the adverb *forwards* to physical movement in the opposite direction to *backwards;* some use *forwards* in the wider adverbial sense of "ahead in space or time"; most use *forward* for all adverbial senses of the word.

In idiomatic phrasal verbs, such as *come forward, put forward, look forward to*, etc., and in the sense of "into a prominent position," the adverb *forward* is never written with a final *s*: □ *She came forward as a witness.* □ *I put forward the proposals at the meeting.*

The word *forward* is also used as a noun (denoting a player or position in various sports) and as a verb: □ *to forward a letter*. See also **-WARD OR -WARDS?**

Forward, should not be confused with *foreword*, the introduction to a book. See also **FOREWORD OR PREFACE?**

founder see **FLOUNDER OR FOUNDER?**

F

foyer This word, meaning "an entrance hall or lobby in a theatre, hotel, etc.," is usually pronounced [*foiĕr*].

• The pronunciations [*foiay*] and [*fwahyay*] are also acceptable, the last of these being an approximation of the French original.

fraction Some people dislike the use of a *fraction* to mean "a small part" or "a little": □ *We flew there in a fraction of the time it takes to go by car.* □ *Could you turn the volume down a fraction, please?*

• A fraction is not necessarily a small part of the whole: nine-tenths is a fraction.

To avoid possible ambiguity or misunderstanding, express a small fraction clearly as such: □ *Why dine out when you can eat at home for a small fraction of the cost?* □ *Only a small fraction of the work has been completed.*

See also **HYPHEN 6.**

-free The adjective *free* is frequently used in combination to indicate the absence of something undesirable or unpleasant: □ *lead-free gasoline* □ *rent-free accommodations* □ *additive-free food* □ *pollution-free water* □ *a trouble-free life.*

• Some careful users object to this usage, preferring to replace some compounds with a paraphrase: □ *accommodations, for which no rent is paid* □ *water that has not been polluted.*

-friendly see **USER-FRIENDLY.**

-ful For nouns ending in *-ful*, such as *cupful, spoonful, sackful, handful, mouthful,* etc., most users prefer the plural form *-fuls*: □ *two cupfuls* □ *three spoonfuls.*

• The plural form *-sful*, as in: □ *three cupsful* □ *two spoonsful,* is regarded by some authorities as rare or old-fashioned and by others as incorrect; it is best avoided.

It is important to recognize the difference between *-ful* and *full:* □ *a bucketful of water* denotes the quantity of water held by a bucket, but not the bucket itself; *a bucket full of water* denotes both the bucket and the water it contains.

The tendency to confuse *-ful* with *full* sometimes leads to the misspelling of both nouns and adjectives, such as *spoonful, doubtful,* etc., with a double *l* (see also **FULLNESS OR FULNESS?**).

fulfill Note the spelling of this word and the derived noun *fulfillment,* with the second *l* doubled. In British English neither *l* is doubled in *fulfil* or *fulfilment;* however, the final *l* of the verb is doubled before a suffix beginning with a vowel, as in *fulfilled* and *fulfilling* (see also **SPELLING 1**).

full see **-FUL.**

fullness or fulness? Either spelling is acceptable, *fullness* being much more frequent.

• In the nouns derived from adjectives ending in *-ful,* the *l* is never doubled: □ *faithfulness* □ *hopefulness.*

fulsome *Fulsome praise, fulsome compliments,* etc., are offensively excessive, exaggerated, or insincere.

• Derived from *full* and the suffix *-some,* the word originally meant "abundant"; its derogatory connotations may have developed from a mistaken etymology that associated *fulsome* with *foul.*

fun The use of the word *fun* as an adjective, meaning "enjoyable" or "amusing," is disliked by many users and is best restricted to informal contexts: □ *a fun game* □ *a fun person.*

function The verb *function* is best avoided where *work, perform, operate, serve, act,* etc., would be adequate or more appropriate, particularly in general, nontechnical contexts: □ *The machine never works* [not *functions*] *properly in very hot weather.* □ *The automatic lock serves* [not *functions*] *as a safety device.*

• Some people also object to the excessive use of the noun *function* as a synonym for "duty," "role," "party," etc.: □ *What are the precise functions of bishops and priests in the modern world?*

fundamental The adjective *fundamental* means "basic," "essential," "primary," or "principal"; it is best avoided where *important, major, great,* etc., would be more appropriate: □ *the fundamental difference between the two systems* □ *a major* [not *fundamental*] *improvement in East-West relations.*

• The noun *fundamental,* which is more frequently used in the plural form, denotes a basic principle, constituent, etc.: □ *the fundamentals of the issue.*

fungi *Fungi,* one of the plural forms of *fungus,* may be pronounced to rhyme with *try* or sometimes *tree;* the *g* may be hard, as in *gum,* or soft, as in *germ.*

• The pronunciations [fung͡gī] and especially [funjī], rhyming with *try,* are the most frequent. The first of these is closer to the singular form, which has a hard *g* sound. See also SPELLING.

Funguses is an alternative plural of *fungus.*

furor *Furor* is the usual spelling of the word, pronounced [fewror] and meaning "uproar" or "craze."

• The British spelling is *furore,* usually pronounced as a three-syllable word stressed on the second syllable [fewrori].

further, furthest see FARTHER, FARTHEST, FURTHER, OR FURTHEST?

gaiety *Gaiety*, meaning "a cheerful and carefree manner" or "festivity," is sometimes misspelled. See also **GAY**.
- Note the middle vowels *-aie-*.

gallant The adjective *gallant*, "brave and courageous," as in: □ *put up a gallant fight*, is stressed on the first syllable [*gal*ănt].
- The sense "courteous to women" is stressed on the second syllable [gă*lant*].

gamble or **gambol?** The verb *gamble* means "take a risk on a game of chance"; *gambol* means "skip and jump playfully."
- The spelling of these words is sometimes confused although their meanings are very different: □ *He went to the casino to gamble.* □ *lambs gamboling in the fields.*

gaol see **JAIL OR GAOL?**

garage This word is pronounced [ga*rahzh*]. The first syllable is stressed in British English: [*garahzh*] or [*garij*].

gases or **gasses?** The plural of the noun *gas* is *gases* or, less commonly, *gasses*.
- *Gasses* is also a form of the verb *gas*, meaning "affect with a gas" or "talk idly." See also **SPELLING 1**.

gauge This word, which means "measure or standard," is frequently misspelled. The *u* comes after the *a* and not before it.
- The correct pronunciation is [*gayj*]. A mispronunciation [*gawj*] may arise from the unusual spelling. The variant spelling *gage* is less frequent.

gay The adjective *gay* is so widely used as a synonym for "homosexual" that its use in the original sense of "cheerful," "merry," or "bright" may be open to misinterpretation in some contexts: □ *a gay bachelor* □ *a gay party.*
- The noun *gay* is principally applied to homosexual men, *lesbian* being the preferred term for homosexual women: □ *a community center for gays and lesbians.* The noun derived from *gay* in the sense "homosexual" is *gayness*; in other senses it is *gaiety*.
  In the sense of "homosexual," *gay* is becoming increasingly acceptable in formal contexts.

gender The word *gender* refers to the grammatical classification of nouns as masculine, feminine, or neuter. The use of *gender* as a synonym for "sex" is avoided by many users in formal contexts: □ *Applications are invited from suitably qualified candidates either sex* [not *gender*].
- The frequency of this usage is attributable both to the use of the word *sex* as a synonym for "sexual intercourse" and to the association in grammar between gender and sex.
  In many languages all nouns are of masculine or feminine gen-

der: the French word for *flower* is feminine; the Italian word for *carpet* is masculine. In English, however, masculine nouns refer to male people, animals, etc., and feminine nouns to female people, animals, etc.: *king, brother, drake,* and *bull* are masculine nouns; *heroine, mother, vixen,* and *cow* are feminine nouns.

See also SEXISM.

gentleman *Gentleman* is used as a synonym for "man" in some formal or official contexts and as a term of politeness: □ *Show the gentleman to his room.* □ *Ladies and gentlemen, may I introduce tonight's guest speaker?*

• The noun *gentleman* has connotations of nobility, chivalry, and good manners: □ *a country gentleman* □ *If you were a gentleman, you'd stand up and give me your seat.*

See also MAN; WOMAN.

geriatric Many people object to the increasing use of the noun and adjective *geriatric* as derogatory synonyms for "old person" or "elderly:" □ *These geriatric drivers should be banned from the roads.* □ *The country is governed by a bunch of geriatrics.*

• *Geriatrics* is the branch of medical science concerned with the diseases of old age and the care of old people; the use of *geriatric* in such contexts as *the geriatric ward of the hospital* is acceptable to all users.

gerunds see INFINITIVE; -ING FORMS.

get In formal contexts *get* may often be replaced with an appropriate synonym, such as *become, buy, obtain, receive,* etc.: □ *It is becoming* [not *getting*] *increasingly difficult to obtain* [not *get*] *impartial advice on financial matters.* If, however, the synonym sounds clumsy or unnatural in context, or causes ambiguity, *get* should be retained or the sentence restructured.

• The same principles apply to phrasal verbs, idioms, and other expressions containing *get,* such as *get out* (escape), *get by* (survive), *get dressed* (dress), *get well* (recover): □ *I often get up/rise at six.* □ *They will get married/marry in the spring.* See also GOT.

gibe, jibe, or **gybe?** The word *gibe,* or its occasional variant spelling *jibe,* means "jeer or taunt:" □ *gibes/jibes and insults.*

• *Jibe,* sometimes spelled *gybe,* is a nautical term referring to the movement of a ship's sail. *Jibe* also means "agree, accord."

girl see WOMAN.

given name see FIRST NAME, CHRISTIAN NAME, FORENAME, GIVEN NAME, OR BAPTISMAL NAME?

glacier This word, which means "a vast area of ice," is pronounced [*glay*sher]. In British English, the first syllable may be pronounced to rhyme with *mass* [*glas*eer] or with *clay* [*glay*seer].

glamorous Some people object to the frequent use of the adjective *glamorous* as a synonym for "beautiful," "romantic," "exciting," "interesting," etc.: □ *a glamorous setting* □ *a glamorous career.*

• The adjective is best restricted to the combination of showy attractiveness, fashion, romance, excitement, charm, and fascination that is known as *glamour:* □ *a glamorous film star* □ *a glamorous lifestyle.*

The *u* of *glamour* (rarely *glamor*) is usually omitted in the adjective *glamorous,* although some dictionaries acknowledge the rare variant spelling *glamourous.*

glasnost *Glasnost*, a Russian word, is used to denote the increased openness, both in East-West relations and in internal policies and reforms, that became a characteristic of the Soviet statesman Mikhail Gorbachev's regime in the mid-1980's: □ *Glasnost is blowing into the Chicago theater community on the winter winds* (*Variety*, Jan. 4-10, 1989). See also **PERESTROIKA**.
• The term is also applied to other Communist countries: □ *Glasnost has come to Albania* (*The Guardian*, June 22, 1987).

gobbledygook The noun *gobbledygook* is used in informal contexts to denote the pretentious or incomprehensible **JARGON** of bureaucrats, especially the circumlocutory language of official documents, reports, etc.
• The alternative spelling *gobbledegook* is in regular use. See also **OFFICIALESE**.

god or **God?** A *god* is any of a number of beings worshiped for their supernatural powers. *God*, written with a capital *G*, is the supreme being worshiped in many religions as the creator and ruler of all: □ *the god of war* □ *the Greek gods* □ *to believe in God* □ *for God's sake.*
• Compounds and derivatives of the noun, whether they refer to a *god* or to *God*, are usually written with a lowercase *g*: □ *godly* □ *godless* □ *godchild* □ *godsend*. The adjectives *God-fearing* and *Godforsaken*, however, are usually written with a capital *G*; *God-fearing* is usually hyphenated; *Godforsaken* is rarely hyphenated.

goodwill or **good will?** The term meaning "a feeling of kindness and concern," as in: □ *a gesture of good will*, can be written either as one word, with or without a hyphen, or as two words. The hyphenated *good-will* is used only as an adjective. *Good will* is a noun phrase. *Goodwill* may be a noun or an adjective.

gorilla see **GUERRILLA OR GORILLA?**

got *Got*, the past participle of *get*, is often superfluous in the expressions *have got* (meaning "possess") and *have got to* (meaning "must"): □ *He has (got) gray hair.* □ *They have (got) to win this game.*
• In informal contexts, especially in negative sentences, questions, and **CONTRACTIONS**, *got* is often retained: □ *We haven't got any milk.* □ *Have you got enough money?* □ *I've got to write to my brother.*

In some contractions, the occasional omission of *got* may cause confusion: □ *She's a cat* may mean "She is a cat" or "She has a cat"; *She's got a cat* is unambiguous.

Used alone, *got* is the past tense of *get*; it should not be used in place of *have* or *have got*: □ *They have/have got* [not *They got*] *three children.* □ *I got a new car last week.*

Gotten is a frequent variant of the past participle *got*, with *gotten* suggesting "acquired": □ *He's gotten a job.* In British English, its use is restricted to such expressions as *ill-gotten gains*.

gourmand or **gourmet?** A *gourmand* enjoys the pleasurable indulgence of eating, with or without regard to the quality of the food. *Gourmet*, the more common and also more complimentary of the two terms, refers only to a connoisseur of fine food or drink: □ *size of the meals will satisfy the gourmand; their quality should please the most discriminating gourmet.* To avoid ambiguity, *gourmand* may be replaced by *glutton* in the sense of "one who eats greedily or to excess."

• Many people object to the increasing use of *gourmet* to describe restaurants, meals, etc., in which the food is elaborate and expensive but not necessarily of high quality.

Gourmand is usually pronounced [*goor*mănd] or [*goor*mon(g)]; *gourmet* is pronounced [*goor*may]. Each word is occasionally stressed on the second syllable.

government In the sense of "the group of people who govern a country, state, etc.," *government* is usually a singular noun: □ *The government is blamed for the rise in unemployment.* It is considered plural in British English: □ *The government have rejected the proposal.*

• See also COLLECTIVE NOUNS; SINGULAR OR PLURAL?

graceful or **gracious?** *Graceful* refers to movement, actions, forms, shapes, etc., that have *grace*, in the sense of beauty, charm, or elegance: □ *a graceful dance.* *Gracious* means "kind," "courteous," "benevolent," or "compassionate": □ *a gracious gift.*

• The two words are not interchangeable, although they may occasionally qualify the same noun: □ *a graceful gesture* is a beautiful or elegant movement; □ *a gracious gesture* is an act of kindness or courtesy.

The adjective *gracious* may also occasionally imply condescension: □ *She thanked the waiter with a gracious smile.* In such expressions as *gracious living*, the word conveys an impression of luxury, comfort, elegance, and indulgence.

graffiti Careful users still object to the widespread use of the plural *graffiti* as a singular noun: □ *Graffiti covers the walls of the community centre.* □ *Some of this graffiti is quite obscene.*

• *Graffito*, the singular of this Italian borrowing, meaning "a little scratch," is used to refer to a single inscription or drawing: □ *The first graffito appeared the day after the room was repainted.*

Note the spelling of the word, particularly the double *f* and the single *t*.

grand- or **great-?** Each of these prefixes is used to denote family relationships that are two or more generations apart. Either prefix may be used for the aunts and uncles of one's parents and the children of one's nephews and nieces, *great-* being somewhat more frequent than *grand-*: □ *grandniece* □ *great-uncle.*

• The prefix *grand-* is always used for the parents of ones parents and the children of one's children: □ *granddaughter* □ *grandfather* □ *grandchild* □ *grandma.*

The prefix *great-* is also used for the parents of one's grandparents and the children of ones grandchildren: □ *great-grandmother* □ *great-grandson* □ *great-grandparent.* (The father of one's *great-grandfather* is one's *great-great-grandfather*, and so on.)

Great takes a hyphen; *grand* is joined to the word without a hyphen.

grass roots Some people object to the widespread use of this term both in political or industrial contexts and as a noun meaning "the fundamental level" or as a hyphenated adjective for "fundamental" or "basic": □ *the grass roots of the problem* □ *at the grass-roots level* □ *support for the party at the grass roots* □ *grass-roots opinion.*

- The noun *grass roots* originally referred literally to the soil immediately below the surface. It was subsequently applied to the ordinary people as opposed to the political leaders of society. The *grass roots* of a trade union or other organization are its rank-and-file members.

gratuitous The adjective *gratuitous* is most frequently used in the sense of "unwarranted" or "uncalled-for": □ *gratuitous violence* □ *gratuitous criticism.*
- The original meaning of the word is "free" or "given without payment."

gray or **gray?** *Gray* is standard in American English; *greyhound* is an exception. In British English, *grey* is more frequent.

great- see GRAND- OR GREAT-?

Great Britain see BRITAIN.

Greek or **Grecian?** The adjective *Greek* means "of Greece, its people, or its language"; the rarer adjective *Grecian* means "in the simple but elegant style of classical Greece": □ *Greek history*; □ *a Grecian vase.*
- The adjective *Grecian* was formerly applied to the art, architecture, literature, culture, etc., of ancient Greece; in these senses it has been largely superseded by *Greek*.

The noun *Greek* denotes a native or inhabitant of Greece; an archaic use of *Grecian* meant a scholar of classical Greek language or literature.

grey see GRAY OR GREY?

grill or **grille?** A *grill* is "a framework of bars used for cooking food." A *grille* is a grating over a window or door.
- These words are occasionally confused, especially because *grille* can also sometimes be spelled *grill*.

grisly or **grizzly?** The spellings of these words may sometimes be confused. *Grisly* means "gruesome": □ *a grisly experience*; *grizzly* means "partly gray": □ *a grizzly bear.*

growth The word *growth* is used adjectivally, in the sense of "rapidly developing or increasing," in economic and commercial spheres: □ *a growth industry* □ *a growth economy.*
- In other contexts it is often better replaced by a paraphrase: □ *Soccer is a growth sport* could well be changed to: *The sport of soccer is increasing in popularity.*

guarantee This word, which is often misspelled, means "an assurance that a certain agreement will be kept": □ *He gave me his guarantee that the car was in good shape.*
- It is worth remembering that the vowels of the first syllable are like those in *guard*: □ *A guarantee guards the rights of the consumer.*

guerrilla or **gorilla?** *Guerrilla* means "fighter within an independent army": □ *a guerrilla war*; a *gorilla* is a large ape. For the fighter the spelling *guerilla* is sometimes used, although *guerrilla* is preferred; it derives from the Spanish *guerra*, "a war," with a double *r*.
- The usual pronunciation of each word is [gĕrilĕ]; however, *guerrilla/guerilla* may be pronounced [gerilĕ] to make it distinct from *gorilla* [gĕrilĕ].

guest The use of the word *guest* as a verb, in the sense "of be a guest (on a television or radio show)," is disliked by some users and is best restricted to informal contexts: □ *She guested on his talk show last month.*

• Unlike *host*, the verb *guest* is not used outside the entertainment industry: □ *He was a guest at* [not *He guested at*] *our wedding.*

guidelines Some people object to the increasing use of the plural noun *guidelines* in place of *advice, policy, instructions rules*, etc.: □ *New guidelines to establish minimum sentences in rape cases* (*The Guardian*, July 28, 1987). □ *The series is within the BBC's guidelines on violence* (*Daily Telegraph*, Aug. 24, 1987).

• The noun *guidelines*, which is rarely used in the singular, is written as one word; the hyphenated form *guide-lines* is an accepted but rare variant.

gut The use of the word *gut* as an adjective, meaning "instinctive," "strong," "basic," or "essential," is best restricted to informal contexts: □ *a gut reaction* □ *a gut feeling* □ *gut issues.*

gybe see GIBE, JIBE, OR GYBE?

gymkhana This word, meaning, "place for athletic contests " or "competition for horses and their riders," is sometimes misspelled.

• It is worth remembering that *gym* is spelled as in *gymnastics,* and the first syllable of *khana* as in *khaki*.

gynecology This word is frequently misspelled. Note the *y* and *e*. The British spelling is *gynaecology.*

gypsy or **gipsy** This word, meaning "wanderer," has two spellings: the rare *gipsy* and *gypsy* . The *g* is usually lowercase.

• Some users prefer the *i* spelling, but the *y* spelling indicates the derivation from Egyptian. At one time this group of migrant people was thought to have originated in Egypt.

hail or **hale?** The noun *hail* means "frozen rain," or as a verb, "call" or "be a native of": □ *hail a taxi* □ *She hails from Scotland.* It should not be confused with *hale*, meaning "vigorous and healthy": □ *hale and hearty* or, as a verb, "force to go": □ *They haled him into court.*

half Although *half* is a singular noun, it is followed by a plural verb when it denotes a number rather than an amount: □ *Half of the books are missing.* □ *Half of the water has evaporated.* In many cases the word *of* is optional: □ *Give him half (of) the money.*

• Such expressions as *a half-hour* and *half an hour*, *a half-dozen* and *half a dozen*, etc., are equally acceptable in most contexts; however, the insertion of an extra indefinite article before *half an hour*, *half a dozen*, etc., is avoided by careful users. See also HYPHEN 4.

hallo see HELLO, HALLO, OR HULLO?

handful Most users prefer to form the plural *-fuls:* □ *handfuls.*

• See -FUL.

hands-on This expression is often used in business and advertising: □ *The head of the business, Sy Newhouse, has some reputation as a hands-on proprietor* (*The Bookseller*, May 15, 1987). □ *This is a vitally important, hands-on role calling for an experienced individual* (*Daily Telegraph*, June 4, 1987).

• The term *hands-on* is often used in the expression *hands-on experience*, practical experience "in ... learning where—students can obtain real experience of possible future jobs—or in business, where there is a similar implication of rolling up one's sleeves and getting involved, rather than simply reading or talking, or in a variety of situations where the practical is seen as improving on the merely theoretical" (Jonathon Green, *Dictionary of Jargon*).

hangar or **hanger?** These words are often misspelled. A *hangar* is a building for storing aircraft; a *hanger* is a small frame on which articles can be hung: □ *coat hanger.*

• To avoid mistakes, remember the *a* in *aircraft* and in *hangar.*

hanged or **hung?** *Hung* is the past tense and past participle for most senses of the verb *hang; hanged* is restricted to the meaning "suspended by the neck until dead," in the context of capital punishment or suicide: □ *He hung up his coat.* □ *The picture was hung in the hall.* □ *The conspirators were hanged for treason.* □ *Her father hanged himself.*

hanger see HANGAR OR HANGER?

hang-up The noun *hang-up* is an informal name for a mental or emotional problem or inhibition: □ *She's got a hang-up about* *answering the phone*. The word should not be used in formal contexts.

• *Hang-up* is usually hyphenated, but it is sometimes written as one unhyphenated word. The plural of *hang-up* is *hang-ups*.

harangue This word, which means "a vehement and lengthy speech," as in: □ *a long harangue about the state of the economy*, is sometimes misspelled.

• The *-gue* ending is the same as in *meringue*.

harass This word, meaning "trouble persistently," is spelled with a single *r* and a double *s*. It is pronounced [hǎ*ras*] or [*har*ǎs] the latter preferred in British English.

• Note that the same spelling rules apply for *harassment*.

hardly In the sense of "only just" or "almost not," the adverb *hardly*, like its synonyms *scarcely* and *barely*, is used with negative force; it is unnecessary to add another negative to the clause or sentence: □ *I can [not can't] hardly see you*. See also -**DOUBLE NEGATIVE**.

• Careful users avoid using *than* in place of *when* in the constructions *hardly ... when, scarcely ... when,* or *barely ... when*: □ *She had hardly begun to speak when* [not *than*] *he interrupted her*. □ *Scarcely had they reached the end of the road when* [not *than*] *the rain began*. This confusion may be due to the use of *than* in the construction *no sooner ... than*: □ *No sooner had I stepped into the bathtub than* [not *when*] *the doorbell rang*.

Hardly is rarely used as the adverbial form of the word *hard*, which functions both as an adjective and as an adverb: □ *a hard surface* □ *to work hard* □ *hard-earned money*.

have got (to) see **GOT**.

he see **HE OR SHE**.

heavy-duty The term *heavy-duty* should be restricted to articles, materials, etc., that are specifically designed to withstand hard wear or frequent use: □ *heavy-duty overalls* □ *heavy-duty fabric*.

• In other contexts, *tough* or *strong* may be adequate or more appropriate.

height This word, which is sometimes misspelled, refers to the distance from the base to the top of an object or a person: □ *the height of the mountain*. It also means "most intense point": □ *at the height of summer*.

heinous This word, meaning "extremely evil": □ *a heinous crime*, is often misspelled and mispronounced. Note the *ei* spelling and the stress on the first syllable [*hay*nǎs].

• The pronunciation [*hee*nǎs] is also acceptable, but [*hī*nǎs] is best avoided.

hello, hallo, or **hullo?** This word of greeting has variant spellings, but *hello* is the most frequent in contemporary usage.

help Many people object to the phrases *cannot/can't/could not/couldn't help but*, as in: □ *I couldn't help but laugh*, preferring either *I couldn't help laughing* or, less frequently, *I couldn't but laugh*.

• The idiomatic *cannot/can't/could not/couldn't help* construction, where *help* means "refrain from," is followed by a present participle. See also **BUT**.

In the sense of "assist" or "contribute," *help* is usually followed by a direct object and/or an infinitive, with or without *to*: □ *These pills will help you (to) sleep.* □ *They all helped (to) tidy the house.* Some users prefer to retain *to* in the absence of a direct object: □ *This money will help to pay for the new car.* □ *This money will help us pay for the new car.*

hemorrhage This noun, meaning "immense loss of blood from blood vessels," is often misspelled. The only double letter is *rr*.
• In British English, the first *e* is changed to *ae*: *haemorrhage*. The same pattern of spelling is followed by *hemorrhoid* (British English, *haemorrhoid*).

hence *Hence* means "from this time" or, more rarely, "from this place"; it is therefore unnecessary to precede the adverb with *from*: □ *The concert will begin three hours hence.*
• The use of *hence* in the sense of "from this place" is largely restricted to very formal or archaic contexts. See also **THENCE**.

Hence is also used to mean "for this reason" or "therefore": □ *My route is more direct; hence it is faster than yours.* □ *Her father drowned at sea, hence her reluctance to go sailing.* In these examples, note that *hence* is often followed by a noun or pronoun rather than a verb; to replace *hence* with *therefore* in the second example would involve rewording: □ *. . . therefore, she is reluctant to go sailing.*

he or **she** The use of *he/him/his* as pronouns of common gender, with reference to a person of unspecified sex, is widely considered to be misleading and sexist, as is the use of *she/her/hers* for the same purpose with reference to jobs or activities that traditionally associated with women: □ *The candidate must pay his own traveling expenses.* □ *This book will be of great value to the student nurse preparing for her examinations.* The most acceptable substitutes for these pronouns are the cumbersome and pedantic expressions *he or she, he/she, his or her,* etc.: □ *If a child is slow to learn he or she will be given extra assistance.* □ *The candidate must pay his or her own traveling expenses.*

In some cases, the problem may be avoided by restructuring the sentence, making the subject plural, or both: □ *Traveling expenses must be paid by the candidate.* □ *Candidates must pay their own traveling expenses.* □ *Children who are slow to learn will be given extra assistance.*
• Various attempts to coin new pronouns, such as *s/he, tey, hesh,* etc., have met with little success; it has also been suggested that the pronoun *it*, already used of babies, should be extended to human beings of all ages. Some consider that the solution is already in the making, with the increasing use of *they, them, their,* and *theirs* as singular pronouns □ *Anyone can attend as long as they pay the admission fee.* (see **THEY**).

hereditary or **heredity?** *Hereditary* is an adjective, meaning "genetically transmitted" or "inherited"; *heredity* is the noun from which it is derived: □ *The disease is not hereditary.* □ *Is intelligence determined by heredity or environment?*
• The two words are sometimes confused, being similar in pronunciation (the *a* of *hereditary* is often elided in speech).

hiccup or **hiccough?** Either spelling of this word is acceptable, but *hiccup* is the more frequent.
• The word refers to a sudden intake of breath resulting in a characteristic sound. In British English, it has the additional informal

sense of "small problem": □ *The project is going well apart from a few minor hiccups.*

high or **tall?** Each of these adjectives means "of greater than average size, measured vertically," but there are differences of sense, usage, and application between them: □ *a high mountain* □ *a tall woman.*

• The adjective *tall* is largely restricted to people, animals, and plants and to things that are narrow in proportion to their height; it is the opposite of *short*: □ *a tall tree* □ *a tall chimney. High* has the additional meaning of "situated at a great above the base"; it is the opposite of *low*: □ *a high branch* □ *a high shelf.*

The two adjectives may be applied to the same noun in different senses: *a high window* is a long way from the floor; *a tall window* is relatively large from top to bottom. The size of the *high window* and the position of the *tall window* are unspecified.

Like other adjectives of magnitude (*long, deep, wide,* etc.), *high* and *tall* are used in combination with specific measurements regardless of size: □ *He is only five feet tall.* □ *The wall is less than four feet high.*

high-profile see PROFILE.

hijack The verb *hijack,* meaning "seize control of (a vehicle in transit)," is increasingly used in figurative contexts: □ *The plane has been hijacked by terrorists.* □ *One of their most successful authors has been hijacked by a rival company.*

• *Highjack* is a rare variant spelling of the verb.

him or **his?** see -ING FORMS.

hire or **rent?** Each verb can mean "have or give temporary use of something in return for payment," *hire* in this sense being more frequent in British English: □ *He hired a suit for the wedding.* □ *We rented an apartment.* □ *They rent/hire (out) cars at competitive rates.* (*Hire* is used in paying for the services of a person.)

• The difference in sense between the two verbs often concerns the length of the period of temporary use and, to some extent, the nature of the item in question: a room or building may be *hired* for a party or conference or *rented* for a longer period of time. Clothes are *hired* (usually for a single occasion) or *rented*; television sets are *rented* (sometimes for a number of years), not *hired*. Cars may be *hired* or *rented.*

his or **her** see HE OR SHE.

historic or historical? The adjective *historic* relates to events, decisions, etc., that are memorable or important enough to earn a place in recorded history; *historical* relates to the study of history and to the past in general: □ *a historic election* □ *historical records* □ *The kings visit to the town was not a historic occasion; it is of historical interest only.* The adjective *historical* is also applied to people, events, etc., that existed or happened in fact, as opposed to fiction or legend: □ *a historical character.*

• The two adjectives are not fully interchangeable, although each may be applied to the same noun. *A historic voyage,* for example, is contrasted with one that is of no lasting significance, whereas *a historical voyage* is contrasted with one that never took place: the voyage of Christopher Columbus to the New World was both *historic* and *historical.* See also A OR AN?

histrionic or **hysterical?** The adjectives *histrionic* and *hysterical* are each used of emotional outbursts but should not be confused: *histrionic* behavior is a display of insincerity, being deliberately exaggerated for melodramatic effect; *hysterical* behavior is the result of an involuntary loss of control.

• The same distinction may be applied to the nouns *histrionics* and *hysterics*, each of which is used with plural verbs, adjectives, etc., in this context (see -ICS).

Histrionics and *histrionic* originally referred to actors and the theater; *hysterics* and *hysterical* relate to the mental disorder of *hysteria.*

hoard or **horde?** A *hoard* is "a store reserved for future use"; a *horde* is "a large crowd": □ *hoardes of tourists.*

• These words are often confused, because they have the same pronunciation.

holistic The adjective *holistic* is used of any system, method, theory, etc., that deals with the whole rather than with individual parts or members: □ *holistic medicine* □ *a holistic approach to life.*

• The term relates to the concept of wholes that are greater than the sum of their parts, of the natural tendency to form such wholes, and of a universe that is composed of such wholes. Many people take care not to overuse or misuse this word.

holocaust The use of the noun *holocaust* to denote any major disaster, especially one that involves great loss of life, is disliked by some users, who prefer to restrict the word to its original meaning of "total destruction by fire": □ *the nuclear holocaust.*

• The *Holocaust*, usually written with a capital *H*, refers to the massacre of the Jews by the Nazis during World War II.

homely The adjective *homely* has the derogatory sense of "plain" or "unattractive": □ *a homely child.* In British English, it is complimentary, meaning "like home," "unpretentious."

• Misunderstanding is most likely to occur when the adjective is applied to a person, in which case it may be replaced by an appropriate synonym.

homogeneous or **homogenous?** These two adjectives are for the most part interchangeable in the sense of "similar, identical, or uniform in nature, structure, or composition," *homogeneous* being the more frequent of the two: □ *a homogeneous mixture.*

• In biology, the adjective *homogenous* specifically refers to correspondence or similarity due to common descent.

The two words are closer in spelling and meaning than in pronunciation: *homogeneous* is usually pronounced [homŏ*jee*neeŭs] and *homogenous* [hŏ*moj*inŭs].

homosexual This word may be pronounced in several ways, two of the most frequent being [hōmō*seks*yooŭl] and [homŏ*seks*yooŭl].

• Some people prefer [hom-] to [hōm-] because, in this case, *homo* is from the Greek *homos*, "same," and not the Latin *homo*, "man." See also GAY.

honorary or **honorable?** *Honorary* means "given as an honor, without the usual requirements or obligations" or "unpaid": □ *an honorary degree* □ an *honorary* member of the *club.* *Honorable* means "worthy of honor" or "showing honor" and is also used as a title of respect: □ *an honorable man* □ *an honorable deed* □ *the Right Honorable Margaret Thatcher.*

• The two adjectives are not interchangeable in any of their senses, but each may be abbreviated to *Hon.*

Note the spellings of the two words: *u* is present in the British spellings of *honour* and *honourable* but absent from the American spelling of these words.

hoofs or **hooves?** Either *hoofs* or *hooves* is acceptable as the plural of *hoof* "the hard bony part of the foot of a horse, cow, etc."

hopefully The use of *hopefully* to mean "it is (to be) hoped (that)" or "I/we hope (that)" is disliked by some users and is best restricted to informal contexts: □ *Hopefully the rain will stop before we leave.*

• The resistance to this usage is based on a number of arguments, of which the most valid is the possible confusion with the traditional adverbial sense of *hopefully* — "with hope" or "in a hopeful manner." Ambiguity is most likely to occur when the adverb is placed directly before the verb: □ *They will hopefully wait for us* may mean "I hope they will wait for us" or "They will wait for us with hope"; *Hopefully they will wait for us* and *They will wait for us hopefully* are somewhat less ambiguous renderings of the two senses. See also **ADVERBS.**

Hopefully is favored by some users as a less cumbersome alternative to "it is (to be) hoped (that)" and a more impersonal alternative to "I/we hope (that)."

horde see **HOARD OR HORDE?**

horrible, horrid, horrific, or **horrendous?** *Horrible* and *horrid* are virtually interchangeable in the sense of "very unpleasant"; *horrific* and *horrendous* convey a stronger sense of horror: □ *a horrid sight* □ *a horrible dream* □ *a horrific attack* □ *the horrendous prospect of nuclear war.*

• All four adjectives are ultimately derived from the Latin verb *horrēre,* meaning "to tremble or bristle (with fear)"; in formal contexts they are principally used in the sense of "causing fear or dread."

The use of *horrible* and *horrid* to mean "disagreeable" or "unkind": □ *a horrid man* □ *a horrible meal,* is best restricted to informal contexts, as is the use of *horrendous* to describe exorbitant prices, very bad weather, etc.

hospitable This word may be stressed on the first syllable [*hospităbl*] or the second syllable [ho*spit*ăbl]. Some users prefer the former, more traditional pronunciation, but the latter is becoming more frequent.

hospitalize The verb *hospitalize,* meaning "send or admit to a hospital," is disliked by some users as an example of the increasing tendency to coin verbs by adding the suffix *-ize* to nouns and adjectives: □ *She was hospitalized last week.*

host The verb *host* meaning "act as host at" or "be the host of" is disliked by some users: □ *He hosted the company's Christmas party.* □ *She is to host the new quiz show.*

• See also **GUEST.**

however The principal adverbial senses of *however* are "nevertheless," "in whatever way," and "no matter how": □ *The car doesn't have a large trunk; it does, however, have plenty of room inside.* □ *However I wash my hair, and however carefully I dry it, it always looks messy.* For the distinction between *however* and *how ever* see **WHATEVER OR WHAT EVER?**

• In the sense of "nevertheless," *however* often serves the same purpose as *but*; careful users avoid using both words in the same sentence or clause unless *however* is being used in one of its other senses: □ *The girl screamed; she did not, however, try to escape.* □ *The girl screamed, but she did not try to escape.* □ *The girl struggled, but however hard she tried, she could not escape.*

Some users always separate *however* (in the sense of "nevertheless") from the rest of the sentence with commas or other punctuation marks; others use punctuation marks only where there is a possibility of ambiguity or confusion. See also COMMA 4.

In the sense of "nevertheless," *however* is usually placed immediately after the word or phrase that it serves to contrast or emphasize: □ *My friend, however, does not like the color* suggests that I like the color but my friend does not; *My friend does not, however, like the color* suggests that my friend likes some other feature of the object in question but does not like the color.

Some users object to the positioning of *however* (in the sense of "nevertheless") at the beginning or end of a sentence, a usage that is best avoided in formal contexts.

hullo see HELLO, HALLO, OR HULLO?

human Some people dislike the use of *human* as a noun, preferring *human being* (or *man, woman, child, person*, etc.): □ *This job can be done more efficiently by a robot than by a human (being).*
• Most dictionaries acknowledge the noun *human* as a synonym for *human being*. See also INHUMAN OR INHUMANE?

humorous This word, meaning "amusing or funny," is sometimes misspelled. *Humor* is spelled *humour* in British English. The second *u* of *humour* is dropped before the suffix *-ous*.
Humorous must not be confused with *humerus*, the long bone in the upper arm.

hung see HANGED OR HUNG?

hygiene This word, meaning "science of maintaining good health," is often misspelled. Note *hy-* and not *hi-* at the beginning of the word, and the *-ie-* in the middle.

hype The word *hype*, used as a noun or verb with reference to extravagant and often deceptive publicity for books, films, etc., is generally regarded as a slang term: □ *The launch owed more to hype than to literary merit* (*Sunday Times*, June 7, 1987). □ *the biggest moneymaking hype in sports history* (*Publishers Weekly*, March 6, 1972). □ *Hyping books is big business* (*The Bookseller*, April 19, 1980).
• The word is of uncertain origin: many authorities associate it with the slang use of *hype* as an abbreviation for *hypodermic*; others have suggested a connection with the prefix *hyper-*, meaning "excessive," as in *hyperbole*.

hyper- or hype-? These two prefixes are often confused, particularly resulting in misunderstanding when each is joined to its relevant suffix. *Hyper-* means "above or excessively": □ *a hyperactive child*; *hype-* means "beneath or under": □ *a hypodermic needle*.

hypercritical see HYPOCRITICAL OR HYPERCRITICAL?

hyphen The principal uses of the hyphen in English are to join two or more words together, either as a fixed compound or to avoid ambiguity, and to indicate that a word has been broken at the end of a line through lack of space.

• There are a number of other situations in which the use of the hyphen is optional.

1 Most standard prefixes are attached without a hyphen: □ *unimportant* □ *multicolored* □ *predetermined.*

Some users prefer to hyphenate words prefixed with *non-* and words in which the absence of the hyphen would result in a doubled vowel: □ *non-flammable* □ *pre-eminent* □ *co-ordinate.* Such words are widely and increasingly accepted in the one-word forms: □ *nonflammable* □ *preeminent* □ *coordinate,* etc. However, the double *i* of words prefixed by *anti-, semi-,* etc., is usually split by a hyphen: □ *anti-inflationary* □ *semi-invalid.*

Words prefixed with *ex-* (in the sense of "former") and *self-* are usually hyphenated: □ *ex-wife* □ *self-sufficient.*

A hyphen is sometimes inserted after the prefix to avoid ambiguity or confusion; for example, to distinguish between the nouns *co-op* (a cooperative) and *coop* (an enclosure), or between the verbs *re-cover* and *recover* (see also RE-), and to clarify the pronunciation and meaning of such words as *de-ice.*

A hyphen is always used to join a prefix to a word beginning with a capital letter: □ *anti-American* □ *un-Christian.*

2 Many compounds can be written with or without a hyphen, depending on convention, frequency of usage, the writers personal preference, or the publisher's style: □ *dining room* or *dining-room* □ *hard-hearted* or *hardhearted.* There is a growing tendency towards minimal hyphenation, with the substitution of two words or one word as appropriate.

Some fixed compounds of three or more words, such as *son-in-law, happy-go-lucky,* etc., are always hyphenated; two-word compound adjectives in which the second element ends in *-ed,* such as *heavy-hearted, blue-eyed, best-dressed,* etc., are usually hyphenated (see also **4** below).

Some compounds derived from phrasal verbs are always hyphenated: □ *broke-down;* some are always solid: □ *break-through;* others may be hyphenated or solid: □ *takeover* or *take-over* □ *run-down* or *rundown.*

3 Compounds of two or more words used adjectivally before the noun they qualify are usually hyphenated: □ a *used-car dealer* sells used cars; □ *dark-chocolate candy* is made of dark chocolate; □ a *three-month-old baby* is three months old; □ a *once-in-a-lifetime opportunity* occurs only once in a lifetime. These hyphens are often essential to avoid ambiguity: □ a *red-wine bottle* is a bottle for red wine; □ a *red wine bottle* may be a wine bottle that is red.

4 Adjectives or participles preceded by an adverb are not hyphenated if the adverb ends in *-ly:* □ a *neatly written letter* □ a *letter that is neatly written.* Compounds containing other adverbs, especially those that may be mistaken for adjectives (*well, ill, best, little, half,* etc.), are usually hyphenated when they are used adjectivally before a noun, to avoid ambiguity: □ a *half-cooked meal* □ *his best-known novel.* When such compounds occur after the noun, the hyphen is sometimes optional.

5 A common element need not be repeated in groups of two or more hyphenated compounds, but the hyphen must not be omitted; the same convention applies to solid compounds, in which the common element may be replaced by a hyphen: □ *long- or short-haired dogs* □ *salesmen and -women.* Some users dislike this convention, preferring to retain the full compound in all cases.

6 A hyphen is inserted when numbers between 21 and 99 are written out in full: □ *twenty-one* □ *thirty-seven* □ *eighty-six* □ *four hundred and fifty-three.* It is used between numbers or dates as the equivalent of *to:* □ *20-30* □ *1914-18.*

A hyphen is also used when fractions are written out, to separate the numerator and denominator: □ *three-tenths* □ *thirteen-sixteenths* □ *two-thirds* □ *forty-one sixty-fourths.*

7 The other major use of the hyphen is at the end of a line, splitting a word that is to be continued at the beginning of the next line.

There are a number of conventions relating to the points at which a word may be divided; these recommended breaks are marked in many dictionaries. There is an increasing tendency for word division to be influenced by phonetic rather than etymological principles; for example, *photog-rapher* [fŏtogrăfĕr], not *photographer.*

A word should always be split between syllables, ideally at a natural break: after an existing hyphen; between the elements of a one-word compound; after a prefix, such as *semi-*, *inter-*, etc.; or before a suffix, such as *-ness*, *-ment*, etc. Words of one syllable should not be broken. Words should not be broken immediately after the first letter or immediately before the last.

It is also important to be sure that the letters on either side of the break will not mislead the reader, especially if they form a word in their own right: □ *mace-rate* □ *the-rapist* □ *mans-laughter,* and that the hyphen will not be mistaken for a fixed hyphen: □ *re-creation* □ *de-crease* □ *re-form.*

8 In handwritten and typewritten texts, a hyphen is sometimes used in place of a DASH.

hype- see HYPER- OR HYPO-?

hypocritical or **hypercritical?** These two words are often confused. *Hypocritical* means "feigning of standards or beliefs"; *hypercritical* means "excessively critical": □ *It would be hypocritical of me to say I enjoyed the concert, when I really thought it was awful.* □ *He's so hypercritical about the way his wife sets the table.*

• As well as being misspelled, these words are sometimes mispronounced. *Hypocritical* is pronounced [hipĕkritikl], *hypercritical* is pronounced [hīpĕrkritikl].

hysterical, hysterics see HISTRIONIC OR HYSTERICAL?

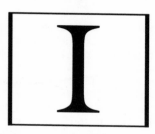

I or me? The subject pronoun *I* and the object pronoun *me* are sometimes confused in informal speech, especially in the phrases *It's me* and *between you and I.*

• After action verbs and prepositions, the object pronoun *me* should be used; before action verbs, the subject pronoun *I* should be used: □ *They have invited my mother, my father, and me* [not *I*] *to the wedding.* □ *He works with Mary and me* [not *I*]. □ *My friend and I* [not *me*] *will help.*

These problems rarely arise when the pronoun stands alone; any confusion may therefore be resolved by mentally removing the other item(s) and assessing the results: □ *They have invited me to the wedding.* □ *He works with me.* □ *I will help.*

The verb *to be*, according to grammatical convention, is an exception: in formal contexts *It is me* is unacceptable to a few careful users, who prefer *It is I*. In informal contexts, however, the idiomatic *It's me* is generally considered to be more natural than the pedantic *It's I* and is acceptable to most users. See also IT.

The phrase *between you and I* is avoided by many users in all contexts, although it is often heard in informal speech. *Between you and me*, which conforms to grammatical convention, is the preferred usage.

See also AS; LET; MYSELF; PRONOUNS; THAN.

-ible see -ABLE OR -IBLE?

-ic or -ical? Many adjectives are formed by the addition of the suffixes *-ic* and *-ical:* □ *cubic* □ *symmeterical* □ *phonetic* □ *geographical.*

• Sometimes either suffix may be added to the same root. The pairs of words thus created may be virtually interchangeable, such as: □ *metric—metrical* □ *philosophic—philosophical*, although one is usually more frequent or more specialized than the other. In other pairs the two words may differ in meaning or usage: see ASSIC OR CLASSICAL?; COMIC OR COMICAL?; ECONOMIC OR ECONOMICAL?; ELECTRIC OR ELECTRICAL?; HISTORIC OR HISTORICAL?; MAGIC OR MAGICAL?; POLITIC OR POLITICAL?

Some adjectives, especially those related to nouns ending in *-ic*, are found only in the *-ical* form: a *critic* may be *critical;* a *skeptic* is *skeptical*. Others, such as *static* or *tragic,* are very rarely, if ever, found in the *-ical* form.

With a rare exception such as *public,* all adverbs derived from adjectives ending in *-ic* or *-ical* have the suffix *-ically:* □ *tragically* □ *critically.*

-ics A number of words ending in *-ics* may be singular or plural nouns, depending on the sense in which they are used: □ *Acous-*

tics is the study of sound. □ *The acoustics of the room are excellent.*

• Such nouns are usually singular when they denote a science or some other area of study or activity: □ *Mathematics was not my favorite subject in school.* □ *Gymnastics is just one of her many hobbies.* □ *Economics is taught in our high school, but politics is not in the curriculum.*

In other contexts, the same nouns may become plural, when they refer to a system, set of principles, group of activities, etc. □ *His politics are very conservative.* □ *What are the economics of the steel industry?*

Some nouns, such as *tactics, statistic,* and *ethics,* may be singular or plural as described above but also exist in a singular *-ic* form: □ *military tactics* □ *vital statistics* □ *professional ethics* □ *her latest tactic* □ *an alarming statistic* □ *the work ethic.*

Nouns relating to behavior, such as *heroics* and *hysterics,* are usually plural.

See also **SINGULAR OR PLURAL?**

identical with or **identical to?** The adjective *identical* may be followed by *with* or *to:* □ *This picture is identical with/to the one we saw in the shop.*

• Some users dislike the phrase *identical to,* considering *with* to be the more acceptable preposition in this context, but *identical to* is becoming more frequent.

identify Some people dislike the frequent use of *identify* as a synonym for "associate," "link," or "connect": □ *They have been identified with a number of extreme right-wing organizations.*

• In the sense of "share the ideas or feelings of," *identify with* is sometimes used reflexively: □ *I cannot identify (myself) with the heroine.*

In commercial and bureaucratic contexts, *identify* is increasingly used as a synonym for "find," "discover," or "recognize": □ *to identify a gap in the market.*

idioms An idiom is a more or less fixed expression, such as *out of hand, in spite of, to come into one's own,* or *step on it,* the meaning of which is distinct from the individual senses of the words it contains. See also **METAPHORS; SIMILES.**

• Many idioms, such as □ *have egg on one's face,* "be shown to be foolish," and □ *be dog tired,* "to be very tired after exertion," are best restricted to informal contexts; others, such as □ *the salt of the earth,* "people regarded as having praiseworthy qualities," are acceptable at all levels.

idiosyncrasy This word is often misspelled, the most frequent error occurring when the ending *-asy* is replaced by *-acy.* The correct ending is like *fantasy* and not like *privacy.*

• Note also that *i* and *y* occur twice each.

idyllic The first *i* of *idyllic* is usually pronounced as in *item,* although it is sometimes pronounced as in *if.*

• The stress occurs on the second syllable in both cases; [īdi*l*ik] or [idi*l*ik].

i.e. see **E.G. AND I.E.**

if The use of *if* in place of *though* often causes ambiguity: □ *The work, if difficult, is rewarding.* □ *The service was good, if not excellent.*

• The first of these examples may mean "the work is difficult but rewarding" or "difficult work is rewarding." It is impossible to ascertain from the second example whether the service was excellent or not.

The use of *if* in place of *whether* may also be confusing in certain contexts: □ *Ask him if it is raining* probably means "Ask him whether it is raining (or not)," but it may also mean "If it is raining, ask him (for a ride, to close the window, etc.)." See also SUBJUNCTIVE; WERE OR WAS?; WHETHER.

if and when Many people object to the frequent use of the phrase *if and when*, which can usually be replaced by *if* or *when* alone: □ *We'll move to a larger house if and when we start a family.*

• The phrase sometimes serves a useful purpose, however. In the example above, the users may not wish to commit themselves on the subject of parenthood: *if* would imply doubt; *when* would imply certainty.

I

ilk The use of *ilk* as a synonym for "*type*" or "*sort*," in the phrase *of that ilk,* is widely accepted in many contexts but is disliked by some users: □ *Jackie Collins and other writers of that ilk.* The word *that* is sometimes replaced by *your, their, his, her,* etc.: □ *Jackie Collins and other writers of her ilk.*

• The phrase *of that ilk* is traditionally used to denote the landed gentry of Scotland, meaning "of that estate": □ *Glengarry of that ilk is Glengarry, laird of Glengarry.* In such contexts the phrase is often misinterpreted as "of that family."

ill see SICK OR ILL?

illegal see ILLICIT, ILLEGAL, OR ILLEGITIMATE?

illegible or **unreadable?** The adjective *illegible* describes something that cannot be deciphered and is therefore impossible to read; *unreadable* often means "uninteresting" or "badly worded," describing something that cannot be read with enjoyment, ease, or understanding: □ *Her handwriting is illegible.* □ *He has produced another unreadable novel.* □ *The document is unreadable; it must be reworded.*

• *Unreadable* may be used as a synonym for "*illegible*" in certain contexts, but it can cause ambiguity: □ *This paragraph is totally unreadable* may be a criticism either of the handwriting (or printing quality) or of the content or wording.

illegitimate see ILLICIT, ILLEGAL, OR ILLEGITIMATE?

illicit or **elicit?** The adjective *illicit* (see ILLICIT, ILLEGAL, OR ILLEGITIMATE?) should not be confused with the verb *elicit*, meaning "draw out" or "evoke": □ *illicit dealings* □ *to elicit the truth.*

• The two words have the same pronunciation [i*lis*it] although *elicit* is often pronounced [ee*lis*it].

illicit, illegal, or **illegitimate?** These adjectives mean "unlawful," but there are differences of sense, usage, and application between them: □ *illicit trade* □ *illegal parking* □ *an illegitimate attack.*

• *Illicit* means "not permitted or approved by law": □ *The Government should seek the cooperation of the unions, business and revenue authorities to eradicate illicit and irregular earnings* (*Daily Telegraph*, June 1, 1987). The word is also used to describe something that is contrary to social custom: □ *an illicit relationship*. See also ILLICIT OR ELICIT?

Illegal means "forbidden by law": □ *The hippies defied the notice to leave public property where they had set up an illegal camp.* The word is also used to describe something that violates the regulations of a sport, etc.: □ *an illegal tackle.*

The adjective *illegitimate* is principally applied to children born of unmarried parents: □ *illegitimate son.* It also describes something that defies reason or logic: □ *an illegitimate explanation.*

illusion see ALLUSION, ILLUSION, OR DELUSION?

illusive, illusory see ALLUSIVE, ELUSIVE, OR ILLUSIVE?

image The frequent use of *image* as a synonym for "reputation" is disliked by some users: □ *This scandal will not be good for the president's image.*

• In many contexts, however, *image* has a wider range of meaning than *reputation:* an advertising campaign can improve the *image,* but not necessarily the *reputation,* of a political party, for example. The *reputation* of a person, product, organization, etc., is largely based on past performance; the word *image* denotes a more general impression, which may also be influenced by presentation, appearance, association, etc.

imaginary or **imaginative?** *Imaginary* means "unreal" or "existing only in the imagination"; *imaginative* means "having or showing a vivid or creative imagination": □ *an imaginary character* □ *an imaginative designer* □ *an imaginative story.*

• The two adjectives are not interchangeable, although either may occasionally be applied to the same noun: □ *an imaginary friend* does not exist; *an imaginative friend* has a lively imagination.

I mean The phrase *I mean* may be used in informal speech to clarify, expand, or correct a previous statement, question, etc.: □ *Is your foot very painful—I mean, too painful to walk on?* □ *She lives in New York, I mean, New Jersey.*

• In some contexts the phrase serves no useful purpose and may be omitted: □ *You could have bought a new umbrella; (I mean) they're not very expensive.*

immanent see EMINENT, IMMINENT, OR IMMANENT?

Immigrant see EMIGRANT OR IMMIGRANT?

Imminent see EMINENT, IMMINENT, OR IMMANENT?

immoral see AMORAL OR IMMORAL?

immunity or **impunity?** *Immunity* is exemption or freedom from obligation or duty; *impunity* is exemption or freedom from punishment or harm: □ *Diplomatic immunity provides foreign ambassadors with immunity from taxation and enables them to break the law with impunity.*

• *Impunity* is a restricted form of *immunity*; the word occurs most frequently in the phrase *with impunity.*

Immunity also means "resistance to disease": □ *This vaccination may not confer total immunity.*

impact The use of *impact* as a synonym for "effect," "impression," or "influence" is best restricted to contexts in which the effect, impression, etc., is particularly powerful: □ *the impact of the government's decision on the stock market* □ *The new packaging has had little effect* [not *impact*] *on sales.*

• Some people object to all figurative uses of the noun, reserving it for physical collisions and their effects: □ *the impact of the bullet on the car door.*

I

The use of *impact* as a verb meaning "affect" is best avoided: □ *The cutbacks impacted secondary education negatively* could be reworded as: *The cutbacks had a bad effect on secondary education.*

impeccable This word, meaning "faultless": □ *She spoke impeccable Italian,* is often misspelled. Note particularly the *-able* ending as in *acceptable,* and not *-ible* as in *sensible.*

imperial or **imperious?** The adjective *imperial* means "of an emperor, empress, or empire; *imperious* means "overbearing" or "arrogant": □ *the imperial palace* □ *an imperious gesture.*

• The two words are sometimes confused in the extended sense of *imperial*—"majestic," "regal," or "commanding": *imperial powers* are those that are as majestic as an emperor's, not those that are domineering and arrogant. Both are derived from the Latin noun *imperium,* meaning "command."

The adjective *imperial* also refers to the British system of weights and measures (pounds and ounces, feet and inches, gallons and pints, etc.), which is gradually being replaced by the metric system.

impious This word should be stressed on the first syllable [impeeŭs].

• This pronunciation contrasts with *impiety,* which is stressed on the second syllable [impíitee].

implement The verb *implement* is best avoided where *carry out, fulfill, accomplish,* or *put into action* would be adequate or more appropriate: □ *His absence will enable us to carry out* [not *implement*] *our plan.*

• Originally a legal term, the verb *implement* is widely used in official contexts: □ *Townsend Thoresen . . . could pull out of an operating deal with a Belgian ferry company if it did not implement safety measures introduced in the wake of the Zeebrugge disaster* (*Daily Telegraph,* June 3, 1987).

As a noun, *implement* denotes a tool or instrument: □ *agricultural implements.* There is a slight difference in pronunciation between the verb and the noun: the final syllable of the verb is sounded [-ment], rhyming with *tent;* the final syllable of the noun is unstressed [-měnt], as in *garment.*

implicit see EXPLICIT OR IMPLICIT?

imply or **infer?** The verb *imply* means "suggest" or "hint at"; *infer* means "deduce" or "conclude": □ *She implied that there would be some layoffs in the factory.* □ *I inferred from what she said that there would be some layoffs in the factory.* To *imply* involves speech, writing, or action; to *infer* involves listening, reading, or observation.

• The two verbs are frequently confused, *infer* being used in place of *imply,* to the extent that some dictionaries now list "*imply*" as an additional sense of *infer.* Many people object to this usage, however; it is therefore advisable to maintain the distinction between the two words. Similarly, the noun *inference* is sometimes used instead of *implication,* but it is preferable to maintain the distinction between these two words: □ *the implications* [not *the inferences*] *of the report.*

Infer is stressed on the second syllable; the final *r* is doubled before *-ed, -ing,* and *-er.* The noun *inference,* in which the stress shifts to the first syllable, has a single *r.* See also SPELLING 1.

important or **importantly?** *More important* (short for *what is more important*) is sometimes regarded as an adverbial phrase, the adjective *important* being changed to *importantly:* □ *His assistants are very conscientious and, more important(ly), they are utterly trustworthy.*
• The phrase *more important* is preferred by many users in formal contexts, although *more importantly* is becoming increasingly acceptable.

impostor or **imposter?** Either spelling of this word, meaning "person who fraudulently pretends to be another person," is correct, although the spelling *impostor* is more frequently used than *imposter.*

impractical or **impracticable?** see PRACTICAL OR PRACTICABLE?

impromptu see EXTEMPORE OR IMPROMPTU?

impunity see IMMUNITY OR IMPUNITY?

in see AT OR IN?; INTO OR IN TO?

inapt or **inept?** The adjective *inapt* means "inappropriate" or "unsuitable"; its synonym *inept* is more frequently used in the sense of "incompetent" or "clumsy": □ *an inapt comparison* □ *an inept mechanic.*
• Both adjectives are ultimately derived from the Latin word *aptus,* meaning "fit," and the negative prefix *in-*; *inept* entered the English language via the Latin adjective *ineptus.*

inasmuch as This phrase may also be written *in as much as,* although *inasmuch as* is far more frequent: □ *The result was significant inasmuch as it demonstrated the power of the individual.* See also INSOFAR AS.

incident The noun *incident* is frequently used in the mass media to denote an action or occurrence that has or is likely to have serious, violent, or political consequences: □ *The latest wave of terrorist attacks was set off by an incident in Belfast.*
• In other contexts the noun *incident* is principally used with reference to events of minor importance: □ *The unfortunate incident was soon forgotten.*

incomparable This word, meaning "without comparison," is often mispronounced. The stress falls on the second syllable and not the third. The correct pronunciation is [inkompĕrĕbl].

incredible or **incredulous?** *Incredible* means "unbelievable"; *incredulous* means "disbelieving": □ *He told her an incredible story.* □ *She looked at him with an incredulous expression.*
• The use of the adjective *incredible* in the sense of "wonderful" or "amazing" should be restricted to informal contexts: □ *We had an incredible holiday.* See also CREDIBLE, CREDITABLE, OR CREDULOUS?

indefinitely This word is often misspelled, the most common error being the substitution of an *a* for the final *i.*
• It is worth remembering that the word *finite* is contained in *indefinitely.*

independence and **independent** These words are sometimes misspelled, the most frequent error being the substitution of an *a* after the final *d.*
• Note, however, that the noun *dependent,* "person who relies on another for financial support," is sometimes spelled *dependant,* with an *a.*

in-depth The adjective *in-depth* is disliked by many users; it can usually be replaced by *thorough* or *detailed*, for which it is an unnecessary synonym: □ *an in-depth knowledge of the latest electronic equipment* □ *an in-depth study of child abuse.*

indexes or **indices?** The noun *index* has two accepted plural forms, *indexes* and *indices.* The use of the plural form *indices,* pronounced [*indiseez*], is largely restricted to mathematics, economics, and technical contexts.

• For other senses of *index,* especially that of "alphabetical list," the plural form *indexes* is preferred by most users: □ *This cookbook has two indexes: one lists recipes by name; the other lists principal ingredients.* □ *Book titles and authors' names are entered in separate indexes.*

Indian The adjective and noun *Indian* may refer to India and its inhabitants or to the indigenous peoples of America: □ *the Indian Empire* □ *an Indian reservation.*

• The common confusion may be blamed on the explorer Christopher Columbus, who mistook the New World for India.

The term *American Indian* is used to distinguish these peoples from the Indians of Asia; it is preferred to the older British term *Red Indian,* which refers to the Indians of North America, and is now generally considered offensive.

An inhabitant of Pakistan, part of the Indian subcontinent, is a *Pakistani.* (Asian Indians and Pakistanis living in Britain are usually referred to as *Asians.*) See also ASIAN OR ASIATIC?

Further confusion may be caused by the term *West Indians,* which refers to inhabitants of the *West Indies* and their descendants.

indices see INDEXES OR INDICES?

indict and **indite** The words *indict* and *indite* are pronounced [in-*dīt*], but they have different meanings. *Indict*—note the *c* that is not pronounced—means "accuse; formally charge"; *indite* is an older word that means "write down."

• The derived nouns are spelled *indictment* and *inditement.*

indifferent The adjective *indifferent* should be followed by *to* or *as to,* not *for* or *about:* □ *He is indifferent to your criticism.* □ *I am indifferent as to the outcome of the trial.*

• The two principal senses of *indifferent* have undergone a gradual change, from "impartial" to "unconcerned" or "uninterested," and from "neither good nor bad" to "below average" or "poor." Used in either of its original senses, or even in one of its modern senses, the word is sometimes open to misinterpretation or confusion: □ *an indifferent referee* may be uninterested, neither good nor bad, or poor.

indiscriminate or **undiscriminating?** Each of these adjectives refers to a lack of discrimination (in the sense of "discernment" rather than "prejudice"); *indiscriminate* has the extended meaning of "random" or "unselective": □ *indiscriminate killings* □ *an undiscriminating palate.*

• There is a tendency for *undiscriminating* to be preferred to *indiscriminate* with direct reference to people: □ *undiscriminating viewers* □ *indiscriminate viewing.* See also DISCRIMINATING OR DISCRIMINATORY?

indispensable This word, meaning "absolutely essential": □ *In* *this job, a car and a telephone are indispensable*, is sometimes misspelled.

• The ending is -*able*, and not -*ible* as in *indestructible*.

indite see INDICT AND INDITE.

individual The use of the noun *individual* in place of *person* is disliked by some users, who reserve *individual* for contexts in which a single person is contrasted with a group: □ *the rights of the individual* □ *the person* [not *individual*] *who wrote this article.*

• The noun *individual* is also used, with a derogatory, contemptuous, or humorous effect, to denote a particular kind of person: □ *an unpleasant individual* □ *an eccentric individual.* This usage is best restricted to informal contexts.

indoor or **indoors?** *Indoor* is an adjective; *indoors* is an adverb: □ *an indoor antenna* □ *to go indoors* □ *Indoor games are played indoors.*

inept see INAPT OR INEPT?

in fact The phrase *in fact* is largely used for emphasis or to expand on a previous statement: □ *This legislation will not, in fact, improve housing conditions in inner-city areas.* □ *I'm not familiar with the machines; in fact, I've used it only once.*

• Since *in fact* means "actually" or "in reality," the addition of *actual* is considered by many users to be superfluous: □ *He often spends his vacations in France, but in (actual) fact he hates the French.*

infamous or **notorious?** Each adjective means "well-known for something bad": *notorious* emphasizes the well-known aspect; *infamous* emphasizes the bad aspect: □ *the execution of this infamous/notorious criminal* □ *his notorious lack of punctuality* □ *That intersection is notorious for accidents.* □ *one of Hitler's most infamous deeds.*

• Note the pronunciation and stress pattern of *infamous* [ĭnfămŭs], which is quite different from that of *famous* [faymŭs].

infectious see CONTAGIOUS OR INFECTIOUS?

infer, inference see IMPLY OR INFER?

infinitive The infinitive of a verb, often preceded by *to*, is its basic form, without any of the changes or additions that relate to tense, person, number, etc.: *(to) go* is the infinitive of the verb from which the past participle *gone* is derived.

• The infinitive is used without *to* after a number of auxiliary verbs: □ *you can leave* □ *they must wait* □ *he may object* □ *we should succeed*, etc.

After a number of other verbs, the infinitive is used with *to*: □ *I hope to see it.* □ *She refused to come.* □ *It never fails to amuse him.* □ *Do you wish to go home?* The infinitive (with *to*) is also used after adjectives and nouns: □ *easy to mend* □ *a book to read.*

In some constructions the infinitive functions as a verbal noun and may be interchangeable with its gerund (see -**ING FORMS**): □ *We love walking/to walk.* □ *He began writing/to write.* □ *To teach/Teaching young children requires great patience.* □ *To find/Finding another job is not always easy.*

In other constructions the infinitive and gerund are not interchangeable: □ *able to win—capable of winning* □ *a tendency to cheat—a habit of cheating* □ *He volunteered to help—he considered helping.*

I

Replacing an infinitive with a gerund sometimes changes the meaning of a sentence: □ *He stopped* [i.e., paused] *to read the notice.* □ *He stopped reading the notice* [i.e,. He finished reading it]. □ *I remembered to lock the door* [i.e., I didn't forget to do it]. □ *I remembered locking the door* [i.e., I recalled having locked it]. See also SPLIT INFINITIVE.

inflammable The adjective *inflammable* describes something that will catch fire and burn easily: □ *This liquid is highly inflammable. Inflammable* may be wrongly interpreted as the opposite of its synonym *flammable* (by analogy with *sensitive-insensitive; visible-invisible; edible-inedible; capable-incapable;* etc.). The potential danger of such confusion has led to a preference, especially on warning signs and labels, for the less ambiguous terms *flammable* (denoting an inflammable substance) and *nonflammable* (denoting a substance that is not [in] flammable).

• *Inflammable* also means easily angered or excited: □ *an inflammable situation.* In this figurative sense it cannot be replaced by *flammable.*

The adjectives *inflammable* and *inflammatory* should not be confused; something *inflammatory* tends to arouse strong or violent feelings: □ *an inflammatory speech.*

inflation Inflation is a general increase in the level of prices: □ *The rate of inflation has risen to 16%.* The word is widely used, especially in informal contexts, to denote the rate of inflation: □ *Inflation has risen to 16%.*

• Inflation is sometimes misinterpreted as being synonymous with the level of prices: □ *They say inflation's going down, but my income isn't going any further than it did.* A fall in (the rate of) inflation does not mean a fall in prices; it simply denotes a slower increase.

inflection *Inflection* is the term used for the change in form that words undergo in order to denote distinctions of number, tense, gender, case, etc. It is also used to describe the grammatical relation of a word to its root by inflection.

• One can say that the word *tables* is formed by inflection from *table; walked* is formed by inflection from *walk; heroine* is formed by inflection from *hero; them* is formed by inflection from *they.*

The spelling *inflexion* is occasionally seen in British English. This spelling is not incorrect, but it is now considered virtually obsolete and *inflection* is the preferred spelling.

inflict see AFFLICT OR INFLICT?

influenza see FLU.

inform The verb *inform* is best avoided where *tell* would be adequate or more appropriate: □ *Please tell* [not *inform*] *your husband that his car is ready.*

• Unlike *tell, inform* should not be followed by an infinitive: □ *They told* [not *informed*] *him to leave.* □ *They informed me of his departure.*

Inform is also used in the sense of "inspire," which is closer to the meaning of the Latin verb *informare,* "give shape to," from which it is derived: □ *His learning informs his whole discourse.*

informant or **informer?** An *informant* is a person who gives information; an *informer* is a person who gives the police information about criminals and their activities: □ *The professor was one of* *the author's most useful informants.* □ *The police were tipped off about the robbery by an informer.*

• The noun *informer* may also be used in the neutral sense of *informant*, but to avoid misunderstanding, it is best restricted to its more specific meaning.

ingenious or **ingenuous?** *Ingenious* means "clever" or "inventive"; *ingenuous* means "innocent," "naïve," or "frank": □ *an ingenious idea* □ *an ingenuous smile.* The two adjectives are not interchangeable, but they are sometimes confused.

• The noun form *ingenuity*, originally derived from *ingenuous* and formerly used for both adjectives, is now restricted to the sense of "cleverness" or "inventiveness"; *ingenuousness* is the noun form of *ingenuous*.

Note the pronunciations of the two adjectives: the *e* of *ingenious* is long, as in *mean*; the *e* of *ingenuous* is short, as in *men*.

-ing forms The *-ing* form of a verb may be a present participle or a gerund (verbal noun): □ *I am learning Japanese* [present participle]. □ *Learning Japanese is not easy* [gerund]. It is sometimes difficult, and often unnecessary, to distinguish between a gerund and a present participle.

• Problems of usage arise when the gerund has its own subject: □ *She disapproves of your using the car.* □ *She disapproves of the house where she spent her childhood being demolished.* According to grammatical convention, the possessive form should always be used in such cases. The substitution of *you* for *your* in the first example (or of *me/him/us/them* for *my/his/our/their* in similar cases) would be unacceptable to many users, even in informal contexts; however, the substitution of *childhood's* for *childhood* in the second example would be clumsy, unidiomatic, and also unacceptable to many users.

Between these two extremes—the simple personal pronoun and the complex noun phrase—the possessive form is used with varying degrees of acceptability.

For personal names and nouns relating to people, animals, etc., the possessive form is usually preferred in formal contexts but is sometimes rejected in informal contexts: □ *She disapproves of Peter's using the car.* □ *She disapproves of the gardener's using the car.* If more than one name or noun is involved, the possessive form is usually rejected in all contexts: □ *She disapproves of Michael and Peter using the car.* □ *She disapproves of the cook and the gardener using the car.*

For abstract nouns and nouns relating to inanimate objects, which are rarely used with the possessive ending *-'s*, the possessive form is usually rejected: □ *She disapproves of the house being demolished.* □ *She disapproves of religion being taught in schools.*

In the four preceding examples, the absence of the possessive ending may cause confusion: the reader or listener is momentarily led to believe that *she disapproves of Michael/the cook/the house/religion.* Such confusion can often be avoided by restructuring the sentence or by replacing the gerund with a noun: □ *She disapproves of the demolition of the house.*

The use of the possessive form with such words as *painting, writing, meeting, cooking,* etc., which may denote either an action or its result, can be ambiguous in some contexts: □ *We were not informed of their meeting* [that they intended to hold a meeting]. □ *We were not informed of their meeting* [that they had met].

In other contexts, the use of the possessive form may alter the meaning of a sentence: □ *They watched the girl dancing* places the emphasis on the girl; □ *They watched the girl's dancing* places the emphasis on the dancing.

See also APOSTROPHE; DANGLING PARTICIPLES; INFINITIVE; PARTICIPLES; 'S OR S'; WANT.

inherent This word, meaning "essential or necessary part of a thing," has two possible pronunciations: [inheerĕnt] or [inherĕnt]. The first of these is the more traditional, but the second is preferred by some users.

inhuman or **inhumane?** Careful users maintain the distinction between *inhuman* and *inhumane*. *Inhumane*, the opposite of *humane*, means "lacking in compassion and kindness; cruel; not merciful": □ *inhumane treatment*. *Inhuman*, the opposite of *human*, is stronger and has a wider scope than *inhumane*. To be *inhuman* means to lack all human qualities, not only compassion and kindness: □ *inhuman violence* □ *inhuman living conditions*.

• *Inhuman* has the additional meaning of "not having human form": □ *An inhuman shape appeared at the window.*

in-law The use of the plural noun *in-laws*, denoting a person's relatives by marriage, is best restricted to informal contexts: □ *My in-laws are coming for dinner on Saturday.*

• The plural of *mother-in-law, father-in-law, son-in-law, daughter-in-law*, etc., is formed by adding *s* to the first element of the compound: *mothers-in-law, fathers-in-law*, etc.

in lieu The phrase *in lieu (of)* is best avoided where *instead (of)* would be adequate or more appropriate: □ *She drove to the airport instead* [not *in lieu*] *of taking the train.*

• *In lieu (of)* is chiefly used in formal contexts with reference to the replacement of one thing with another or others of equivalent value or importance: □ *If they have to work on Christmas Day, they should be given time off in lieu.* □ *We are sending two bottles of dessert wine in lieu of the champagne you ordered.*

The word *lieu* may be pronounced [loo] or [lew].

inoculation This word is often misspelled, the most frequent error being the addition of an extra *n* as in *innocent*. Also, note the single *c* and the single *l*.

in order that and **in order to** The phrase *in order that* is followed by *may, might, shall*, or *should* rather than *can, could, will*, or *would*: □ *He moved his suitcase in order that we might* [not *could*] *open the door.* □ *She drove him to the station in order that he should* [not *would*] *not miss his train.*

• These restrictions do not apply to the simpler expression *so that* (see SO), which is often preferable to *in order that* in such contexts.

If the subordinate clause has the same subject as the main clause, *in order that* may be replaced by *in order to* followed by an infinitive: □ *He moved his suitcase in order to open the door.*

The phrase *in order to* is best avoided where *to* would be adequate: □ *He turned the key to* [not *in order to*] *open the door.*

input Many people object to the use of the noun *input* as a synonym for "contribution": □ *We hope to have some input from the teaching staff at tomorrow's meeting.* □ *positive input,* "approval or encouragement" □ *negative input,* "criticism."

• As a noun, *input* may be used to denote the power, energy, data, etc., put into a system or machine, or the resources, labor, raw materials, etc., required for production.

The verb *input* refers to the process of entering data into a computer: □ *Travel agents will be able to input data directly to a central computer.* In other contexts, use of the verb *input* is generally deprecated, other verbs being preferred: □ *contribute* [not *input*] *ideas to a meeting* □ *provide with* [not *input*] *equipment.*

inquiry or **enquiry?** The spellings of the nouns *inquiry* and *enquiry* (and of the verbs *inquire* and *enquire*) are completely interchangeable. Some British users, however, maintain that *enquire* and *enquiry* are used for simple requests for information: □ *He enquired after her health.* □ *directory enquires,* and *inquire* and *inquiry* are used for investigations, especially official ones: □ *The police are now inquiring into the events that led up to his disappearance.* □ *Leaders are calling for a public inquiry into the causes of the disaster.*

insofar as This expression may be written *insofar as* or *in so far as,* the first being more frequent: □ *I'll help you insofar as it is appropriate.*

• See also INASMUCH AS.

in spite of see DESPITE OR IN SPITE OF?

install or **instal?** Either spelling of this word is correct, although the first is much more frequently used: □ *install a new central-heating system.*

• If the spelling *instal* with a single *l* is followed, then this *l* doubles before the suffixes beginning with a vowel: *installing, installed, installer, installation.*

Installment is spelled with a double *l*. In British English, *instalment* has a single *l*.

instantly or **instantaneously?** The adverbs *instantly* and *instantaneously* are virtually interchangeable in the sense of "immediately" or "without delay": □ *He replied instantly/instantaneously.*

• *Instantaneously* has the additional meaning of "very quickly" or "almost simultaneously": □ *She was hit by the car and died instantaneously.*

instill This word, meaning "allow to enter gradually," is often misspelled. Note the double *l*. It ends in a single *l* in British English, which must be doubled before a suffix is added: *instilled.* See also SPELLING 1.

institute or **institution?** Each noun is used to denote certain professional bodies and established organizations founded for research, study, charitable work, the promotion of a cause, etc.: □ *National Institutes of Health* □ *the Smithsonian Institution.* The nouns also denote the buildings or premises used by these organizations.

• *Institution* has a range of additional meanings: "the act of instituting": □ *the institution of a new electoral system;* "an established social custom or practice": □ *the institution of marriage;* "a school or hospital": □ *an educational institution* □ *He spent years in a mental institution.*

I

The verb *institute* means "establish," "initiate," or "install."

insurance see ASSURANCE OR INSURANCE?

insure see ASSURE, ENSURE, OR INSURE?

integral Some people object to the frequent use of the phrase *integral part*, in which the adjective *integral* is often superfluous: □ *The study of local history is an integral part of the syllabus.* Most parts are *integral*—i.e., "essential to the completeness of the whole"—by definition.

• In many contexts, the word *integral* would be better replaced by *essential, important*, etc.: □ *Cash registers have become an integral part of even the most backward industries in these competitive days.*

The usual pronunciation of *integral* is [íntigrăl], stressed on the first syllable; the variant pronunciation [intégrăl], stressed on the second syllable, is disliked by many users.

integrate The verb *integrate* is widely used in the sense of "make or become part of a social group": □ *One of the aims of our organization is to integrate ethnic minorities into the community.* □ *Newcomers to the village often find it difficult to integrate.*

• In other contexts *integrate* is often better replaced by *mix, amalgamate, join, combine*, etc.: □ *a new television program that combines* [not *integrates*] *learning with entertainment.*

Note the spelling of *integrate*, which does not begin with the prefix *inter-*.

intense or **intensive?** *Intense* means "extreme" or "very strong"; *intensive* means "concentrated" or "thorough": □ *intense pain* □ *intense heat* □ *intensive training* □ *an intensive search.* The two adjectives are not interchangeable, although each may be applied to the same noun: *intense/intensive study.*

• Each adjective has additional senses: *intense* describes a person who has very strong and deep feelings; *intensive* has specialized meanings in grammar and agriculture and is used in such compounds as *intensive care* and *labor-intensive.*

inter see INTERMENT OR INTERNMENT?

inter- or **intra-?** The prefix *inter-* means "between" or "reciprocally"; *intra-* means "within": □ *intercontinental* □ *interdependent* □ *intravenous* □ *intramural.*

• The two prefixes should not be confused: *international* means "of two or more nations"; *intranational* means "within one nation."

The prefix *intra-* is most frequently found in medical contexts: □ *intracranial* □ *intramuscular* □ *intrauterine.*

interface In science, computing, etc., the noun *interface* denotes a surface forming a common boundary or a point of communication. Its extended use as a synonym for "interaction," "liaison," "link," "(point of) contact," etc., is disliked by many people: □ *the interface between professionals and lay people in the caring professions* □ *the interface of history and literature* □ *at the interface between design and technology.*

• The verb *interface* is also best restricted to technical contexts: □ *The office microcomputers will interface with the main computer.*

interment or **internment?** *Interment* means "burial"; *internment* means "imprisonment": □ *the interment of the corpse* □ *the internment of the terrorists.*

• The two words should not be confused.

The noun *interment* and the verb *inter* (from which it is derived) are formal words that refer to the depositing of a dead body in the earth or in a tomb.

The noun *internment* is derived from the verb *intern,* which refers to the confinement of enemy aliens, prisoners of war, etc.

In each of these nouns and verbs the stress falls on the second syllable.

The noun *intern,* stressed on the first syllable, is a name for someone in the final stages of professional training, especially in medicine.

internecine The adjective *internecine* may refer to slaughter or carnage, mutual destruction, or conflict within a group: □ *an internecine battle* □ *internecine warfare* □ *an internecine dispute.*

• The first of these, the original meaning of the word, is the least frequent of the three. It is pronounced [intĕrneesin] or [intĕrnessin]; in British English, the word is pronounced [intĕrneesīn].

internment see INTERMENT OR INTERNMENT?

interpretative or **interpretive?** Either adjective may be used, but *interpretive* is the more frequent of the two: □ *The appendix contains interpretive/interpretative notes on the text.*

in that The phrase *in that* means "because" or "to the extent that": □ *He is unsuitable for the job in that he has no relevant experience.* □ *The two machines are different in that one is fully automatic and the other is manually controlled.*

• In some contexts, however, *in that* may be better replaced by *because* or one of its synonyms: □ *We are in financial difficulties because* [not *in that*] *my wife has become unemployed.*

in the near future The phrase *in the near future* is disliked by some users as an unnecessarily wordy substitute for *soon:* □ *The company will be relocating in the near future.*

in this day and age The cliché *in this day and age* is best avoided where *nowadays, today, now,* etc., would be adequate or more appropriate: □ *In this day and age, a good education is not a passport to a successful career.*

into or **in to?** *Into* is a preposition with a variety of meanings; *in to* is a combination of the adverb *in* and the preposition or infinitive marker *to:* □ *I went into the house.* □ *I went in to fetch a book.* □ *I went in to supper.*

• It is important to recognize and maintain the distinction between these uses.

As prepositions, *into* and *in* are occasionally interchangeable: □ *He put the letter into/in his pocket. Into* usually suggests movement from the outside to the inside, whereas *in* suggests being or remaining inside. In many contexts the two prepositions are not interchangeable: □ *They sailed into the harbor at four o'clock.* □ *They sailed in the harbor all afternoon.*

in toto The Latin phrase *in toto* means "entirely" or "completely": □ *He did not disagree in toto.*

• It is acceptable, but not necessary, to use italics when writing or printing this expression.

intra- see INTER- OR INTRA-?

intrinsic or **extrinsic?** The adjective *intrinsic* means "inherent," "essential," or originating from within: □ *The discovery is of* *great intrinsic interest. Extrinsic,* the opposite of *intrinsic,* is less frequent in general usage: □ *The document is of extrinsic interest only.*

• The *intrinsic* value of a penny, for example, is the value of the metal from which it is made; its *extrinsic* value is one cent.

introvert see **EXTROVERT OR INTROVERT?**

invalid The adjectival sense of "not valid" is pronounced with the stress on the second syllable [in*val*id]. The noun sense of "someone who is ill" is pronounced with the stress on the first syllable, either as [*in*vălid] or the British [*in*văleed].

• The verb sense, "disable," or, usually followed by *out,* the British "remove from active service because of illness or injury," may be pronounced [*in*vălid], [*in*văleed], or [invă*leed*].

inverted commas see **QUOTATION MARKS.**

invite The use of the word *invite* as a noun, in place of *invitation,* is disliked and avoided by many users, even in informal contexts: □ *Have you had an invite to their party?* □ *Thank you for your invitation, which I am very pleased to accept.*

• Note that the stress pattern of the noun *invite* is different from that of the verb: the noun is stressed on the first syllable; the verb is stressed on the second syllable. See also **STRESS.**

involve Some people object to the frequent use of the verb *involve* and its derivatives in place of more specific or more appropriate synonyms: □ *This proposal will entail* [not *involve*] *further cuts in expenditure.* □ *Some changes may be necessary* [not *involved*]. □ *I have a number of questions concerning* [not *involving*] *teaching methods and discipline.* □ *These fingerprints are evidence of his participation* [not *involvement*] *in the robbery.*

• Some authorities recommend that *involve* and its derivatives be restricted to the sense of entanglement and complication: □ *the chairman's involvement in the scandal* □ *a long-winded and involved account of the incident.*

inward or **inwards?** *Inward* is principally used as an adjective, as well as an adverb meaning "toward the inside": □ *inward feelings* □ *to push inward.*

• The adverb *inwards* is more frequently used in British English. See also **-WARD OR -WARDS?**

I.Q. This abbreviation for "intelligence quotient": □ *the average I.Q. must always be written with capital letters.*

• The abbreviation with lowercase letters, *i.q.,* stands for *idem quod,* a Latin phrase meaning "the same as."

ironic, ironical, ironically see **IRONY.**

iron out The phrasal verb *iron out* is widely used in the metaphoric sense of "settle," "resolve," "solve," or "remove": □ *We have a few more problems to iron out before work can begin.*

• It is best avoided, however, in contexts that may be associated with its literal meaning of "smooth with an iron": □ *The laundry workers have ironed out their difficulties.* □ *The last stumbling block was ironed out at yesterday's meeting.*

irony Irony is the use of words to express the opposite of their accepted meaning, often for satirical or humorous effect.

• Some people object to the frequent use of the noun *irony* and its derivatives with reference to something paradoxical, incongruous, or odd: □ *She resigned when they rejected her proposals; the iro-*

ny of the situation is that they have now adopted the system she proposed. □ *It's ironic that he should win a ski trip just after breaking his leg.* □ *Ironically, it was the police sergeant's car that was stolen.*

The adjectives *ironic* and *ironical* are both in use, *ironic* being the more frequent.

Irony may be used as a form of *sarcasm*, but the two words should not be confused: an *ironic* remark is more witty and less cruel than a *sarcastic* remark.

irrefutable This word, meaning "impossible to be disproved": □ *irrefutable evidence*, may be stressed on the second or on the third syllable: [irefyootăbl] or [irifyootăbl]. The second pronunciation is becoming more common.

irrelevant This word is frequently misspelled. Note the double *r* and the vowels *i-e-e-a*.

irreparable This word, meaning "unable to be repaired," is often mispronounced. The stress should fall on the second syllable and not the third [irepărăbl].

irrespective The word *irrespective* is most frequently used in the prepositional phrase *irrespective of*, meaning "regardless of": □ *Applications are invited from all suitably qualified candidates, irrespective of age, sexual orientation, nationality, disability or religion.*

• The expression *irrespectively of* is generally considered to be unidiomatic.

Unlike *regardless*, *irrespective* should not be used adverbially in other contexts: □ *It soon began to rain, but they carried on with their game regardless* [not *irrespective*]. The word *irregardless*, a blend of *irrespective* and *regardless*, is unacceptable to careful users.

-ise see -IZE OR -ISE?

-ism Some people object to the increasing use of the suffix *-ism*, in the sense of "discrimination," to coin new words modeled on the nouns *racism* and *sexism*: □ *legislation against ageism* □ *the controversial issue of heterosexism.*

• The use of the suffix to form new nouns in the conventional sense of "doctrine" or "system" is acceptable in moderation: □ *the prospect of another four years of Reaganism.*

-ist or -ite? Each of these suffixes may be used to denote an adherent, follower, advocate, or supporter of a particular doctrine: □ *Stalinist* □ *Reaganite* □ *communist* □ *laborite*. The suffix *-ite* is sometimes used in a derogatory manner: people who call themselves *Trotskyists*, for example, may be described by opponents of *Trotskyism* as *Trotskyites*; it also means "inhabitant of" □ *Brooklynite* or "descendant of": □ *Israelite*.

• The suffix *-ist*, which is also used to form adjectives, may face the same objection as -ISM: □ *ageist principles* □ *heterosexist attitudes.*

it The pronoun *it* has a wide range of uses: to replace an abstract noun or the name of an inanimate object, as the subject of an impersonal verb, etc.: □ *He washed the towel and hung it out to dry.* □ *It hasn't rained for a week.* □ *I find it difficult to make new friends.* □ *It's obvious that she doesn't like him.* For this reason, the use of *it* may sometimes cause ambiguity or confusion: □ *She took her purse out of her handbag and put it on the table* [the purse or the handbag?]. □ *You can open the window if it gets too hot* [the window or the weather?].

• The constructions *it is/was . . . who* and *it is/was . . . that* should be used only for emphasis: □ *It was she who broke the window, so I don't see why you should pay for the repair.* □ *It's the weather that's making me feel tired—I'm not ill.*

In such constructions, the verb following *who* or *that* agrees with the pronoun or noun that follows *is* or *was*, not with the word *it*: □ *It's I who wish* [not *wishes*] *to complain.* □ *It was they who were* [not *was*] *at fault.* □ *It is the books that make* [not *makes*] *the trunk so heavy.* (Note the use of *I* and *they*, rather than *me* and *them*; see also I OR ME?; PRONOUNS.)

The construction is not used with *where* or *when*: □ *It is in France that the best cheeses are to be found* [not *It is France where . . .*]. □ *It was in 1986 that he won the championship* [not *It was 1986 when . . .*].

The construction, however, should not be confused with such statements as *It was dark when we arrived* and *It's snowing where my parents live* or such expressions as *it is believed that . . .* and *it is possible that . . .* .

See also ITS OR IT'S?; THAT OR WHICH?

italics The word *italic* denotes a sloping typeface that is used for a variety of purposes in English. In handwritten or typewritten texts, underlining is generally used to indicate italics.

• The principal uses of italics are:

1 For the titles of books, newspapers, magazines, plays, films, works of art, musical works, etc.: □ *The New York Times* □ *Newsweek* □ *Gone with the Wind* □ *the Mona Lisa.*

2 For the names of ships, boats, trains, aircraft, etc.: □ *the U.S.S. Enterprise.*

3 For the Latin names of plants, animals, etc.: □ The tiger, *Panthera tigris,* is found in Asia.

4 For foreign words and phrases that are not fully integrated into the English language: □ This was his *pièce de résistance.* □ The teacher is *in loco parentis.* It is sometimes difficult to judge whether a foreign word or phrase should be italicized or not. Some dictionaries offer guidance on this matter.

5 To indicate stress or emphasis: □ Is it *still* raining? □ I don't *like* spiders, but I'm not afraid of them. Excessive italicization for the purpose of stress or emphasis is avoided by careful users.

6 To draw attention to a particular word, phrase, or letter: □ How do you pronounce *controversy*? □ Her name is spelled with a double *s.*

-ite see -IST OR -ITE?

its or **it's?** *It's*, a contraction of *it is* or *it has*, should not be confused with *its*, the possessive form of *it*: □ *It's easy to tell the difference.* □ *It's been raining for several hours.* □ *The lion has escaped from its cage.* See also APOSTROPHE; CONTRACTIONS; 'S OR S?

• The insertion of an apostrophe in the possessive form *its* is wrong in all contexts, although it occasionally finds its way into print: □ *It's aim is to encourage new ideas and developments in the field*

I

of learning and teaching English (advertisement for The English-Speaking Union, *The Guardian,* Feb. 6, 1980).

The omission of the apostrophe in the contraction *it's* is less frequent but equally unacceptable.

-ize or **-ise?** The sound [-īz] at the end of many verbs is usually spelled *-ize:* □ *baptize* □ *realize* □ *recognize* □ *organize,* etc. Most modern dictionaries, partly because of the American international influence, list *-ize* as the preferred spelling, giving *-ise* as an accepted variant. The use of *-ise* is generally as common as *-ize* in British English.

• There is etymological justification for both spellings, the suffix being derived via the French *-iser* from the Latin *-izare* and the Greek *-izein.*

Whichever spelling is preferred, it is important to be consistent within a single piece of writing, both in the choice of other *-ize/-ise* words and in the spelling of any derivatives ending in *-ization/-isation, -izer/-iser, -izable/-isable,* etc.

There are a number of *-ise* verbs that cannot be spelled *-ize;* the most common of these are *advertise, advise, chastise, circumcise, comprise, compromise, despise, devise, enfranchise, excise, exercise, improvise, revise, supervise, surmise, surprise,* and *televise.*

Verbs ending in *-yze,* such as *analyze* and *paralyze,* are spelled *-yse* in British English.

Some people object to the modern tendency to create new verbs by the addition of *-ize/-ise* to a noun or adjective: □ *pedestrianize* □ *hospitalize* □ *prioritize* □ *finalize.*

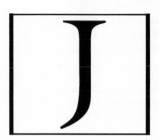

jail or **gaol?** *Jail* is the accepted spelling. In British English, *gaol* is also acceptable, although *jail* is preferred by many people.

jargon Jargon is the technical language used within a particular subject or profession, such as science, computers, medicine, law, accounting, etc.: □ *Rollover is banking jargon for refinancing or reinvesting of funds.*

• The term is also used to denote the complex, obscure, pretentious, or euphemistic language used by journalists, sociologists, advertisers, bureaucrats, politicians, etc.: □ *In sociological jargon, the class system has been replaced with a series of socioeconomic groups.*

Jargon of both types is acceptable, and often indispensable, in professional journals and in written or spoken communications between members of the same group. It should be avoided, however, in articles, brochures, insurance policies, etc., that are to be read and understood by lay people and in conversations with members of the general public. Jargon should not be used to impress, intimidate, confuse, or mislead the outsider. See also JOURNALESE; OFFICIALESE.

Jargon sometimes finds its way into everyday language in the form of CLICHÉS or vogue words, e.g. *interface, traumatic, user-friendly.* Such words and expressions are disliked and avoided by many users.

Jargon should not be confused with DIALECT OR SLANG.

jealousy see ENVY OR JEALOUSY?

jeopardize This word, meaning "expose to danger," is often misspelled, the most frequent error being the omission of the letter *o*.

• Note that the vowel pattern is the same as in *leopard.*

jewelry or **jewellery?** *Jewelry* is the standard spelling. *Jewellery,* however, is more frequent in British English.

• The preferred pronunciation is [*joo*ĕlree] rather than the dialectal or nonstandard [*jool*ĕree].

jibe see GIBE, JIBE, OR GYBE?

job action *Job action,* or the British term *industrial action,* may denote any of a number of measures (such as a strike, sit-in, etc.) used dissatisfied employees to put pressure on their employers: □ *The job action by factory workers may end soon.* The term is, however, misleading and contradictory, as for example a strike is characterized by *a lack* of action, rather than action.

• The expression *job action,* which originated in the late 1960's, is not confined to industry (in the sense of "manufacturing or commercial enterprises"): teachers, hospital staff, etc., may also undertake job actions.

jodhpurs This word for "riding trousers" is often misspelled, the *h* being either incorrectly placed or omitted completely.

• The word originates from *Jodhpur*, a city in India, hence the unusual spelling.

journalese *Journalese* is a derogatory name for the style of writing or language that is considered to be typical of newspapers.

• It is characterized by the use of CLICHÉS and short sensational synonyms, e.g. *ax, bid, probe*, which occur especially in headlines.

Careful users avoid such techniques and devices in formal writing. See also JARGON.

judgment or **judgement?** There are two spellings for this word. *Judgment* is more common. In British English, however, *judgement* is probably more frequent.

• Some authorities that follow the British spelling *judgement* in general contexts prefer the spelling *judgment* in legal works.

Whichever spelling of *judg(e)ment* is adopted, it is advisable to be consistent in the spelling of this word and words such as *abridg(e)ment* and *acknowledg(e)ment.*

judicial or **judicious?** *Judicial* means "of judgment in a court of law" or "of the administration of justice"; *judicious* means "having or showing good judgment" or "prudent": □ *judicial proceedings* □ *a judicious choice.*

• The two adjectives are not interchangeable, although each may be applied to the same noun: □ *a judicial decision* is the decision of a court of law; □ *a judicious decision* is a wise decision.

Judicial may also mean "of a judge; impartial; fair"; it is in this sense that it is most likely to be confused with *judicious.*

juncture The phrase *at this juncture* refers to a critical point in time; many people object to its frequent use in place of *now*: □ *The leader's resignation at this juncture would have a disastrous effect on the member's morale.* □ *I suggest that we take a short break for refreshments now* [not *at this juncture*].

• This use of *juncture* has developed from its meaning of "concurrence or conjunction of events or circumstances." The noun is rarely used in its original sense, as a synonym of "junction" or "joint."

junta This word, which comes from Spanish, refers to a controlling political council and has various pronunciations. The preferred pronunciation is [*huun*tă], with alternatives such as [*jun*tă] and [*juun*tă].

just *Just* has a variety of adverbial senses: "at this moment," "exactly," "only," etc. For this reason, it must be carefully positioned in a sentence in order to convey the intended meaning: □ *Your son has just eaten two cakes* [i.e., a short time ago]. □ *Your son has eaten just two cakes* [i.e., not one or three, etc.]. □ *Just your son has eaten two cakes* [i.e., only your son; no one else]. Transposing *just* and *not* may also change the meaning of a sentence: □ *I'm just not tired.* □ *I'm not just tired; I'm hungry too.*

• In the sense of "in the very recent past," *just* should be used with the perfect tense in formal contexts: □ *They have just arrived at the station.* Its use with the past tense in this sense (*They just arrived . . .*) is becoming more frequent but is avoided by many careful users in formal contexts.

Just may be used in place of, but not in addition to, *exactly:* □ *That's just* [not *just exactly*] *what I need.*

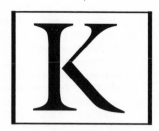

kaleidoscope This word is sometimes misspelled. Note particularly the *-ei-* and the first *o* from the Greek *eidos,* meaning "form."
• The correct pronunciation is [kălīdŏskōp].

karat see CARAT, KARAT, OR CARET?

kerb see CURB OR KERB?

key Some people object to the increasingly frequent use of the word *key* as an adjective, in the sense of "fundamental," "essential," "crucial," "most important," "indispensable," etc.: □ *key aide* □ *setting up a policy committee that will make key decisions* (*Sunday Times,* Aug. 23, 1987).
• In many contexts it is better replaced by one of its synonyms.

kid The use of the noun *kid* as a synonym for "child" or "young person" is best restricted to informal contexts: □ *Things were very different when I was a kid.* □ *One of the local kids broke the window.* □ *Have you got any kids?*

kilo The word *kilo,* pronounced [keelō], is most frequently used as an abbreviation for *kilogram:* □ *a kilo of sugar* □ *50 kilos of coal.*
• Some dictionaries also list *kilo* as an abbreviation for *kilometer,* but this usage is less frequent.

kilometer This word may be stressed on the first syllable [kilŏmeetĕr] or on the second syllable [kilomitĕr].
• Each of these pronunciations is widely accepted, but the second is probably becoming more current. See also METER OR METRE?; STRESS.

kindly The word *kindly* may be used as an adjective, meaning "kind" or "sympathetic," or as an adverb, meaning "in a kind way": □ *a kindly policeman* □ *a kindly smile* □ *They treated us kindly.*
• The adjective *kindly* has no one-word adverbial form: □ *He smiled in a kindly manner.*
    The adverb *kindly* is also used in polite or angry requests or commands: □ *Patrons are kindly requested to refrain from smoking.* □ *Kindly allow me to tell you what happened.* □ *Would you kindly take your hand off my knee!* In such contexts it is often better replaced with please.

kind of In formal contexts the phrases *kind of, sort of,* and *type of,* in which *kind, sort,* and *type* are in the singular, should be preceded by *this* or *that* (rather than *these* or *those)* and followed by a singular noun: □ *this kind of story* □ *that sort of biscuit.*
• Such expressions as *these kind of stories, those sort of biscuits,* etc., are sometimes heard in informal contexts but are disliked and avoided by careful users.
    A plural noun may be used if the expression is rephrased: □ *Sto-*

ries of this kind are very popular. Note that the verb agrees with *stories,* not *kind.*

Where more than one kind, sort, or type is concerned, the whole expression may be put into the plural: □ *She specializes in detective stories and horror stories: these kinds of stories are very popular.* In such cases, the noun that follows *kinds/sorts/types of* may remain in the singular: . . . *these kinds of story are very popular.* (Note that the verb here agrees with *kinds,* not *story.*)

The same principles apply to *kind of, sort of,* and *type of* in other contexts: □ *a different type of vegetable* □ *many different types of vegetable/vegetables.* See also **SINGULAR** OR **PLURAL?** Do not use *a* or *an* after the *of:* □ *a type of vegetable,* not *a type of a vegetable.*

The use of *kind of* or *sort of* in place of *rather* or *somewhat* is best restricted to informal contexts: □ *I sort of like him.* □ *It's kind of warm in here.* The spelling *kinda* is sometimes used in writing to denote "kind of" in casual speech.

kneeled or **knelt?** Either word may be used as the past tense and past participle of the verb *kneel. Knelt* is more frequent: □ *He knelt on the grass,* but *kneeled* is also seen.

• See also **-ED** OR **-T?**

knit or **knitted?** *Knitted* is the more frequent form of the past tense and past participle of the verb *knit,* especially in the literal sense: □ *I (have) knitted a sweater for the baby.* □ *She was wearing a knitted jacket.*

• *Knit,* an alternative form of the past tense and past participle, is largely restricted to figurative contexts, especially in combination with an adverb before a noun: □ *a closely knit family* □ *a well-knit story.*

know see **YOU KNOW.**

knowledgeable This word, meaning "having clear knowledge or understanding," is sometimes misspelled. Note that the final *e* of *knowledge* is retained before the suffix *-able.*

lacquer This word is sometimes misspelled. The word ends in *-er*, and not *-eur* as in *liqueur*.

laden or **loaded?** *Laden*, a past participle of the verb *lade*, is principally used as an adjective, meaning "weighed down" or "burdened"; *loaded* is the past tense and past participle of the verb *load*: □ *The tree was laden with apples.* □ *We overtook a heavily laden truck.* □ *He (has) loaded the car.* The verb *lade*, meaning "load with cargo," is rarely used in modern times in any other form, except in the term *bill of lading*.

• *Loaded* is also used as an adjective in literal and figurative senses: □ *a loaded gun* □ *a loaded question*, "one that contains hidden implications or is misleading."

The two adjectives should not be confused: □ *The van is laden with furniture* implies that the van is weighed down or full to overflowing with furniture; □ *The van is loaded with furniture* simply means that the van contains furniture.

lady see WOMAN.

laid, lain see LAY OR LIE?

lama or **llama?** The spelling of these words is sometimes confused. A *lama* is a Lamaist monk, the order of Lamaism being a form of Buddhism of Tibet and Mongolia. A *llama* is a South American mammal related to the camel. Note the double *l* at the beginning of this word.

lamentable This word has two pronunciations. The traditional pronunciation is [*lam*ĕntăbl].

• The stress may also fall on the second syllable [lămentăbl], although this is disliked and avoided by some users.

lasso A *lasso* is a rope with a noose, used for catching horses or cattle. There are two acceptable pronunciations, although the standard [lasō] is the more frequent.

• The second pronunciation [lasoo] is frequent in British English.

last To avoid ambiguity, the adjective *last* should be replaced, where necessary, with an appropriate synonym, such as *latest, final,* or *preceding:* □ *His latest* [not *last*] *novel was published in June.* □ *His final* [not *last*] *novel was published in June.* □ *The final* [not *last*] *chapter of the book contains a list of useful addresses.* □ *The preceding* [not *last*] *chapter of the book contains a list of useful addresses.*

• *Last* may be retained where the context makes its meaning clear: □ *His last novel was published posthumously.* □ *The identity of the narrator is not revealed until the last chapter.*

lather This word is pronounced to rhyme with gather. A pronunciation rhyming with *father* is becoming more frequent in contemporary British usage.

• [*lay*thĕr] is incorrect.

latter see FORMER OR LATTER?

launch The verb *launch* is widely used in the figurative sense of "set in motion," "start," or "introduce": □ *The campaign will be launched next month.* □ *They have just launched their new perfume.*

• *Launch* is also used figuratively as a noun: □ *He gave a party to celebrate the launch of his latest novel.*

Some people object to the frequency of this usage, replacing *launch* with an appropriate synonym wherever possible.

lavatory see TOILET, LAVATORY, LOO, OR BATHROOM?

lawful, legal, or **legitimate?** Each of these adjectives means "authorized by law," but there are differences of sense, usage, and application for them: □ *the lawful owner* □ *a legal contract* □ *a legitimate organization.*

• *Lawful* means "allowed by law" or "rightful"; it is largely restricted to formal contexts or set phrases, such as *one's lawful business.*

Legal is more widely used, having the additional meaning of "relating to law": □ *the legal profession* □ *legal advice* □ *the legal system* □ *legal action.*

The adjective *legitimate* is principally applied to children born in wedlock: □ *the king's legitimate son.* It also means "reasonable," "logical," "genuine," or "valid": □ *a legitimate excuse* □ *a legitimate reason.*

lay or **lie?** The verb *lay*, which is usually transitive—i.e., has an object—is often confused with *lie*, which is intransitive—i.e., does not have an object: □ *I'll lay the towel on the sand to dry.* □ *She's going to lie down for a while.*

• Careful users maintain the distinction between the two verbs in all contexts.

This confusion is probably due to the fact that the word *lay* also serves as the past tense of *lie*: □ *The baby lay in his crib and screamed.* □ *You'd better lay the baby in his crib.*

The past participle of *lie* is *lain;* the word *laid* (note the spelling) is the past tense and past participle of *lay:* □ *They have lain in the sun for too long.* □ *We (have) laid our coats on the bed.*

This verb *lie,* meaning "rest in a horizontal position," should not be confused with the unrelated verb *lie,* meaning "be untruthful." The past tense and past participle of the latter are regular: □ *He (has) lied about his age.* The present participle of these two verbs is *lying;* the present participle of the verb *lay* is *laying.*

The verb *lay* has a number of specific uses: □ *to lay eggs* □ *to lay the table* □ *to lay one's fears,* etc. The expression to *lay low,* meaning "to bring down," should not be confused with to *lie low,* meaning "to stay in hiding."

The verb *lay* is rarely used without a direct object, a notable exception being the sense of "produce eggs": □ *If the hens don't lay, there will be no eggs for breakfast.* The verb *lie* almost never has a direct object.

lead or **led?** These two words are often confused. *Lead* means "guide by going in front": □ *He was leading the walking party,* and is pronounced [leed]. The past tense of this verb is *led.* This is sometimes wrongly spelled as *lead,* because the pronunciation is the same as that of the metal: □ *as heavy as lead,* pronounced [led].

leading question A *leading question* suggests or prompts the expected or desired answer, such as: □ *Did you see the defendant stab his wife with a kitchen knife?* □ *Do you approve of the wholesale slaughter of innocent animals for their fur?*

• Many people object to the frequent use of the term with reference to questions that are challenging, unfair, embarrassing, etc.: □ *"Are there going to be any layoffs at the factory?" "That's a leading question."*

leak The use of the verb and noun *leak* with reference to the unofficial, surreptitious, or improper disclosure of secret information is acceptable in most contexts: □ *Details of the report were leaked to the press.* □ *The senator's secretary denied all responsibility for the leak.*

• The verb *leak* is used both transitively and intransitively in this sense: □ *He leaked the story.* □ *The story leaked out.*

leaned or **leant?** Either word may be used as the past tense and past participle of the verb *lean:* □ *She leaned/leant forward to open the window,* although *leaned* is more common.

• *Leaned* may be pronounced [leend] or [lent]; *leant* is always pronounced [lent]. See also -**ED** OR -**T?**

leaped or **leapt?** Either word may be used as the past tense and past participle of the verb *leap:* □ *They leaped/leapt across the ditch,* although *leapt* is more frequent (*lept* is a rare variation).

• Leaped may be pronounced [leept] or [lept]; *leapt* is always pronounced [lept]. See also -**ED** OR -**T?**

learn or **teach?** The use of the verb *learn* in place of *teach* is wrong: □ *He's teaching* [not *learning*] *me to swim.*

• To *learn* is to gain knowledge; to *teach* is to impart knowledge. See also **LEARNED** OR **LEARNT?**

learned or **learnt?** Either word may be used as the past tense and past participle of the verb *learn:* □ *Have you learned/learnt the words of the song?* The more frequent form is *learned.*

• The past tense and past participle *learned* may be pronounced [lernd] or [lernt]; it should not be confused with the two-syllable adjective *learned* [lernid], meaning "erudite": □ *a learned professor.* See also -**ED** OR -**T?**; **LEARN** OR **TEACH?**

leave or **let?** The use of the verb *leave* in place of *let,* especially in the expressions *let go* and *let be,* is regarded as incorrect and avoided by many users: □ *You mustn't let* [not *leave*] *go of the rope.* □ *I told the children to let* [not *leave*] *him be.* The expressions *leave alone* and *let alone,* however, are virtually interchangeable in the sense of "refrain from disturbing, bothering, interfering with, etc.": □ *Leave/Let the dog alone.*

• *Leave alone* also means "allow or cause to be alone," in which sense it cannot be replaced by *let alone:* □ *Please don't leave me alone—I'm afraid of the dark.*

Let alone is also used as a set phrase meaning "not to mention" or "still less": □ *They can't afford chopped beef, let alone steak.* See also **LET**.

led see LEAD OR LED?

leeward This word has two possible pronunciations. The generally accepted pronunciation is [*lee*wărd], but [loord] is common in nautical contexts.

legal see LAWFUL, LEGAL, OR LEGITIMATE?

legendary The use of the adjective *legendary* in the sense of "very famous or notorious" may be misleading or confusing: □ *the legendary Robin Hood helped the poor.* □ *Listening to recordings of the legendary Andrés Segovia during the 1930's* . . . *(Reader's Digest,* June 1987).
• The context of the second example makes it clear that Andrés Segovia existed in fact, not legend, but the first example is ambiguous.

legible or **readable?** The adjective *legible* describes something that can be deciphered and read; *readable* often describes something that may be read with interest, enjoyment, or ease: □ *legible handwriting* □ *a very readable novel.*
• *Readable* is also used as a synonym for "legible": □ *The text is barely readable without a magnifying glass.*
   See also ILLEGIBLE OR UNREADABLE?

legitimate see LAWFUL, LEGAL, OR LEGITIMATE?

leisure This word, meaning "time spent free from work," is sometimes misspelled. Note the *ei*, which does not conform to the usual "i before e" rule.
• *Leisure,* commonly pronounced [*lee*zhăr], is pronounced [*le*zhĕ] in British English.

lend or **loan?** The word *lend* is used only as a verb; *loan* is used principally as a noun: □ *He lent me his pen.* □ *Thank you for the loan of your lawn mower.* The use of *loan* as a verb is becoming increasingly acceptable, however, with reference to the lending of large sums of money, valuable works of art, etc.: □ *The bank will loan us the money we need to finance the new venture.* □ *This picture has been loaned to the gallery.*
• The use of the verb *lend* in place of *borrow* is wrong: □ *Can I borrow* [not *lend*] *your umbrella, please?* To *lend* is to give for temporary use; to *borrow* is to take for temporary use.

lengthwise or **lengthways?** Either word may be used as an adverb: □ *Fold the sheet lengthwise/lengthways before ironing it,* but *lengthwise* is more frequent.
• As an adjective, *lengthwise* is also preferred to *lengthways.* See also -WISE OR -WAYS?

lengthy The adjective *lengthy* means "tediously, excessively, or unusually long"; it should not be used in place of *long* as a neutral antonym for *short*: □ *The children became very restless during the principal's lengthy speech.* □ *She has long* [not *lengthy*] *hair and brown eyes.*
• *Lengthy* may be pronounced [*lenk*thi] or [*leng*thi]. Note the consonant sequence -*ngth*- in the spelling.

leopard This word is sometimes misspelled. The most frequent error is the omission of the *o*, which is not pronounced.

less see FEWER OR LESS?

let Used in the imperative, *let* should be followed by an object pronoun rather than a subject pronoun: □ *Let them try.* □ *Let him finish his meal first.* □ *Let Paul and me* [not *I*] *see the letter.*

• *Let's,* an informal contraction of *let us,* is used to introduce a suggestion or proposal made to the other member(s) of one's group: □ *Let's stay here.*

The preferred negative form of *let's* is *let's not,* although *don't let's* is also used in British English: □ *Lets not go to the party.* See also LEAVE OR LET?

letter writing There are a number of conventions relating to the style and layout of a formal or semiformal letter.

1 The sender's address, followed by the date, should appear at the top of the letter, usually in the right-hand corner. The recipient's name and address appear below this, on the left-hand side of the page. Punctuation of the address—no comma at the end of each line, no periods after the final line—is optional.

2 The salutation (*Dear Sir, Dear Madam, Dear Miss Jones, Dear Mr. Brown,* or, increasingly, *Dear James Chapman,* etc., where the writer wants to avoid the formality of *Dear Mr. Chapman* and the informality of *Dear James*) is set on a separate line, beginning with a colon (a comma in British English). See also ABBREVIATIONS; MS., MRS. OR MISS?

3 The letter itself should be divided into paragraphs, with or without indentation. The style and content of the letter depend on the level of formality.

4 The letter is closed with any of a number of fixed phrases, the most frequent being *Sincerely yours.* Like the salutation, this phrase is set on a separate line, beginning with a capital letter and ending with a comma, but it is often placed on the right-hand side of the page.

5 The signature is usually followed by the senders name, title, and office (if appropriate).

6 Some of these conventions also apply to informal letters: the position of the sender's address, the punctuation and layout of the salutation and closing phrase, etc. An informal letter may begin with the recipient's first name and end with any of a number of expressions, such as *Best wishes, Yours, Love,* etc. The recipient's name and address is usually omitted, and it is rarely necessary to add the sender's name after the signature.

leukemia This word is sometimes misspelled. Note the two sets of vowels: *eu* and *ia.* The British English spelling is *leukaemia.*

level The noun *level* serves a useful purpose in a variety of literal and figurative senses but is sometimes superfluous or unnecessarily vague: □ *a high level of unemployment* (high unemployment) □ *an increase in the noise level* (more noise) □ *decisions made at the management level* (decisions made by the management).

liable or **likely?** Each adjective is used to express probability, followed by an infinitive usually with *to. Liable* refers to habitual probability, often based on past experience; *likely* refers to a specific probability that may be without precedent: □ *The dog is liable to bite strangers.* □ *The dog is likely to bite you if you pull his tail.* □ *The shelf is liable to collapse when it is filled with books.* □ *The shelf is likely to collapse if it is filled with books.* Careful users maintain the distinction between the two words.

• The adjectives *apt* and *prone,* which are similar in sense and usage to *liable,* principally refer to disposition, inclination, or tendency: □ *He is apt/prone to lose his temper.*

Liable also means "responsible (for)" or "subject (to)": ☐ *She is liable for their debts.* ☐ *He is liable to epileptic attacks.* *Prone* is interchangeable with *liable* in the second of these senses: ☐ *She is prone to indigestion.* See also LIKELY.

liaison The noun *liaison* and its derived verb *liaise* are often misspelled; the most frequent error is the omission of the second *i*.
• Some people object to the widespread use of *liaison* and the more colloquial *liaise* as synonyms for "communication," "communicate," or "(maintain) contact," and the use of *liaison* to refer to an illicit sexual relationship: ☐ *Closer liaison between teachers and social workers might have prevented this tragedy.* ☐ *Overseas travel will be necessary to liaise with subsidiaries and distributors in Europe, South America, and the Far East.* ☐ *His wife found out about his liaison with his secretary.*

libel or **slander?** Each word refers to defamatory statements: *libel* is written, drawn, printed, or otherwise recorded in permanent form; *slander* is spoken or conveyed by gesture.
• In informal contexts *libel* is often used in place of *slander*.
Each word may be used as noun or verb. The final *l* of *libel* is not doubled before a suffix beginning with a vowel except in British English; the final *r* of *slander* is never doubled. See also SPELLING 1.

library The pronunciation of this word is [*lī*brări]. Careful users avoid dropping either *r*.

license or **licence?** The noun as well as the verb is spelled *license*: ☐ *a marriage license* ☐ *poetic license* ☐ *to license a driver* ☐ *(un)licensed driver* ☐ *license plate.* In British English, the noun is spelled *licence*.

lichen This word has two variant pronunciations [*lī*kĕn] or [*lī*tchĕn]. Most people prefer the first of these, which is the same pronunciation as for *liken*.

licorice There are two possible pronunciations of this word. The traditional pronunciation [*lik*ŏris] is preferred by some, but [*lik*ŏr-ish] is also acceptable and is more widely used. The British spelling is *liquorice*.

lie see LAY OR LIE?

lieu see IN LIEU.

lieutenant This word is often misspelled, the most frequent errors occurring in the first syllable: *lieu*-. The pronunciation of this syllable varies. The most frequent pronunciation is as in *loot*, in nautical contexts the pronunciation is as in *let*, and in British English, the pronunciation is as in *left*.

lifelong or **livelong?** The adjective *lifelong* means "lasting or continuing for a lifetime": ☐ *my lifelong friend* ☐ *his lifelong admiration for her work.* The adjective *livelong*, meaning "very long" or "whole," is chiefly used in the old-fashioned poetic expression *all the livelong day.*
• *Lifelong* is usually written as a solid compound, the hyphenated form *life-long* being an accepted but rare variant.
Livelong, which is etymologically unrelated to the word *live*, is pronounced [*liv*long].

life style Some people object to the frequent use of the term *life style*, a synonym for "way of life," by advertisers, journalists, etc.: ☐ *urban life style* ☐ *consumer life style values* ☐ *The spread of*

AIDS is likely to have tremendous effects on the personal life styles of many people.

• Kenneth Hudson (*The Dictionary of Even More Diseased English*) notes a connection between life style and possessions: "Cars, houses, vacations, clothes, and furniture have a great deal to do with 'life styles.' A naked savage living in a reed hut . . . would be allowed 'a way of life,' but not a 'lifestyle.'"

There is an increasing tendency for *life style* to be written as a one-word compound, *lifestyle*. It is sometimes hyphenated (*life-style*), especially when used adjectivally.

lighted or **lit?** Either word may be used as the past tense and past participle of the verb *light*. *Lighted* is perhaps the more frequent of the two. □ *Have you lighted the fire?* □ *He lighted his pipe.* □ *The hall was lighted by candles.*

• Used adjectivally before a noun, *lighted* is the preferred form: □ *a lighted torch* □ *a lighted match* □ *a lighted cigarette*. If the adjective is modified by an adverb, however, *lighted* may be replaced by *lit*: □ *a well-lit room* □ *a badly lit stage*.

lightning or **lightening?** These two words are often confused. *Lightning* is a flash of light produced by atmospheric electricity: □ *thunder and lightning*. *Lightning* is also used as an adjective to describe things that happen very quickly: □ *the lightning attack*. *Lightening* is the present participle/gerund of the verb *lighten*: □ *lightening someone's load*.

light-year A *light-year* is a unit of distance, not time; careful users avoid such expressions as: □ *It happened light-years ago.* □ *The wedding seemed light-years away.*

• A *light-year* is the distance traveled by light in a vacuum in one year (approximately 5.8 trillion miles); the term is used in astronomy.

likable or **likeable?** Either spelling of this word is acceptable, but *likable* is preferred. See SPELLING 3.

like The use of *like* as a conjunction, introducing a clause that contains a verb, is disliked by many users and is best avoided in formal contexts, where *as, as if,* or *as though* should be used instead: □ *The garden looks as if* [not *like*] *it has been neglected for many years.* □ *As* [not *like*] *the principal said, corporal punishment is not used in this school.*

• The use of *like* as a preposition, introducing a noun, pronoun, or noun phrase, is acceptable in all contexts: □ *The garden looks like a jungle.* □ *Like the principal, she disapproves of corporal punishment.* □ *His sister writes like him.* □ *Like you and me, they are amateur photographers.* (Note that the preposition *like* is followed by the object pronouns *him, me,* etc., not the subject pronouns *he, I,* etc.)

The use of *as* in place of the preposition *like* may change the meaning of the sentence: □ *As your father, I have a right to know.* □ *Like your father, I have a right to know.* □ *She plays like a professional.* □ *She plays as a professional.* In other contexts, the two prepositions may be virtually interchangeable: □ *He was dressed as/like a policeman.* □ *They treat me like/as an idiot.*

See also AS; SUCH AS OR LIKE?

likeable see LIKABLE OR LIKEABLE?

likely The adverb *likely*, meaning "probably," is not often used on its own in formal contexts; it is usually preceded by *very, quite, more,* or *most:* □ *They will very likely arrive tomorrow morning.* □ *I'll most likely see you at the party.*

• Some people avoid the problem by using *probably* or by rephrasing the sentence to make *likely* an adjective: □ They will probably arrive tomorrow morning. □ They are likely to arrive tomorrow morning.

As an adjective, *likely* may stand alone or be modified by an adverb: □ a likely effect □ a more likely explanation. See also LIABLE OR LIKELY?

limited Some people object to the use of the adjective *limited* as a synonym for "small," "little," "few," etc.: □ *a limited income* □ *with limited assistance* □ *of limited education.*

• *Limited* is best reserved for its original meaning of "restricted": □ Their powers are limited. □ We have a limited choice. □ He finds it difficult to work in a limited space.

lineage or linage? The noun *lineage*, pronounced [*lineeij*], means "line of descent" or "ancestry"; the noun *linage*, pronounced [*lĩnij*], means "number of printed or written lines": □ *the emperor's lineage* □ *payment based on linage.*

• Neither word is in frequent use: *lineage* is largely restricted to formal contexts, *linage* to the world of printing and publishing.

Lineage is also used as a variant spelling of *linage,* in which case it is pronounced [*lĩnij*].

linguist The noun *linguist* may denote a person who knows a number of foreign languages or a specialist in linguistics, the study of language. □ *Mr. Evans, an accomplished linguist, was a great help to us on our European tour.* □ *At yesterday's lecture, the linguist Noam Chomsky expounded his theory of language structure.*

• A *modern linguist* is someone who can speak or is studying modern languages such as French, German, and Spanish. Although the noun *linguist* is rarely ambiguous in context, it may be replaced, if necessary, by the synonym *polyglot* (for the first sense) or *linguistician* (for the second sense).

liquefy or liquify? Each spelling of this word is acceptable, although the first is generally preferred.

liqueur or liquor? The spellings of these words are sometimes confused. A *liqueur* [li*ker*] or, less commonly, [lik*yoor*] is a sweet alcoholic drink taken after a meal. *Liquor* [*lĩkĕ*] is any alcoholic beverage.

liquify see LIQUEFY OR LIQUIFY?
liquor see LIQUEUR OR LIQUOR?
lit see LIGHTED OR LIT?

literally The use of the adverb *literally* as an intensifier, especially in figurative contexts, is disliked by many users: □ *It literally rained all night.* □ *I was literally tearing my hair out by the time they arrived.*

• The effect of this usage may be misleading or ambiguous: □ We were literally starving, or quite absurd: □ She literally laughed her head off.

As the opposite of figuratively, *literally* may be used to indicate that a metaphoric expression is to be interpreted at its face value: □ The dog had literally bitten off more than it could chew.

literature Some people object to the use of the noun *literature*, with its connotations of greatness, to denote brochures, leaflets, and other written or printed matter: □ *They're sending us some literature about vacations in the Far East.*

• The principal objection is not that *literature* is an unnecessary synonym for some other noun—it has no one-word equivalent in general use for this sense—but "that so reputable a word should be put to so menial a duty" (H.W. Fowler, *A Dictionary of Modern English Usage*).

little see FEW; FEWER OR LESS?

live The adjective *live*, meaning "not prerecorded": □ *a live broadcast* □ *live music*, is increasingly used in the extended sense of "actually present": □ *They have never performed in front of a live audience.*

• This usage inevitably leads to humorous associations with the principal meaning of *live*—i.e., "living" or "alive"—in contrast to "dead." See also AID.

livelong see LIFELONG OR LIVELONG?

living room see LOUNGE.

llama see LAMA OR LLAMA?

loaded see LADEN OR LOADED?

loan see LEND OR LOAN?

loath, loth, or **loathe?** *Loath* and its rare variant *loth* are adjectives meaning "unwilling" or "reluctant"; *loathe* is a verb meaning "detest": □ *He was loath/loth to move.* □ *He loathes working in New York. Loath* and *loathe* are frequently confused: □ *Half the doctors polled did not recommend treatment for patients who cholesterol levels were above 240. . . . Some were loathe to intervene even when readings approached 300* (*Weight Watchers Magazine*, February 1989).

• The adjectives *loath* and *loth* are pronounced [lōth], with the final *th* sound of *bath*; the verb *loathe* is pronounced [lōdh], with the final *th* sound of *bathe*.

Note the spelling of the adjective *loathsome,* which may be pronounced [lodhsŏm] or sometimes [lothsŏm].

locate The verb *locate* and its derived noun *location* are best avoided where *find, situate, place, position,* etc., would be adequate or more appropriate: □ *I can't find* [not *locate*] *my keys.* □ *The shrub should be planted in a sheltered position* [not *location*]. □ *Offices in a prestigious part of the city* [not *a prestigious city location*].

longevity This word, meaning "long span of life," is usually pronounced [lonjevĭtee] although [longjevĭtee] is also frequently used.

• The pronunciation [longgevĭtee] is nonstandard.

longitude This word, referring to the distance west or east of the Greenwich meridian, may be pronounced with a *j*-sound [lonjitood] or occasionally with a *g*-sound [longgitood].

loo see TOILET, LAVATORY, LOO, OR BATHROOM?

look-alike The noun *look-alike* denotes someone who closely resembles another person, usually a famous person: □ *a Michael Jackson look-alike* □ *the Elvis look-alike competition.*

• *Look-alike* is sometimes written as a one-word compound, but the hyphenated form is more frequent.

loose or **loosen?** The verb *loose* means "release," "set free," or "undo"; the verb *loosen* means "make or become less tight": □ *She loosed the lion from its cage.* □ *He loosened his belt.* The two verbs are not interchangeable.

• The adjective *loose*, which means "free" or "not tight," may be applied to something that has been *loosened:* □ *The lion was loose.* □ *His belt was loose.*

The verb *loose* is less frequent in modern times. It is occasionally confused with the verb *lose,* which is similar in spelling and pronunciation (*loose* is pronounced [loos]; *lose* is pronounced [looz]).

lose see **LOOSE OR LOOSEN?**

lot The expressions *a lot (of)* and *lots (of)* are best avoided in formal contexts, where they may be replaced by *many, much, a great deal (of), a good deal (of),* etc.: □ *We have many* [not *lots of*] *books.* □ *They received a great deal of* [not *a lot of*] *help.*

• See also **MANY; MUCH; SINGULAR OR PLURAL?**

loth see **LOATH, LOTH, OR LOATHE?**

lots see **LOT.**

lounge The word *lounge* denotes a room with comfortable furniture in a hotel, theater, club, or airport: □ *Coffee will be served in the lounge.* □ *The passengers waited in the lounge.*

• In British English, the *lounge* of a private house or flat is the room used for relaxation, recreation, and the reception of guests, as opposed to the *dining room:* □ *She showed the visitors into the lounge.* Some people consider the synonyms *sitting room* and *living room* to be less pretentious than *lounge.*

The noun *parlor,* an old-fashioned synonym for *lounge,* is derived from the French verb *parler,* meaning "to speak": □ *The maid has tidied the parlor.* The word *parlor* also has a number of specific uses: □ *beauty parlor* □ *ice-cream parlor.*

The term *drawing room* (short for *withdrawing room*), another synonym, has connotations of grandeur and formality: □ *The ladies retired to the drawing room.*

Sitting room, living room, drawing room, and *dining room* are sometimes hyphenated or written as a single word.

low-key Some people object to the frequent use of the adjective *low-key,* meaning "of low intensity," in place of *modest, restrained, subdued, unassertive,* etc.: □ *The reception was a very low-key affair.*

• The variant *low-keyed* is also used from time to time.

low-profile see **PROFILE.**

lunch or **luncheon?** Each noun denotes a midday meal: a *luncheon* is usually a formal social occasion; *lunch* is often a light informal meal or a fuller meal at which business is conducted: □ *The First Lady was the guest of honor at the luncheon.* □ *We stopped at a fast-food place for lunch.* □ *They discussed the terms of the contract at their business lunch.*

• The use of *luncheon* as a synonym for "lunch" is generally considered to be old-fashioned, surviving only in such terms as *luncheon meat* and *luncheon invitation.*

luxuriant or **luxurious?** *Luxuriant* means "profuse," "lush," or "fertile"; *luxurious* means "sumptuous" or "characterized by luxury": □ *luxuriant vegetation* □ *a luxurious hotel.* The two adjectives are not interchangeable: *luxuriant* is principally applied to things that produce abundantly; *luxurious* to things that are very comfortable, expensive, opulent, self-indulgent, etc.

• The noun *luxury* is also used as an adjective, meaning "desirable but not essential": □ *luxury items*. Its use as a synonym for "luxurious," especially in advertisements: □ *a luxury car* □ *a luxury hotel*, etc., is disliked by some.

lying see LAY OR LIE?

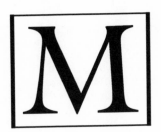

machinations This word, meaning "devious plots or conspiracies," is traditionally pronounced [*mak*inayshŏns], although the alternative pronunciation [*mash*inayshŏns] is becoming increasingly common.

macro- and **micro-** *Macro-* means "large"; *micro-* means "small." Each prefix is used in scientific and technical terms, such as: □ *macroeconomics* □ *microorganism* □ *macrobiotics* □ *microwave* □ *macrocosm* □ *microcosm* □ *macroscopic* □ *microscopic* □ *microprocessor* □ *microchip*. The use of *macro-* and *micro-* in other contexts, e.g. □ *macrocontract* □ *microskirt*, in place of the adjectives *large, great, small, tiny*, etc., is best avoided.

• The insertion of a hyphen between the prefix *macro-* or *micro-* and a word beginning with a vowel is optional: *macroeconomics* and *microorganism*, for example, may be replaced with *macroeconomics* and *micro-organism*. See also HYPHEN 1.

Madam or **Madame?** *Madam* is a polite term of address for a woman; the word may be written with a capital or lowercase *m:* □ *Would madam like a cup of coffee?* □ *Can I help you, Madam?* *Madame*, written with a capital *M*, is the French equivalent of *Mrs:* □ *Wax models of famous people are displayed at Madame Tussaud's* □ *Madame Bovary*.

• The usual English pronunciation of each word is [*mad*ăm]; *Madame* is pronounced [mă*dam*] or [mă*dahm*], Anglicized forms of the French pronunciation.

Madam is also used as an impersonal salutation in LETTER WRITING and as a formal title of respect: □ *Dear Madam* □ *Madam President*. In these uses the word is always written with a capital *M*.

Mesdames, the plural of the French word *Madame*, also serves as the plural form of *Madam*. It is usually pronounced [may*dahm*] in English.

The noun *madam* also denotes a woman who runs a brothel.

magic or **magical?** The adjective *magic* is more closely related to the art or practice of magic than *magical*, which is used in the wider sense of "enchanting": □ *a magic wand* □ *a magic potion* □ *a magic spell* □ *a magical experience* □ *the magical world of make-believe*.

• The two adjectives are virtually interchangeable in many contexts, although *magic* is retained in certain fixed expressions, such as: □ *magic carpet* □ *magic lantern*, etc., and *magical* is sometimes preferred for things that happen as if by magic: □ *a magical transformation*. *Magic*, but not *magical*, is also used in informal contexts to mean "wonderful": □ *The whole evening was magic!*

157

magnitude The noun *magnitude* is best avoided where *size, extent, importance, greatness,* etc., would be adequate or more appropriate: □ *the magnitude of the problem.*

• The expression *of the first magnitude* is used in astronomy to describe the brightness of a star; its figurative use, in the sense of "greatest" or "most important," is disliked by some people: □ *a disaster of the first magnitude.*

Mahomet see MOSLEM OR MUSLIM?

major Some people dislike the frequent use of the adjective *major* in place of *great, important, chief, principal, serious,* etc.: □ *There was certainly major news interest in the details of the background of a man convicted of murdering five members of his family (Daily Mail,* June 18, 1987).

• Although *major* is an accepted synonym for these words, it should not be used to excess.

majority and **minority** *Majority* means "more than half of the total number"; *minority* means "less than half of the total number": □ *the majority of the books* □ *a minority of his friends.*

• *Majority* and *minority* should not be used to denote the greater or lesser part of a single item: □ *the greater part* [not *the majority*] *of the house* □ *less than half* [not *the minority*] *of the meal.*

A *majority* may be as small as 51 percent; a *minority* may be as large as 49 percent. For this reason, *majority* and *minority* are best avoided where *most, a few,* etc., would be more appropriate.

Majority and *minority* may be singular or plural nouns. If the people or items in question are considered as a group, a singular verb is used; if they are considered as individuals, a plural verb is used: □ *Only a minority was in favor of the proposal.* □ *The majority have refused to pay.* See also COLLECTIVE NOUNS; SINGULAR OR PLURAL?

The two nouns also denote the difference between the greater and lesser numbers; in this sense they are always singular: □ *The Republican candidate's majority has increased.*

male or **masculine?** The adjective *male* refers to the sex of a person, animal, or plant; it is the opposite of *female:* □ *a male kangaroo* □ *male chauvinist. Masculine* is applied only to people (or their attributes) or to words (see GENDER); it is the opposite of *feminine:* □ *masculine strength.*

• With reference to people, *male* is used only of the sex that does not bear children; it is used to distinguish men or boys from women or girls but has no further connotations: □ *We have a male French teacher and a female German teacher.*

Masculine, on the other hand, may be used of both sexes; it refers to characteristics, qualities, etc., that are traditionally associated with men: □ *a masculine walk* □ *masculine clothes.*

The noun *male* is best reserved for animals and plants, *man* and *boy* being the preferred terms for male human beings, unless the question of age makes these nouns inappropriate: □ *Hemophilia is almost exclusively restricted to males.*

See also BOY; CHAUVINISM; MAN.

malevolent, malicious, or **malignant?** Each of these adjectives means "wishing harm to others," but there are differences of sense, usage, and application for them: □ *a malevolent look* □ *malicious gossip* □ *cruel, malignant intentions.*

- *Malignant* is the strongest of the three, describing an intense desire for evil. It is common in medical contexts, in the sense of "cancerous," "resistant to treatment," or "uncontrollable": □ *a malignant tumor.*

The adjectives *malevolent* and *malicious* are interchangeable in many contexts. *Malicious,* the more frequent, is also used in law with reference to premeditated or willful harm: □ *malicious intent* □ *malicious mischief.*

man Many people consider the use of the noun *man* as a synonym for "person" to be ambiguous and/or sexist: □ *the best man for the job* □ *All men are equal.* With reference to individual human beings of unspecified sex, it is usually possible to use *person, people, worker(s), citizen(s),* etc., in place of *man* or *men:* □ *the best person for the job* □ *All people are equal.*

- Idiomatic expressions, such as *the man in the street, to a man, as one man,* or *be one's own man,* and compounds, such as *manhole, manpower, man-made,* or *man-hour,* should not be changed but may be replaced with a synonym or paraphrase if necessary: □ *without exception* (for *to a man*) □ *be independent* (for *be one's own man*) □ *work force* (for *manpower*) □ *synthetic* (for *man-made*).

Some users also object to the verb *man,* preferring *operate, staff, work, run,* etc.

See also **BOY; CHAIR; GENTLEMAN; MALE** OR **MASCULINE?; MANKIND; SEXISM; WOMAN.**

manageable This word, meaning "able to be controlled": □ *manageable in small numbers,* retains the *-e-* to indicate the softness of the *g.*

mandatory The adjective *mandatory* is usually pronounced [*man*dătŏree].

- The British alternative pronunciation [man*day*tŏri] is disliked by most users and is best avoided.

Some people object to the frequent use of *mandatory* as a synonym for "compulsory," "obligatory," or "essential": □ *A degree in archeology is desirable, but not mandatory, for this job.*

maneuver This word is sometimes misspelled. Note the vowel sequence *-eu-* and the *-er* ending. In British English, the spelling is *manoeuvre.* The *-oe-* vowels were traditionally printed as a single letter *œ,* but this is not often seen nowadays.

- The derived adjective is maneuverable (in British English, *manoeuvrable*).

mankind The use of the noun *mankind* to denote human beings collectively may be confused with its second sense of "men in general" (as opposed to *womankind,* meaning "women in general"): □ *the future of mankind.*

- The word *humankind,* coined as a replacement for the first sense of *mankind,* is disliked by many users. *Humanity* may be ambiguous, having the additional meaning of "kindness," but *the human race* is acceptable to most: □ *the future of the human race.* See also **MAN.**

mantel or **mantle?** A *mantel* or, more commonly, a *mantelpiece* is a shelf forming part of an ornamental structure around a fireplace. A *mantle* is a cloak or something that covers: □ *shrouded in a mantle of secrecy.*

• The spelling *mantle* is also possible for the fireplace shelf but is much rarer.

many In formal contexts the adjective *many* may be used in place of the informal expressions *a lot (of)* and *lots (of)* (see **LOT**). *Many* is also used in informal contexts, especially in negative and interrogative sentences: □ *She doesn't buy many clothes.* □ *Have you got many pets?* In some positive sentences, however, *a lot of* and *lots of* are more idiomatic than *many* in informal contexts: □ *We have a lot of* [not *many*] *books.*

• *Many* denotes a large number (as opposed to *much,* which denotes a large amount: □ *There is much work to be done*); it is therefore used with a plural verb: □ *Many have disappeared.* □ *Many houses were destroyed*; however, in the idiomatic expressions *many a . . .* and *many's the . . .* a singular verb is used: □ *Many a child has dreamed of becoming a film star.* □ *Many's the time I've walked down this road.*

margarine The usual pronunciation of this word has a soft *g* [*mahr*jărin].

• The original pronunciation, with a hard *g*, as in *Margaret,* is now rarely used, even though it is more in keeping with the spelling and the etymology of the word.

marginal Some people object to the use of the adjective *marginal* as a synonym for "small" or "slight": □ *marginal changes* □ *a marginal improvement* □ *a marginal effect* □ *a student of marginal ability.*

• *Marginal* means "close to a margin or limit," sometimes with reference to a lower limit: □ *marginal profits* □ *a ceremony of marginal, not primary, importance.*

Marginal is also used to describe land on the edge of producing profitably.

masculine see **MALE OR MASCULINE?**

masterful or masterly? *Masterful* means "domineering"; *masterly* means "very skillful": □ *His masterful approach made him unpopular with the staff.* □ *West Germany reached the fifth World Cup final with a display of masterly efficiency* (*The Guardian,* May 26, 1986).

• The two adjectives relate to different senses of the noun *master,* from which they are both derived: "person in authority" (*masterful*) and "expert" (*masterly*).

Masterful is sometimes used in place of *masterly:* □ *a masterful performance by the soloist,* but many users prefer to maintain the distinction between the two words.

materialize The use of the verb *materialize* in place of *happen* or *turn up* is disliked by some users: □ *The threatened strike is unlikely to materialize.* □ *Her friends didn't materialize so we left without them.*

• In formal contexts the word is best restricted to its original meaning of "make or become real": □ *They watched in horror as the spirit materialized before their very eyes.*

mathematics see -**ICS**.

matrimony This word, describing the state of marriage, is sometimes mispronounced.

• The correct pronunciation is [*matri*mōnee] with the stress on the first syllable.

mattress Note the double *t* and the double *s* in this word, which is often misspelled.

maximal, maximize see MAXIMUM.

maximum The noun and adjective *maximum* refer to the greatest possible quantity, amount, degree, etc.: □ *a maximum of twenty guests* □ *the maximum dose.*

• The noun *maximum* has two plural forms, usually in technical contexts: *maximums* and *maxima.*

The adjective *maximum* is more frequent than its synonym *maximal.*

The verb *maximize* means "increase to a maximum"; it is best avoided where *increase* would be adequate or more appropriate: □ *The initial plan is to maximize sales of existing products.* Some people also dislike the use of *maximize* to mean "make maximum use of": □ *to maximize resources.*

may or **might?** *Might* is the past tense of *may* (see CAN OR MAY?): □ *She may win.* □ *May we sit down?* □ *I thought she might win.* □ *He said we might sit down.* In the last two examples, *might* cannot be replaced with *may.* In the first two examples, however, *might* can be substituted for *may* with a slight change of meaning: □ *She might win* expresses a greater degree of doubt or uncertainty than *She may win.* □ *Might we sit down?* is a more tentative request than *May we sit down?*

• *May* and *might* are also used in the perfect tense. *May have* expresses a possibility that still exists; *might have* expresses a possibility that no longer exists: □ *She may have won; I didn't hear the result.* □ *She might have won if she hadn't fallen.*

maybe or **may be?** *Maybe*, meaning "perhaps": □ *Maybe the letter will come tomorrow*, is often confused with the phrase *may be*, the verb *may* and the verb *be*: □ *It may be that she has missed the train.*

me see I OR ME?

me or **my?** see -ING FORMS.

mean see I MEAN.

meaningful The adjective *meaningful* should be avoided where *important, significant, serious, worthwhile*, etc., would be adequate or more appropriate: □ *a caring, loving, and meaningful relationship* □ *a meaningful experience.*

• *Meaningful* is best reserved for its literal sense of "having meaning": □ *meaningful utterances* □ *a meaningful smile* □ *a highly meaningful pause.*

means In the sense of "method," *means* may be a singular or plural noun; in the sense of "resources" or "wealth," it is always plural: □ *A means of reducing engine noise was developed.* □ *Several different means of transportation were used.* □ *His means are insufficient to support a large family.* See also SINGULAR OR PLURAL?

meantime or **meanwhile?** *Meantime* is chiefly used as a noun, in the phrases *in the meantime* and *for the meantime*; *meanwhile* is chiefly used as an adverb: □ *He wrote a letter in the meantime.* □ *We have enough for the meantime.* □ *Meanwhile, I had phoned the police.*

• *Meantime* may also be used as an adverb, in place of *meanwhile*, and *meanwhile* as a noun, in place of *meantime*, but these uses are less frequent. Use *meantime* as a single word except for the astronomical sense of *mean time,* written as two words.

media The word *media,* frequently used to refer to television, radio, newspapers, etc., as means of mass communication, is one of the plural forms of the noun *medium:* □ *The media act as publicity agents for writers.* □ *Television is an influential medium.*

• The plural of *medium* in the sense of "spiritual intermediary" is *mediums.* Either plural form may be used for other senses of the noun: "agency through which something is transmitted": □ *the mediums* [or *media*] *of air and water for transmitting sound,* "means of communication": □ *English and French are the media* [or *mediums*] *of instruction.*

The increasing use of *media* as a singular collective noun is unacceptable to many people and is best avoided: □ *Dr. Habgood . . . reminded him that perhaps the media was not the best forum for airing subtle points about the Incarnation* (The Guardian, July 5, 1984). *Media* is also used adjectivally in front of other nouns: □ *a media event* is an event that is deliberately created for extensive coverage by the mass media.

medieval or **mediaeval?** The two spellings of this word are acceptable. The spelling *medieval* is standard and now more frequent.

mediocre This word, meaning "of indifferent quality," is sometimes misspelled. Note the ending -*cre.*

• Some users object to such expressions as *quite mediocre* and *very mediocre,* since something either is or is not mediocre.

medium, mediums see MEDIA.

meet with The phrasal verb *meet with* has the sense of "experience" or "receive": □ *I hope he hasn't met with an accident.* □ *Does it meet with your approval?*

• The use of *meet with* in the sense of "have a meeting with" is frequent, but it is disliked by some: □ *We met with the managing director this morning.*

The phrasal verbs *meet up with* and, a less frequent term, *meet up* are regarded as unnecessary synonyms for "meet" and are best avoided, especially in formal contexts: □ *I met (up with) her at the theater.* □ *They met (up) in the park.*

mega- Some people object to the increasing use of the prefix *mega-,* meaning "great" or "large," in nontechnical contexts, as in: □ *megabuck* □ *mega-trend* □ *mega-merger* □ *mega-bid.*

• In science, the prefix *mega-* means "one million": a *megaton* is one million tons. In computer usage, the prefix *mega-* means 2^{20}: a *megabyte* is 1,048,576 bytes.

melted or **molten?** *Melted* is the past tense and past participle of the verb *melt;* it is also used as an adjective: □ *The chocolate (has) melted.* □ *Serve the asparagus with melted butter. Molten* is used only as an adjective, meaning "melted" or "liquefied": □ *molten iron* □ *molten rock.*

• The use of the adjective *molten* is restricted to substances that become liquid at very high temperatures.

mental The use of the adjective *mental* as a synonym for "stupid," "foolish," "mentally ill," "mentally deficient," etc., should be restricted to very informal contexts: □ *They must be mental to set off in such terrible weather.* □ *Her youngest son's a bit mental, and the other children tease him.*

• The principal meaning of *mental* is "of or involving the mind": □ *mental illness* □ *mental arithmetic.* The adjective is also used in the sense of "relating to disorders of the mind": □ *a mental hospital* □ *a mental patient.*

meretricious or **meritorious?** *Meretricious* means "superficially attractive" or "insincere"; *meritorious* means "having merit" or "praiseworthy": □ *meretricious glamour* □ *a meritorious deed.* Each adjective is fairly formal in usage.

• The adjective *meretricious* originally meant "of a prostitute"; like *meritorious,* it is ultimately derived from the Latin verb *merēre,* meaning "to earn" or "to deserve."

Note the spellings of the two words, particularly the second vowel: *meretricious* has the *e* of its Latin root; *meritorious* has the *i* of *merit.*

meta- Some people object to the increasing use of the prefix *meta-* in the sense of "transcending" or "of a higher order": □ *A suggestion of metafiction, of uncertainties found to be themselves fictionally productive* (*London Review of Books,* June 25, 1987).

• The prefix has a number of other accepted meanings: "change": □ *metamorphosis;* "after," "behind," or "beyond": □ *metatarsus.*

metal or **mettle?** These two words, which have the same pronunciation, are sometimes confused. A *metal* is one of a group of mineral substances that are good conductors of heat and electricity. *Mettle* means "strength of character": □ *He was given no chance to prove his mettle.*

• The confusion may arise from the fact that *mettle* was originally derived from *metal.*

metallurgy This word, meaning "the science of metals," is usually pronounced [met*ă*lŭrjee], although sometimes stressed on the second syllable [met*a*lŭjee].

metamorphosis The usual pronunciation of this word is [met*ă*morfōsis] with the stress on the third syllable.

• The alternative pronunciation [met*ă*mawfōsis] is possible but disliked by many people.

metaphors *Metaphors* are figures of speech in which a word or phrase is used, not with its literal meaning, but to suggest an analogy with something else. The comparison is implicit, not introduced by *like* or *as:* □ *the winds of change* □ *an icy voice* □ *stone deaf.*

• Many expressions used in everyday speech are metaphoric, but they are so frequently used that they are hardly thought of as metaphors: □ *the arm of a chair* □ *a branch of a bank,* and many occur in well-known idioms: □ *not up my alley* □ *feel under the weather* □ *if you play your cards right.*

Metaphors have been used very successfully with striking effect in literature. There are biblical examples: □ *Thy word is a lamp unto my feet* (Psalm 119:105) and countless poetic ones: □ *I see a lily on thy brow . . . and on thy cheek a fading rose* (Keats, *La Belle Dame Sans Merci*); however, as used by modern politicians and journalists, metaphors can often be tired and overworked: □ *the cure for unemployment* □ *fighting against inflation* □ *light at the end of the tunnel.*

Mixed metaphors, where two or more different metaphors are

used in one sentence, should be avoided: □ *In resurrecting these allegations, they are just fueling the flames of racism.* □ *The committee's task was to iron out all the bottlenecks in the system.*

meter or **metre?** A *meter* is a measuring instrument: □ *gas meter* □ *speedometer.* A *meter* is also the basic metric measurement of length and is used in derived measurements: □ *kilometer* □ *millimeter.* The British spelling of this sense is *metre.*

• *Meter* is also the technical term for the regular rhythmic arrangement of syllables in poetry. Note that in compounds describing such measures, the spelling *-meter* is also followed: □ *pentameter,* "a line having five stresses."

methodology The noun *methodology* denotes a body or system of methods, rules, principles, etc., used in a particular area of activity: □ *the methodology of teaching.*

• The use of the noun in other contexts, especially as a synonym for "method": □ *experimental design methodology* □ *unstructured pragmatic methodologies,* is disliked by many people and is best avoided.

meticulous The adjective *meticulous* is widely used and accepted as a synonym for "painstaking" or "scrupulous": □ *meticulous attention to detail* □ *a meticulous secretary.*

• Some people, however, object to the use of the adjective in a complimentary manner, restricting it to the pejorative sense of "fussy" or "excessively careful": □ *If you weren't so meticulous, you'd have finished the cleaning hours ago.*

Meticulous originally meant "timid," being ultimately derived from *metus,* the Latin word for "fear."

metre see METER OR METRE?

mettle see METAL OR METTLE?

mezzanine This word, meaning "intermediate story between two floors," is usually pronounced [*mez*ăneen]. The alternative [*mets*ăneen], is sometimes used and is closer to the original Italian.

• The last syllable in each pronunciation should rhyme with *keen* and not with *line.*

micro- see MACRO- AND MICRO-.

middle see CENTER OR MIDDLE?

midwifery This word is sometimes mispronounced. The perferred pronunciation is [mid*wif*ĕree].

• In an alternative pronunciation, *wif* may be pronounced like *wife.*

might see CAN OR MAY?; MAY OR MIGHT?

migraine The usual pronunciation of this word, meaning "a severe and recurrent headache," is [*mi*grayn].

• The alternative pronunciation [*mee*grayn] is also acceptable, especially in British English.

mileage or **milage?** *Mileage* is the more frequent spelling of this word, *milage* being a rare variant: □ *The exceptionally low mileage makes this car a good buy.* See also SPELLING 3.

• In its figurative sense of "benefit" or "usefulness," the noun is avoided by some users in formal contexts: □ *All the cars below have air bags. Buy one and add mileage to your life* (advertisement, *The New York Times,* Dec. 28, 1988)

militate or **mitigate?** The verb *militate,* which is usually followed by the preposition *against,* means "have a powerful influence or effect": □ *His left-wing opinions militated against his* *appointment.* The verb *mitigate* means "moderate" or "make less severe": □ *mitigating circumstances* □ *The judge's decision did little to mitigate the suffering of the bereaved parents.*

• The two verbs are occasionally confused, *mitigate* being wrongly used in place of *militate.*

millennium This word is often misspelled, the most frequent error being the omission of the second *n*: □ *Over the millenia, as earth movements cause new formations* (*Readers Digest* advertisement for *Marvels and Mysteries of the World around Us,* 1987).

• Spelling mistakes may be avoided by associating the word, which means "a thousand years," with the double *l* of *milligram* and *millimeter* (from Latin *mille,* "thousand") and the double *n* of *annual* and *perennial* (from Latin *annus,* "year").

millionaire The word *millionaire* is sometimes misspelled. It has a double *l* but only one *n.*

mimic This word, meaning "imitate": □ *He likes mimicking the teachers,* is sometimes misspelled. Note that a *k* is added before the suffixes *-ed, -ing,* and *-er. Mimicry* does not, however, have a *k.* See also SPELLING 1.

miniature *Miniature,* meaning "small in size," is sometimes misspelled. Note the spelling *-iat-.*

minimal, minimize see MINIMUM.

minimum The noun and adjective *minimum* refer to the smallest possible quantity, amount, degree, etc.: □ *a minimum of four employees* □ *the minimum requirements.*

• The noun *minimum* has two plural forms, usually in technical contexts: *minimums* or *minima.*

The frequent use of *minimal* in the sense of "very small" is disliked by some users: □ *The response to our advertisement was minimal—we received only two applications.* □ *minimal effort.* The verb *minimize* means "reduce to a minimum"; it is best avoided where *reduce* would be adequate or more appropriate: □ *The new safety regulations should minimize the danger.* Some people also object to the widely accepted use of *minimize* to mean "play down" or "belittle": □ *to minimize one's achievements.*

minority see MAJORITY AND MINORITY.

minus The use of the preposition *minus* in the sense of "without" or "lacking" is best restricted to informal contexts: □ *She came home minus her umbrella.*

• Some people also avoid using the noun *minus* as a synonym for "disadvantage" in formal contexts: □ *Having to move is one of the minuses of my new job.* See also PLUS.

minuscule This word is often misspelled, the most frequent error being the substitution of an *i* for the first *u.* The word is pronounced [minŭskyool].

minutiae The plural noun *minutiae,* meaning "small, minor, or trivial details," may be pronounced [minewshiee] or [minew-shiī]: □ *The minutiae of the problem are of no interest to me.*

• *Minutia,* the singular form of the noun, is rarely used.

The noun *minutiae* is best avoided where *details* would be more appropriate: □ *discuss the details* [not *minutiae*] *of the contract.*

Note the spelling of *minutiae,* particularly the three final vowels *-iae.*

miscellaneous This word, meaning "of a variety of items," is sometimes misspelled. Note particularly the *sc* and the *-eous* ending.

mischievous The correct pronunciation of this word is [mis*chiv*ŭs].
- The mispronunciations [mis*cheev*ŭs] and [mis*cheev*iŭs] are heard from time to time but are avoided by careful speakers. The word is often misspelled: particular attention should be paid to the order and position of the vowels.

Miss see MS., MRS. OR MISS?

misspelled or **misspelt?** *Misspelled* is the past tense and past participle of the verb *misspell:* □ *You have misspelled my name.* An occasionally used variant is *misspelt.*
- See also -ED OR -T?
    Misspelled may be pronounced [mis*speld*] or [mis*spelt*]; *misspelt* is always pronounced [mis*spelt*].
    Note the spellings of the two words, particularly the double *l* of *misspelled* and the double *s* of each word.

mistrust see DISTRUST OR MISTRUST?

misuse see ABUSE OR MISUSE?

mitigate see MILITATE OR MITIGATE?

mix Some people object to the increasing use of the noun *mix* in place of *range:* □ *A wide mix of subjects will be taught at the college.*
- In the sense of "combination" or "mixture," *mix* is found in compounds such as *sound mix,* "the various sounds that are coordinated in a recording or live performance." Some users, however, object to its use in formal contexts.

moccasin This word, used to describe a soft leather shoe without a heel, is sometimes misspelled. Note the double *c* but single *s.*

modern or **modernistic?** The adjective *modern* means "of the present time" or "contemporary"; *modernistic* means "characteristic of modern trends, ideas, etc.," and is sometimes used in a derogatory way: □ *modern society* □ *modernistic architecture.*
- *Modern* has a wider range of sense and usage than *modernistic,* which is largely restricted to objects, designs, thoughts, etc., that are conspicuously modern or unconventional.

modus vivendi The Latin phrase *modus vivendi* is principally used in English to denote an arrangement or compromise between conflicting parties: □ *This modus vivendi enabled them to complete the job without further disruption.*
- The literal meaning of the phrase *modus vivendi* is "way of living," but some people object to its use in place of the English expression *way of life.*
    The word *modus* is pronounced [*mō*dŭs]; *vivendi* may be pronounced [vi*ven*dee] or sometimes [vi*ven*dī].

Mohammed see MOSLEM OR MUSLIM?

molten see MELTED OR MOLTEN?

momentary or **momentous?** *Momentary* means "lasting for a very short time"; *momentous* means "of great significance": □ *a momentary lapse* □ *a momentous decision.*
- The two adjectives relate to different senses of the noun *moment,* from which they are derived: "a very short time" (*momentary*) and "significance" (*momentous*).
    Note the difference in stress between the two adjectives: *momentary* is stressed on the first syllable, *momentous* on the sec-

ond. The adverb *momentarily* should also be stressed on the first syllable [*momĕntĕrĕlee*]; the variant pronunciation [mōmĕn*terri*-lee] is unacceptable to some people.

mongoose The plural of the noun *mongoose* is *mongooses;* the word should not be treated as a compound of the noun *goose* (the plural of which is *geese*).
• *Mongoose* is derived from the word *mangūs*, of Indian origin, and is etymologically unrelated to *goose*.

moot The adjective *moot*, meaning "debatable" or a newer sense of "merely academic," rarely occurs outside the fixed phrase *a moot point:* □ *Whether she will accept this offer is a moot point.*
• The verb *moot*, meaning "put forward for debate," is most frequently used in the passive in formal contexts: □ *The subject was mooted at our last meeting.*

moral or **morale?** These two spellings are sometimes confused. *Moral* means "concerned with the principles of right and wrong": □ *the gradual erosion of moral standards. Morale* is the extent of confidence and optimism in a person or group: □ *After the election defeat, the party's morale sank to an all-time low.*
• *Moral* is stressed on the first syllable [*morăl*]. *Morale* is stressed on the second syllable [mo*ral*].

more The adverb *more* is used to form the comparative of a number of adjectives and adverbs: □ *She is more intelligent than her sister.* □ *The trains run more frequently in the summer months. More* should not be used with adjectives that already have the comparative ending *-er*, such as *happier, older,* etc.
• Other uses of the word *more*—as the comparative of *much* or *many*, or in the sense of "further" or "additional"—may lead to confusion: □ *She has more beautiful dresses* may mean "Her dresses are more beautiful (than mine/yours/etc.)," "She has other dresses that are more beautiful (than this one)," "She has a greater number of beautiful dresses (than you/me/etc.)," or "She has other beautiful dresses (in addition to this one)."

The phrase *more than one,* although it implies a plural subject, is used with a singular verb: □ *More than one accident has happened at this intersection.* If the sentence is reworded, however, a plural verb is used: □ *More accidents than one have happened at this intersection.*

See also **COMPARATIVE** AND **SUPERLATIVE; SINGULAR** OR **PLURAL?**

mortgage This word is sometimes misspelled, the most frequent error being the omission of the silent *t*.

Moslem or **Muslim?** The preferred spelling for a follower of the Islamic faith is *Moslem*, rather than the newer spelling *Muslim*.
• *Moslem* is pronounced [*mahz*lem]; *Muslim* is pronounced [*muuz*lim] or [*muz*lim].

The most accepted spelling of the name of the prophet of Islam is *Mohammed*, rather than *Muhammad* or *Mohomet*.

most The adverb *most* is used to form the superlative of a number of adjectives and adverbs: □ *This is the most expensive picture in the shop.* □ *The prize will be awarded to the child who writes the most imaginatively. Most* should not be used with adjectives that already have the superlative ending *-est*, such as *saddest, youngest,* etc.

• Other uses of the word *most*—as the superlative of *much* or *many*, or in the sense of "very"—may cause ambiguity: □ *This teacher has the most intelligent pupils* may mean "This teacher has the greatest number of intelligent pupils" or "This teacher's pupils are the most intelligent"; □ *She danced most gracefully* may mean "She danced very gracefully" or "She danced more gracefully than the other dancers." See also COMPARATIVE AND SUPERLATIVE.

The use of *most* in place of *very* is generally best avoided, although it is acceptable in certain contexts: □ *I am most grateful for your assistance.* □ *He spoke most rudely of his former employers.*

The adverb *mostly*, meaning "mainly" or "usually," should not be confused with *most*: □ *He writes mostly* [not *most*] *for children.* □ *Old people are most* [not *mostly*] *at risk.* In some contexts the substitution of *most* for *mostly*, or vice versa, changes the meaning of the sentence: □ *Our friends are mostly helpful.—Our friends are most helpful.* □ *The shop sells most books.—The shop sells mostly books.*

motif or **motive?** These words are sometimes confused. A *motif* is a recurrent feature that establishes a pattern throughout a work of art, etc.: □ *a design with a feather motif.* A *motive* is a reason for a course of action: □ *no apparent motive for the crime.*

motivation The use of the noun *motivation*, which means "incentive" or "drive," in place of *reason* or *motive* is disliked and avoided by many users: □ *his reason* [not *motivation*] *for deserting his wife and family.*

• Some people also object to the frequent use of the noun in its accepted sense of "providing with an incentive" in the context of industrial psychology: □ *the motivation of the work force.* As Roland Gribben remarked in the *Daily Telegraph* (June 30, 1987): "Motivation is a grossly overworked and abused term for getting the best or more out of people."

Similar objections may be applied to the use of the verb *motivate* in place of *cause* and of *motivated* as a synonym for "keen": □ *an action that may cause* [not *motivate*] *her to change her mind* □ *a highly motivated sales manager.*

motive see MOTIF OR MOTIVE?

movable or **moveable?** This word has two different spellings. Each is acceptable although the first spelling *movable*, which omits the *e* before the suffix *-able*, is more frequent in contemporary usage.

• See also SPELLING 3.

mowed or **mown?** Either word may be used as the past participle of the verb *mow*: □ *Have you mowed/mown the grass yet?*

• When the participle is used as an adjective, *mown* is preferred to *mowed*: □ *a neatly mown lawn* □ *new-mown hay.*

The past tense of the verb *mow* is always *mowed*: □ *I mowed the grass yesterday.*

Mr. see MS., MRS., OR MISS?

Ms., Mrs., or **Miss?** *Ms.*, *Mrs.*, and *Miss*, shortened forms of the archaic title *Mistress*, are used before the names of girls and women, according to age and marital status, in letter writing and as polite terms of address.

• *Miss* is traditionally used for girls, unmarried women, and married women who have retained their maiden name: □ *Miss Mary Baker* □ *Miss Davies* □ *Miss Elizabeth Taylor*. In formal contexts, two or more girls or unmarried women with the same surname should be referred to as *the Misses Brown/Smith*/etc. rather than *the Miss Browns/Smiths*/etc.

Mrs., pronounced [*misiz*], is used before a woman's married name: □ *Mrs. Anne Johnson* □ *Mrs. Peter Johnson* □ *Mrs. Johnson.*

Ms., pronounced [*miz*], is used before the name of a woman of unknown or unspecified marital status. It was introduced as a feminine equivalent of the masculine title *Mr.*, which makes no distinction between married and unmarried men. Because of feminist associations, however, the title *Ms.* is disliked by some people. *Ms.* is most frequently used in place of *Miss* but is best avoided when referring to elderly unmarried women or young girls. See also SEXISM.

The titles *Ms., Mrs.,* and *Mr.* are usually written with a period. See also ABBREVIATIONS.

much The use of the adjective *much* in positive sentences is best restricted to formal contexts: □ *They own much land.* □ *There is much work to be done.*

• Even in formal contexts, some users prefer to replace *much* with *a large amount of, a great deal of,* etc.: □ *They own a large amount of land.* □ *There is a great deal of work to be done.*

In informal contexts, *much* may be replaced with *a lot of* or *lots of:* □ *There is a lot of work to be done.* See also LOT.

In negative and interrogative sentences, *much* is acceptable in all contexts: □ *They don't own much land.* □ *Is there much work to be done?*

See also MANY; VERY.

mucous or **mucus?** These two words are sometimes confused. *Mucous* is the adjective from the noun *mucus; mucus* is the secretion produced by *mucous membranes.*

Muhammad see MOSLEM OR MUSLIM?

multi- Some people object to the increasing use of the prefix *multi-*, meaning "many," to coin new adjectives that are often better expressed by a paraphrase: □ *a multiuse device* □ *a multistage process* □ *multilateral decisions.*

• In neologisms of this kind, a hyphen is sometimes inserted between the prefix and the word to which it is attached.

Muslim see MOSLEM OR MUSLIM?

must The auxiliary verb *must* expresses obligation, compulsion, necessity, resolution, certainty, etc.: □ *We must obey the rules.* □ *They must go.* □ *I must finish writing this letter.* □ *You must be very thirsty.* In other tenses, and in the negative, *must* is usually replaced by *have to*: □ *We had to obey the rules.* □ *They don't have to go.*

• The negative form *must not* (or *mustn't*) expresses prohibition: □ *They must not go.*

The past tense *must have* is used only to express certainty: □ *You must have been very thirsty.*

The use of *must* as a noun, meaning "something necessary or essential," is best restricted to informal contexts: □ *Waterproof clothing is an absolute must for a sailing trip.*

mustache This word is sometimes misspelled. The most frequent error is the substitution of *ou* for *u*. The British English spelling, however, is *moustache*. Note also the *-che* ending.

mutual, common, or **reciprocal?** A *mutual* action or emotion is done or felt by each of two or more people to or for the other(s): □ *mutual help / destruction / admiration / hatred / etc.* □ *The feeling is mutual.*

• The adjective *mutual* is superfluous in such phrases as: □ *a mutual agreement* □ *a mutual exchange* □ *their mutual love for each other.*

The frequent use of *mutual* in place of *common*, meaning "shared" or "joint," is disliked by many users: □ *a mutual friend* □ *mutual interests* □ *a mutual problems*; however, the other senses of *common* can cause ambiguity: □ *a common friend* may mean "an unsophisticated or rude friend" as well as "a friend shared by two people." Thus, expressions such as □ *our joint friend* □ *the friend we have in common* □ *the friend we share* should be used instead.

Reciprocal and *mutual* are synonymous in the principal sense of the latter: □ *reciprocal help* □ *reciprocal hatred*. *Reciprocal* can also be used to describe an action or emotion that is done or felt in return: □ *He praised her new novel, and she expressed reciprocal admiration for his latest film.*

my or **me?** see -ING FORMS.

myself The use of the pronoun *myself* for emphasis is acceptable to most users but disliked by some: □ *I disapprove of such behavior myself.* □ *I myself have never met her.*

• *Myself* should not be used in place of *I* or *me* in the following sentences and similar constructions: □ *My sister and I* [not *myself*] *will do the gardening.* □ *The bill was paid by Richard and me* [not *myself*]. See also I OR ME?; SELF.

mythical or **mythological?** *Mythical* means "imaginary"; *mythological* means "of mythology": □ *a mythical danger* □ *a mythological kingdom.*

• Each adjective means also "of a myth or myths," in which sense they are virtually interchangeable: □ *a mythical/mythological character.*

naïve, naive, or **naïf?** This word, meaning "innocent" or "credulous," is most commonly spelled *naïve* or *naive*.

• *Naïf*, the French masculine adjective, is no longer used, *naïve* (or *naive*) being used to describe people of both sexes.

The derived noun is most commonly spelled *naïveté* or *naivety*, although the variants *naiveté* and *naïvety* are also found.

Naïve is pronounced [nīeev] or [naheev]. *Naïveté* is pronounced [naheevtay].

naked or **nude?** A person wearing no clothes at all may be described as *naked* or *nude:* □ *pictures of naked/nude men.*

• The adjective *naked,* however, has a wider range of usage and application than *nude,* which is largely restricted to artistic or pornographic human nakedness or to nudism: □ *nude photography* □ *nude sunbathing* □ *a naked* [not *nude*] *body buried in a shallow grave* □ *naked* [not *nude*] *children playing in the sand.*

Naked is also used as a synonym for "bare" or "uncovered" in other contexts: □ *a naked flame* □ *the naked truth.*

naphtha This word, meaning "petroleum," is sometimes misspelled. Note particularly the *phth.*

• Note also the spellings of the compounds *naphthalene* and *naphthene.*

nation see COUNTRY OR NATION?

naturalist or **naturist?** A *naturalist* is a person who studies animals and plants or an advocate of naturalism (in art, literature, philosophy, etc.); a *naturist,* more frequent in British English, is a nudist: □ *Naturalists will appreciate the flora and fauna of the island.* □ *Naturists can take advantage of its secluded beaches.*

nature Such phrases as *of this/that nature* and *in the nature of* are often better replaced by more concise or less vague expressions: □ *Crimes like that* [for *of that nature*] *should be severely punished.* □ *This new method of assessment is like* [for *in the nature of*] *an examination.*

• The word *nature* is used in other unnecessary circumlocutions: □ *a problem of a difficult nature* is *a difficult problem* □ *a remark of a flippant nature* is *a flippant remark,* etc.

naturist see NATURALIST OR NATURIST?

naught or **nought?** *Naught* means "nothing" and is used in idiomatic expressions such as *set at naught,* "consider unimportant," and *come to naught,* "produce no successful results": □ *All our plans came to naught.* It is also used to represent the figure *0* (zero): □ *The number 100 has two naughts,* although some prefer the variant spelling *nought* for the sense of "zero."

nauseous The use of the adjective *nauseous* in the sense of "nauseated" or "suffering from nausea" is becoming acceptable but is best avoided in formal contexts: □ *I feel sick* [not *nauseous*].

• The principal meaning of *nauseous* is "nauseating" or "causing nausea": □ *a nauseous smell*.

naval or **navel?** These two words are sometimes confused. *Naval* is used to describe something connected with a navy: □ *a naval officer* □ *naval warfare*. The *navel* is the small depression in the middle of the abdomen where the umbilical cord was formerly attached.

nearby or **near by?** There is often confusion as to whether this term should be one word or two. *Nearby* is the preferred form for both adjectival and adverbial senses: □ *nearby towns*; *near by* is rarely used.

necessarily There are two possible pronunciations for this word. In the traditional pronunciation, the first syllable is stressed [nesĕsĕrĕlee], but this is very difficult to say unless one is speaking slowly and carefully. Many users prefer the alternative pronunciation, which has the main stress on the third syllable [nesĕserrălee].

necessary This word, meaning "essential," is often misspelled. Note the single *c* and double *s*.

neé *Née,* the feminine form of the French word for "born," is used to indicate the maiden name of a married woman: □ *Mrs. Susan Davies, née Eliot.*

• The pronunciation of *née,* which is sometimes written without an accent, is [nay].

Née should not be used to indicate a man's original name or pseudonym or a remarried woman's previous married name: □ *Ringo Starr, born* [not *née*] *Richard Starkey* □ *Jacqueline Onassis, formerly* [not *née*] *Jacqueline Kennedy.*

need *Need* may be used as a full verb, in the sense of "require" or "be obliged," or as an auxiliary verb, indicating necessity or obligation: □ *We need help.* □ *Your daughter needs to wear glasses.* □ *He need not leave.* □ *Need she reply?*

• The use of *need* as an auxiliary verb is indicated by the absence of *-s* in the third person singular and the omission of *to* in the following infinitive.

The auxiliary verb *need,* in fact, is used only in questions and negative sentences (see the last two examples above) and in certain constructions that have negative force, such as: □ *All she need buy is food.* □ *He need do no more than wait.* □ *You need only ask.* □ *Nobody need suffer.*

The full verb *need* may also be used in questions and negative sentences: □ *He doesn't need to leave.* □ *Does she need to reply?* In the sense of "require," *need* is followed by the *-ing* form of the verb or by a past participle preceded by *to be,* not by the past participle alone: □ *This shirt needs washing* [not *washed*]. □ *This shirt needs to be washed.*

needless to say The idiomatic expression *needless to say* is frequently used for emphasis, especially in informal contexts: □ *Needless to say, the unions intend to campaign against the proposed legislation.*

• The expression is disliked by those who choose to interpret it literally, but it is acceptable to most people.

negative A negative word is one that is used to deny or contradict something. Words such as *no, not, nobody, never,* and *nothing* make the clause in which they appear a negative one. Care must be taken as to where a negative word is placed in a sentence. □ *She didn't explain definitely* does not have the same meaning as: □ *She definitely didn't explain.* Usually the negative word is placed with the clause whose truth is being denied: □ *He said he had never been there.*

• The exception is with verbs such as *believe, think, expect, imagine,* etc., where the negative word is generally placed beside the verb: □ *I dont think you know what you're talking about.* □ *She didn't expect them before dark.*

The adjective *negative* is now often used in a very general way to mean not only "lacking in positive features," but also "pessimistic; unenthusiastic": □ *You're taking a rather negative view.* □ *I felt very negative about all his suggestions.*

neglectful, negligent, or **negligible?** *Neglectful* and *negligent* mean "careless" or "heedless"; *negligible* means "very small," "trivial," or "insignificant": □ *a neglectful mother* □ *a negligent driver* □ *a negligible effect.*

• The adjectives *neglectful* and *negligent* are not completely synonymous: *negligent* often implies habitual or more serious neglect or negligence, which may be punishable by law.

Note the spelling of *negligible,* especially the two *i's.*

Negress, Negro see BLACK.

neither As an adjective or pronoun, *neither* is used with a singular verb: □ *Neither towel is clean.* □ *Neither of the towels is* [not *are*] *clean.*

• In the *neither . . . nor* construction, a singular verb is used if both subjects are singular, and a plural verb is used if both subjects are plural: □ *Neither his brother nor his sister has* [not *have*] *been invited.* □ *Neither his parents nor his friends have been invited.*

The use of a plural verb with the pronoun *neither* or with singular subjects in a *neither . . . nor* construction is avoided by careful users, especially in formal contexts, but nevertheless occurs with some frequency: □ *Neither the coal industry nor British Rail are likely to be privatized in the short term* (*Daily Telegraph,* June 3, 1987).

When a combination of singular and plural subjects occurs in a *neither . . . nor* construction, the verb traditionally agrees with the subject that is nearer to it: □ *Neither his brother nor his parents have been invited.* □ *Neither his friends nor his sister has been invited.* The same principle is applied to singular subjects that are used with different forms of the verb: □ *Neither you nor he has* [not *have*] *been invited.* □ *Neither my husband nor I have* [not *has*] *been invited.* If the resulting sentence sounds awkward or unidiomatic it may be reordered or rephrased.

The alternatives presented in a *neither . . . nor* construction should be grammatically balanced: □ *She traveled neither by boat nor train* may be changed to: □ *She traveled neither by boat nor by train* or: □ *She traveled by neither boat nor train.*

As a pronoun, *neither* should be used only of two alternatives: □ *There are two cars outside, but neither is mine.* □ *None* [not *Neither*] *of the three candidates arrived on time.* The use, however, of the *neither . . . nor* construction with three or more subjects is acceptable to some people: □ *They eat neither meat nor fish nor eggs.*

The first syllable of *neither* may be pronounced to rhyme with *tree* or *try.* The pronunciation [needhĕr] is more frequent.

See also DOUBLE NEGATIVE; EITHER; NOR.

nephew There are two different pronunciations for this word. In American English, [nefĕw] is standard, while in British English, [nevĕw] is also heard.

never The use of *never saw/took/went/*etc. in place of *did not see/take/go/*etc., usually for emphasis, is avoided by careful users in all but a few informal spoken contexts: □ *I never said a word! Never* means "at no time" and should not be used when referring to a single occasion: □ *I never met his wife.* □ *I did not meet his wife in town yesterday.*

• *Never* is sometimes used informally as a substitute for a simple negative when expressing surprise: □ *He never expected that to happen.* □ *We never thought it would work.* □ *I never knew you could play the guitar.*

nevertheless see NONETHELESS OR NEVERTHELESS?

next or **this?** The adjective *this* is often used in place of *next* with reference to days of the current week, months of the current year, etc.: □ *I'm not going to the club this Friday.* □ *She's getting married this September.*

• As a result, the use of *next* in similar contexts may lead to ambiguity or confusion: the phrase *next Friday,* used on a Tuesday, for example, may mean "three days from now" or "ten days from now."

nice The adjective *nice,* in the sense of "pleasant," "agreeable," "kind," "attractive," etc., is often better replaced with an appropriate synonym, especially in formal contexts: □ *an attractive* [not *nice*] *garden* □ *a pleasant* [not *nice*] *afternoon.*

• In the sense of "subtle" or "precise," *nice* is acceptable in all contexts: □ *a nice distinction.*

Nice is ultimately derived from the Latin adjective *nescius,* meaning "ignorant"; it was originally used in the now-obsolete sense of "foolish."

niche This word may be pronounced to rhyme with *pitch* or *leash.*

• The second of these pronunciations is closer to the French origin, but the Anglicized [nich] is the more frequent.

no see NO ONE OR NO-ONE?; YES AND NO.

nobody see NO ONE OR NO-ONE?

noisome The adjective *noisome* means "offensive" or "noxious"; it has no connection, etymological or otherwise, with the noun *noise:* □ *a noisome smell.*

• *Noisome* is derived from the verb *annoy.* It is largely restricted to formal contexts.

non- The prefix *non-* is used to form a simple or neutral antonym of the word to which it is attached: □ *a nonprofessional golfer* □ *non-Christian religions.*

• The prefix *un-,* attached to the same words, may have stronger negative force: an *unprofessional* or *un*-Christian act, for example, violates professional ethics or Christian principles.

Many people object to the frequent use of the prefix *non-* to coin unnecessary antonyms: □ *nonpresence* (for *absence*) □ *nonper-*

manent (for *temporary*) □ *nonsuccess* (for *failure*) □ *nonobligatory* (for *optional*).

See also HYPHEN 1; INFLAMMABLE.

none The use of a singular or plural verb with the pronoun *none* depends on the sense and context in which it is used: □ *None of the milk was spilled.* □ *None of my friends has/have seen the film.* In the first of these examples, *none*, like *milk*, must be used with a singular verb. In examples of the second type, some people prefer a singular verb in formal contexts, especially if *none* is used in the sense of "not one." In informal contexts, or in the sense of "not any," a plural verb may be used.

See also SINGULAR OR PLURAL?

nonetheless or **nevertheless?** These two synonyms are sometimes confused. Traditionally *none the less* was written as three separate words, but now each of these words is written as a single word.

nonflammable see INFLAMMABLE.

no one or **no-one?** Most users prefer the two-word compound *no one* to the hyphenated form *no-one*. Unlike *anyone, everyone,* and *someone, no one* should not be written as a one-word compound.

• The pronoun *no one* and its synonym *nobody* are interchangeable in all contexts. Each is used with a singular verb but is sometimes informally followed by a plural personal pronoun or possessive adjective (see THEY): □ *No one/Nobody likes to see their children suffer.*

nor *Nor* is used in place of *or* in the *neither . . . nor* construction (see NEITHER) and to introduce a negative alternative that stands as a separate clause: □ *I speak neither German nor Spanish.* □ *She hasn't been to America, nor has her sister.* □ *He never watches television, nor does he listen to the radio.*

• In many other contexts *nor* and *or* are interchangeable: □ *The library is not open on Thursday mornings, nor/or on the weekend.* □ *We have no food to eat nor/or clothes to wear.*

Many users prefer *or* to *nor* where the negative force of an auxiliary verb covers both alternatives: □ *They cannot sing or dance.* □ *She has not done her homework or had her supper yet.*

The use of *nor* at the beginning of a sentence is informally acceptable: □ *Nature is slow to compensate for deforestation. Nor has man been able to make good the damage* (*Daily Telegraph,* July 13, 1987).

north, North, or **northern?** As an adjective, *north* is always written with a capital *N* when it forms part of a proper name: □ *North America* □ *the North Sea.* The noun *north* is usually written with a capital *N* when it denotes a specific region, such as the northern part of the country: □ *House prices are lower in the North.* In other contexts, and as an adverb, *north* is usually written with a lower-case *n:* □ *We traveled north for ten days.* □ *The wind is blowing from the north.*

• The adjective *northern* is more frequent and usually less specific than the adjective *north:* □ *the northern part of the country* □ *in northern France.*

Like *north, northern* is written with a capital *N* when it forms part of a proper name, such *as Northern Ireland.* With or without a capital *N,* it also means "of the North": □ *a Northern/northern region.*

no sooner see HARDLY.

nostalgia The noun *nostalgia* and its derivatives are most frequently used with reference to a wistful or sentimental yearning for the past: □ *She remembered the seaside vacations of her childhood with a deep nostalgia.* □ *Listening to old records always makes me nostalgic.* Some people object to this usage, restricting the term to its original meaning of "homesickness."

• The use of the adjective *nostalgic* in the sense of "causing nostalgia," rather than "feeling nostalgia," is also disliked and avoided by some users: □ *the nostalgic sound of the church bells.*

not The position of the word *not* in a negative sentence may affect its meaning and can sometimes lead to ambiguity: □ *All children are not afraid of the dark.* □ *We did not go because it was raining.* □ *He is not trying to win.* □ *He is trying not to win.* The first of these examples, which literally means "No children are afraid of the dark," is easily reworded: □ *Not all children are afraid of the dark.* The second example may be reordered or expanded for clarity: □ *Because it was raining, we did not go.* □ *We did not go because it was raining; we went because we were bored.*

• See also NOT ONLY . . . BUT ALSO.

notable see NOTICEABLE OR NOTABLE?

nothing but The phrase *nothing but . . .* should be used with a singular verb, even if the noun that follows *but* is plural: □ *Nothing but crumbs was* [not *were*] *left on the plate.*

• When *nothing but* is followed by an infinitive, the word *to* is omitted: □ *They have done nothing but cry since you left.*

noticeable or **notable?** The adjective *noticeable* means "perceptible" or "obvious"; *notable* means "remarkable" or "worthy of note": □ *a noticeable change in temperature* □ *a notable achievement.* The two words should not be confused.

• The final e of the verb *notice* is retained in the adjective *noticeable*, whereas the final e of *note* is omitted in *notable.*

not only . . . but also The words or clauses that follow *not only* and *but also* must be grammatically balanced: □ *I have lost not only my purse but also my car keys* [not *I have not only lost . . .*]. □ *They not only broke the world record for long-distance swimming but also raised several thousand dollars for charity* [not *They broke not only . . .*].

• In informal contexts the word *also* is often omitted: □ *He not only arrived late but (also) left early.*

notorious see INFAMOUS OR NOTORIOUS?

nought see NAUGHT OR NOUGHT?

nouns The main division of nouns is into countable and uncountable nouns. Countable nouns are those that can be preceded by *a* or *the* or a number or word denoting number: □ *a goat* □ *three lemons* □ *the priest* □ *several books.* Uncountable nouns are not able to be counted because they are nouns of mass: □ *flour* □ *water* □ *coffee.* Some words can be countable or uncountable, according to how they are used: □ *Have a beer.* □ *Beer is fattening.*

• Proper nouns refer to a single particular person or thing and begin with a capital letter: □ *Tom Jones.* Exceptionally, proper nouns can be made plural: □ *the two Germanys.*

Nouns can often be used as adjectives, when they sometimes

form one word with another noun, or are hyphenated, or remain as two words: □ *mailbox* □ *man-eater* □ *birthday present.* They are more likely to be hyphenated when the two nouns are used together adjectivally: □ *birthday-cake decorations* □ *coffee-table book.* See also **HYPHEN 3.**

The use of nouns as verbs has a long history. We use the verb *to question* without thinking that *question* was originally a noun. Such phrases as: □ *to paper a room* □ *to can fruit* □ *to pencil it in* are also so frequently used as to be wholly acceptable; however, more modern examples of functional shift, such as: □ *Will you bill me for that?* □ *They host dinner parties every month.* □ *He trashed their policies,* are disliked by many people.

nubile The adjective *nubile,* derived from the Latin word for "marriageable," is frequently applied to any sexually attractive young woman, especially in jocular or informal contexts: □ *His friend's nubile sister was sunbathing in the garden.* Some people object to this usage, restricting the term to its original meaning.

• The use of the adjective *nubile* to describe attractive married women or unattractive unmarried women is therefore best avoided.

nude see **NAKED OR NUDE?**

number The phrase *a number of* . . . is usually used with a plural verb; the phrase *the number of* . . . is used with a singular verb: □ *A number of pupils were late.* □ *The number of pupils has increased.*

• See also **SINGULAR** OR **PLURAL?**

numbers Numbers that occur in printed or written texts may be expressed in figures or written out in full, according to the nature of the work, the context, the writer's personal preference, or the publisher's house style.

• In mathematical, scientific, technical, commercial, or statistical texts, numbers are usually expressed throughout in figures.

In other works specific measurements or sums of money, page numbers, and dates are usually expressed in figures.

Some writers and publishers spell out numbers from one to ten only; some spell out numbers from one to twenty; others spell out all numbers up to one hundred. It is important to be reasonably consistent within a single piece of writing, but some users prefer not to mix figures and words in the same sentence: □ *There are nine boys and fifteen* [not *15*] *girls in his class.* □ *We invited 130 guests, but only 80* [not *eighty*] *turned up.*

The time may be expressed in words or figures: □ *twenty past three* □ *3:20* □ *eight o'clock* □ *8 o'clock.*

Times using the 24-hour clock are written as figures: □ *1300 hours.* See also **A.M.** AND **P.M.**; **DATES.**

Numbers of four or more digits are separated by commas into groups of three: □ *45,069* □ *3,728,960.* Four-digit numbers are sometimes printed or written without commas: □ *5069* □ *8960.*

See also **HYPHEN 6.**

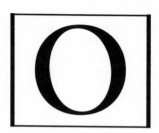

O or oh? *O*, always written as a capital, is a rarer, more poetic variant of the interjection *oh:* □ *O come, all ye faithful.* □ *O* [or *Oh*], *for the school holidays!* □ *"I can't come and see you later, I'm afraid." "Oh well, never mind."* □ *She burst into tears, crying, "Oh dear! Oh dear!"* □ *I just thought . . . oh, never mind.*

objective or **subjective?** The adjective *objective* means "not influenced by personal feelings, beliefs, or prejudices"; its antonym *subjective* means "influenced by personal feelings," etc.: □ *This is a subjective opinion: I find it hard to be objective when we're discussing my own daughter's career.*

• Some users consider the adjectives to be unnecessary synonyms for *fair, impartial, personal, biased,* etc.

The noun *objective* is best avoided where *goal, aim, purpose, object,* etc., would be adequate or more appropriate: □ *the purpose* [not *objective*] *of this meeting.* □ *Our aim* [not *objective*] *is to provide equal opportunities for all.*

obliged or **obligated?** Each of these adjectives may be used in the sense of "morally or legally bound": □ *He felt obliged/obligated to report the accident.*

• The use of *obligated* is largely restricted to formal contexts.

Obliged has the additional meaning of "physically constrained" or "compelled": □ *They were obliged to remain in their seats.*

oblivious The adjective *oblivious* is often used in the sense of "unaware" or "heedless": □ *He remained in the shelter of the tree, oblivious of the fact that the rain had stopped.*

• Some people object to this usage, restricting the adjective to its original sense of "no longer aware" or "forgetful": □ *Oblivious of the need for caution, she came out of the car to photograph the lions.*

The frequent use of the phrase *oblivious to,* rather than *oblivious of,* is unacceptable to some users but is now more frequent: □ *oblivious to the dangers* □ *oblivious to my presence.*

observance or **observation?** The noun *observance* denotes either the act of complying or a ritual custom or practice; *observation* denotes either the act of watching or noticing or a remark or comment: □ *observance of the rules* □ *religious observances* □ *their observation of human behavior* □ *an observation made by his client.*

occasion The verb *occasion* is best avoided where *cause, bring about,* etc., would be adequate: □ *The accident was caused* [not *occasioned*] *by faulty brakes.*

• Note the spelling of the word *occasion,* particularly the double *c* and single *s.*

178

occurrence This word is often misspelled. Note the double *c* and double *r*, as also in *occurred* and *occurring*.

oculist see OPTICIAN, OPHTHALMOLOGIST, OPTOMETRIST, OR OCULIST?

of The preposition *of* should never be substituted for the verb *have:*
□ *They should have* [not *of*] *refused.* This substitution, caused by the similarity in pronunciation between the two words when unstressed, is wrong.
• The use of such phrases *as of a Friday, of an evening,* etc., in place of *on Fridays, in the evening,* etc., should be restricted to informal contexts: □ *I go shopping of a Tuesday afternoon.*
See also OFF; 'S OR S'?; SINGULAR OR PLURAL?

of course The phrase *of course* serves a number of useful purposes, but it should not be used to excess.
• It has a variety of connotations, some of which may cause offense.
Used for emphasis, either alone or to introduce a reply, the phrase may convey impatience or politeness: □ *"Did you remember to mail my letter?" "Of course (I did)."* □ *"May I use your telephone?" "Of course (you may)."*

Used in the sense of "naturally" or "admittedly," it may be patronizing, superior, sympathetic, or apologetic: □ *It is, of course, impossible to communicate with the dead.* □ *I knew his uncle, of course. I don't believe you ever met him, did you?* □ *Of course, you're tired—you've had a long journey.* □ *I may be wrong, of course.*

off The use of the preposition *off* in place of *from*, to indicate the source of an acquisition, is considered wrong by many people, even in informal contexts: □ *I bought if from* [not *off*] *my sister.*
• The redundant phrase *off of* is also wrong and should be avoided in all contexts: □ *He jumped off* [not *off of*] *the fence.* □ *Take your feet off* [not *off of*] *the table.*
The word *off* is usually pronounced to rhyme appoximately with *scoff;* the variant pronunciation [awf] is generally considered to be old-fashioned or affected.

offense This word, meaning "action causing displeasure; illegal act," is sometimes misspelled. Note the *-s-* (*-c-* in British English: *offence*).
• The derived adjective is spelled *offensive.*

official or **officious?** The adjective *official* means "authorized," "formal," or "of an office"; *officious*, which is generally used in a derogatory manner, means "interfering," "bossy," "self-important," or "offering unwanted advice or assistance": □ *an official strike* □ *an official visit* □ *an officious clerk.* The two words should not be confused.
• In the field of diplomacy, the adjective *officious* means "informal" or "unofficial": □ *an officious agreement.* This sense is not in general usage.

officialese Officialese is a derogatory name for the style of writing or language that is considered to be typical of official forms, reports, memorandums, letters, leaflets, and other bureaucratic documents. Some prefer the term *bureaucratese.*
• Known informally as *gobbledygook,* officialese is characterized by the use of pompous and wordy language, obscure jargon, and

long unintelligible sentences. An example quoted by Tom Vernon in *Gobbledegook* is from a Department of Employment form: □ *In certain circumstances that condition may be modified to enable those persons who claim benefit early in their insurance life to treat as paid in one tax year all class 1 (standard rate) contributions paid in the period starting with the year in which they first became liable for such contributions, and ending with the day from which benefit is claimed.*

Widely satirized in the media, government departments have tried in recent years, with some success, to eliminate officialese by simplifying vocabulary and circumlocutory phrases, shortening sentences, and personalizing instructions. See also JARGON.

officious see OFFICIAL OR OFFICIOUS?

often The words *oftener* and *oftenest* are accepted by some users as comparative and superlative forms of the adverb *often*, but most users prefer *more often* and *most often*, especially in formal contexts: □ *It rains most often in the autumn.* □ *Which car do you use more often?*

• The *t* of *often* is rarely sounded, the most frequent pronunciation of the word being [ofĕn]. The pronunciation [oftĕn] is heard from time to time, but the variant [awfĕn], which sounds somewhat like *orphan,* is generally considered to be old-fashioned or affected.

oh see O OR OH?

O.K. or okay? The term *O.K.* or *okay*, denoting agreement or approval, may be used as an adjective, adverb, noun, or verb: □ *That's O.K.* □ *The meeting went O.K.* □ *Has she given us the O.K./okay?* □ *They are unlikely to O.K./okay the suggestion.*

• As the term is most frequently used in informal speech, the variations in its written form are not of great importance.

Inflectional endings are sometimes added: □ *The project has been O.K.'d/okayed by the committee.*

The two-letter form *O.K.* is sometimes written without periods: □ *It looks OK to me.*

older, oldest see ELDER, ELDEST, OLDER, OR OLDEST?

omelet This word is sometimes misspelled. The preferred spelling is *omelet* (in British English, *omelette*). Note the first *e*.

• The word is pronounced [omlet].

on see ONTO OR ON TO?; UPON OR ON?

one The pronoun *one*, representing an indefinite person, is to be followed by *one's, oneself,* etc., rather than by *his, himself,* etc.: □ *One should be kind to one's friends.*

• If the resulting sentence sounds clumsy or unidiomatic, it may be paraphrased: □ *When one lives on one's own, one often talks to oneself,* for example, may be changed to: *People who live on their own often talk to themselves.*

In informal contexts, however, *one* is usually followed in such contexts by *his, himself,* etc.: □ *One often talks to himself.* □ *One should be kind to his friends.* This usage can lead to ambiguity: in the last example, *his friends* may refer to the friends of some other person.

When the pronoun *one* represents a specific person, it is always followed by *his, her,* etc.: □ *The twins' tastes are not identical: one drinks her [not one's] coffee black, the other drinks it with cream.*

In formal contexts the impersonal pronoun *one* is generally preferred to *you*. The use of *one* in place of *I* or *we*, however, is widely considered to be affected and is best avoided, especially in informal contexts: □ *I have* [not *One has*] *never been very good at sports.* □ *We hope* [not *One hopes*] *that the situation will improve.* See also **YOU**.

The constructions *one in three/five/ten/*etc. and *one of the . . .*, followed by a plural noun, should be used with a singular verb: □ *One in four teachers is in favor of corporal punishment.* □ *One of the eggs is broken;* however, the constructions *one of those . . . who* and *one of the . . . that* are usually followed by a plural verb: □ *He is one of those people who are never satisfied.* □ *It is one of the shortest books that have ever been published.* See also **SINGULAR OR PLURAL?**

In some contexts the word *one* is superfluous: □ *His smile was not a friendly one,* for example, may be more concisely expressed as: *His smile was not friendly.*

See also **EACH OTHER OR ONE ANOTHER?**

onerous This word, meaning "demanding or troublesome": □ *onerous tasks*, has two acceptable pronunciations: [onĕrŏs] and the less frequent [ōnĕrŏs].

ongoing Many people object to the use of the adjective *ongoing* in place of *continuing, developing, in progress,* etc.: □ *ongoing research* □ *an ongoing investment program in manufacturing technology.* The cliché *ongoing situation* is also widely disliked.

• The word *ongoing* sometimes appears in hyphenated form: □ *We put you through the world's most advanced management training courses, followed by on-going personal development* (*Executive Post*, May 28, 1987).

on-line The term *on-line*, which relates to equipment that is directly connected to and/or controlled by a central computer, is hyphenated. Its antonym is *off-line*, also hyphenated.

only In some written sentences, the adverb *only* must be carefully positioned, as near as possible to the word it refers to, in order to convey the intended meaning: □ *She eats fish only on Fridays* [i.e., not on other days]. □ *She eats only fish* [i.e.,nothing else] *on Fridays.* □ *Only she* [i.e., She is the only one who] *eats fish on Fridays.*

• In speech, where the stress and intonation of the sentence should eliminate any ambiguity, and in informal written sentences that are not open to misinterpretation, *only* may be placed in its most idiomatic position—i.e., between the subject and the verb: □ *They have only sold three books.*

The use of *only* as a conjunction, in place of *but* or *however*, is best restricted to informal contexts: □ *I'd like to go to Canada, only I can't afford the trip.*

Some people object to the use of the phrase *only too* as an intensifier, reserving it for the sense of "regrettably": □ *I am very* [not *only too*] *pleased to help.* □ *The new container, which is supposed to be childproof, is only too easy to open.*

See also **NOT ONLY . . . BUT ALSO.**

onomatopoeia *Onomatopoeia* is the formation of words that imitate the sound associated with an object or action: □ *cuckoo* □ *moo* □ *clang* □ *croak* □ *hiss* □ *twitter.*

• It also refers to the use of words, usually in poetry, in such a way as to suggest the sound described. An example is:

Keeping time, time, time,
In a sort of Runic rhyme,
To the tintinnabulation that so musically wells
From the bells, bells, bells, bells.

(Edgar Allan Poe, *The Bells*)

on-stream The British term *on-stream* relates to an industrial process or plant that is in production or about to go into production or operation or to the launching of a new advertising campaign, etc.: □ *Works Manager . . . required to undertake full responsibility for one of the existing factories, but with the potential to assume control of new installations as they come "on-stream"* (*Executive Post*, August 27, 1987).

• It is usually possible to replace the phrase *come on-stream* with *open, begin,* etc.

onto or **on to?** The preposition *onto* may be written as one or two words: □ *She drove onto/on to the pavement. On to* may also be a combination of the adverb *on* and the preposition or infinitive marker *to,* in which case it should not be written as one word: □ *She drove on to London.* □ *She drove on to find a hotel.*

onward or **onwards?** *Onward* is used as an adjective or an adverb meaning "ahead": □ *onward motion* □ *to march onward.*

• The adverb *onwards* is more frequently used in British English. See also **-WARD OR -WARDS?**

operative The frequent use of the noun *operative* in place of *worker,* especially in nonindustrial contexts, is disliked by many users: □ *a strike by cleaning operatives at the hospital.* It can also refer to a detective or spy.

optician, ophthalmologist, optometrist, or **oculist?** Each of these four nouns denotes someone concerned with defects or diseases of the eye.

• The word *optician,* which is probably the most familiar, refers to someone who makes and sells glasses (and other optical equipment).

An *ophthalmologist* is a doctor who specializes in eye diseases.

An *optometrist* is qualified to test eyesight and prescribe corrective lenses.

Oculist is synonymous with *ophthalmologist.*

The word *ophthalmologist* is sometimes misspelled, the most frequent error being the omission of the first *h.* It is usually pronounced [ofthal*molō*jist]; the pronunciation of the first syllable to rhyme with *hop,* rather than *scoff,* is disliked by some users.

optimal see **OPTIMUM.**

optimistic Many people object to the frequent use of the adjective *optimistic* as a synonym for "hopeful," "confident," "cheerful," "favorable," "encouraging," etc.: □ *She is optimistic that the car will be found.* □ *They have produced an optimistic report on the company's prospects.*

• In general usage *optimistic* principally relates to a tendency to see or expect the best or to take a favorable view of things: □ *Throughout his illness he remained optimistic.*

optimize see **OPTIMUM.**

optimum The adjective and noun *optimum* refer to the most favorable or advantageous condition, amount, degree, etc.: □ *the optimum speed* □ *A temperature of 15° C. is the optimum.*

• The noun *optimum* has two plural forms, usually in technical contexts: *optimums* and *optima*.

The frequent use of the adjective *optimum* and its synonym *optimal* in the sense of "best" is disliked by many users: □ *a manufacturing program designed to make optimum use of all available resources* (*Executive Post*, July 16, 1987). □ *A combination of olive oil and butter will produce the optimal result.*

The verb *optimize* means "make the most of" or "make as efficient as possible": □ *to optimize the potential of the business* □ *to optimize the production process.*

optometrist see OPTICIAN, OPHTHALMOLOGIST, OPTOMETRIST, OR OCULIST?

or When *or* connects two or more singular subjects, a singular verb is used: □ *Perhaps Peter or Jane knows* [not *know*] *the answer.* A plural verb is used if each subject is plural: □ *Carrots or parsnips are served with this dish.*

• In a combination of singular and plural alternatives, the verb traditionally agrees with the subject that is nearer to it: □ *One large pot or two small ones are needed.* □ *Two small pots or one large one is needed.* The same principle is applied to singular subjects that are used with different forms of the verb: □ *Are you or your wife going to the concert?* If the resulting sentence sounds inelegant or unidiomatic, a second verb may be added: □ *Am I the winner or is he?*

The use of *or* at the beginning of a sentence is informally acceptable: □ *We may go to London tomorrow. Or we may stay at home.*

For the use of a comma before *or* in a series of three or more items, see COMMA 1. The conjunction *or* may also be preceded by a comma in other contexts, especially if it introduces a synonym rather than an alternative: □ *the policy of glasnost, or openness.*

See also AND/OR; EITHER; NOR.

oral see AURAL OR ORAL?; VERBAL OR ORAL?

ordinance or **ordnance?** An *ordinance* is a decree or regulation; the noun *ordnance* denotes military supplies or artillery.

• Neither word is in frequent use: *ordinance* is largely restricted to local government contexts; *ordnance* is restricted to military contexts.

The similarity in spelling often leads to confusion of the two words.

orient or **orientate?** Each form of the verb is acceptable: *orient*, the standard form, is preferred by some users as the shorter and simpler alternative, but *orientate* is the more frequent in British English.

• To *orient* originally meant "to face east"; the variant *orientate* was perhaps a BACK-FORMATION from the noun *orientation*. The verb is often used reflexively, meaning "get one's bearings" or "adjust oneself to new surroundings": □ *They found it difficult to orient/orientate themselves in the unfamiliar town.*

The past participle is increasingly used in the sense of "inclined toward": □ *a commercially orientated service* □ *a science-oriented course.* Many people dislike this usage, which is generally avoidable and often quite superfluous: examples include the local government service designed *to meet locality-oriented needs* rather than "to meet the needs of the locality" and job advertisements that call for experience in *product-orientated development* (product development) or *engineering-orientated environments* (engineering).

ostensible or ostentatious? *Ostensible* means "apparent"; *ostentatious* means "showy": □ *the ostensible reason for her absence* □ *an ostentatious display of grief.*

• Each adjective is ultimately derived from the Latin verb *ostendere,* meaning "show," and neither is complimentary: *ostensible* has connotations of falseness or deception; *ostentatious* suggests pretentiousness or vulgarity.

other than The use of *other than* as an adverbial phrase is disliked by some users: □ *They were unable to escape other than by squeezing through the narrow window.*

• Its adjectival use, however, is acceptable to all: □ *There was no means of escape other than the narrow window.*

Other than is best avoided where apart from would be more appropriate: □ *There was a narrow window; apart from* [not *other than*] *that, there was no means of escape.*

The construction *other . . . than* should not be replaced by *other . . . but* or *other . . . except:* □ *He had no other friend than* [not *but*] *me.* □ *Every other card than* [not *except*] *yours arrived on time.* If the word *other* is omitted, however, *but* or *except* may be substituted for *than.*

otherwise Some people object to the frequent use of *otherwise* as an adjective or pronoun: □ *All essays, finished or otherwise, must be handed in tomorrow morning.* □ *The entire work force, union members and otherwise, went on strike. Otherwise* may be replaced by *not* in the first of these examples and by *others* in the second.

• The use of *otherwise* in combination with an adverb is acceptable to all: □ *The window was broken, accidentally or otherwise, by one of your children.*

In the sense of "or else," *otherwise* should not be preceded by *or:* □ *Turn the volume down; otherwise, you'll wake the baby.*

ought The auxiliary verb *ought,* expressing duty, obligation, advisability, expectation, etc., is always followed by an infinitive with *to:* □ *They ought to visit her more often.* □ *Ought we to have invited your sister?* □ *The meat ought to be cooked by now.*

• The negative and interrogative forms *didn't ought to, hadn't ought to, did we ought to, had I ought to,* etc., are regarded as wrong by careful users.

Ought to can occasionally be replaced by should: □ *The meat should be cooked by now.* In most contexts, however, *ought* expresses a stronger sense of duty, obligation, advisability, etc., than *should.* See also SHOULD OR WOULD?

our or us? see -ING FORMS.

outdoor or outdoors? *Outdoor* is an adjective; *outdoors* is an adverb: □ *outdoor sports* □ *outdoor pursuits* □ *to play outdoors* □ *Outdoor clothes are worn outdoors. Out-of-doors,* used as adjective or noun, is hyphenated.

• The word *outdoors* is also used as a noun: □ *the great outdoors.*

outlet Some people object to the frequent use of the noun *outlet* in place of *shop*: □ *The product is available at a number of retail outlets.*

• In commercial contexts *outlet* also means "market": □ *The company has yet to find outlets for its solar-powered lights.*

outrageous This word, meaning "shocking or unconventional": □ *outrageous manners,* is sometimes misspelled. The *e* of *outrage* is retained before the suffix *-ous* to indicate the softness of the *g.*

outward or **outwards?** *Outward* is used as an adjective or adverb meaning "towards the outside": □ *the outward journey* □ *to pull outward.*

• The adverb *outwards* is more frequently used in British English. See also **-WARD OR -WARDS?**

over see **ABOVE OR OVER?**

overall The word *overall* is best avoided where *total, whole, comprehensive, general, average, inclusive, altogether,* etc., would be adequate or more appropriate: □ *his general* [not *overall*] *appearance* □ *the total* [not *overall*] *cost of the project* □ *The journey will take five days altogether* [not *overall*].

• In some contexts *overall* is superfluous: □ *an overall increase in production.*

The use of the word *overall* in its original sense of "from end to end" is acceptable to all users: □ *the overall length of the room.*

overkill The frequent use of the noun *overkill* in the sense of "excess" is disliked by some users: □ *In the coverage of the election, the media have been accused of overkill.*

• The noun is particularly undesirable in contexts that may be associated with the literal meaning of the verb *kill:* □ *We must avoid overkill in the presentation of our antiabortion campaign.*

The term *overkill* originally denoted a greater capacity than necessary for destruction, with specific reference to nuclear weapons.

overly Many people object to the use of the adverb *overly* in place of *too, excessively,* etc.: □ *She was not overly enthusiastic about my idea.* □ *He is overly sensitive to the slightest criticism.*

• In some contexts the need for *overly* can be obviated by attaching the prefix *over-,* with or without a hyphen, to the relevant adjective: □ *overenthusiastic* □ *oversensitive.*

overview The noun *overview* is best avoided where *survey, summary,* etc., would be adequate or more appropriate: □ *a general overview of the situation.*

owing to see **DUE TO, OWING TO, OR BECAUSE OF?**

package The word *package* and the expression *package deal* are widely used to denote a set of proposals or offers that must be accepted or rejected as a whole: □ *a new package of measures dealing with pay and working conditions.*

• In other contexts *package* is often better omitted or replaced with a more appropriate noun: □ *Japan's recent announcement of a substantial package of extra spending* (*Sunday Times*, June 7, 1987). □ *Hammicks has spent over £100,000 on a retail design package* (*The Bookseller*, May 22, 1987).

Some people also object to the frequent use of the verb *package* in place of *present*: □ *the different ways in which the major political parties were packaged during the election campaign.*

palate This word, meaning "the top part of the inside of one's mouth" or "sense of taste": □ *a cleft palate* □ *He has a sensitive palate*, is sometimes misspelled. It should not be confused with *palette*, the board on which an artist mixes colors, or *pallet*, a flat platform used in stacking and moving stored goods, and also a hard bed or straw mattress.

palpable The use of the adjective *palpable* in the extended sense of "easily perceived," in place of *obvious, manifest, plain*, etc., is disliked by some people: □ *a palpable lie.*

• Derived from the Latin verb *palpare*, meaning "touch," *palpable* was originally restricted to what could be touched or felt: □ *palpable warmth.*

panacea The noun *panacea* denotes a universal remedy for all ills; it should not be used with reference to individual problems or troubles: □ *They consider desegregation to be a panacea for racial conflict.*

• Often used disparagingly, the word is more frequently found in figurative contexts than in its literal sense of "cure-all."

Note the spelling of *panacea*, which is derived from the prefix *pan-*, meaning "all," and the Greek word for "cure." It is pronounced [panăseeă].

panic The word *panic* adds a *k* before the suffix *-y* and suffixes beginning with an *e* or *i* such as *-ed, -er*, and *-ing*: □ *panicky* □ *They panicked.* □ *Stop panicking!* See also SPELLING 1.

paradigm The noun *paradigm* is best avoided where *example, model, pattern*, etc., would be adequate or more appropriate: □ *a paradigm of enterprise and initiative* □ *a paradigm of the problems faced by the unemployed.*

• *Paradigm* specifically denotes a clear or typical example; it should not be confused with the noun *paragon*, meaning "model of excellence."

186

The *g* of *paradigm*, pronounced [parrădīm], is silent. In the adjective *paradigmatic*, pronounced [parrădigmatik], the *g* is sounded.

paraffin This word is sometimes misspelled. Note the single *r* and double *f*, as in *raffle*.

paragon see PARADIGM.

paragraphs A paragraph, a subdivision of a written passage, usually deals with one particular point or theme. It expresses an idea that, though it relates to the sense of the whole passage, can to some extent stand alone.

• There is no specified length for a paragraph. It can be one sentence or over a page long; however, very short successive paragraphs, as found in advertisements and popular journalism, can have a rather disjointed effect, whereas very long paragraphs can give the impression of heavy material that can be read through only in a slow, laborious manner. The most effective writing usually mixes longer and shorter paragraphs.

A paragraph starts on a new line and is indented. In a passage of dialogue, each act of speech normally starts a new paragraph.

parallel This word is sometimes misspelled. Note the single *r*, the double *l*, and then the single *l*.

• The spelling of some derived forms and compounds varies: □ *paralleling* or sometimes *parallelling* □ *paralleled* or sometimes *parallelled* □ *parallelism* □ *parallelogram* □ *unparalleled*.

paralyze This word is sometimes misspelled. The spelling is *paralyze* (in British English, *paralyse*).

• See also -IZE OR -ISE?

parameter Many people object to the frequent use of the noun *parameter*, a mathematical term, as a synonym for "limit," "boundary," "framework," "characteristic," or "point to be considered": □ *A business must operate within the parameters of time, money, and efficiency.* □ *". . . outside the parameters of my ministry"* ("Amen," NBC-TV, Jan. 7, 1989). □ *What are the parameters of the problem?*

• Note the pronunciation of *parameter*, which is stressed on the second syllable [păramitĕr].

paranoid The adjective *paranoid* principally relates to a mental disorder (*paranoia*) characterized by delusions of persecution or grandeur: □ *Often, he* [a schizophrenic] *feels himself to be persecuted—a paranoid delusion that occasionally leads to* violence (*Readers Digest*, June 1987).

• Some people object to the frequent use of *paranoid* and *paranoia* with reference to any intense suspicion, distrust, anxiety, fear, obsession, etc.: □ *It gives me an interest-free overdraft . . . so I don't have to get paranoid at the end of the month* (Midland Bank advertisement, *Sunday Times*, June 7, 1987).

The word *paranoid* is also used as a noun. Its synonym *paranoiac*, pronounced [parrănoiak] or [parrănoïik], is less frequent.

Note the spelling of *paranoia*, particularly the last three vowels.

parentheses Parentheses are also known as brackets. They are used to enclose supplementary or explanatory material that interrupts a complete sentence: □ *William James (1842-1910) was the brother of the novelist Henry James.* □ *He asked his uncle (a farmer who's always awake by sunrise) to wake him at nine.* The

P

material in parentheses could be removed without changing the meaning or grammatical completeness of the sentence. These are used, in preference to commas or dashes, when the interruption to the sentence is noticeable.

• Punctuation within parentheses is that appropriate to the parenthetic material. Punctuation of the sentence containing the parentheses is unaffected, except that any punctuation that would have followed the word before the first parenthesis is placed after the second: □ *Worst of all, their confidence is undermined by a lurking fear of the meaninglessness of those basic questions in themselves (is this good? is this right?), which yet they find themselves unable to cease from asking* (Richard Hoggart, *The Uses of Literacy*). If the parenthetic material comes at the end of a sentence, the period is placed outside the second parenthesis. The only time when a period appears at the end of a parenthetic sentence is when the material in parentheses comes as a full sentence between two sentences, rather than within a sentence: □ *He came from a humble background. (His mother was a charwoman.) Yet he mixed with people of all classes.*

Parentheses are also used for letters or numbers in a series: □ *The union demanded (1) higher wages, (2) shorter hours, (3) safer working conditions. . . .* They are also used to indicate alternatives or brief explanations: □ *boy(s)* (meaning ''boy'' or ''boys'') □ *it took a fortnight (two weeks)* □ *the S.E.C. (the Securities and Exchange Commission).* See also BRACKETS.

parenting The word *parenting*, which means ''being a parent'' or ''parental care,'' is increasingly used to emphasize the joint responsibility of the parents in all aspects of a child's upbringing and to avoid the sexual stereotypes and traditional roles associated with the words *mother* and *father* and their derivatives: □ *the advantages of shared parenting* □ *a guide to parenting the gifted child.*

• This expression is disliked by those who object to the use of nouns as verbs.

parliament The noun *parliament*, meaning ''legislative authority, assembly, or body,'' is usually written with a capital *P* when it denotes a specific parliament, especially that of the United Kingdom: □ *The issue will be debated in Parliament this afternoon.*

• The usual pronunciation of *parliament* is [pärlămĕnt]; the pronunciations [pärlimĕnt] and [pärlyămĕnt] are accepted variants. Note the spelling of the word, particularly the central vowels.

parlor see LOUNGE.

partially or **partly?** Each adverb means ''not completely'' or ''to some extent,'' but there are differences of sense, usage, and application for them: □ *facilities for the blind and partially sighted.* □ *The course consists partly of oral work and partly of written work.*

• In some contexts the two adverbs are virtually interchangeable: □ *a partly/partially successful attempt.* It can be helpful to think of *partly* as meaning ''concerning one part; not wholly'': □ *The woman's face was partly hidden* [i.e. only part of her face was hidden] *by her veil.* □ *The art treasures were partly on permanent loan to the museum and partly in the possession of the Adams family. Partially* may then be used to mean ''to a limited extent; not completely": □ *The woman's face was partially hidden* [i.e. her whole face may have been hidden but to a limited degree] *by her veil.* □ *His hopes were partially frustrated by the lack of full commitment by his fellow workers.*

In actual usage, however, such guidelines tend to be ignored, and the words are used interchangeably, with *partly* being the more frequent.

participles All verbs have *present participles*, which are formed with *-ing:* □ *seeing* □ *walking,* and *past participles,* formed with *-d* or *-ed* for regular verbs and in other ways for irregular verbs: □ *loved* □ *finished* □ *given* □ *gone* □ *thought.*
• *Participles* are often used as adjectives: □ *broken promises* □ *a leaking tap.* They are also used, with an inversion of the usual sentence construction, to introduce a sentence such as: □ *Sitting in the corner was an old man.* □ *Attached to his wrist was a luggage label.* Care should be taken with such introductory participles, because they are sometimes used to link items that are quite unrelated: see DANGLING PARTICIPLES.

The pronunciation most frequently used is [*partisipl*].

See also -ED OR -T?; -ING FORMS.

particular Used for emphasis, the adjective *particular* is often superfluous: □ *Do you have any particular preference?* □ *This particular dress was worn by Vivien Leigh in "Gone with the Wind."*
• Many people dislike this usage, reserving the adjective for what is exceptional, special, specific, or worthy of note: □ *This discovery is of particular importance.*

partly see PARTIALLY OR PARTLY?

past or **passed?** These spellings are sometimes confused. *Passed* is the past tense and past participle of *pass:* □ *We passed the station.* □ *The years have passed by so quickly.*
• *Past* is used for all other forms: noun, adjective, preposition, and adverb: □ *Your past is catching up with you.* □ *the past weeks* □ *She ran past the sign.* □ *It's five past three.* □ *The plane flew past.*

patent This word is pronounced [*patĕnt*] in all senses □ *to patent/ apply for a patent for a new invention* □ *patent leather shoes,* and as the adverb *patently* [*patĕntlee*]: □ *It is patently obvious she's lying.*
• In British English [*paytĕnt*] is used for all senses.

pathetic The use of the adjective *pathetic* in the derogatory sense of "contemptible" or "worthless" is best restricted to informal contexts: □ *The comedian made a pathetic attempt to mimic the President.* □ *Don't be so pathetic!*
• The principal sense of *pathetic* is "arousing pity or sorrow": □ *The sick child made several pathetic attempts to stand up.*

patriot This word, meaning "a person who loves his or her country," has two acceptable pronunciations [*paytreeŏt*] or the British [*patriŏt*].

patron see CLIENT OR CUSTOMER?

peaceable or **peaceful?** The adjective *peaceable,* meaning "disposed to peace," "peace-loving," or "not aggressive," is principally applied to people: □ *the peaceable inhabitants of the town* □ *a peaceable temperament.* *Peaceful,* the more frequent of the two

P

adjectives, means "characterized by peace," "calm," or "not violent": □ *a peaceful scene* □ *a peaceful demonstration:* □ *peaceful coexistence.*
• Note the spelling of *peaceable,* particularly the second *e* (see also SPELLING 3).

pedigree The noun *pedigree* denotes an ancestral line or line of descent, specifically that of a purebred animal; its use as a synonym for "record" or "background" is disliked by some users: □ *a pedigree of success spanning over 50 years in the radio and television rental and retail field* (*Executive Post,* July 16, 1987).

pejorative This word, meaning "disparaging," can be pronounced in two ways. The pronunciation [pĕjorǎtiv] is used more frequently than the more traditional [peejŏrǎtiv].

peninsula or **peninsular?** These two spellings are sometimes confused. A *peninsula* is a long narrow section of land that is almost surrounded by water but is joined to the mainland. The adjective is *peninsular:* □ *the Peninsular War of 1808 to 1814.*

pensioner see SENIOR CITIZEN OR OLD-AGE PENSIONER?

people *People* is usually a plural noun, but in the sense of "nation," "race," or "tribe" it may be singular or plural: □ *a nomadic people of Africa* □ *all the peoples of the world* □ *The French people are renowned for their culinary expertise.* The use of the alternative plural form *persons* to denote a number of human beings is best restricted to formal contexts: □ *No more than eight persons may use the elevator.* □ *There are four people* [not *persons*] *in the waiting room.*
• With reference to a group or body of human beings, the word *people* is preferred in all contexts: □ *a meeting place for young people* □ *representatives of the people.*

per The preposition *per,* meaning "for each" or "in each," is often better replaced by *a* or *an:* □ *four times a* [not *per*] *month* □ *50 cents a* [not *per*] *mile.* In some contexts, however, *per* must be retained: □ *Use two ounces of cheese per person.* □ *The parking-lot attendant charges five dollars per car per day.*
• Many people consider the use of *per* in place of *according to* to be colloquial: *We did the work per their instructions.*
See also AS PER; PER ANNUM; PER CAPITA; PERCENT; PER SE.

per-, pre-, or **pro-?** These three prefixes sometimes cause confusion in the spelling and usage of certain pairs of words.
• See PERSECUTE OR PROSECUTE?; PERSPECTIVE OR PROSPECTIVE?; PRECEDE OR PROCEED?; PREREQUISITE OR PERQUISITE?; PRESCRIBE OR PROSCRIBE?

per annum The Latin phrase *per annum,* meaning "for each year," is best restricted to formal contexts: □ *You will be paid a salary of $12,000 per annum.*
• In other contexts the more informal phrase *a year* is preferred: □ *It costs several hundred dollars a year, excluding gasoline costs, to keep this car on the road.* See also PER.

per capita The adverbial or adjectival phrase *per capita* is widely used in English in the sense of "for each person": □ *the minimum cost per capita* □ *a per capita allowance of eight dollars.*
• Some people object to this usage as an inaccurate translation of the Medieval Latin phrase, which literally means "by heads": □ *The estate will be divided per capita.*

percent *Percent* is used adverbially, in combination with a number, in the sense of "in or for each hundred": □ *an increase of 25 percent* □ *75 percent of the students.*

• The use of *percent* as a noun, meaning "one-hundredth" or "a percentage," is disliked by some users: the phrase *half a percent,* for example, is better replaced by *one-half of 1 percent.* See also PERCENTAGE.

Percent is usually written as one word without a period; however, in British English the two-word form *per cent* is preferred. In informal contexts, the symbol % is sometimes used.

See also SINGULAR OR PLURAL?

percentage Many people object to the use of a *percentage* to mean "a small part," "a little," or "a few": □ *Only a percentage of the work force will be present.* A percentage may be as small as 1 percent or as large as 99 percent; in the sense of "proportion," the noun often needs a qualifying adjective for clarity: □ *A small percentage of the money is used for administration costs.* □ *A large percentage of the stock was damaged in the fire.*

• *Percentage* is sometimes better replaced by *number, amount, part,* or *proportion; a high percentage* by *many* or *much; a lower percentage* by *fewer* or *less,* etc.

The use of the noun *percentage* as a synonym for "advantage" or "profit" is best restricted to informal contexts: □ *There's no real percentage in sending your children to a private school.*

perceptible, perceptive, or **percipient?** The adjective *perceptible* means "perceivable," "noticeable," or "recognizable"; *perceptive* means "observant," "discerning," or "sensitive": □ *a perceptible change* □ *a perceptive remark.*

• *Percipient,* which is virtually synonymous with, but less frequent than, *perceptive,* is largely restricted to formal contexts: □ *a percipient writer.*

The adverbs *perceptibly* and *perceptively* are often confused, being similar in spelling and pronunciation: □ *The children were perceptibly quieter when their teacher was present.* □ *She spoke perceptively of the composer's orchestral works.*

perestroika *Perestroika,* a Russian word, is used to denote the restructuring or economic and social reform program in the Soviet Union under Mikhail Gorbachev in the late 1980's. *Perestroika* was also the title of a book by Gorbachev published in 1987: □ *the success of perestroika depends on Mr. Gorbachev's leadership, the responsiveness of the Soviet people and the system's ability to adapt* (Senator Bill Bradley, *The New York Times,* January 3, 1989).

• See also GLASNOST.

perfect Many people avoid using such adverbs as *very, rather, more, most, less, least,* etc., to qualify the adjective *perfect,* meaning "faultless," "unblemished," "complete," or "utter": □ *This book is in less perfect condition than that one.* □ *It was the most perfect diamond that he had ever seen.* The expressions *nearly perfect* and *almost perfect,* however, are widespread.

• The pronunciation of the adjective *perfect* is different from that of the verb. The adjective is stressed on the first syllable [*per*fikt]; the verb is stressed on the second syllable [per*fekt*].

period The principal use of the period as a punctuation mark is to end a sentence that is neither a direct question nor an exclamation.

• See also EXCLAMATION POINT; QUESTION MARK; SENTENCES.

In creative writing, reference books, etc., the period may also mark the end of a group of words not conforming to the conventional description of a sentence: □ *He had four drinks. Four very large drinks.*

A period is also used in decimals □ *3.6 inches of rain.* Periods are also used in many ABBREVIATIONS.

A period is sometimes called a *stop,* a *point,* or (in British English) a *full stop.*

See also BRACKETS; QUOTATION MARKS; SEMICOLONS.

perk see PREREQUISITE OR PERQUISITE?

perpetrate or **perpetuate?** *Perpetrate* means "commit" or "perform"; *perpetuate* means "cause to continue" or "make perpetual": □ *to perpetrate a crime* □ *to perpetuate a tradition.* The two verbs should not be confused.

perquisite see PREREQUISITE OR PERQUISITE?

per se The Latin phrase *per se,* meaning "by itself" or "in itself," is best restricted to formal contexts: □ *The discovery is of little importance per se.*

• Note the spelling and pronunciation of the word *se* [say].

persecute or **prosecute?** *Persecute* means "harass" or "oppress"; *prosecute* means "take legal action against": □ *They were persecuted for their beliefs.* □ *Trespassers will be prosecuted.* The two verbs should not be confused.

person Many people prefer to use the noun *person,* rather than *man,* to denote a human being whose sex is unspecified: □ *We need to hire another person for the job.*

• The substitution of *person* for *man* in such words as *chairman, salesman, statesman, spokesman, layman, craftsman,* etc., is a more controversial issue: □ *Margaret Thatcher, world statesperson, mingling with her peers at the summit in Venice* (*The Guardian,* June 8, 1987). □ *Mrs. Liz Forsdick . . . will act as "linesperson" in the third qualifying-round game* (*The Guardian,* Oct. 9, 1981).

Some users apply the terms *chairman, salesman,* etc., to both men and women: □ *The chairman of the CBI's Smaller Firms Council, Mrs. Jean Parker* (*The Guardian,* April 21, 1987). Others use the more or less acceptable feminine forms *chairwoman, saleswoman,* etc. for women: □ *The appointment was announced yesterday by ChildLine's chairwoman, Miss Esther Rantzen* (*The Guardian,* May 14, 1987). See also CHAIR; MAN; SEXISM.

As a general rule, the substitution of *person* for *man,* in any context, is best avoided if a simpler or more idiomatic solution can be found: the use of *someone else* instead of *another person, nobody* instead of *no person, crew of four* instead of *four-person crew,* etc.

Person has two plural forms, *persons* and *people:* see also PEOPLE.

personal see PERSONALLY; PERSONNEL.

personally The use of the adverb *personally* for emphasis is disliked by some users: □ *I personally prefer to spend my holidays at home.*

• Similar objections may be raised to the unnecessary use of the adjective *personal* in such expressions as: □ *a personal friend* □ *her personal opinion* □ *a personal visit,* etc.

In some contexts, however, *personally* and *personal* may serve the useful purpose of distinguishing between the unofficial and the official, the private and the professional, etc.: □ *I personally think you should accept their offer, but as your attorney must advise you to make further inquiries.* □ *He is a business acquaintance but not a personal friend.*

personnel Many people object to the frequent use of the noun *personnel* in place of *staff, work force, workers, employees, people,* etc.: □ *They do not have enough personnel for the increased workload.* The word *personnel* is principally used to denote the employees of a large company or organization, considered collectively, or the department that is concerned with their recruitment and welfare: □ *hospital personnel* □ *the personnel officer.*

• *Personnel* may be a singular or plural noun, but it should not be used with a specific number: □ *We are moving four people* [not *personnel*] *from the sales office to the production department.* Note the spelling of *personnel,* particularly the double *n* and the second *e,* and the pronunciation of the word, with the primary stress on the last syllable [persŏnel]. *Personnel* is sometimes confused with the adjective *personal:* □ *There will be strong prospects of long-term personnel development for . . . the truly commercial engineer* (*Sunday Times,* June 7, 1987).

persons see PEOPLE.

perspective or **prospective?** *Perspective* is a noun, meaning "view," "aspect," or "objectivity"; it should not be confused with the adjective *prospective,* meaning "expected," "likely," or "future": □ *a different perspective* □ *a prospective employer.*

• In painting, drawing, etc., the noun *perspective* principally refers to the representation of three-dimensional objects and their relative sizes and positions on a flat surface. Its figurative use in the phrase *in perspective* is derived from this sense: □ *You must try to put things in perspective: the loss of one customer is relatively unimportant when the future of the company is at stake.*

perturb see DISTURB OR PERTURB?

phenomena see PHENOMENON OR PHENOMENA?

phenomenal The use of the adjective *phenomenal* as a synonym for "extraordinary," "remarkable," "prodigious," or "outstanding" is disliked by some: □ *a phenomenal achievement.*

phenomenon or **phenomena?** *Phenomena* is the plural form of the noun *phenomenon:* □ *This phenomenon is of great interest to astronomers.* □ *Such phenomena are not easy to explain.*

• The use of *phenomena* as a singular noun, a frequent error, is wrong: □ *"The development of the Muslim community in Britain is only a recent phenomena and needs proper research,"* Mr. Ayman Ahwal, London spokesman of the World Muslim League, said (*The Times of London,* Aug. 18, 1987).

philosophy The noun *philosophy* is best avoided where *idea, view, policy,* etc., would be adequate or more appropriate: □ *My philosophy is that children should be seen and not heard.* □ *The company has a philosophy of sound management practices at the local level.*

phlegm This word causes problems with spelling and pronunciation. Note the initial *ph-* spelling, pronounced [f], and the silent *g*. The word is pronounced [flem].

phobia A *phobia* is an abnormal or irrational fear or aversion: □ *He has a phobia about flying.* □ *She has a phobia of spiders.*
• The noun should not be used as a synonym for "dislike," "dread," "obsession," "inhibition," etc.: □ *She has a phobia of losing her car keys.* □ *He has a phobia about undressing in front of other people.*

phone The use of the noun and verb *phone* in place of *telephone* is becoming increasingly frequent and acceptable. The shortened form *phone* is best avoided, however, in formal contexts: □ *The phone's ringing.* □ *You'd better phone the doctor.* □ *The cost of your telephone call will be refunded.* □ *Please write or telephone for an application form.*
• See also ABBREVIATIONS; APOSTROPHE.

phony or **phoney?** The more frequent spelling of this word, meaning "fake," is *phony*. *Phoney* with an *e* is preferred in British English.

photo The use of the noun *photo* in place of *photograph* is best avoided in formal contexts: □ *Did you take a photo of the baby?* □ *This pass is not valid without a photograph of the holder.* The plural of *photo* is *photos*.
• The word *photo*, however, is generally used as a shortened form of the verb *photograph*. See also ABBREVIATIONS; APOSTROPHE.

physiognomy Note the spelling of this word, which means "the outward appearance of a person considered to show the person's character." The *g* is pronounced in American English, silent in British English.

picnic This word adds a *k* before the suffixes *-er*, *-ed*, *-ing:* □ *picnickers* □ *They picnicked in the woods.* See also SPELLING 1.

pidgin or **pigeon?** These two words may sometimes be confused. *Pidgin* is a language that is a mixture of two other languages: □ *pidgin English.* A *pigeon* is a usually gray bird with short legs and compact feathers: □ *the pigeons in Central Park.*
• *Pigeon* also has the informal sense of "someone easily tricked": □ *The con man waited for a pigeon.*

pigmy see PYGMY OR PIGMY?

piteous, pitiable, or **pitiful?** Each of these adjectives means "arousing or deserving pity," in which sense they are virtually interchangeable in many contexts. There are, however, slight differences of usage and application □ *a piteous cry* □ *a pitiable figure* □ *a pitiful sight.*
• Note the spelling of *piteous*, the least frequent of the three adjectives, in which the *t* is followed by *e* rather than *i* (as in *pitiable* and *pitiful*).
Pitiable and *pitiful* have the additional meaning of "arousing or deserving contempt": □ *Their pitiful offer of a two percent raise was immediately rejected by the union.*

pivotal The frequent use of the adjective *pivotal* in the sense of "crucial or important" is disliked by some users: □ *a pivotal decision.*
• Note the pronunciation of *pivotal*, which is stressed on the first syllable [pívõtäl].

plain or **plane?** These spellings are sometimes confused. The main noun sense of *plain* is "level, treeless expanse of land": □ *the vast plains of the prairie.* *Plane* as a noun is a shortened form of airplane, a carpenter's tool, or a surface in geometry. See also **PLANE.**

• *Plain* has several adjectival senses, including "straightforward," "simple," "clear"; the adjectival use of *plane* means "flat": □ *a plane surface.*

plaintiff or **plaintive?** These spellings are sometimes confused. A *plaintiff* is the person who starts legal action in a court; *plaintive* means "mournful and melancholy": □ *a plaintive song.*

plane The use of the noun *plane* as a shortened form of *airplane* is acceptable in most contexts: □ *What time does your plane leave?* □ *More than 250 people were killed in the plane crash.*

• See also **ABBREVIATIONS; APOSTROPHE; PLAIN OR PLANE?**

platform The use of the noun *platform* to denote the declared policies and principles of a political party or candidate is disliked by a few users but is acceptable to most: □ *Their platform will win them few votes in the forthcoming election.*

playwright see **DRAMATIST OR PLAYWRIGHT?**

pleaded or **pled?** *Pleaded* is the usual form of the past tense and past participle of the verb *plead:* □ *"Save my child," she pleaded.* □ *They had pleaded with him to stay.*

• *Pled* is a dialectal variant of *pleaded.*

plenty The use of *plenty* as an adverb, in place of *quite* or *very*, is regarded by some as nonstandard: □ *The house is plenty big enough for us.* □ *She was plenty upset when she heard the news.*

• The adjectival use of *plenty* without *of* is also unacceptable to many users: □ *They have plenty toys to play with.*

plurals The regular way to form plurals for English words is to add an *-s*, except for words ending in *-s*, *-x*, *-ch*, *-sh*, and *-z*, where *-es* is added: □ *ships* □ *houses* □ *buses* □ *foxes* □ *churches* □ *sashes* □ *buzzes.* Of course, there are many irregularly formed plurals. Words ending in a consonant and then *-y* have *-ies* in the plural: □ *fairies* □ *ponies*, except for proper nouns, which have *-s* or *-ies:* □ *the two Germanys.* □ *the two Sicilies.* Some words ending in *-f* or *-fe* have *-ves* in the plural: □ *halves* □ *wives*, while others simply add *-s*, and others allow a choice: □ *beliefs* □ *hoofs—hooves.* Some words ending in *-o* add *-es*, others just an *-s*. It is impossible to formulate a general rule here, although note the frequently used *potatoes* and *tomatoes*, which both end with *-es*. Note also that shortened forms ending in *-o* just add *-s:* □ *photos* □ *pianos* □ *radios* □ *stereos* □ *videos.* Some nouns ending in *-s* are already plural and cannot be pluralized: □ *trousers* □ *spectacles* □ *scissors.* With various animal names the plural form is the same as the singular: □ *deer* □ *sheep* □ *bison.* See also **FISH OR FISHES?**

• Several English words have plurals not formed in any of the ways described above: □ *man—men* □ *child—children* □ *mouse—mice* □ *goose—geese* □ *foot—feet.* There is no rule about these words and one cannot generalize from them; the plural of *mongoose* is *mongooses* [not *mongeese*].

Foreign words sometimes take a regular English plural and sometimes the plural of the appropriate language. Often either is regarded as correct: □ *châteaus/châteaux.* If the word is in general English use, then it is more likely to take an English plural, but if it is considered a foreign word and would be printed in italics, then it takes the plural of the appropriate language.

Difficulties often arise with the plurals of compound nouns. The general rule is that, when the qualifying word is an adjective, the noun is made plural: □ *courts-martial* □ *poets laureate*, though in less formal usage, the second word is made plural: □ *poet laureates*. If both words are nouns, the second is made plural: □ *town clerks*, although *a woman teacher* becomes *women teachers*. In compounds of a noun, and a prepositional phrase or adverb, the noun is made plural: □ *mothers-in-law* □ *hangers-on* □ *men of war*. If no words in the compound are nouns, then *-s* is added at the end: □ *forget-me-nots* □ *go-betweens* □ *grown-ups*.

On using singular or plural verbs, see **SINGULAR** OR **PLURAL?**

plus The prepositional use of *plus* in the sense of "with the addition of" is acceptable in informal contexts: □ *My savings, plus the money my grandmother left me, are almost enough to buy a car.* • Note that the verb agrees with *savings;* if the sentence is reordered to make *money* the principal subject, a singular verb must be used: □ *The money my grandmother left me, plus my savings, is almost enough to buy a car.*

Some people avoid using the noun *plus* as a synonym for "advantage": □ *Being within walking distance of the station is one of the pluses of living here.*

The expression *an added plus* is tautological and should be avoided.

The use of *plus* in the sense of "and" or "with" should also be restricted to informal contexts: □ *He's afraid to go sailing because he can't swim, plus he suffers from seasickness.* □ *She was met at the airport by her son plus his new girlfriend.*

See also **MINUS**.

p.m. see **A.M.** AND **P.M.**

poetess see **-ESS**.

poignant This word, meaning "sharp" or "emotionally moving," is usually pronounced [*poy*nyănt] although in British English [*poy*nănt] is also acceptable. The *g* is silent.

politic or political? *Politic* means "prudent," "shrewd," or "cunning"; *political* means "of politics, government, policy making," etc.: □ *a politic decision* □ *a political party*. The two adjectives should not be confused.

• *Politic* was originally synonymous with *political*. This sense of the word survives only in the expression the *body politic*, meaning "the state."

Note the different stress patterns of the two words: *politic* is stressed on the first syllable, *political* on the second.

politics see **-ICS**.

pore or pour? These spellings are sometimes confused. *Pore* as a verb means "study intently": □ *They pored over the map; pour* means "cause to flow": □ *She poured the tea*. The noun *pore* refers to a minute opening in the skin.

Portuguese This word is sometimes misspelled; note the *-e-* following the second *u*.

position To *position* is to put carefully and deliberately in a specific place: the verb is best avoided where *place, put, post, situate, locate*, etc., would be adequate or more appropriate: □ *She posi-*

tioned the mat on the carpet to hide the stain. □ *He put* [not *positioned*] *his dirty plate on top of the others.* □ *The offices are situated* [not *positioned*] *in the middle of town.*
• Some people also dislike the unnecessary use of the noun *position* in many contexts. It is usually possible to replace the verbal phrase *be in a position to,* for example, with *be able to* or *can:* □ *I am not in a position to answer your questions.*

possessives The two ways of showing that a noun is one of possession are the apostrophe and the use of the word *of:* □ *Anne's car* □ *the company's profits* □ *the rabbits' food* □ *members of the squad.*
• The apostrophe is used more frequently than *of,* and there is no firm rule as to where it is appropriate to use *of.* One can say either: □ *the table's leg* or *the leg of the* table, but where there is a recognized phrase containing *of:* □ *the Valley of the Rocks,* an apostrophe cannot be substituted. *Of* is usually used for inanimate things; when it is used for people an apostrophe is sometimes used as well: □ *a friend of Peter's.* It is also often used for geographical regions: □ *the wines of France* □ *the cities of Europe.*

In cases of joint possession, the apostrophe belongs to the last owner mentioned: □ *Tom and Lucy's house* □ *Beaumont and Fletcher's plays.* With a compound noun the last word takes the apostrophe: □ *the lady-in-waiting's dress* □ *the county court's judge.*

Care should be taken with such phrases as: *one of the residents' dogs* which might mean "the dog(s) belonging to one of the residents" or "one of the dogs belonging to one of the residents" or "one of the dogs jointly owned by the residents." It is better to rephrase such an expression to avoid ambiguity. See also **APOSTROPHE.**

post- Some people object to the frequent use of the prefix *post-,* meaning "after," to coin new adjectives, often of a futuristic nature: □ *post-nuclear Britain* □ *post-feminist literature* □ *Mr. Steel said the aim would be to create an "effective and electable alternative to government in the post-Thatcher period"* (*Daily Telegraph,* September 7, 1987).

posthumous This word causes problems with spelling and pronunciation. In speech the *h* is silent [*postyoomŭs*]; the first syllable is not as in *post,* but as in *positive.*

pour see **PORE OR POUR?**

practical or **practicable?** The adjective *practical* has a wide range of senses; the principal meaning of *practicable* is "capable of being done or put into practice." A *practicable* suggestion is simply possible or feasible; a *practical* suggestion is also useful, sensible, realistic, economical, profitable, and likely to be effective or successful: □ *It may be practicable to create jobs for everyone, but this would not be a practical solution to the problems of unemployment.*
• Careful users maintain the distinction between the two words, which is also applicable to their antonyms, *impractical* and *impracticable:* □ *It's impractical to use the washing machine when you only have a couple of shirts to wash.* □ *It's impracticable to use the washing machine when there is a power cut. Unpractical* is a less frequent antonym of *practical.*

Additional senses of *practical* include "not theoretical," "suitable for use," "skilled at doing or making things," and "virtual": □ *a practical course in first aid* □ *a more practical layout for the kitchen* □ *My brother is not a very practical man.* □ *She has practical control of the company.*

See also PRACTICALLY.

practically The adverb *practically* is widely used as a synonym for "almost," "nearly," "virtually," etc.: □ *I practically broke my ankle.*

• Some people dislike this usage, which can lead to confusion with one of the more literal senses of the word: □ *It is practically impossible,* for example, may mean "It is impossible in practice" or "It is almost impossible."

See also PRACTICAL OR PRACTICABLE?

practice or **practise?** The noun as well as the verb is *practice*: □ *the doctor's practice* □ *the doctor who practices in our town.*

• In British English, the verb is spelled *practise.*

practitioner This word is sometimes misspelled, the most frequent error being the substitution of *c* or *s* for the final *t*.

pray or **prey?** These spellings are sometimes confused. The verb *pray* means "ask God for something": □ *pray for forgiveness.* The noun *prey* means "animals hunted for food": □ *birds of prey.*

• Spelling mistakes may be avoided if *pray* is associated with *prayer.*

pre- see HYPHEN 1; PER-, PRE-, OR PRO-?; PREWAR.

precautionary measure The phrase *precautionary measure* can usually be replaced by the noun *precaution,* which denotes a measure taken to avoid something harmful or undesirable: □ *The police closed the road as a precaution(ary measure) against flooding.*

precede or **proceed?** *Precede* means "come before," "go before," or "be before"; *proceed* means "continue," "go on," or "advance": □ *September precedes October.* □ *The text is preceded by an introduction.* □ *I am unable to proceed with this work.* □ *They proceeded to dismantle the car.*

• The two verbs should not be confused or misspelled: note the different spelling but identical pronunciation of the second syllables, -*cede* and -*ceed* [-*seed*].

precedence or **precedent?** The noun *precedence* means "priority" or "superiority"; the noun *precedent* denotes a previous example that may serve as a model (in a court of law or elsewhere): □ *Should this work take precedence over our other commitments?* □ *The guests were seated in order of precedence.* □ *The committee's decision has set a precedent for future claims.* □ *This result is without precedent.*

• Each noun is derived from the verb *precede* (see PRECEDE OR PROCEED?); to interchange them is wrong.

The pronunciation of *precedence* is [presĭdĕns]. The noun *precedent* is pronounced [presĭdĕnt], but the rarer adjective is pronounced [preseedĕnt].

precipitate or **precipitous?** The adjective *precipitate* means "rushing," "hasty," "rash," or "sudden"; *precipitous* means "like a precipice" or "very steep": □ *a precipitate decision* □ *their precipitate departure* □ *a precipitous slope.*

• The substitution of *precipitous* for *precipitate* is disliked by some users but acknowledged by many dictionaries. *Precipitate*, however, should not be used in the sense of "precipitous."

The word *precipitate* is also used as a verb and as a noun. In the pronunciation of the adjective and noun, the final syllable is usually unstressed [pris*i*pität]. The verb has the same primary stress pattern, but the final syllable is pronounced to rhyme with *gate* [pris*i*pitayt].

precondition see CONDITION OR PRECONDITION?

predict or **predicate?** To *predict* is to foretell; the verb *predicate* means "affirm," "declare," or "imply": □ *It is impossible to predict the result of tomorrow's game.* □ *They predicated that the accident had been caused by negligence.*

• *Predicate*, however, is also widely used as a synonym for "base" or "found": □ *Her decision was predicated on past experience.*

In grammar and logic, the word *predicate* is also used as a noun. The verb is pronounced [*predi*kayt]; the noun is pronounced [*predi*kät].

preface see FOREWORD OR PREFACE?

prefer The elements that follow the verb *prefer* should be separated by *to*, not *than*: □ *I prefer cricket to football.* □ *She prefers watching television to reading a book.*

• If these elements are infinitives, the preposition *to* (and the second infinitive marker *to*) may be replaced by *rather than* in informal contexts: □ *He prefers to walk rather than (to) drive.* In formal contexts the sentence should be rephrased: □ *He would rather walk than drive.* □ *He prefers walking to driving.*

Careful users avoid qualifying the verb *prefer* and its derived adjective *preferable* with such adverbs as *more, most,* etc.: □ *Which dress do you prefer* [not *prefer most*]? □ *Quiet background music is acceptable, but complete silence is preferable* [not *more preferable*].

The verb *prefer* is stressed on the second syllable; the final *r* is doubled before *-ed, -ing,* and *-er*. In the adjective *preferable*, the adverb *preferably*, and the noun *preference*, the stress shifts to the first syllable, and the final *r* is not doubled. See also SPELLING 1.

prefixes and **suffixes** Prefixes and suffixes are elements attached to a word in order to form a new word. Prefixes are attached to the beginnings of words and include: □ *un-* □ *dis-* □ *anti-* □ *non-* □ *ex-*. Suffixes are attached to the ends of words and include: □ *-ism* □ *-ful* □ *-dom* □ *-ology* □ *-ship*.

• Prefixes are sometimes used with hyphens, sometimes not: □ *disenchanted* □ *ex-husband*: see HYPHEN 1.

There are some cases where a word cannot stand alone without its prefix: □ *uncouth* □ *disgruntled* □ *disheveled* □ *unkempt*, although *gruntled, kempt*, etc., are occasionally used jocularly.

Most affixes are in productive use: they can be attached to any appropriate nouns; however, new coinages involving affixes are often disliked: see, for example, MACRO- AND MICRO-.

prelude The frequent use of the noun *prelude* in the sense of "introduction" is disliked by some users: □ *The leaders had an informal meeting this morning as a prelude to next week's summit in Geneva.*

• The noun *prelude* is principally used to denote a piece of music: □ *one of Chopin's preludes.*

premier The adjective *premier* is best avoided where *foremost, principal, first,* etc., would be adequate or more appropriate: □ *We consulted one of the country's premier authorities on the subject.*
• *Premier* is pronounced [pri*myir*], the first syllable having the short *i* of *it,* not the long *e* of *theme.*

premiere Some people dislike the use of the word *premiere* as a verb, meaning "give the first performance of": □ *The film will be premiered in New York.*
• The verb is also used intransitively: □ *The play premiered in the West End.*

The noun *premiere,* meaning "first performance," is acceptable to all: □ *the world premiere of Andrew Lloyd Webber's latest musical.*

Premiere may be pronounced [pri*myir*] or [*premiĕr*]. It is sometimes spelled with a grave accent on the second *e,* as in the French word from which it is derived: *première.* See also **ACCENTS**.

premises The noun *premises,* denoting a building (or buildings) and any accompanying land or grounds, is always plural: □ *Their new premises are on the other side of the railroad tracks.*
• The singular noun *premise,* which is not used in this context, means "assumption" or "proposition"; it has the variant spelling *premiss* in British English.

premiss see **PREMISES**.

prepositions Prepositions are such words as: □ *at* □ *with* □ *of* □ *up* □ *before* that show the relation of a noun or noun equivalent to the rest of the sentence.
• One often hears of the grammatical rule that one should never end a sentence with a preposition. It is true that prepositions, as their name implies, usually precede the noun or pronoun to which they are attached: □ *It was under the chair.* □ *They drove to Birmingham,* but it certainly does not have to be in this position. □ *Which village did you stay in?* and *In which village did you stay?* are each possible, although the latter sounds more formal. In some cases it is hardly possible to put the preposition anywhere but at the end of the sentence: □ *What is he up to?* □ *It isn't worth worrying about.* A reliable rule is that the preposition should be placed where it sounds most natural.

The "rule" about ending a sentence with a preposition originated in the fact that a Latin sentence cannot end with a preposition, but there is no reason for this fact to have any implication for English usage.

A preposition does not need to be repeated when it applies to two elements of a sentence: □ *They went to France and Italy.* □ *He behaved with tact and discretion,* although the preposition must be repeated if ambiguity might otherwise arise. □ *They were arguing about physical fitness and about drinking alcohol* could have a different meaning if the second *about* were omitted.

prerequisite or **perquisite?** A *prerequisite* is a precondition; a *perquisite* is a benefit, privilege, or exclusive right: □ *A degree is not a prerequisite for a career in journalism.* □ *A company car is often regarded as a perquisite.*
• In the sense of "incidental benefit," the noun *perquisite* is usually shortened to *perk:* □ *one of the perks of the job.*

See also **PREREQUISITE OR REQUISITE?**

prerequisite or **requisite?** Each of these words may be used as noun or adjective. *Requisite* relates to anything that is required, necessary, essential, or indispensable; *prerequisite* relates to something that is required in advance: □ *Does the building have the requisite number of fire exits?* □ *The shop sells pens, paper, and other writing requisites.* □ *Physical fitness is prerequisite to/a prerequisite of success in sports.* See also **PREREQUISITE OR PERQUISITE?**

prescribe or **proscribe?** To *prescribe* is to set down as a rule or to advise or order as a remedy; to *proscribe* is to condemn, prohibit, outlaw, or exile: □ *The union has prescribed a new procedure for dealing with complaints.* □ *Surrogate motherhood has been proscribed in Britain.* □ *Proscribing the doctor's habit of prescribing* (*Daily Telegraph* headline, Sept. 1, 1987).
• The two verbs are similar in pronunciation but almost opposite in meaning: a *prescribed* book is recommended, whereas a *proscribed* book should not be read; a *prescribed* drug should be taken, whereas a *proscribed* drug is banned.

presently Some people object to the increasingly frequent use of the adverb *presently* in place of *currently, at present,* or *now:* □ *the senator, presently leader of the opposition.* □ *The company presently manufactures components for the electronics industry.*
• The meaning these users prefer for *presently* is "soon." □ *We walked on a little further, and presently we reached the inn.* □ *I'll phone him presently.*

pressure or **pressurize?** The verb *pressure,* which literally means "apply pressure to," is frequently used in the figurative sense of "coerce": □ *They were pressured into accepting the raise.*
• The literal meaning of the verb *pressurize* is "increase the pressure in," but it is also used figuratively in British English: □ *Airplane cabins are pressurized to maintain normal atmospheric pressure at high altitudes.* □ *They were pressurized into accepting the raise.*
     The figurative use of *pressurize* and *pressurized* is disliked and avoided by some British users, especially in potentially ambiguous contexts: □ *The ability to work effectively in a pressurized stimulating environment is essential* (*Daily Telegraph,* June 24, 1987).

prestige The noun *prestige,* denoting the high status, esteem, or renown derived from wealth, success, or influence, is pronounced [presteezh] or sometimes [presteej].
• *Prestige* is also used adjectivally: □ *a prestige company* □ *a prestige car.* See also **PRESTIGIOUS.**

prestigious The adjective *prestigious* is frequently used in the sense of "having or conferring prestige": □ *new ways of raising money for the country's most prestigious opera house* □ *The company will shortly be relocating to prestigious new offices in the city.*
• The original meaning of *prestigious* was less complimentary: derived from the Latin word for "conjuring tricks," it was used as a synonym for "fraudulent" or "deceitful."
     Prestigious has the pronunciation [prestijüs]

presume see **ASSUME OR PRESUME?**

presumptuous or **presumptive?** *Presumptuous* means "bold," "forward," or "impudent"; *presumptive* means "based on presumption or probability" or "giving reasonable grounds for belief": □ *It's rather presumptuous of him to make such a request.* □ *This is only presumptive evidence.*

• The adjective *presumptive* is also used in the term *heir presumptive,* which denotes a person whose right to succeed or inherit may be superseded by the birth of another.

Note the spelling of *presumptuous,* particularly the second *u.*

pretense, pretension, or **pretentiousness?** The noun *pretense* denotes the act of pretending; a *pretension* is a claim; *pretentiousness* means "ostentation" or "affectation": □ *She made a pretense of closing the door.* □ *He has no pretensions to fame.* □ *Their pretentiousness does not impress me.*

• In some contexts *pretense* may be used in place of *pretension,* especially to denote a false or unsupported claim; each noun may be used in the sense of "pretentiousness."

Compare the spellings of *pretension* and *pretentiousness,* particularly the *s* of the former and the second *t* of the latter. In British English, the *s* of *pretense* is replaced with *c: pretence.*

prevaricate or **procrastinate?** To *prevaricate* is to be evasive, misleading, or untruthful; to *procrastinate* is to delay, defer, or put off: □ *She prevaricated in order to avoid revealing her husband's whereabouts.* □ *He procrastinated in the hope of avoiding the work altogether.*

• The two verbs should not be confused: *prevaricate* is partially derived from the Latin word *varus,* meaning "crooked"; *procrastinate* contains the Latin word *cras,* meaning "tomorrow."

prevent When the verb *prevent* is followed by an *-ing* form in formal contexts, the *-ing* form should be preceded either by *from* or by a possessive adjective or noun: □ *They prevented me from winning.* □ *They prevented Andrew from winning.* □ *They prevented my winning.* □ *They prevented Andrew's winning.*

• In informal contexts, the last example may be considered unnatural or unidiomatic and the word *from* may be omitted from the first two examples: □ *They prevented me/Andrew winning.* See also **-ING FORMS.**

preventive or **preventative?** Either word may be used as an adjective or a noun, but *preventive* is the more frequent: □ *preventive measures* □ *preventive surgery* □ *This drug is used as a preventive/preventative.*

• Some users consider *preventative* to be a needlessly long variant.

In medical and technical contexts, the adjective is used with reference to procedures that forestall disease, damage, breakdown, etc., rather than curing or repairing it: □ *preventive medicine* □ *preventive maintenance.*

prewar This word, sometimes hyphenated, is usually a one-word compound. See also **HYPHEN 1.**

• *Prewar* is generally used as an adjective: □ *prewar conditions* □ *reverting to prewar practices.* Its adverbial use is less frequent, the phrase *before the war* being preferred by some users: □ *These houses were built prewar/before the war.*

In general usage, *prewar* usually refers to the period preceding World War II, but in some contexts the reference may be to World War I or, more rarely, to a different war. This usage can occasionally lead to ambiguity or confusion: □ *prewar prices in Asia.*

prey see **PRAY OR PREY?**

price see COST OR PRICE?

prima facie This Latin phrase is used adverbially or adjectivally in the sense of "at first sight," "(based) on first impressions," or "apparently true": □ *Her argument seems reasonable prima facie.* □ *There is prima facie evidence to support his case.* The adjective may be hyphenated: *prima-facie.*
 • Largely restricted to formal contexts, the phrase is pronounced [*prīmǎ fayshee*].

primarily Some users prefer to stress this word on the first syllable [*prīmǎrěli*]; the pronunciation with the stress on the second syllable [*prīmerrělee*] is the standard pronunciation. See also STRESS.

prime Some people dislike the frequent use of the adjective *prime* in the sense of "best," "most important," "principal," etc., especially when it is applied to something that is not of the highest quality, significance, or rank: □ *in prime condition* □ *the prime position* □ *a prime example.*

primeval This word, meaning "of the first ages," is usually spelled *primeval,* but in British English it may also be spelled *primaeval.*

principal or **principle?** These two spellings are often confused. The adjective *principal* means "of the most importance": □ *the principal cause;* the noun *principal* refers to the head of an organization: □ *the principal of a school. Principle* is always a noun and refers to a fundamental truth or standard: □ *moral principles.* The adjectival form is *principled.*
 • *In principle* means "in theory," whereas *on principle* means "because of the principle."

principal parts The principal parts of a verb are the main inflected forms from which all the other verb forms can be derived. In English they usually include the infinitive, the present participle, the past tense, and past participle. The principal of *give,* for example, would be: □ *give, giving, gave, given.* Often the past tense and past participle are the same and do not both have to be listed: □ *walk, walking, walked.* The present participle is not always included when it is derived regularly, as in: □ *know, knew, known.*

principle see PRINCIPAL OR PRINCIPLE?

prioritize The verb *prioritize,* meaning "put in order of priority" or "give priority to," is disliked by many users as an example of the increasing tendency to coin new verbs by adding the suffix *-ize* to nouns and adjectives: □ *The methods of increasing output have been prioritized.* □ *Are we expected to prioritize this work?*
 • An editorial comment in the *Oxford English Dictionary Supplement* notes that this is a word "that at present sits uneasily in the language." See also -IZE OR -ISE?

prior to Many people object to the unnecessary use of the phrase *prior to* in place of the simpler and more natural preposition *before:* □ *Players and singers rehearsed the works during the afternoon prior to performing them in the evening* (Chichester Observer, July 16, 1987).
 • The use of *prior* as an adjective is acceptable to all: □ *I would like to come but unfortunately have a prior engagement.*

prise see PRIZE OR PRISE?

pristine The use of *pristine* to mean "spotlessly clean," "pure," or "as good as new" is acceptable to most users: □ *a pristine table-*

cloth □ *Located in a pristine setting, Black Bear Woods Resort pedestal homes offer panoramic views of three surrounding ski areas in Canaan Valley* (advertisement, *The Washington Post,* Jan. 6, 1989).

• A few people object to this usage, restricting the adjective to its earlier sense of "original" or "primitive": □ *The pristine severity of the Benedictine rule was moderated in the course of time.*

The second syllable of *pristine* is pronounced to rhyme with *mean.*

privacy The standard pronunciation is [*prīvasee*].
• This word has two pronunciations: [*privăsi*] and [*prīvăsi*] in British English.

privilege This word, meaning "special right or advantage," is often misspelled. Note particularly the vowels: the two *i*'s and the two *e*'s. Remember also that there is no *d* as in *ledge.*

prize or **prise?** For the meaning "to force open," either spelling can be used, but *prize* is more common: □ *In the end we managed to prize the lid off.*
• *Prize* is the only possible spelling for the noun meaning "a reward" and the verb "value greatly": □ *Gloria won first prize in the competition.* □ *The thieves made off with most of their prized possessions.* In British English, the spelling *prise* is more common than *prize* for the sense "to force open."

pro- see PER-, PRE-, OR PRO-?

probe In the headline language of popular newspapers, the noun *probe* is often used in place of the longer *inquiry* or *investigation:* □ *Crucial questions the BBC poll probe must answer (Sunday Times,* June 21, 1987). See also **JOURNALESE.**
• In medicine a *probe* is a slender instrument for examining a wound or cavity; *space probes* examine and investigate the expanse beyond the earth's atmosphere.

In nontechnical contexts *probe* is more frequently used as a verb: □ *After further gentle probing, Mark revealed some new details of the incident.*

proceed see PRECEDE OR PROCEED?

procrastinate see PREVARICATE OR PROCRASTINATE?

prodigal *Prodigal* means "recklessly wasteful," "extravagant," or "lavish": □ *Her brother has always been prodigal with his money.* □ *They were prodigal of praise.*
• The use of the adjective *prodigal* to mean "returning home after a long absence" (based on a misunderstanding of the word in the New Testament parable of the prodigal son, Luke 15:11–32) is disliked and avoided by some careful users: □ *Prodigal performers from the Bosham Players are to return home 40 years on (Chichester Observer,* June 25, 1987).

The use of the noun *prodigal,* however, in the extended sense of "returned wanderer" or "repentant sinner," rather than the traditional sense of "spendthrift," is acceptable to most: □ *The prodigal has returned.*

prodigy or **protégé?** The noun *prodigy,* meaning "marvel," is used to denote an exceptionally talented person, especially a child: □ *Tracy Austin, then 14, was starting to be acknowledged as one of the first child prodigies in professional tennis (Daily Telegraph,* June 22, 1987). A *protégé* is someone who receives help, guidance, protection, patronage, etc., from a more influential or experienced person: □ *one of Lord Olivier's protégés.* The two nouns should not be confused.

• Derived from the French word *protéger,* meaning "to protect," the noun *protégé* has the (optional) feminine form *protégée.*

productivity The noun *productivity,* frequently used in industrial contexts, relates to efficiency or rate of production; it is not synonymous with *output,* which denotes the amount produced: □ *a productivity bonus* □ *The installation of new machinery will increase the company's productivity; employing more workers will only increase its output.*

professional The adjective *professional* is applied to people who are engaged in a profession or who take part in a sport or other activity for gain: □ *doctors, lawyers, and other professional people* □ *a professional golfer/actor/writer/musician.* The noun *professional* is used to denote such people.

• In general usage the word *professional,* in the sense of "(person) engaged in a profession," may refer to any career that requires advanced learning and/or special training, such as law, medicine, theology, accountancy, engineering, teaching, nursing, and the armed forces. Many users object to the wider application of the term as a noun that means other middle-class occupations: □ *a marketing professional* □ *sales professionals* □ *recruitment professionals.*

Note the spelling of the word *professional,* which has one *f* and a double *s.*

professor This word is sometimes misspelled. Note the single *f,* double *s,* and the *-or* ending.

profile The noun *profile* is widely used in the expression *keep a low profile,* meaning "be inconspicuous or unobtrusive" or "avoid attention or publicity": □ *The group has kept a low profile since the arrest of its leader.* This usage is disliked by some.

• Two adjectival compounds, *low-profile* and *high-profile,* have developed from this use: □ *a low-profile investigation* □ *In Glasgow on Monday, he [Neil Kinnock] . . . continued his high-profile, ticket-only rallies with his wife, Glenys* (*Sunday Times,* May 31, 1987). See also **VISIBLE**.

The noun *profile* is also used alone in a further extension of this sense: □ *She [Joan Bakewell] is credited with raising the profile of arts coverage on television* (*Sunday Times,* Aug. 23, 1987). □ *You can't risk loss of profile, market share, and media appeal* (*The Bookseller,* May 29, 1987).

prognosis see **DIAGNOSIS OR PROGNOSIS?**

program or **programme?** These words may be used as nouns or verbs. The preferred spelling is *program.* In British English the spelling *program* is restricted to the computing sense of "(provide with) a series of coded instructions": □ *a computer program* □ *to program a computer.* The British noun is usually *programme.* The word's meanings include "broadcast," "list," "plan," and "schedule": □ *a television program* □ *a theatre program* □ *the program for tonight's concert* □ *a research program* □ *a housing program* □ *the program of events.*

• The verb *program* means "plan," "schedule," or "cause to conform to particular instruction," though some object to this usage:

P

□ *The new road is programmed for completion next spring.* □ *He has been programmed to respond in this way.*

The final *m* of program is usually doubled before *-ed, -ing, -er,* and *-able.*

The spelling *programme* was adopted from the French in the 19th century; *program* was the original spelling of the word in British English.

prohibit see FORBID OR PROHIBIT?

project The word *project,* as a noun, meaning "scheme or plan," is usually pronounced [projekt]. The alternative [prŏjekt] is sometimes heard but is avoided by careful users.

• The verb *project* meaning "protrude" or "estimate for the future" is pronounced [prŏjekt].

prolific The adjective *prolific* means "very productive"; it is applied to the person or thing that produces rather than to what is produced: □ *A prolific author, she writes two or three new novels every year.*

• Many people object to the use of *prolific* as a synonym for "abundant" or "numerous": □ *Her prolific novels deal with a wide range of subjects.*

prone see LIABLE OR LIKELY?

pronouns Pronouns are words that are used to replace nouns or noun phrases to refer to something or someone: □ *I* □ *she* □ *him* □ *it* □ *you* □ *they,* etc. The main difficulty that arises with pronouns is in the use of the personal pronoun, because many people are confused by the subject and object forms. Such phrases as: □ *Everything comes to he who waits.* □ *It was up to Julia and I,* though incorrect, are frequently used. Remember that after verbs and prepositions, the object pronoun (*me, him, her, us, them*) should be used: □ *Everything comes to him who waits.* □ *It was up to Julia and me.* The confusion can be resolved by mentally changing the sentence slightly: □ *Things come to him* [not *he*]. □ *It was up to me* [not *I*]. Before verbs, the subject pronouns (*I, he, she, we, they*) should be used: □ *I* [not *me*] *and my friend will come.* □ *She* [not *her*] *and her colleague are arguing.* See also I AND ME?

• Perhaps because of this uncertainty about the personal pronoun, another frequent mistake is the use of a reflexive pronoun (formed with *-self*) instead of a personal pronoun: □ *It was written by another author and me* [not *myself*].

A further difficulty with pronouns is that of uncertainty of reference. This ambiguity can occur in sentences containing *it:* □ *We took the bus although it was late.* It is unclear whether the bus was late or the time was late. See also IT.

pronunciation Most people now accept that there is no one standard form of English pronunciation that is correct. There is great regional variety within the United States and further variations in the speech of other English-speaking countries, and there is nothing incorrect about a pronunciation that is standard to a particular community or region.

• It is perfectly valid, then, for an American to say [misl] and for a British speaker to say [misīl]. There is, however, still the possibility of mispronunciations, where a certain pronunciation is not an accepted regional variation and would generally be regarded as a mistake—for example, pronouncing *gist* as [gist] instead of [jist]. It should also be noted, though, that pronunciation is not static; it changes over the years and new pronunciations that were originally resisted by careful speakers sometimes eventually become the standard form.

A frequent mistake is to misspell *pronunciation* as *pronunciation*. The recommended pronunciation is [prōnunseeayshun], not [prănownsiayshăn].

propeller This word for a rotating device with blades is usually spelled with the ending *-er*, though *-or* is occasionally found.

proper nouns see CAPITAL LETTERS; NOUNS.

prophecy or **prophesy?** These spellings and pronunciations are sometimes confused. The noun meaning "prediction" is spelled *prophecy* and pronounced [*prof*ĕsee]. The verb meaning "to utter predictions" is spelled *prophesy* and pronounced [*prof*isī].

• *Advice* and *advise* are a similar noun-verb combination, spelled with a *c* for the noun and an *s* for the verb.

proportion The noun *proportion* denotes a ratio; it is best avoided where *part, number, some,* etc., would be adequate or more appropriate: □ *The proportion of female students to male students has increased.* □ *Some* [not *A proportion*] *of his friends are unemployed.*

• Such phrases as a *small(er) proportion* and a *large(r) proportion* may be replaced by *few, less, many, more,* etc.: □ *many* [not a *large proportion*] of our employees □ *less* [not a *smaller proportion*] of their money.

Some people also dislike the use of the plural noun *proportions* in place of size or dimensions: □ *Men of his proportions have difficulty finding clothes that fit.* □ *They set sail in a ship of enormous proportions.*

proscribe see PRESCRIBE OR PROSCRIBE?

prosecute see PERSECUTE OR PROSECUTE?

prospective see PERSPECTIVE OR PROSPECTIVE?

prostate or **prostrate?** The word *prostate* refers to a gland around the base of the bladder in men and other male mammals: □ *He's going into the hospital to have his prostate (gland) removed.*

• It should not be confused with the adjective *prostrate*, which means "lying face downwards," "exhausted," or "overcome": □ *He stepped over the prostrate body of the prisoner.* □ *They were prostrate with anguish.*

The word *prostrate*, stressed on the first syllable, is also used as a verb. In British English, the verb is stressed on the second syllable.

protagonist Some people object to the frequent use of the noun *protagonist* to denote a supporter, especially a leading or notable supporter, of a cause, movement, idea, political party, etc.: □ *British Rail has been the chief protagonist of the pro-Tunnel view over recent years* (*The Guardian*, March 19, 1980). □ *I would find myself a protagonist of a movement to introduce sanctions on those who do not use these established trade tools* (*The Bookseller*, Jan. 2, 1987). In such contexts, *protagonist* may be better replaced by an appropriate synonym, such as *champion, advocate,* or *proponent.*

• The traditional meaning of *protagonist* is "the leading or principal character in a play or story": □ *Wheeler and Webb then added a third series, starting with "Murder Gone to Earth" (1937), . . . in which the protagonist was a country doctor (Daily Telegraph,* Aug. 5, 1987). In this sense it should not be necessary to qualify the noun with such adjectives as *chief, main, leading, principal,* etc.

protégé see PRODIGY OR PROTÉGÉ?

pro tem The expression *pro tem* is a shortened form of the Latin phrase *pro tempore,* meaning "for the time (being)" or "temporarily": □ *Mr. Jones will take charge of the sales department pro tem.*

proved or **proven?** *Proved* is the past tense of the verb *prove* and the usual form of its past participle □ *They (have) proved their innocence.*

• As a variant form of the past participle, *proven* is largely restricted to the Scottish legal phrase *not proven.* It is also more frequently used as an adjective: □ *a proven remedy* □ *proven skills* □ *a proven liar.*

The accepted pronunciation of the word *proven* is [proovĕn], although the pronunciation [prōvĕn] is also heard from time to time, particularly in the Scottish legal phrase *not proven.*

proverbial The cliché *the proverbial . . .* is often used when (part of) a proverb or other idiomatic expression is quoted: □ *It's like leading the proverbial horse to water.* □ *We found ourselves up the proverbial creek.*

• The use of the adjective *proverbial* as a synonym for "famous" or "notorious" is disliked by some: □ *the proverbial British weather.*

provided or **providing?** The expressions *provided (that)* and *providing (that)* mean "on the condition (that)": □ *You may have a dog provided/providing that you look after it yourself.*

• Some consider *provided (that)* to be more acceptable than *providing (that).* The inclusion or omission of *that* is optional in most contexts.

The use of *provided* or *providing* in place of *if* is usually unnecessary and sometimes wrong: □ *I'll clean the windows this afternoon if/provided/providing it doesn't rain.* □ *We'll miss our train if* [not *provided/providing*] *we don't leave soon.*

psychiatry The branch of medicine dealing with problems of the mind is known as *psychiatry.* Note the spelling of the first syllable: *psych-,* which is from the Greek *psychē,* "soul."

• Other words that have this same stem include: □ *psychic* □ *psychiatrist* □ *psychoanalysis* □ *psychological.*

publicly This word is sometimes misspelled; there is no -*k*- before the suffix -*ly.*

• This word does not conform to the normal rule that adjectives ending in -*ic* have an adverb ending in -*ically,* as in *tragically.*

punctuation The primary purpose of punctuation is to clarify the writer's meaning. In speech the meaning is conveyed by the use of emphasis and pauses; punctuation has to serve the same purpose with written language. Lack of punctuation or incorrect punctuation can lead to misunderstanding and ambiguity.

• The importance of punctuation in conveying meaning can be illustrated by the various levels of punctuation in the following sentences: □ *My son who is a psychiatrist said George is insane.* The sense here is that one of my sons was commenting on George's mental state. □ *My son, who is a psychiatrist, said George is insane.* The suggestion here is that I have only one son and he was commenting on George's mental state. □ *"My son, who is a psychiatrist," said George, "is insane."* Here George is commenting on his son's mental state.

Punctuation is sometimes a matter of rules and sometimes a matter of style or personal preference. A heavily punctuated passage of writing is unpleasant to read and, in general, it is preferable to use the minimum amount of punctuation consistent with conveying the meaning clearly.

See also APOSTROPHE; BRACKETS; CAPITAL LETTERS; COLON; COMMA; DASH; ELLIPSIS; EXCLAMATION POINT; HYPHEN; ITALICS; PARAGRAPHS; PERIOD; QUESTION MARK; QUOTATION MARKS; SEMICOLONS; VIRGULE.

pygmy or **pigmy?** Each of these spellings is acceptable, although the *y* spelling is preferred by some users, because it shows the word's Greek origin: *pygmaios,* "dwarfish."

• *Pygmy* may be written with an initial capital letter when it is used to refer to a member of one of the tribes of equatorial Africa.

P

quality The word *quality* is often used adjectivally as a synonym for "excellent" or "of superior quality": □ *quality goods* □ *quality fiction* □ *a quality newspaper*. Some people object to this usage on the grounds that the noun *quality* does not always denote excellence: the quality of a product, service, etc., may be good, mediocre, or bad.

quantum leap Many people object to the frequent use of the term *quantum leap* (or *quantum jump*) to denote a great change or advance: □ *Sir Geoffrey has failed to convince the South African government that it must make the "quantum leap" to negotiations with Mr. Nelson Mandela and the African National Congress* (*The Guardian*, July 30, 1986).
• The term is borrowed from the field of physics, in which it refers to a sudden transition that is discernible but far from great.

quasi The Latin word *quasi*, meaning "as if," may be combined with adjectives, in the sense of "seemingly," "partly," or "almost,' or with nouns, in the sense of "resembling," "so-called," or "apparent": □ *quasi-religious* □ *quasi-official* □ *quasi splendor*.
• The hyphen is sometimes omitted, but the words are never written as a one-word compound.
Quasi may be pronounced [*kwayzī*] or [*kwahzee*].

quay This word for "landing place" is sometimes misspelled. Although pronounced like *key*, note its totally different spelling.

query The verb *query* is best avoided where *ask* or *question* would be more appropriate: □ *"Where do you live?" she asked* [not *queried*].
• The word *query* has connotations of doubt: a *query* is a question prompted by doubt; to *query* is to cast doubt on: □ *They accepted his statement without query.* □ *We queried the bill.*

question see BEG THE QUESTION; LEADING QUESTION; QUESTION MARK; RHETORICAL QUESTION.

question mark The primary use of the question mark is as a substitute for a period at the end of a sentence that is a direct question: □ *Where are you going?* and at the end of a quoted question, within the quotation marks: □ *"Where are you going?" he asked.* It is not used for an indirect question: □ *He asked me where I was going.*
• A question mark may appear after a question that is not a complete sentence: □ *Beer? Wine? Red or white?* It may also appear after a sentence that is not actually in question form but in which the rising intonation of speech would indicate an interrogative: □ *You can't mean that?* □ *She's really going to do it?*
A question mark usually follows a request: □ *Could I possibly*

210

have a cup of tea? If the request is more of an instruction, especial-ly if it is lengthy, it may end with a period, not a question mark: □ *Would all ladies who wish to travel to the gardens by bus kindly remain here for a short time.*

If a verb of thinking follows a direct question, it takes a question mark, but not if the question is in the past, where it has the force of reported speech: □ *Where are they now, I wonder?* □ *Where were they now, I wondered.* One would not write: □ *Where are they now? he wonders,* although it is occasionally possible for a ques-tion mark to appear in the middle of a sentence: □ *The question Why me? is one that cannot be answered.* This usage is disliked by some people who insist that, as a question mark has the force of a period, it cannot appear except at the end of a sentence, or in quotes or parentheses.

A question mark can be used to show that a fact is dubious: □ *Ambrose Bierce (1842?–1914).* It is sometimes also used, hu-morously or ironically, to express doubt: □ *my devoted (?) little brother,* but writers should use a question mark in this way only in very informal contexts. Similarly, double question marks and the combination of question marks and exclamation points should be avoided in formal writing.

questionnaire This word is sometimes misspelled. Note the double *n,* unlike the single *n* in *millionaire.*
• The traditional pronunciation of the first syllable was [kest-], but in contemporary usage the first syllable is pronounced as in *ques-tion:* [kweschŏnair].

quick The use of the word *quick* as an adverb should generally be avoided in formal contexts: □ *Please reply quickly* [not *quick*] *to avoid disappointment.* □ *Come quick!*
• The comparative and superlative forms *quicker* and *quickest* are more informal than *more quickly* and *most quickly:* □ *Some plants grow more quickly/quicker than others.* □ *The East German ath-lete ran the most quickly/quickest. Quicker* may be preferred to *more quickly* when the adverb is preceded by *any:* □ *Can you drive any quicker?*

The use of the adverb *quick* in fixed combinations, such as *quick-drying paint, quick-frozen food,* etc., is acceptable in all contexts.

quiet or **quieten?** Each of these verbs may be used to mean "soothe, calm, or allay" or "make or become quiet"; in the second of these senses the verb is often followed by *down. Quiet* is preferred in both senses.
• In British English the verb *quiet* is largely restricted to the first sense and formal usage and *quieten* to the second: □ *We must try to quiet his doubts.* □ *The children quietened down when their mother appeared.*

quit or **quitted?** Either word may be used as the past tense and past participle of the verb *quit.*
• *Quit* is becoming increasingly frequent, particularly in informal contexts: □ *They quit/quitted the building without delay.* □ *He has quit/quitted his job.*

quite In the usual sense of "completely," "totally," or "entirely," the adverb *quite* is generally used with adjectives that cannot be qualified by *very:* □ *a quite excellent result* □ *a quite unneces-*

sary remark □ *It is quite impossible!* □ *The ring is quite worth-less.* Used with other adjectives, *quite* sometimes has the meaning "somewhat," "fairly," or "rather": □ *They are quite use-ful.* □ *The film is quite frightening.*

• In some contexts, however, the adverb may be ambi-guous: □ *The room is quite clean.* □ *The bucket is quite full.*

In the sense of "fairly," the adverb *quite* usually precedes the in-definite article: □ *quite an easy question* □ *quite a long time.* The adjectival use of the expression *quite a/an,* meaning "remarkable" or "exceptional," is best restricted to informal contexts: □ *She has quite a collection.* □ *That was quite a meal.*

quitted see QUIT OR QUITTED?

quotation marks Quotation marks are used at the beginning and end of direct quotations: □ *He said, "I'm going out now."* □ *"All right," she replied, "but don't be late."* Only the words actually spoken are placed within the quotation marks; they are not used in reported speech: □ *"I am tired," she said.* □ *She said that she was tired.* In reported speech, though, one might use quotation marks in order to draw attention to the fact that the speaker has used certain words, particularly if one wished to dissociate oneself from the expression used: □ *He said he was in an "ongoing situation."*

• Periods and commas come inside the quotation marks; semico-lons and colons are placed outside. Question marks and exclama-tion points are placed inside or outside, depending on the sense. The convention in British English, however, has been for punctua-tion to come inside the marks only when it is part of the actual quo-tation. The comma usually also comes within the quotation marks when it is followed by *he said, Martha replied,* etc.: □ *"I wish," she said, "you would go away."* In sentences where the quoted matter is not followed by *he said* or similar, then the comma is out-side. □ *He loves Kipling's "If", and is constantly quoting it.*

Double quotation marks should be used, but when there is a quotation within a quotation, single marks must be used inside double ones: □ *She commented, "I wish he wouldn't call me 'sweetie.'"*

Quotation marks are used instead of italics for various short liter-ary and musical works (see TITLES). They are also sometimes used by writers to indicate slang or as an apology for using a par-ticular word or expression: □ *I gather my writing is thought to lack "pizzazz."* They are also used in various specialized writings to in-dicate meanings or interpretations: □ *The word hence means "from this time."*

quote The noun *quote* (short for *quotation*) and the plural form *quotes* (short for *quotation marks*) are best restricted to informal contexts: □ *It's a quote from Shakespeare.* □ *The newspaper arti-cle was full of quotes.* □ *Should the last sentence be in quotes?*

• The word *quote* is also used in speech to introduce a direct quo-tation: □ *The chairman said, quote, there will be no further layoffs this year, unquote.* (The addition of *unquote* at the end is optional.)

racism or **racialism?** Each of these nouns is used in the sense of "racial prejudice or discrimination," *racism* being more frequent than the older *racialism* in modern usage: □ *The company was accused of racism in its recruitment policy.*
• *Racism* and *racialism* also refer to the theory that some races (or one particular race) are superior to others. See also **BLACK**.

rack or **wrack?** These two words are sometimes confused. *Rack* is used for a framework for storing or displaying things: □ *a luggage rack* □ *a shoe rack.* *Rack* is also used for the torturing frame. As a verb, *rack* means "cause to suffer pain": □ *racked with uncertainty* □ *nerve-racking;* one also *racks one's brains.* The expression *rack and ruin,* "a state of collapse," may also be spelled *wrack and ruin.* Seaweed is *wrack.*

racket or **racquet?** Either spelling is acceptable for describing the implement used in sports for striking the ball: □ *tennis racket/racquet; racquet* is preferred in *racquetball.*
• The spelling *racket* has the additional noun senses "loud noise": □ *That music is a terrible racket,* and "illegal business": □ *involved in a drug racket.*

raise or **raze?** The verb *raise* means "move to a higher position": □ *He raised the trophy high; raze* means "destroy completely": □ *The city was razed to the ground.* The two spellings should not be confused.

raise or **rise?** Each of these verbs means "move to a higher or upright position" or "increase." *Raise* is transitive, whereas *rise* is intransitive: □ *She raised her arm.* □ *They may raise the price.* □ *I watched the smoke rise.* □ *The temperature was rising.*
• The verb *raise* is also used in the sense of "bring up," "rear," or "breed": □ *He was raised in Kentucky.* □ *We raise Highland cattle. Rise,* an irregular verb, has a number of specialized uses: □ *She rose at dawn.* □ *The dough has risen.*
  The noun *rise* means "increase": □ *a rise in temperature* □ *a rise in unemployment. Raise* is used in place of *rise* to denote an increase in salary, wages, etc.: □ *He asked for a raise;* this usage is widely heard in American English, but is only gradually coming into use in British English.
  See also **ARISE OR RISE?; RAISE OR RAZE?**

raison d'être The phrase *raison d'être,* of French origin, is used in English to denote a reason or justification for existence; it is best avoided where *reason, explanation,* etc., would be adequate or more appropriate: □ *Helping the bereaved is the organization's raison d'être.* □ *The White House spokesman explained the reason* [not *raison d'être*] *for the Government's change of policy.*

213

• Note the spelling of the phrase, particularly the circumflex accent on the first *e*. The Anglicized pronunciation is [*rayzon detrĕ*].

rapt or **wrapped?** These spellings are sometimes confused. The adjective *rapt* means "engrossed or absorbed": □ *rapt with wonder* □ *They listened with rapt attention*. *Wrapped* is the past tense of the verb *wrap*, meaning "enfold": □ *She wrapped the shawl around the baby*.

• Note that *wrapped* can also be used figuratively: □ *He is completely wrapped up in his work.*

rara avis The phrase *rara avis*, denoting a rare or an unusual person or thing, is often better replaced by the noun *rarity:* □ *The dedicated employee who is prepared to work long hours without reward is a rara avis*.

• Of Latin origin, the phrase literally means "rare bird." The usual pronunciation of *rara avis* is [*reră ayvis*] or sometimes [*rară ayvis*].

rather The adverb *rather* may be used with *would* or *had*, but *would* is more frequent in modern usage, *had* being rather formal: □ *They would/had rather watch television than listen to the radio*. □ *She would/had rather you stayed at home*.

• The contraction *'d*, which may represent either *would* or *had*, is often used in informal contexts: □ *I'd rather write than telephone*. See also **SHOULD** OR **WOULD?**

The substitution of *rather than* for *than* after a comparative is wrong: □ *He is more interested in the customs and traditions of Colonial Virginia than* [not *rather than*] *in the political events of the period*.

Some people object to the use of *rather* before *a* or *an* when the following noun is qualified by an adjective, preferring *It's a rather expensive car* to *It's rather an expensive car*. If the noun is not qualified by an adjective, *rather* must precede the indefinite article: □ *He's rather a coward*.

ravage or **ravish?** These two verbs should not be confused. *Ravage* means "cause great damage to" and "devastate"; to *ravish* is "to delight or enrapture": □ *The country was ravaged by war.* □ *They were ravished by the beauty of the sunset.*

• *Ravish* has the additional meaning of "rape" or "carry off by force": □ *She was ravished by her captors*.

Both verbs are largely restricted to formal contexts. The word *ravage* is also used as a noun, in such phrases as the *ravages of time*, and the word *ravish* in the adjectival form *ravishing:* □ *You look ravishing in that dress*.

raze see **RAISE** OR **RAZE?**

re The use of the preposition *re*, meaning "with reference to" or "in the matter of," should be restricted to the heading or opening of a business letter or memo: □ *Re: Interest rates for personal loans*. □ *Re your advertisement in* Life.

• In other contexts *re* can usually be replaced by *about, concerning*, etc.: □ *I am producing a documentary about* [not *re*] *the problems faced by single parents*. □ *We have received many letters of complaint concerning* [not *re*] *the proposed route for the new bypass*.

Re is usually pronounced to rhyme with *bee*. The pronunciation [*ray*] is also heard from time to time, but is incorrect.

re- The prefix *re-*, meaning "again," should be followed by a hyphen in compounds that might be confused with existing or more familiar words. Such verbs as *re-sound* and *re-sign* (meaning "sound again" and "sign again"), for example, are thus distinguished from the verbs *resound* and *resign*.

• See also **RECOUNT OR RE-COUNT?**; **RECOVER OR RE-COVER?**; **RECREATION OR RE-CREATION?**; **REFORM OR RE-FORM?**; **REPRESENT OR RE-PRESENT?**; **RESORT OR RE-SORT?**

The use of a hyphen in the words *re-educate, re-election, re-entry, re-examine,* etc., is optional. See also **HYPHEN 1**.

Careful users avoid the tautological addition of the adverbs *back* and *again* to verbs that begin with the prefix *re-*: □ *She returned* [not *returned back*] *to Canada in 1945.* □ *I refer you to the opening paragraph* [not *I refer you back*]. □ *We are redecorating the lounge* [not *redecorating again*]. □ *He made me rewrite the article* [not *rewrite again*]. The use of *again* in the last example would imply that the article had been written more than twice: □ *He was not satisfied with my second draft and made me rewrite the article again.*

reaction The noun *reaction*, which denotes a spontaneous or automatic response, is best avoided where *reply, response, answer, opinion,* etc., would be more appropriate: □ *On hearing the alarm, his reaction was one of panic.* □ *We had hoped for a more favorable response* [not *reaction*] *from the committee.* □ *Please study these proposals and give me your opinion* [not *reaction*].

• A *reaction* can occur only in response to something else; the word should not be used in place of *effect, influence,* etc.: □ *What was the effect* [not *reaction*] *of the news on her family?* or □ *What was the reaction of her family to the news?*

readable see **LEGIBLE OR READABLE?**

real Many people object to the frequent use of the adjective *real* in place of *important, serious,* etc., or simply for emphasis: □ *a real achievement* □ *a real problem* □ *the real facts* □ *in real life.*

• The adverbial use of *real* in the sense of "really" or "very" is colloquial: □ *He's real clever.*

realistic The frequent use of the adjective *realistic* as a synonym for "sensible," "practical," "reasonable," etc., is disliked by many users: □ *a realistic proposal* □ *a realistic alternative* □ *a realistic offer.*

really The excessive use of the adverb *really* is best avoided, even in informal contexts. *Really* can often be replaced by a different intensifier, such as *very, extremely, thoroughly, truly,* etc., or omitted altogether: □ *It was really late when they arrived and we were really worried.* □ *Wait until the paint is really dry.* □ *I really enjoyed that vacation.* □ *She really hates her job.*

reason Careful users regard the tautological construction *the reason is/was because* as wrong, preferring *the reason is/was that* or a simpler paraphrase using *because* alone: □ *The reason for the delay is that* [not *because*] *there was road construction in progress.* □ *The reason I opened the window was that* [not *because*] *there was a wasp in the room.* □ *I opened the window because there was a wasp in the room.*

• Similar objections are raised to the use of such constructions as *the reason is due to, the reason was on account of,* etc.

The phrase *the reason why* is acceptable to some users but disliked by others. In most instances *why* may be replaced by *that* or omitted altogether; if a noun can be substituted for the verb, the phrase *the reason for* may be used instead: □ *the reason (that) he resigned; the reason for his resignation.*

receipt This word, meaning "written confirmation that something has been paid or received," is sometimes misspelled. Note the *-ei*-spelling, and the silent *p*. See also **SPELLING 5.**

reciprocal see **MUTUAL, COMMON, OR RECIPROCAL?**

reckon The use of the verb *reckon* in place of *think*, expressing a personal opinion, is best restricted to informal contexts: □ *He reckons the other team will win.*
• In the sense of "consider" or "regard," however, *reckon* is acceptable in all contexts: □ *She is reckoned to be one of the most talented musicians of her generation.*

recommend This word, meaning "praise or suggest as suitable," is often misspelled. Note the single *c* and double *m*.

reconnaissance This word, meaning "exploration or survey of an area for military intelligence purposes," is often misspelled. Note the double *n* and double *s*.
• Note also the spelling of the verb *reconnoiter* meaning "make a reconnaissance."

recount or **re-count?** The preferred spelling is *recount*. The verb *recount* means "narrate": □ *He recounted his experiences during the war.* The verb *recount* also means "count again," and the noun *recount*, which is used more frequently than the verb, means "second count": □ *to demand a recount of the votes.* Except in the sense of "narrate," *recount* is sometimes spelled with a hyphen: *re-count.* See **RE-.**

recourse, resort, or **resource?** Similarities in the sense, usage, form, and pronunciation of these words may lead to confusion. Each of the three can refer to a source of help or an expedient: □ *Violence was our only recourse/resort/resource.*
• In the expressions *have recourse/resort to* and *without recourse/resort to, recourse* and *resort* are virtually interchangeable but cannot be replaced by *resource. Recourse* is the more frequent noun in such contexts, *resort* being used as a verb in similar constructions: □ *I hope he will not have recourse to violence.—I hope he will not resort to violence.* □ *They settled the dispute without recourse to violence.—They settled the dispute without resorting to violence.*
  In the expression *as a last resort/resource* the nouns *resort* and *resource* are interchangeable but cannot be replaced by *recourse. Resort* is generally considered to be the more idiomatic choice in such contexts: □ *She turned to violence as a last resort.*

recover or **re-cover?** These two spellings are sometimes confused. *Recover* means "regain": □ *She recovered her health. Re-cover,* with a hyphen, means "give a new cover to": □ *The decorators re-covered the chair.* See **RE-.**

recreation or **re-creation?** The spellings of these words are sometimes confused. *Recreation* means "relaxation; leisure (pursuit)": □ *recreation grounds. Re-creation,* a word less frequently used, is "a new creation": □ *the re-creation of the Wild West for the film set.* See **RE-.**

redundant Some people object to the frequent use of the adjective *redundant* in place of *unnecessary, superfluous, irrelevant, unimportant,* etc.: □ *Our second car will become redundant when my husband starts commuting by train.* □ *The cancellation of the dinner dance made the baby-sitting problem redundant.* In British English, *redundant* means "laid off or dismissed from work."

refer The verb *refer* is stressed on the second syllable; the final *r* is doubled before *-ed, -ing,* and *-er.* In the noun *reference,* the stress shifts to the first syllable, and the second *r* is not doubled.
• See also **SPELLING 1.**
For the use of the adverb *back* with the verb *refer,* see **RE-.**

referendum The noun *referendum* has two plural forms, *referendums* and *referenda. Referendums* is the more frequent in general usage: □ *Their proposed referendums on nuclear disarmament and the return of capital punishment will be welcomed by many.*

reform or **re-form?** These spellings are sometimes confused. The verb *reform* means "change by improvement": □ *plans to reform the tax system. Re-form,* with a hyphen, means "form again": □ *After a lapse of seven years, the club decided to re-form.* See **RE-.**

refute or **deny?** The verb *refute* means "prove to be false"; *deny* means "declare to be false": □ *He refuted their accusations by producing a receipt for the camera.* □ *He denied their accusations but was unable to prove his innocence.* The use of *refute* in place of *deny* is avoided by many careful users but nevertheless occurs with some frequency.

regard In the sense of "consider," the verb *regard* should be used with the preposition *as:* □ *She regards her mother as her friend.* □ *This novel is regarded as the author's masterpiece.* Compare **CONSIDER.**
• The verb *regard* has a number of other senses and is also used in the prepositional phrase *as regards,* meaning "with respect to," "about," or "concerning": □ *As regards your suggestion, the committee will discuss it at tomorrow's meeting. As regards* should not be confused with the phrases *with regard to* and *in regard to,* in which the word *regard* is a noun and does not end in *s.* In mid-sentence, these compound prepositions are often better replaced by *about, concerning, regarding.*
The noun *regard* is used in a variety of other expressions. *Have regard for* means "show consideration for." □ *They have no regard for her safety.* The plural noun *regards,* meaning "greetings," occurs in such expressions as *with kind regards* (used to close a letter) and *give one's regards to:* □ *Please give my regards to your daughter when you see her.*

regardless see **IRRESPECTIVE.**

rein or **reign?** These spellings are sometimes confused. *Reins* are the leather straps that control a horse; *reign* means "exercise (of) royal authority": □ *pull at the reins* □ *the reign of King Henry VIII.*
• The noun *rein* is also used in such expressions as *give free rein to,* "allow freedom to," and *keep a tight rein on,* "control strictly." A *reign* is the period of a monarch's rule. □ *King Henry VIII's reign lasted from 1509 to 1547. Reign* is also used to describe a powerful prevalent power or influence: □ *the reign of terror in Uganda under Idi Amin.* □ *Peace has reigned in Europe since 1945.*

R

reiterate The verb *reiterate* means "repeat" or "say or do repeatedly"; it should not be used with the adverb *again* (see also RE-):
□ *The politician was simply reiterating the promises made in the party manifesto.*

relation or **relationship?** Each of these nouns may be used in the sense of "connection," but they are not interchangeable in all contexts: □ *Is there any relation/relationship between unemployment and crime?* □ *This evidence bears no relation* [not *relationship*] *to the case.* □ *What is his relationship* [not *relation*] *to the deceased?*
• The noun *relationship* is preferred for human connections, *relation* for more abstract connections.

A similar distinction may be applied to the use of *relationship* and the plural noun *relations* in the sense of "mutual feelings or dealings": □ *business relations* □ *an intimate relationship* □ *the government's relations with the unions* □ *his relationship with his wife.* See also RELATION OR RELATIVE?

relation or **relative?** Either noun may be used to denote a person connected to another by blood, marriage, or adoption: □ *Most of her relations/relatives are going to the wedding.* □ *I have a distant relative/relation in Canada.*
• See also RELATION OR RELATIONSHIP?

relatively The adverb *relatively* implies comparison; many people object to its use as a synonym for "fairly," "somewhat," "rather," etc., where there is no comparison: □ *After the heat of the kitchen, the lounge felt relatively cool.* □ *Our records are fairly* [not *relatively*] *up-to-date.*

relevant This word is sometimes misspelled. Note particularly the second *e*.

relocate The verb *relocate*, frequently used in business and industrial contexts, is widely regarded as a pretentious synonym for "move": □ *the latest major firm to relocate to Florida* □ *Unemployment in the North is forcing many families to relocate.*

remedial or **remediable?** *Remedial* means "intended as a remedy"; *remediable* means "able to be remedied": □ *remedial treatment* □ *a remediable problem.* The two adjectives should not be confused. *Remedial* is specifically applied to teaching aimed at helping overcome deficiencies: □ *remedial education* □ *a remedial course.*
• *Remediable* is less frequent than its antonym *irremediable*: □ *The damage is irremediable.*

Each adjective is stressed on the second syllable, unlike the word *remedy* from which they are derived. *Remedial* is pronounced [rimeediäl]; *remediable* is pronounced [rimeediäbl].

reminiscent This word is sometimes misspelled. Note particularly the *-sc-*, as in *scent*.

renege The traditional pronunciation of this word, which means "not keep (a promise, agreement, etc.)," is [rineeg], but [rinig] is also frequently used and is acceptable.

rent see HIRE OR RENT?

repair see FIX OR REPAIR?

repairable or **reparable?** Each of these adjectives means "able to be repaired"; careful users apply *repairable* to material objects and *reparable* to abstract nouns: □ *The car is badly damaged but repairable.* □ *His loss is scarcely reparable.*

• The two adjectives relate to different senses of the verb *repair:* "mend" or "restore" (*repairable*) and "remedy" or "make good" (*reparable*).

Reparable, which is stressed on the first syllable [rĕpărăbl], is less frequent than its opposite *irreparable:* □ *These allegations have done irreparable harm to his political career.*

Repairable is stressed on the second syllable [ripairăbl]; its opposite is *unrepairable.*

repel see REPELLENT OR REPULSIVE?

repellent or **repulsive?** *Repellent* and *repulsive* mean "causing disgust or aversion." *Repulsive* is the stronger of the two adjectives, both of which are ultimately derived from the Latin verb *repellere,* meaning drive back, "repel": □ *His deformed body was a repellent sight.* □ *The partially decomposed corpse was a repulsive sight.* □ *The principles of Communism are repellent to some; the doctrines of Nazism were repulsive to many.*

• The adjective *repellent* is also used in combination to mean "driving away" or "resistant": □ *insect-repellent spray* □ *water-repellent fabric. Repellant* is a less frequent spelling of the noun and adjective *repellent.*

The verb *repel* is a weaker synonym of *repulse.* The use of the verb *repulse* in the sense of "disgust" is disliked by some users, who restrict it to the sense of "drive back" or "rebuff": □ *The inhabitants repulsed the invading army.* □ *He repulsed her offer of friendship. Repel* may be used in any of these senses.

repercussions The word *repercussions* is best avoided where *result, consequence, effect,* etc., would be adequate or more appropriate: □ *the repercussions of a ban on smoking in restaurants.*

• The noun *repercussion* literally means "reverberation" or "rebound"; in figurative contexts it should be restricted to indirect or far-reaching effects: □ *the repercussions of a serious accident at one of the nuclear-power plants.*

repertoire or **repertory?** The noun *repertoire* principally denotes the musical or dramatic works, poems, jokes, etc., that a person or group is able or prepared to perform: □ *That song is not in her repertoire.*

• The word *repertory* is also used in this sense but is more frequently applied to a company of actors that presents a *repertoire* of plays at the same theater: □ *a repertory company* □ *a repertory theater* □ *to act/be performed in repertory.*

repetitious or **repetitive?** The adjective *repetitive* means "characterized by repetition"; *repetitious* means "characterized by unnecessary or tedious repetition": □ *a repetitive rhythm* □ *repetitious arguments.*

• *Repetitive,* the more frequent of the two adjectives, is also sometimes used in the derogatory sense of *repetitious,* but careful users avoid this usage: □ *a lengthy, repetitious* [not *repetitive*] *description of the ceremony.*

replace or **substitute?** The verb *replace* means "take the place of"; the verb *substitute* means "put in the place of": □ *I substituted his painting for her photograph.* □ *Her photograph was replaced*

R

with *his painting*. □ *His painting was substituted for her photograph*. □ *His painting replaced her photograph*.

• *Substitute* is used with the preposition *for*; *replace* may be used with the preposition *with* or *by* (especially in passive sentences): □ *Her photograph was replaced by his painting*.

All the examples above refer to the act of removing her photograph and putting his painting in its place. The two verbs are often confused in such contexts, *substitute* being used instead of *replace*, but careful users maintain the distinction between them.

replica Some people object to the frequent use of *replica* in place of *copy, duplicate, reproduction, model*, etc.: □ *He bought a plastic replica of the Statue of Liberty*. □ *This article is a replica of yesterday's editorial*.

• The noun *replica* principally denotes an exact copy of a work of art, especially one made by the original artist.

represent or **re-present?** The spellings are sometimes confused. *Represent* means "act in place of": □ *The team will represent the whole school*. *Re-present*, with a hyphen, means "present again": □ *He re-presented the series of lectures the following autumn*.

repulse, repulsive see REPELLENT OR REPULSIVE?

requisite see PREREQUISITE OR REQUISITE?

resort or **re-sort?** The noun *resort* means "place of rest or recreation": □ *seaside resorts* or a source of help: □ *the last resort*. The verb *resort* means "turn to": □ *I hope he will not resort to violence*. The verb *re-sort*, with a hyphen, means "sort again": □ *re-sort all the index cards*.

• *Resort*, both as a noun and as a verb, is pronounced with a *z* [riz*ort*]; *re-sort* is pronounced with an *s* [rees*ort*].

resort, resource see RECOURSE, RESORT, OR RESOURCE?

respective and **respectively** The words *respective* and *respectively* should be used only where there would be a risk of ambiguity or confusion in their absence: □ *The workers explained their respective problems to the foreman*. □ *Toys and furniture are sold on the second and third floors, respectively*. Without *respective*, the first example could imply that all the workers had the same problems; without *respectively*, the second example might suggest that toys and furniture are sold on both floors.

• In other contexts, the words are often unnecessary or inappropriate: □ *Paul and Sarah got into their (respective) cars and drove away*. □ *Each book must be returned to its (respective) shelf*. □ *She worked (respectively) in Paris, Vienna, and Rome*.

respite This word, meaning "relief, delay" : □ *no respite from the toil*, is often mispronounced. The stress falls on the first syllable, unlike *despite*, which has the stress on the second syllable.

• The second syllable may be pronounced [res*pit*] or [res*pīt*] although most users prefer the former pronunciation.

restaurateur Note the spelling for this formal word for a person who runs a restaurant. There is no *n* as in *restaurant*.

• Restaurateur is pronounced [rest*ĕrĕter*].

restive or **restless?** The adjective *restive* means "resisting control"; *restless* means "fidgety" or "agitated": □ *The teacher tried to discipline his restive pupils*. □ *Some of the congregation became* *restless during the long sermon.* The use of *restive* in place of *restless* is disliked by careful users.

resuscitate This word, meaning "revive": □ *All attempts to resuscitate him with the kiss of life failed,* is often misspelled. Note particularly the *-sc-* in the middle of the word.

return see RE-.

reveille This word is pronounced [revĕlee].
• Note also the spelling; the word is derived from the French *réveiller,* "awaken."

revenge or **avenge?** Each of these verbs refers to the act of repaying a wrong. The person who *revenges* is usually the offended or injured party; a person who *avenges* is usually a third party acting on behalf of another: □ *I will revenge myself on those who humiliated me.* □ *He planned to avenge his brother's death by drowning the murderer's daughter.* □ *He avenged his murdered brother.*
• This distinction is not observed by all users in all contexts, however, and *revenge* is often interchangeable with *avenge.* See also REVENGE OR VENGEANCE?

revenge or **vengeance?** Each of these nouns may be used in the sense of "retaliation" or "retribution": □ *The destruction of her parent's home was an act of revenge/vengeance.*
• Some users associate *revenge* with the subjective or personal act of revenging and *vengeance* with the objective or impersonal act of avenging (see REVENGE OR AVENGE?): □ *They humiliated me, but I will take my revenge.* □ *He sought vengeance for the murder of his brother.*

reversal or **reversion?** *Reversal* is the act of reversing; *reversion* is the act of reverting: □ *the reversal of this trend* □ *reversion to his former way of life.* The two nouns should not be confused.

review or **revue?** These two spellings are sometimes confused. *Review,* as a noun, is a "critical appraisal": □ *a review of her latest novel* or a "reassessment": □ *The warden ordered an urgent review of prison security.* A *revue* is a light theatrical show consisting of sketches, songs, etc.: □ *the annual Christmas revue.*
• *Revue* may also be spelled *review,* but this usage is best avoided in order to maintain the distinction between the two words.

rhetorical question A rhetorical question is one that is asked for effect, and to which no answer is expected: □ *What is the world coming to?* □ *How can people behave like that?* The question is sometimes asked so that it can be answered immediately by the speaker: □ *Why are we on strike? I will tell you why . . . .*
• A rhetorical question is sometimes just a rephrased statement, put in question form for greater emphasis: □ *Was there ever a more unfortunate person?*

rheumatism This word for an illness that causes pain in the muscles or joints is sometimes misspelled. Note particularly the first syllable *rheu-.*

rhinoceros The name of this animal is often misspelled. Note particularly the *rh-,* and the *c* in the middle of the word.

rhythm This word is frequently misspelled. Note particularly the first *h* and the *y.*

ribald This adjective, meaning "coarse or crude": □ *ribald language,* is often mispronounced. The pronunciation is [rĭbăld].

R

• The alternative [*rī*bawld] is regarded as unacceptable by careful users.

ricochet This word, used to describe bullets, etc., that rebound, is usually pronounced [*rī*kŏshay]; [*rī*kŏshet] is a British variant. There are alternative present and past participles: *ricocheting* [*rī*-kŏshaying] or *ricochetting* [*rī*kŏsheting] and *ricocheted* [*rī*kŏshayd] or *ricochetted* [*rī*kŏshetid].

right or **rightly?** Each of these adverbs may be used in the sense of "correctly" or "properly." *Right* is generally placed after the verb, *rightly* before the verb: □ *Have I spelled your name right?* □ *He rightly stopped at the school crossing.* □ *You're not holding your fork right.* □ *She rightly held her fork in her left hand.*

• The phrase *if I remember right/rightly* is a notable exception to this rule.

Right has a number of other adverbial uses: □ *Turn right at the next intersection.* □ *They went right home.* □ *We live right at the top of the hill. Rightly* also means "justly" or "suitably": □ *She was rightly annoyed by their behavior.* □ *Am I rightly dressed for the trip?* The two adverbs are not interchangeable in any of these senses.

In informal contexts, *right* is sometimes used to mean "very" and *rightly* to mean "with certainty": □ *We're right pleased to see you.* □ *He doesn't rightly know.*

rigor or **rigour?** *Rigor,* meaning "harsh conditions; severity": □ *the rigors of winter,* is spelled like the medical *rigor:* □ *rigor mortis.*

• Note that in British English, the first sense is spelled *rigour.*

rigorous This word is sometimes misspelled. There is only one *u* in *rigorous.*

rigour see **RIGOR OR RIGOUR?**

rip-off Derived from the slang *rip off,* meaning "steal" or "cheat," the noun *rip-off* is principally applied to overpriced goods or the practice of charging exorbitant prices: □ *This handbag is an absolute rip-off—it's not even made of real leather.* □ *I had to pay $10 to get in—it's a rip-off!*

• Extending this sense of "exploitation," *rip-off* is also used to denote an inferior film, book, etc., that seeks to exploit the success of another by imitation.

The noun *rip-off* should not be used in formal contexts.

rise see **ARISE OR RISE?; RAISE OR RISE?**

road or **street?** Generally the noun *road* is used to denote a thoroughfare between towns or cities; a *street* is a thoroughfare in a city or its suburbs: □ *a country road* □ *a one-way street* □ *the road to Miami* □ *the streets of Washington* □ *their 42nd Street store.* There are, however, numerous exceptions to this rule, especially in the naming of roads and streets.

rob, robbery see **BURGLARIZE, BURGLE, ROB, OR STEAL?**

role Some people object to the frequent use of the noun *role* as a synonym for "place," "function," "position," "part," etc.: □ *the role of religion in modern society* □ *a proven track record in a sales role* □ *A new manager is now sought to play a key role in determining the company's future strategy.* The noun *role* is principally used to denote the part played by an actor. In psychology and sociology, it refers to the part played by an individual in a social situation: □ *role reversal* □ *role-playing.*

• The word is sometimes spelled with a circumflex accent over the *o*, as in the French word from whichit is derived: □ *rôle.* It should not be confused with the English noun *roll,* to which it is etymologically related.

roofs or **rooves?** The plural of the word *roof,* "covering of a building," is *roofs,* pronounced [roofs] or [roovz].

• The spelling of the plural *rooves* is much less frequent.

root see ROUT OR ROUTE?

roughage This word, meaning "coarse food," is sometimes misspelled. Note the *-gh-* in the middle of the word.

round see AROUND OR ROUND?

rouse see AROUSE OR ROUSE?

rout or **route?** The noun *rout* means "overwhelming defeat" or "disorderly retreat"; the noun *route* means "road" or "course": □ *They put the enemy to rout.* □ *The procession took a different route.*

• The risk of confusion is greater when the words are used as verbs, especially in the past tense: □ *They routed the enemy.* □ *The procession was routed along a different road.*

The phrasal verb *rout out,* meaning "find by searching" or "force out," is a variant of the verb *root,* meaning "rummage," and is etymologically unrelated to the verb *rout* discussed above.

Rout is pronounced [rowt], rhyming with *out,* in all its senses and uses; the pronunciation of *route* is identical with that of *root* or sometimes *rout.*

rural or **rustic?** Each of these adjectives relates to the countryside, country life, country people, farming, etc. *Rural* is used as a neutral opposite of urban; *rustic* has connotations of simplicity, crudeness, quaintness, or lack of sophistication: □ *rural schools* □ *a rural setting* □ *rural areas* □ *rustic food* □ *a rustic cottage* □ *rustic manners.* Careful users maintain the distinction between the two words.

S

's or s'? Possessive nouns are usually formed by adding *'s* to singular nouns, an apostrophe to plural nouns that end in *s*, and *'s* to irregular plural nouns that do not end in *s:* □ *Jane's pen* □ *the boy's father* □ *the director's cars* □ *women's clothes.*

• In the possessive form of a name or singular noun that ends in *s, x,* or *z*, the apostrophe may or may not be followed by *s*. The final *s* is most frequently omitted in names, especially names of three or more syllables that end in the sound [z]: □ *Euripides' tragedies* □ *Berlioz' operas.* For words of one syllable, *'s* is generally used: □ *St. James's Palace* □ *the fox's tail* □ *Liz's house* □ *the boss's secretary.* The presence or absence of the final *s* in other possessives of this group depends on usage, convention, pronunciation, etc.: □ *the princess's tiara* □ *Jesus' apostles* □ *the rhinoceros'(s) horn* □ *Kansas'(s) capital.*

See also APOSTROPHE; CONTRACTIONS; -ING FORMS; POSSESSIVES; SAKE.

sacrilegious This word, which means "showing disrespect toward something holy," sometimes causes problems with spelling. Note the position of the first *i* and *e*, which are in the opposite order in the word *religious.*

sake The noun *sake* is usually preceded by a possessive adjective or noun: □ *for their sake* □ *for Edward's sake* □ *for pity's sake* □ *for old times' sake.*

• If the preceding noun ends in the sound [s], the possessive form is not used, although an apostrophe may be added: □ *for goodness sake* □ *for conscience' sake.*

Such expressions as *for all our sakes* and *for both their sakes,* using the plural form of *sake*, are disliked by some users but acceptable to most. They may be replaced by *for the sake of us all, for the sake of both of them,* etc.

salary or wage? Each of these nouns denotes the money paid to employees at regular intervals in return for their services. A *salary* is usually paid monthly or biweekly to professional people or nonmanual workers; a *wage* is usually paid weekly to manual workers or servants: □ *My salary barely covers our mortgage payments and living expenses.* □ *the minimum wage for factory workers.*

• The noun *wage* is often used in the plural form *wages:* □ *a bricklayer's wage(s).* □ *He seems to spend most of his wages on cigarettes and alcohol.* The noun *wages* is not used with a singular verb, except in the well-known biblical quotation *the wages of sin is death* (Romans 6:23).

salivary This word has two possible pronunciations. The more traditional pronunciation has the stress on the first syllable [salivăree].

224

The pronunciation [sǎ*liv*ǎree], with the stress on the second syllable, is a less frequent variant.

salmonella This word is sometimes mispronounced. The pronunciation is [salmö*ne*lǎ].
- Unlike the *l* in salmon, the first *l* in *salmonella* is clearly sounded. The world *salmonella* has, in fact, nothing to do with *salmon;* it is named after the American veterinary surgeon Daniel Elmer Salmon (1850-1914), who first identified this genus of bacteria.

salubrious or **salutary?** *Salubrious* means "wholesome" or "conducive to health"; *salutary* means "beneficial," "causing improvement," or "remedial": □ *a salubrious climate* □ *a salutary warning* □ *We decided to look for a more salubrious hotel.* □ *Spending a few days in prison can be a salutary experience for young offenders.*
- The adjective *salutary* was formerly synonymous with *salubrious* and is still used in this sense today. Both adjectives are ultimately derived from the Latin word *salus,* meaning "health."

same The use of *same* as a pronoun is best restricted to business or official contexts: □ *I enclosed my passport, as requested; please return same by registered mail.* This usage is widely regarded as stilted. Another pronoun, such as *it* or *them*, can usually be substituted for *same.* □ *He found an old blanket and used it* [not *same*] *to line the dog's basket.*
- Nouns qualified by the adjective *same* are usually followed by as: □ *He works for the same company as his brother-in-law.* □ *She sent me the same book as you gave her last Christmas.* In the second example and similar sentences, *as* is often omitted or replaced by *that*: □ *the same suit that he wore for his wedding.* This usage is disliked and avoided by a few users.

sank, sunk or **sunken?** The past tense of the verb *sink* is *sank* or *sunk*, *sank* being the more frequent. The usual form of its past participle is *sunk*, *sunken* being largely restricted to adjectival use: □ *The dog sank its teeth into the man's leg.* □ *One of the boats has sunk.* □ *We are diving for sunken treasure.*

sarcasm, sarcastic see IRONY.

sat see SITTING OR SAT?

says This word is sometimes mispronounced. The form of the verb *say* used in the present tense with *he, she,* or *it* is *says*, pronounced [sez].

scallop The standard pronunciation of this word, which means "a shellfish with two flat fan-shaped shells," is [*skol*ŏp]. An alternative that rhymes with *gallop* is often heard, but avoided by careful users.

scarcely see HARDLY.

scarify The verb *scarify* should not be used in place of *scare*, to which it is unrelated in meaning and origin. *Scarify* tends to be used in formal contexts and means "scratch or break up the surface of": □ *to scarify the skin before administering a vaccine* □ *to scarify the topsoil of a field.* In figurative contexts, it is used in the sense of "wound with harsh criticism": □ *a scarifying review.*
- The traditional pronunciation of *scarify* is [*skarr*ifī], the pronunciation [*skair*ifī] being an accepted and frequent variant.

scenario The noun *scenario* is frequently used to denote a projected or imagined future state of affairs or sequence of events: □ *a sce-*

nario in which the superpowers would have recourse to nuclear weapons. Many people object to the frequency of this usage, especially in contexts where *plan, program, scene, situation,* etc., would be adequate or more appropriate.

• The principal meaning of *scenario* is "outline or synopsis of a play, film, opera," etc. The word is usually pronounced [sinariō]; the variant pronunciation [sinairiō] is also frequent.

sceptic see SKEPTIC OR SCEPTIC?

schedule This word, meanings "plan or timetable": □ *The train was behind schedule again,* is pronounced [*sked*yool]. The word is usually pronounced [*shed*yool] in British English.

• The verb *schedule,* "to plan," should not be overused.

schism The traditional pronunciation of this word, meaning "separation into opposed groups," is [sizm], with a silent *ch.* The alternative pronunciation [skizm] is perfectly acceptable.

schizophrenic The adjective *schizophrenic* relates to the mental disorder *schizophrenia,* which is characterized by hallucinations, delusions, social withdrawal, emotional instability, loss of contact with reality, etc.: □ *Another sufferer believes during a schizophrenic attack that he is in command of a spaceship, 2,000 years in the future (Readers Digest,* June 1987).

• The use of the adjective *schizophrenic* in the extended sense of "inconsistent," "contradictory," "unpredictable," "capricious," etc., is disliked and avoided by most users.

Note the spelling of *schizophrenic* and *schizophrenia* and the difference in pronunciation between the two words: *schizophrenic* is pronounced [skitsŏ*frenik*], with a short *e; schizophrenia* [skitsŏ*freeneea*] has a long *e.*

scone The pronunciation of this word is a favorite topic for debate; [skōn] and [skon] are equally acceptable.

• The parish of *Scone* in East Scotland, the original site of the stone on which Scottish kings were crowned, is pronounced [skoon].

Scotch, Scots, or **Scottish?** Each of these adjectives means "of Scotland," but there are differences of usage and application.

• *Scottish,* the most frequent, is used in a wide range of contexts: □ *Scottish history* □ *a Scottish town* □ *Scottish Gaelic* □ *a Scottish name* □ *Scottish dancing* □ *a Scottish poet.*

The adjective *Scotch* was formerly used for such purposes but is now restricted to a number of fixed phrases, in the sense of "produced in Scotland" or "associated with Scotland": □ *Scotch whisky* □ *Scotch broth* □ *Scotch mist.*

Scots is usually applied to people: □ *the Scots Guards* □ *a Scotsman* □ *a Scotswoman.* The last two examples may be replaced by the noun *Scot,* which means "a native or inhabitant of Scotland": □ *She married a Scot.* The collective name for the people of *Scotland* is the *Scots* or the *Scottish.* The noun *Scots* also denotes a variety of English spoken in Scotland.

In some contexts, two of the adjectives are interchangeable: □ *a Scotch/Scots pine* □ *a Scottish/Scotch terrier* □ *a Scottish/Scots accent.*

sculpt or **sculpture?** The verbs *sculpt* and *sculpture* are synonymous and virtually interchangeable in all contexts: □ *He sculpted/sculptured a copy of the Venus de Milo in marble.* □ *She paints and sculpts/sculptures in her attic studio.*

seasonal or **seasonable?** *Seasonal* means "of or occurring in a particular season"; *seasonable* means "suitable for the season" or "opportune": □ *seasonal vegetables* □ *seasonal work* □ *seasonable weather* □ *seasonable advice*. The two adjectives should not be confused.

second or **secondly?** see FIRST OR FIRSTLY?

seize This word, meaning "take eagerly or by force": □ *He seized the money and ran*, is sometimes misspelled. Note the order of the vowels *-ei-*, which does not correspond to the usual "i before e" rule. See also SPELLING 5.

self The use of the word *self* as a pronoun is disliked and avoided by many users, even in informal contexts: □ *tickets for husband and self.*

• The noun *self* and its plural form *selves* are acceptable to all users: □ *his usual self* □ *their true selves*.

The suffixes *-self* and *-selves* are used to form the reflexive pronouns *myself, yourself, ourselves, themselves*, etc.: □ *She killed herself and her three children*. Some people object to the use of these pronouns for emphasis: □ *The house itself will be demolished next week*. □ *He has not driven the car himself*. See also MYSELF.

The prefix *self-* is almost always attached with a hyphen: □ *self-addressed* □ *self-confident* □ *self-propelled* □ *self-sufficient*. See also HYPHEN 1.

self-starter The frequent use of the noun *self-starter*, especially in job advertisements, to denote a person with initiative who can work without supervision, is disliked by many users: □ *We need an ambitious self-starter with experience in production control and personnel management.*

semicolons The semicolon is a useful punctuation mark but, unlike many of the other punctuation marks, there is no occasion when its use is compulsory. It is mainly used between clauses that are linked by sense but are not joined by a conjunction and that could each stand as a separate sentence: □ *I am very tired; I am also hungry.* □ *The night was dark; the rain fell in torrents.*

• It is frequently used before such phrases as *however, nonetheless, nevertheless*: □ *This precaution is recommended; however, it is not compulsory.*

In sentences where clauses already contain commas, the semicolon is often used to separate the clauses: □ *T.S. Eliot, though born in America, was a British subject; he lived, worked, and died in England*. The semicolon can also be used in order to establish subsets in a long list or series separated by commas: □ *Applicants must have a graduate degree, preferably in English; a lively writing style, a knowledge of magazine publishing, and proven experience; and an ability to work under pressure, to cooperate with colleagues, and to work flexible hours.*

senior citizen This expression is used for an elderly person, especially with reference to one over the age of retirement. *Senior citizen* is considered a euphemism by most: □ *There are courses for senior citizens at the university.* □ *Senior citizens are entitled to reduced bus and train fares.*

sensual or **sensuous?** Each of these adjectives relates to the gratification of the senses. Something that is *sensual* appeals to the body,

S

arousing or satisfying physical appetites or sexual desire; something that is *sensuous* appeals to the senses, sometimes especially the mind, being esthetically pleasing or spiritually uplifting: □ *to indulge in the sensual pleasures of eating and drinking* □ *the sensual movements of the exotic dancer* □ *the sensuous movements of the ballerina* □ *to appreciate the sensuous music from Segovia's guitar.*

• The use of the adjective *sensual* sometimes implies disapproval, whereas *sensuous* is generally used in a favorable manner.

sentences A sentence can be defined as a "grammatically complete unit consisting of one or more words, which starts with a capital letter and ends with a period, question mark, or exclamation point.

• The old rule that "All sentences must contain a subject and a verb" holds true for most kinds of writing, but it is a rule that is often informally broken. □ *Whatever for?* □ *For heaven's sake!* □ *Yes, of course.* Verbless sentences are often used for stylistic effect, particularly in order to emphasize or qualify a previous statement: □ *He's as rich as a king. Possibly richer.*

Sentence structure and word order in English are partly a matter of rules and partly a matter of style. The normal word order is subject-verb-object; for example: □ *The dog bit the mailman* cannot be changed to *The mailman bit the dog* without changing the sense of the sentence; however, one can choose one's word order in sentences such as: □ *After lunch we could go for a walk.—We could go for a walk after lunch.* □ *Even more delicious is her chocolate mousse.—Her chocolate mousse is even more delicious.*

separate This word is often misspelled. Note the vowels; the most frequent error is to write an *e* for the first *a*.

septic see SKEPTIC OR SEPTIC?

sergeant The spelling of *sergeant* is often a source of error. A *sergeant* in an army, etc., is usually a middle-ranking noncommissioned officer or an officer in a police force. A *sergeant major* is a noncommissioned officer of the highest rank. A *sergeant-at-arms* is an officer in a legislative body or social club; the British spelling for this sense is *serjeant-at-arms.*

serial see CEREAL OR SERIAL?

service The verb *service* is best avoided where *serve* would be adequate or more appropriate: □ *It was easy to see why provincial centers were not always well serviced; the importers are mostly concentrated in Istanbul (The Bookseller, June 5, 1987).* □ *A national organization has been formed to service the local groups.*

• The principal meaning of the verb *service* is "overhaul": □ *The mechanic serviced the car.*

serviceable This word, meaning "ready to be used; durable": □ *The television had been repaired and was now serviceable,* is sometimes misspelled. The *e* is retained before the suffix *-able*, indicating the soft *c* sound.

• See also SPELLING 3.

sexism The use of sexist language can often be avoided by the substitution of neutral synonyms or simple paraphrases, without recourse to clumsy or controversial neologisms. Those opponents of sexism who coin such expressions as *the artist's mistress-piece* and *to person the telephones* do little to further their cause.

• The most frequent examples of sexism include the use of the noun *man* in place of *person;* *lady* or *girl* in place of *woman;* *he, him,* and *his* as pronouns of common gender; and the titles *Mrs.* and *Miss.* See **HE OR SHE; MAN; MS., MRS., OR MISS?; WOMAN.**

The problems of sexism arising from occupational titles fall into three categories. The words *engineer* and *nurse,* for example, are of neutral gender but are traditionally associated with men and women, respectively. For this reason the terms *female engineer, male nurse,* etc., are sometimes used to avoid confusion. This is often quite unnecessary: □ *Dr. Tony Butterworth, 40, a former male nurse, has been appointed Britain's first Professor of Community Nursing at Manchester University* (*Daily Telegraph,* June 2, 1987).

The ban on sexual discrimination in job advertisements has encouraged the substitution of neutral synonyms for occupational titles that specify sex: *foreman* and *charwoman,* for example, may be replaced by *supervisor* and *cleaner; policeman* and *policewoman* by *police officer; salesman* and *saleswoman* by *sales representative* or *shop assistant.* See also **PERSON.**

The use of feminine suffixes is also disliked by some users: □ *the comedienne Lucille Ball.* □ *Her sister is an usherette at the local cinema.* □ *He married a successful authoress.* See also **-ESS.**

Shakespearean or **Shakespearian?** This word, meaning "of or having the characteristics of Shakespeare": □ *a Shakespearean sonnet,* may end with *-ean* or occasionally with *-ian.*

shall or **will?** The traditional distinction between *shall* and *will* is that *shall* is used in the first person and *will* in the second and third persons as the future tense of the verb *to be* and that *will* is used in the first person and *shall* in the second and third persons to express determination, compulsion, intention, willingness, commands, promises, etc.: □ *I shall wash the dishes later.* □ *He will come back tomorrow.* □ *We will not obey you.* □ *They shall apologize immediately.*

• In informal contexts the problem rarely arises, the contraction *'ll* being used to represent both *shall* and *will* in all persons.

The distinction between *shall* and *will* is now more simply defined, *shall* being used in all persons to express determination, compulsion, etc., and *will* as the future tense of the verb *to be,* with an increasing tendency to use *will* in all senses. Modern usage in England is following this trend, although *shall* is retained in official contexts: □ *Passengers shall remain seated until the vehicle is stationary.*

The use of *shall* and *will* in questions is a more complex issue. □ *Shall I stay?* can mean "Do you want me to stay?" □ *Shall we go?* is a suggestion or proposition. □ *Will I/we win?* means "Am I/ Are we going to win?" □ *Shall you pay the bill?* can mean "Are you going to pay the bill?" □ *Will you pay the bill?* is a request.

See also **SHOULD OR WOULD?**

she see **HE OR SHE.**

sheared or **shorn?** *Sheared* is the past tense of the verb *shear; sheared* or *shorn* is its past participle: □ *They sheared the sheep.* □ *They have sheared/shorn the sheep.* □ *You will be shorn of your power.*

• The past participle *sheared* is used in the technical sense of "deformed," "distorted," "fractured," or "broken": □ *The head of the screw has sheared off.*

Shorn is also used adjectivally: □ *a shorn lamb* □ *his shorn hair.*

sheik The preferred pronunciation of this word, which means "an Arab chief or ruler," is [shayk]. The alternative pronunciation [sheek] is not generally accepted.

• Note the spelling of this word; the spelling *sheikh* is an accepted variant.

shibboleth The noun *shibboleth* is frequently used to denote a catchword, slogan, maxim, cliché, etc., especially one that is old-fashioned or obsolescent: □ *We were unimpressed by his speech, in which he did little more than repeat the old shibboleths of the party.*

• *Shibboleth* traditionally refers to a custom or practice that serves to distinguish the members of one party, sect, race, etc., from those of another. In the Old Testament (Judges 12:6), the word is used as a test to distinguish the Ephraimites, who could not pronounce the sound [sh], from the Gileadites.

shined or **shone?** *Shone* is the past tense and part participle for most senses of the verb *shine; shined* is restricted to the meaning "polished": □ *The sun (has) shone all day.* □ *He shone his torch on the statue.* □ *They (have) shined our shoes.*

ship see BOAT OR SHIP?

shone see SHINED OR SHONE?

shorn see SHEARED OR SHORN?

should or **would?** In reported speech, conditional sentences, and other indirect constructions, the use of *should* and *would* follows the pattern of *shall* and *will* (as the future tense of the verb *to be*); *would* is always used in the second and third persons and often replaces *should* in the first person: □ *We said we should/would stay until Saturday.* □ *She thought you would fail.* □ *If you were in trouble, I should/would help you.* □ *He would open the door if he had the key.* See also SHALL OR WILL?

• A similar convention applies to the use of *should* and *would* in polite or formal constructions: □ *We should/would be delighted to see you.* □ *I should/would like to buy a pair of sandals.* □ *She would be pleased to oblige.* □ *They would prefer to play outside.*

In informal contexts, the distinction between *should* and *would* does not often arise, the contraction *'d* being used to represent both *should* and *would* in all persons.

In the sense of "ought to," *should* is used in all persons: □ *We should visit her more often.* □ *You should be able to see it from here.* There is sometimes a risk of ambiguity in the first person: □ *I thought I should accept their offer* may be a paraphrase of "I thought I ought to . . ." or the past tense of "I think I shall. . . ."

In the sense of "used to," *would* is used in all persons: □ *When we were on vacation, we would sometimes spend all day on the beach.* □ *Before his retirement he would always get up at seven o'clock.*

See also RATHER; SUBJUNCTIVE.

shrank, shrunk, or **shrunken?** *Shrank* is the past tense of the verb *shrink* and *shrunk* the usual form of its past participle, the variant *shrunken* being more frequently used as an adjective: □ *He*

shrank from telling her the truth. □ *My sweater has shrunk.* □ *A shrunken old woman stood in the doorway.*
• The use of *shrunk* in place of *shrank* is acknowledged by several authorities.

sibling The noun *sibling*, which denotes a brother or sister, is a useful word that is unfortunately disliked by many users and largely restricted to formal contexts and sociological jargon: □ *the twins' relationship with their siblings* □ *sibling rivalry.*
• The use of *sibling* and *siblings* to simplify such sentences as: □ *He would like to have a sibling* [rather than *a brother or sister*] *to play with* and: □ *All her siblings* [rather than *brothers and sisters*] *have left home* has yet to gain general acceptance:

sic The Latin word *sic*, meaning "so" or "thus," is used in printed or written text (often in a quotation) to indicate that an unlikely, unexpected, or questionable usage or misspelled word or phrase has in fact been accurately transcribed: □ *He spoke of a need for "more thorough analysation [sic]" of the results.*
• *Sic* is enclosed in brackets and inserted immediately after the word or phrase it refers to. The use of italics is optional.

sick or **ill?** *Sick* and *ill* are interchangeable in most contexts, *ill* being the more formal of the two adjectives. In British English, to feel *sick* is to feel nauseated; to feel *ill* is to feel unwell: □ *She was sick yesterday* usually means "she vomited yesterday"; □ *She was ill yesterday* means "She was not well yesterday."
• The adjective *ill* is not usually used in this sense before a noun, *sick* being preferred: □ *a sick* [not *ill*] *man.* (*Ill* may, however, precede a noun in the sense of "bad": □ *ill fortune* □ *ill treatment* □ *ill health.*) *Sick* is also used with reference to absence from work because of illness: □ *off sick* □ *sick pay* □ *sick leave.*

siege This word, meaning the "surrounding of a fortified place to force a surrender," is sometimes misspelled. Note the order of the vowels *-ie-*, which conforms to the normal "i before e" rule. See also **SPELLING 5.**

significant The adjective *significant* means "having meaning": □ *a significant detail* □ *a significant gesture.*
• Its frequent use as a synonym for "important," "large," "serious," etc., is disliked by some users: □ *a significant writer* □ *a significant increase* □ *a significant problem.*

silicon or **silicone?** *Silicon* is an element that occurs in the earth's crust and is used in alloys, glass manufacturing, and the electronics industry: □ *silicon chip. Silicone* is a compound that contains *silicon* and is used in lubricants, polishes, and cosmetic surgery: □ *silicone rubber.*
• The two words should not be confused. The final syllable of *silicon* is usually unstressed; the final syllable of *silicone* rhymes with *bone.*

similes A simile is a figure of speech that, like a metaphor, suggests a comparison or analogy, but a simile expresses the comparison explicitly and is usually introduced by *like* or *as:* □ *teeth like pearls* □ *wide as the ocean.*
• Similes are used in many well-known idioms: □ *good as gold* □ *dry as dust* □ *plain as day*, and many similes are so overworked as to have become clichés: □ *to run like the wind* □ *a voice like thunder* □ *sly as a fox.*

Similes can, however, be used to good effect, particularly in humorous or ironic prose: □ *Jeeves coughed one soft, low, gentle cough like a sheep with a blade of grass stuck in its throat* (P.G. Wodehouse, *The Inimitable Jeeves*). □ *The term "computer virus" spread into use like, well, a virus during 1988, but the outbreak came too late . . .* (The Associated Press, Jan. 3, 1989). They are more often used seriously in poetry:

Life, like a dome of many-colored glass,
Stains the white radiance of Eternity.
(Shelley, *Adonais*)

simplistic The adjective *simplistic* means "oversimplified" or "naive"; it should not be used in place of *simple*: □ *a simplistic explanation of the theory of relativity* □ *a simple* [not *simplistic*] *explanation for her behavior.*

• Simplistic is generally used in a derogatory manner: □ His simplistic solution to the problem was rejected without further discussion.

simultaneous This word, meaning "happening at the same time," may cause problems with pronunciation. The usual pronunciation is [sīmŭl*tay*neeŭs].

since see AGO OR SINCE?; BECAUSE, AS, FOR, OR SINCE?

sine qua non The expression *sine qua non*, which is largely restricted to formal contexts, denotes an essential or indispensable condition or requirement: □ *Mutual trust is a sine qua non of a successful marriage.*

• Of Latin origin, the phrase literally means "without which not." The word *sine* may be pronounced [*sī*nee] or [*si*nay]; *qua* may be pronounced [kway] or [kwah]; *non* may rhyme with *gone* or *bone*.

singular or **plural?** As a general rule, a singular verb is used with a singular subject and a plural verb is used with a plural subject. Problems arise when the subject is a noun or phrase that can be singular or plural or when a singular subject is separated from the verb by a number of plural nouns (or vice versa): □ *A list of the names and addresses of new members is* [not *are*] *available on request.*

• Such nouns as audience, government, jury, committee, family, crowd, herd, etc., and other collective nouns followed by of (a bunch of flowers, a flock of geese, a gang of thieves, etc.), are used with a singular verb if the people or items in question are considered as a group and with a plural verb if they are considered as individuals. See also COLLECTIVE NOUNS; COMMITTEE; GOVERNMENT; -ICS; KIND OF; MAJORITY AND MINORITY; NUMBER. Any corresponding pronouns or possessive adjectives should agree with the chosen verb: □ Members of the audience were asked to remain in their [not its] seats. □ The jury has to consider all the evidence before it [not they] can reach a verdict. □ Harvard plays Yale. British English treats groups more frequently as plural: □ Oxford play Cambridge.

Measurements, sums of money, percentages, etc., are used with a singular verb if they are considered as a single entity: □ Four yards is all we need. □ Ten dollars is not enough. □ Fifteen percent is a generous increase.

Two or more nouns joined with and are used with a plural verb unless they represent a single concept: □ His sister and her friend *were killed in the accident.* □ *Gin and tonic is a popular drink.* On the other hand, nouns and phrases joined to the principal subject with *as well as, together with, plus,* etc., are regarded as parenthetical; the verb agrees with the principal subject alone: □ *A valuable painting, as well as her engravings, was destroyed in the fire.* □ *Her engravings, together with a valuable painting, were destroyed in the fire.*

See also ANY; EITHER; MORE; NEITHER; NONE; ONE; OR; PLUS; THERE IS OR THERE ARE?

siphon or **syphon?** This word, meaning "(draw off liquid by means of a) tube using atmospheric pressure," can be spelled with an *i* or a *y.*

• Some users prefer the *i* spelling, which reflects the original Greek *siphōn.*

sitting or **sat?** The substitution of *sat,* the past participle of the verb *sit,* for the present participle *sitting* is found in some dialects of English: □ *They were sitting* [in some dialects *sat*] *in the garden.*

• *Sat* is correctly used in the passive form of the transitive verb *sit:* □ *We were sat at this table by the headwaiter.*

sitting room see LOUNGE.

situation In the sense of "state of affairs," the noun *situation* often serves a useful purpose, but it should not be used to excess: □ *We discussed our financial situation with the bank manager.* □ *They are trying to improve the unemployment situation.*

• In some contexts, *situation* is superfluous: □ *a crisis situation* is a crisis; □ *an interview situation* is an interview. See also ONGOING.

sixth Careful users pronounce this word [siksth]; the pronunciation [sikth] should be avoided in careful speech.

sizable or **sizeable** The preferred spelling is *sizable,* with *sizeable* a variant. See SPELLING 3.

skeptic or **sceptic?** A *skeptic* is a person who has doubts about accepted beliefs or principles, and is pronounced [*skep*tik].

• The British spelling *sceptic,* pronounced [*sep*tik], should not be confused with *septic,* an adjective meaning "infected with harmful bacteria": □ *A septic wound.*

skeptical see CYNICAL OR SKEPTICAL?

skillful The adjective *skillful,* meaning "possessing skill," is sometimes misspelled. Note the double *l* in *skillful.* The final *l* of *skill* is dropped in British English before the suffix *-ful: skilful.*

slander see LIBEL OR SLANDER?

slang Slang is unauthorized language, often but not necessarily coarse, standing in the linguistic hierarchy between general informal speech and the specific vocabularies of professional and occupational jargon. Innovative and dramatic, slang is the most ephemeral of language, continually coining new terms and discarding old ones, which are either abandoned to obscurity or transferred into the respectability of the standard language.

• Slang includes shortening of words: □ *biz* (business) □ *vibes* (vibrations); onomatopoeic words: □ *buzz* □ *zap;* rhyming slang or abbreviations of it: □ *skin* and *blister* (sister) □ *plates* (feet, from *plates of meat);* terms from the criminal and drug subcultures: □ *grass* or *pot* (marijuana) □ *stretch* (time spent in prison) □ *speed* (an amphetamine drug).

S

A sparing use of slang can be effective, except when the context is too formal for it to be appropriate however, slang often becomes obsolete or old-fashioned very quickly, and the use of out-of-date or overworked slang can make speech or writing seem dated and tedious.

sled, sledge, or **sleigh?** Each of these nouns denotes vehicles that are used on snow for transport or recreation.

• *Sled* is the most frequent (*sledge* in British English). *Sleigh* usually refers to a large sled that is pulled by animals; the smaller sled that is used for sliding downhill is also known as a toboggan: □ *a picture of friends riding a sleigh* □ *children playing on their sleds.*

sleight The word *sleight,* most frequently used in the phrase *sleight of hand* ("dexterity in using the hands to perform conjuring tricks, etc.") is sometimes misspelled and mispronounced. Note the *-ei-* spelling and the pronunciation [slīt] not [slayt].

slough *Slough* is usually pronounced [slow], rhyming with *how,* in the sense "swamp; state of hopeless dejection": □ *in the slough of despond,* and [sluf] when referring to the castoff skin of a snake or the verb "shed or abandon."

slow The use of the word *slow* as an adverb should generally be avoided in formal contexts: □ *Time passes slowly* [not *slow*] *in prison.* □ *You'd better drive slow in this fog.*

• The comparative and superlative forms *slower* and *slowest* are more informal than *more slowly* and *most slowly:* □ *She eats more slowly/slower than you.* □ *Michael works the slowest/most slowly. Slower* may be preferred to *more slowly* when the adverb is preceded by *any:* □ *I can't walk any slower.*

The use of the adverb *slow* in fixed combinations, such as *slow-motion, slow-moving traffic,* etc., is acceptable in all contexts.

smear The increasing use of the noun *smear* to denote a defamatory attack, often involving slander or libel, is disliked by some users: □ *Their allegations of professional misconduct are the latest in a series of smears.* □ *the victim of a smear campaign.*

• The noun is particularly frequent in the headline language of popular newspapers.

smelled or **smelt?** Either word may be used as the past tense and past participle of the verb *smell:* □ *The cake smelled/smelt delicious. Smelled* is much more frequent than *smelt.* See also **-ED OR -T?**

• *Smelled* may be pronounced [smeld] or [smelt]; *smelt* is always pronounced [smelt].

so The phrase *so that,* expressing purpose, is sometimes reduced to *so* in informal contexts. In formal speech and writing, the word *that* should be retained: □ *The gate had been left open so (that) we could drive in.*

• To introduce a result or consequence, *so* may be used alone in all contexts: □ *The gate had been left open, so we drove in.*

The phrase *so as,* which also expresses purpose, is followed by an infinitive with *to* and should not be confused with *so that:* □ *She wore gloves so as not to leave fingerprints.* □ *She wore gloves so that* [not *as*] *she would not leave fingerprints. So as to* is best avoided where *to* would be adequate: □ *He closed the window (so as) to keep out the rain.*

See also **AS; IN ORDER THAT** AND **IN ORDER TO; SO-CALLED.**

so-called The adjective *so-called* is generally used in an ironic sense, implying that the following word is inaccurate or inappropriate: □ *a so-called friend* □ *their so-called supporters* □ *so-called simplified spelling* (letter, *Newsweek*, June 27, 1988).

• The increasing use of the adjective in neutral contexts is disliked by some users: □ *The so-called gray market regularly comes under fire.*

Used without a hyphen after the noun it qualifies, *so called* may be interpreted more literally: □ *the bobwhite, so called because of its characteristic cry.*

sociable or **social?** *Sociable* means "friendly," "companionable," or "convivial"; *social* means "of society" or "promoting companionship": □ *a sociable guest* □ *a sociable dinner party* □ *a social worker* □ *a social club.*

• The two adjectives are not interchangeable in these senses, although each may be applied to the same noun: □ *a sociable evening with friends at the pub* □ *a social evening for new members.*

Each word also means "gregarious," *sociable* being used in the sense of "liking the company of others" and *social* in the sense of "living with others": □ *She is more sociable than her sister, who hardly ever goes out.* □ *Ants are social insects.*

somebody or **someone?** The pronoun *somebody* and its synonym *someone* are interchangeable in all contexts.

• Each is used with a singular verb but is sometimes informally followed by a plural personal pronoun or possessive adjective (see **THEY**): □ *Somebody/Someone has parked their car in our driveway.*

somersault Note the spelling and pronunciation of this word, which means "acrobatic roll." The first two syllables are pronounced like *summer*, but are spelt *somer-*; the last syllable is pronounced like *salt*, but spelled *-sault*.

sometime or **some time?** These spellings are occasionally confused. *Sometime* is used as an adverb to mean "at some point in time": □ *I'll come and see you sometime*, and as an adjective to mean "former": □ *John Cooper, the sometime president of our club.* *Some time* means "a period of time": □ *I need some time to think.* □ *I've been worried about her for some time now.*

sooner see **HARDLY.**

sophisticated The adjective *sophisticated* is frequently applied to machines or devices, in the sense of "complex" or "advanced": □ *Diabetic? Now you can greatly reduce your risk . . . with this sophisticated equipment* (advertisement, *The Washington Post*, Dec. 27, 1988).

• This usage may be extended to the methods or techniques involved in producing such equipment: □ *sophisticated technology.* When it is extended to people, however, there is a risk of confusion with the principal sense of the adjective, "refined" or "cultured": □ *the best-documented U.F.O. case in history—one which has managed to perplex and astonish some of the most sophisticated scientists in the world* (*The Bookseller*, June 5, 1987).

sort of see **KIND OF.**

source The use of the word *source* as a verb, meaning "find a source," is disliked by many users: □ *He had difficulty sourcing the material for his thesis.*

south, South, or **southern?** As an adjective, *south* is always written with a capital *S* when it forms part of a proper name: □ *South America* □ *the South Pole.* The noun *south* is usually written with a capital *S* when it denotes a specific region, such as the southern states: □ *The secession of the South precipitated the Civil War.*

• In other contexts, and as an adverb, *south* is usually written with a lowercase *s:* □ *Many birds fly south for the winter.* □ *Only the south wall of the city remains intact.* □ *The island of Tasmania lies to the south of Australia.*

The adjective *southern* is more frequent and usually less specific than the adjective *south:* □ *the southern slopes* □ *in southern Italy.*

Like *south, southern* is written with a capital *S* when it forms part of a proper name, such as the *Southern Hemisphere.* With or without a capital *S,* it also means "of the South": □ *a Southern/southern region.*

sowed or **sown?** Either word may be used as the past participle of the verb *sow,* but *sown* is the more frequent: □ *I have sown/ sowed some more lettuce in the garden.*

• The past tense of the verb *sow* is always *sowed:* □ *They sowed the field with wheat.*

span see SPUN OR SPAN?

-speak Some people object to the increasing use of the suffix *-speak,* meaning "jargon" or "characteristic language," which is usually attached to nouns, proper names, or prefixes and is derived from the term *newspeak* coined by George Orwell in his novel *Nineteen Eighty-Four:* □ *computerspeak* □ *techspeak* □ *Joyrides bill themselves as "the travel sickness tablet for children," which is, to say the least, a cheeky bit of marketing-speak (Sunday Times,* Aug. 16, 1987).

• In view of its etymology, it is appropriate that the suffix should have established itself in the English language during the 1980's.

spearhead The verb *spearhead* is best avoided where *lead* would be adequate: □ *an opportunity exists for a profit-oriented manager who can spearhead the company's continued expansion.*

speciality see SPECIALTY OR SPECIALITY?

specially see ESPECIALLY OR SPECIALLY?

specialty or **speciality?** *Specialty* is used to denote a special skill or interest or a product, service, etc., that is specialized in: □ *Wildlife photography is his specialty.* □ *Steak tartare is a speciality of the house.*

• In British English, the noun *speciality* is more frequent than *specialty.*

species This word is normally pronounced [*speesheez*]. The alternative pronunciation [*speeseez*] is avoided by careful users.

spectrum The noun *spectrum* is best avoided where *range* would be adequate or more appropriate: □ *a wide spectrum of experience* □ *across the whole spectrum* □ *at the other end of the political spectrum.*

• The noun *spectrum* principally denotes the series of colors produced when white light is dispersed. It has two plural forms: *spectra* and *spectrums.*

speeded or **sped?** *Sped* is the past tense and past participle of the verb *speed* in the sense of "move or go quickly"; *speeded* relates to the sense of "drive at excessive speed" and to the phrasal verb *speed up*, meaning "accelerate": □ *We sped through the water.* □ *The days have sped by.* □ *He has never speeded on a highway.* □ *The workers speeded up when the supervisor arrived.*

spelled or **spelt?** Either word may be used as the past tense and past participle of the verb *spell:* □ *Have I spelled/spelt your name right? Spelled,* however, is much more frequent than *spelt.*
   • See also -ED OR -T? *Spelled* may be pronounced [speld] or [spelt]; *spelt* is always pronounced [spelt].

spelling English spelling is notoriously difficult to learn, for native English speakers as well as foreign students. It is to some extent governed by rules, however, some of which are described below.
   • **1 Doubling of consonants** Final consonants are sometimes doubled when a suffix starting with a vowel is added. With single-syllable words, this rule applies when the final consonant is preceded by a single vowel: □ *hit—hitting* □ *drop—dropped.* If the word has more than one syllable, the consonant is doubled if the last syllable is stressed and the final consonant is preceded by a single vowel: □ *refer—referred* □ *infer—inferred.* A final *-c* is not doubled, but is changed to *ck* before *-ed, -ing,* and *-er:* □ *panic—panicked.*
   2 y and i When a suffix is added to a word that ends in *-y,* the *y* becomes an *i* only if the preceding letter is a consonant: □ *silly—sillier* □ *hurry—hurried.* Exceptions are: □ *said* □ *laid* □ *paid* and in words where a suffix beginning with an *i* is added, such as *-ing:* □ *try—trying.*
   3 Final -e When a suffix beginning with a vowel is added to a word with a silent final *-e,* the *e* is dropped: □ *rate—rating.* A growing trend is to drop the *-e-* before the suffixes *-able* and *-age:* □ *like—likeable* □ *size—sizeable.* If the word ends in *-ge* or *-ce,* the *e* is not dropped before *a* and *o:* □ *outrageous* □ *peaceable.* The *e* is not dropped if the suffix begins with a consonant: □ *excitement,* except with words ending *-ue:* □ *due—duly.* □ *True—truly.*
   4 -ly suffix When *-ly* is added to a word that word remains unchanged unless ending in *-ll* or *-le,* which lose this ending: □ *nice—nicely* □ *full—fully* □ *noble—nobly.* Exceptions are: □ *truly* □ *duly* □ *wholly.*
   5 ie and ei The rule "*i* before *e* except after *c*" applies to most words in which the sound those letters represent is [ee]: □ *believe* □ *grief* □ *deceive* □ *ceiling. Seize* and *weird* are exceptions. When the sound represented is [ay], then *ei* is used: □ *beige* □ *reign* □ *neighbor.*
   See also -ABLE OR -IBLE?; -IZE OR -ISE?; PLURALS.

spelt see SPELLED OR SPELT?

spilled or **spilt?** Either word may be used as the past tense and past participle of the verb *spill:* □ *He has spilled/spilt his coffee.* □ *The children spilled/spilt out of the school.*
   • See also -ED OR -T?
   Spilled may be pronounced [spild] or [spilt]; *spilt* is always pronounced [spilt].

split infinitive A split infinitive occurs when an adverb is inserted between *to* and the infinitive form of a verb: □ *to boldly go.* The practice is widely disliked but very widely used: □ *Nor is there* *much confidence in the . . . capacity to vigorously prosecute the killing* (*The New York Times*, Dec. 28, 1988).

• Split infinitives have a long history, and the objection to them is comparatively recent. As with the opposition to ending sentences with prepositions, grammarians based their objections on the rules of Latin grammar.

Since so many people dislike split infinitives, it is probably best to try to avoid them, at least in formal speech and writing. They can sound awkward or unpleasant, particularly when more than one word comes between *to* and the verb: □ *He tries to on the one hand explain.* . . . There are some sentences, however, in which it is preferable to split an infinitive in order to avoid ambiguity: □ *He failed to entirely comprehend me.* The revised ordering *He entirely failed to . . .* or *He failed to comprehend me entirely* would suggest complete, not partial, failure. □ *We expect to further modernize our services.* The revised ordering *We expect further to modernize . . .* suggests *moreover.* □ *They were plotting secretly to destroy the files.* Was the plotting or the intended destruction secret? □ *I would not expect anyone who has not read Joyce fully to understand the play.* Read Joyce fully or understand fully?

Another argument for disregarding the rule is that sometimes the rhythm of spoken English makes the split infinitive sound natural and its avoidance awkward. Compare: □ *I hope to really enjoy myself* with *I hope really to enjoy myself.*

spoiled or **spoilt?** Either word may be used as the past tense and past participle of the verb *spoil:* □ *The bad weather spoiled/spoilt our holiday,* with *spoiled* the more frequent.

• See also **-ED** OR **-T?**

Spoiled may be pronounced [spoild] or [spoilt]; *spoilt* is always pronounced [spoilt].

spontaneity The traditional pronunciation of this noun, meaning "the quality of behaving in a natural, impulsive way," is [spontă-neeitee], but the pronunciation [spontănayitee] is probably more frequently heard.

spoonful Most users prefer to form the plural *-fuls:* □ *spoonfuls.* See **-FUL.**

spouse The use of the noun *spouse* in place of *husband* or *wife* is best avoided where the sex of the person is known: □ *The broadcaster Sue Baker and her husband* [not *spouse*] *were the guests of honor.*

• The words *spouse* and *spouses* may, however, serve as useful replacements for the phrases "husband or wife," "husbands and wives," etc., especially in formal contexts: □ *Please give details of any other properties owned by you or your spouse.* □ *Use of the car pool is restricted to members and their spouses.*

The noun *spouse* is usually pronounced [spows], the pronunciation [spowz] being an accepted variant.

spun or **span?** *Spun* is the past tense and part participle of the verb *spin* in modern usage; *span* is an archaic form of the past tense: □ *He spun the wheel.* □ *This yarn has been spun by hand.*

squalor This word, meaning "filth; wretchedness": □ *the squalor of the slums,* is sometimes misspelled. The ending is *-or,* as in *tremor* and the *l* is not doubled.

stalactite or **stalagmite?** *Stalactites* and *stalagmites* are tapering masses of calcium carbonate that form in limestone caves. A *stalactite* hangs from the roof; a *stalagmite* rises from the floor.
  • The classic method of distinguishing between the two words is to associate the first *t* of *stalactite* with that of *top* and the *g* of *stalagmite* with that of *ground*.

stanch or **staunch?** Either word may be used as a verb, meaning "stop (the flow of)," *staunch* being less frequent than *stanch* in modern usage: □ *I stanched/staunched the flow of blood with a handkerchief.* □ *This offer is no remedy to recruitment and retention problems within our universities: it won't staunch the brain drain* (*The Guardian*, Feb. 7, 1987).
  • *Stanch* is a rare variant of the adjective *staunch,* meaning "loyal" or "firm": □ a *staunch supporter.*
     The word *stanch* is pronounced [stonch] or [stahnch]. *Staunch* is occasionally pronounced in the same way, but its usual pronunciation is [stawnch], rhyming with *launch.*

standing or **stood?** The substitution of *stood,* the past participle of the verb *stand,* for the present participle *standing* is found in some dialects of English: □ *She was standing* [in some dialects *stood*] *in front of the mirror.*
  • It is correct, although not common, to use *stood* in the passive form of the transitive verb *stand:* □ *The bottle should be stood in a cool place for two hours.*

stank or **stunk?** Either word may be used as the past tense of the verb *stink,* but *stunk* is the only form of its past participle: □ *The room stank/stunk of cigarette smoke.* □ *These boots have stunk* [not *stank*] *of manure since my visit to the farm last week.*

state-of-the-art The adjective *state-of-the-art,* which relates to the current level of technical achievement, development, knowledge, etc., is disliked by some users: □ *state-of-the-art computer technology.*
  • It is best avoided where *modern* or *up-to-date* would be adequate or more appropriate: □ *They* [Venture Scouts] *use state-of-the-art camp stoves for cooking* (*Daily Telegraph,* July 31, 1987).

stationary or **stationery?** These two words are often confused. *Stationary* means "not moving": □ *a stationary car; stationery* means "writing materials": □ *office stationery.*
  • To avoid confusion, remember that *stationery* contains an *e,* as in *letter.*

statistics see -ICS.

staunch see STANCH OR STAUNCH?

stay or **stop?** The substitution of the verb *stop* for *stay* in the sense of "reside temporarily" or "remain" is found in some dialects of English: □ *We stayed* [in some dialects *stopped*] *with my sister for a few days.*
  • The use of the verb *stop* with reference to a break in a journey is generally acceptable: □ *We stopped at my sister's house for a cup of tea on the way home.*

steal see BURGLARIZE, BURGLE, ROB, OR STEAL?

stereo This word has the alternative pronunciations [stereeō] and [steereeō], each of which is acceptable, although the former is more frequent in contemporary usage.

S

stiletto Note the spelling of this word, which refers to a small dagger. The spelling has a single *l*, but a double *t*.
- The plural is either *stilettos* or *stilettoes*, the former being accepted by more authorities.

stimulant or **stimulus?** Each of these nouns is used to denote something that stimulates activity. *Stimulant* is specifically applied to drugs, alcohol, etc., whereas *stimulus* is a more general synonym for "incentive": □ *Caffeine is a stimulant.* □ *They responded to the stimulus of competition.* A *stimulant* increases activity; a *stimulus* initiates activity.
- The plural of *stimulus* is *stimuli*, which is usally pronounced [stimewlī], sometimes [stimewlee].

stood see STANDING OR STOOD?

stop see STAY OR STOP?

story or **storey** The spelling *story* is preferred. It means "level of a building": □ *He lives on the second story*, or "a tale": □ *Tell me a story*; its plural is *stories*.
- In British English, the sense "level of a building" is spelled *storey*, with the plural *storeys*.

straightaway or **straight away?** This expression, meaning "without delay": □ *I'll be going home straightaway*, may be written as one word or sometimes as two.

straitened or **straightened?** These words are sometimes confused. *Straitened* means "restricted": □ *in straitened circumstances*. *Straightened* means "made straight": □ *She straightened her hair*.
- The two words have different origins: *straitened* comes from *strait*, and is ultimately derived from the Latin *stringere*, "to bind tightly." *Straighten* comes from *straight* and from Old English *streccan*, "to stretch."

straitjacket and **straitlaced** A *straitjacket*, a constricting jacket used to restrain a violent person, and also in extended senses, "something that restricts," is sometimes spelled *straightjacket*: □ *Eurotunnel will overnight make cross-Channel communications fast, efficient and dependable. A change from the straightjacket we're in now* (Sunday Times, June 28, 1987). In the same way, *straitlaced*, meaning "puritanical," is sometimes spelled *straightlaced*: □ *a very straitlaced maiden aunt*.
- For the origin of *strait* and *straight*, see STRAITENED OR STRAIGHTENED?

strata see STRATUM OR STRATA?

stratagem or **strategy?** A *stratagem* is a scheme, trick, or ruse; *strategy* is the art of planning a campaign: □ *to devise a new stratagem* □ *the strategy involved in a game of chess*.
- The use of *strategy* in the extended sense of "plan" or "method" overlaps with that of *stratagem*.

Both nouns are ultimately derived from the Greek word for "a general" and are principally applied to warfare, a *stratagem* being an artifice for deceiving the enemy and *strategy* being the science or art of conducting a war.

stratum or **strata?** *Strata* is the plural form of the noun *stratum*: □ *from a different social stratum* □ *in one of the upper strata of the rock*.
- The use of *strata* as a singular noun is wrong, but nevertheless is

occurring with increasing frequency, especially in figurative contexts: □ *that strata of society.*

street see ROAD OR STREET?

stress Some languages have a fairly regular stress pattern, but English stress patterns are varied and subject to change over time. As foreign words become absorbed into the English language, they often change their stress to a more English-sounding one: □ *bureau* □ *chauffeur.*

• Two-syllable words are more likely to be stressed on the first syllable, but when a word serves both as a noun and a verb, it is normally stressed on the first syllable as a noun, but the second as a verb: □ *permit* □ *rebel* □ *present* □ *conflict* □ *insult.*

Most three-syllable words have their stress on the first syllable. Words with four or more syllables usually have their stress on the second or third syllable. Some people find difficulty in pronouncing those multisyllabic words that traditionally have been stressed on the first syllable, and such words are coming to be pronounced with the stress on a later syllable: □ *applicable* □ *demonstrable* □ *formidable.*

stringed or **strung?** *Stringed* is an adjective derived from the noun *string; strung* is the past tense and past participle of the verb *string:* □ *a stringed instrument* □ *a twelve-stringed guitar* □ *His tennis racket was strung by an expert.* □ *The children (have) strung decorations around the room.*

• *Strung* is also used adjectivally before a noun, often in combination with an adverb: □ *a newly strung violin.*

stunk see STANK OR STUNK?

stupefy This word, meaning "bewilder or amaze," is sometimes misspelled. Note the ending *-efy* (like *putrefy*), in spite of the spelling of the related word *stupid.*

stupor This word, meaning "a drowsy dazed state": □ *in a drunken stupor,* is sometimes misspelled. Note the final *-or,* as in *torpor,* rather than *-our.*

subconscious or **unconscious?** Each of these adjectives means "without (full) awareness," but *subconscious* implies a greater degree of consciousness than *unconscious:* □ *a subconscious desire* □ *unconscious resentment.*

• In psychology, each word relates to parts of the mind that can influence behavior.

Unconscious has the additional senses of "not conscious," "unaware," and "unintentional": □ *He lay unconscious for two hours.* □ *They were unconscious of the danger.* □ *It was an unconscious insult.*

subjective see OBJECTIVE OR SUBJECTIVE?

subjunctive The subjunctive is the grammatical mood of a verb used to express a conditional content about possibilities or wishes rather than facts. With most verbs, the subjunctive form is its third-person singular form minus the *s,* but *to be* has the past tense subjunctive *were.* The subjunctive is largely falling into disuse but survives in such idioms as: □ *be that as it may* □ *as it were* □ *far be it from me* □ *come what may.*

• The main use of subjunctives is in clauses introduced by *that* and expressing a proposal, desire, or necessity: □ *It is vital that she leave immediately.* □ *I suggested to Mark that he drop in for cof-*

fee sometime. □ *They demanded that he answer their questions.* This usage is less popular in British English, in which *should* is often inserted before the verb: □ *It is vital that she should leave immediately.*

The other use of subjunctives is in clauses introduced by *if, though,* or *supposing:* □ *If you were to go, you might regret it.* □ *It's not as though he were a bachelor.* It is now very unusual to use such a construction with any subjunctive form other than *were.*

See also IF; WERE OR WAS?

subpoena This word, as a noun referring to a writ requiring a person to appear in court, is sometimes misspelled. Note particularly the *-oe-* of *poena.* The pronunciation [sŭpeena] is more frequent than [sŭbpeena].

• The word comes from the Latin *sub poena,* meaning "under penalty."

The present participle of the verb *subpoena,* meaning "issue with a subpoena," is *subpoenaing;* the past tense and past participle are *subpoenaed.*

subsequent see CONSEQUENT OR SUBSEQUENT?

subsidence The traditional pronunciation of this word, which means "falling or sinking": □ *cracks due to subsidence,* is [sŭbsidĕns].

• The alternative pronunciation [subsidĕns] is also widely used and is generally acceptable.

substitute see REPLACE OR SUBSTITUTE?

subsume The verb *subsume* means "incorporate within a larger category or group" or "classify under a general rule or heading"; it should not be used as a pretentious synonym for "include" or "contain": □ *The concept of a classless society is subsumed within the doctrine of Marxism.*

such The use of the construction *such . . . that* (or *such . . . who*) in place of *such . . . as* is avoided by careful users: □ *such tools as* [not *that*] *are needed for the job* □ *such people as* [not *who*] *are eligible for retirement income.*

• The construction *such . . . that* may, however, be used to indicate a result: □ *He earns such a pittance that he can't afford to buy food for his family.*

The use of *such* or *such a/an* before an adjective preceding a noun, in the sense of "so" or "very," is disliked by a few users but acceptable to most: □ *Such careless driving should not go unpunished.* □ *I have never seen such a small house.* □ *You have such beautiful clothes.* □ *It was such a difficult question.*

See also SUCH AS OR LIKE?

such as or **like?** *Such as* introduces an example; *like* introduces a comparison: □ *Dairy products, such as milk and cheese, should be kept in a cool place.* □ *Dairy products, like fresh meat, should be kept in a cool place.* □ *He directed several horror films, such as "Dracula."* □ *He directed several horror films like "Dracula."*

• The potentially ambiguous use of *like* in place of *such as* is disliked by some people but frequently occurs in general usage: □ *Comedy classics like "Family Ties," "Cheers," and "Webster" are part of a Paramount tradition . . .* (advertisement, *Variety,* Jan. 4-10, 1989). The use of *such as* in place of *like* is largely restricted to formal contexts: □ *Shoes such as these are ideal for indoor sports.*

Careful users avoid substituting *such as* for *as:* □ *When the post office is closed, as* [not *such as*] *on Sundays, stamps may be obtained from the machine outside.* □ *The pizza can be cooked in a number of ways, as by* [not *such as by*] *baking it in a hot oven for 20 minutes.* In the second example, *as by* may be replaced by *such as.*

suffixes see PREFIXES AND SUFFIXES.

summon or **summons?** To *summon* is to send for, call upon, or muster; to *summons* is to serve with a legal summons (an order to appear in court): □ *I was summoned to the managing director's office.* □ *He was summonsed for speeding.*

• The verb *summon* may be used in place of the verb *summons:* □ *He was summoned for speeding.*

Of the two words, only *summons* is used as a noun: □ *I received a summons from the managing director.* □ *He received a summons for speeding.*

sunk, sunken see SANK, SUNK, OR SUNKEN?

super- Some people object to the frequent use of the prefix *super-*, in the sense of "surpassing all others" or "to an excessive degree," to coin new nouns and adjectives: □ *a superbug that is resistant to most antibiotics* □ *those superfit people who put the rest of us to shame.*

• See also MACRO- AND MICRO-; MEGA-.

supercilious This word, meaning "haughty in a condescending, disdainful manner," is sometimes misspelled. Note the single *c* and single *l*.

superlative see COMPARATIVE AND SUPERLATIVE.

supersede This word, meaning "replace," is sometimes misspelled. The most frequent mistake is to confuse the *-sede* ending with the *-cede* ending of *precede.*

• *Supersede* comes from the Latin *supersedēre*, "to sit above."

supervise *Supervise*, meaning "oversee": □ *She supervised the plans for the party*, is sometimes misspelled; the *-ise* ending cannot be spelled *-ize:* see -IZE OR -ISE?

• Note also the *-or* ending of *supervisor*, not *-er.*

supplement see COMPLEMENT OR SUPPLEMENT?

suppose or **supposing?** Either word may be used to introduce a suggestion or hypothesis, *suppose* being preferred by some users in formal contexts: □ *Suppose/Supposing we sell the car?* □ *Suppose/Supposing the train is late.*

• Only *supposing* can be used in the sense of "if" or "assuming": □ *I'll buy her some chocolates on the way home, supposing the corner shop is still open.*

surprised *Surprised* is followed by the preposition *by* in the sense of "taken unaware," and by *at* in the sense of "amazed": □ *The thief was surprised by the owner of the car.* □ *I was surprised at her ignorance.*

• In the second sense *surprised* may also be followed by an infinitive with *to* or a clause introduced by *that:* □ *He was surprised to see you.* □ *They were surprised that we won.*

The idiomatic use of a DOUBLE NEGATIVE in such sentences as *I shouldn't be surprised if it doesn't rain* is acceptable to most users in informal contexts, provided that the meaning is clear. The construction is best avoided if there is a risk of ambiguity.

S

S

surveillance This word, meaning "careful observation," is usually pronounced [servayĕns]. The pronunciation [servayĕns], imitating the French original, sounds rather affected.

susceptible The adjective *susceptible* is followed by the preposition *to* in the sense of "easily influenced or affected" and by *of* in the formal sense of "capable" or "admitting" □ *susceptible to flattery* □ *susceptible to hay fever* □ *susceptible of a different interpretation.*
• Note that *susceptible* ends in *-ible*, not *-able*. The *-sc-* combination can also cause spelling mistakes.

swam or **swum?** *Swam* is the past tense of the verb *swim*; *swum* is the past participle: □ *The dog swam to the shore.* □ *the lake where they had swum.*

swap or **swop?** Each spelling is acceptable for this informal word meaning "exchange": □ *to swap stamps. Swap* is the more traditional spelling; *swop* is a rare variation.
• The Middle English *swappen*, from which the word originates, meant "to strike," from the custom of striking or shaking hands on a bargain.

swat or **swot?** These spellings are sometimes confused. *Swat* means "strike with a blow": □ *to swat flies.* This word may also be spelled *swot*, although this spelling is disliked by many careful users. *Swot* is an informal British word meaning "study hard": □ *swotting for exams.*

swelled or **swollen?** Either word may be used as the past participle of the verb *swell. Swelled* is the more neutral form; *swollen* often indicates an undesirable or harmful increase or expansion: □ *The population has swelled in recent years.* □ *The disaster fund was swelled by a generous contribution from the mayor.* □ *His wrist has swollen to twice its normal size.*
• The past tense of *swell* is always *swelled*: □ *The population swelled.* □ *His wrist swelled.*
   Swollen is the usual form of the adjective: □ *She crammed a few more sweets into her swollen pockets.* □ *My ankle is badly swollen.* The adjective *swelled* is largely restricted to the informal phrase *swelled head*, denoting conceit, which is usually *swollen head* in British English.

swingeing Note the pronunciation and spelling of this word, which means "severe": □ *swingeing cuts in public expenditure.* The word is pronounced [swinjing]; the *-e-* distinguishes it from *swinging* and indicates the softness of the *g*. See also SPELLING 3.
• The word derives from Old English *swengan*, "to beat or shake."

swollen see SWELLED OR SWOLLEN?

swop see SWAP OR SWOP?

swot see SWAT OR SWOT?

syndrome Some people object to the frequent use of the noun *syndrome* in nonmedical contexts to denote any set of characteristics, actions, emotions, etc.: □ *She is suffering from the only-child syndrome.*
• In medicine, the noun *syndrome* denotes a group of signs and symptoms indicating a physical or mental disorder: □ *Down's syndrome.*

synergy In technical contexts, the noun *synergy* (or *synergism*) denotes the combined action and increased effect of two or more drugs, muscles, etc., working together. The introduction of the noun *synergy* into general usage is disliked by some: □ *the synergy of the merged companies.*

synonymous Note the spelling of this word, particularly the position of the *y*'s and *o*'s.

• The phrase *synonymous with* literally means "being a synonym of," but in general contexts it is frequently used in the sense of "closely associated with": □ *The verb "jump" is synonymous with "leap."* □ *Our name is synonymous with excellence.* □ *An expensive car is synonymous with the yuppie life style.*

syphon see SIPHON OR SYPHON?

S

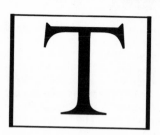

-t see -ED OR -T?

tactics see -ICS.

tall see HIGH OR TALL?

target The noun *target* is now most frequently used in its metaphorical meaning of "aim or goal." The verb form is more recent, and is often followed by *at*: □ *The advertising campaign is to be carefully targeted at the 18-25 age group.*

• Although many people object to the use of *target* as a verb, it has a long history: the *Oxford English Dictionary* cites an example from 1837.

Note that the final *t* is not doubled in front of suffixes: □ *targeted* □ *targeting*.

Target is often used in expressions such as □ *target date*, meaning "the date set for the completion of work," etc.: □ *target markets* □ *consumer-targeted material*.

tariff This word is sometimes misspelled. Note the single *r* and the double *f*.

task force A *task force* is a group of people formed in order to undertake a particular objective, often of a military nature: □ *The captain led a task force to blow up the bridge.*

• The most frequent use refers to subsections of the armed forces dispatched to deal with particular crises; however, it is sometimes used in a civilian context: □ *A police task force is to investigate the rise in crime.*

tautology Tautology is the avoidable repetition of an idea already expressed in different words: □ *a new innovation* □ *a brief moment.* Many well-established English phrases contain *tautologies*: □ *to mix together* □ *free gift*, etc.

• It is not difficult to avoid the cruder tautologies: □ *a dead corpse* □ *an empty bottle with nothing in it*, but many tautologies arise unintentionally from carelessness about the meanings of words. To speak of *unlawful murder* is tautologous because *murder* means "unlawful killing." In □ *She repeated it again*, *again* is redundant as *repeat* means "to say again." People also speak of □ *SALT talks* □ *OPEC countries* □ *the CNN network*, presumably not realizing that the word following the abbreviation is a repetition of the final word of the abbreviation.

Tautologies are in general to be avoided but can sometimes be used deliberately for emphasis: □ *a tiny little speck*.

teach see LEARN OR TEACH?

technical or **technological?** *Technical* means "having or concerned with special practical knowledge of a scientific or mechanical subject"; *technological* means "concerned with applied science" and is used particularly of modern advances in technical processes: □ *technical difficulties* □ *technical college* □ *a technological breakthrough.*

• The prefix *techno-* can be used to relate to each adjective, but is mainly connected with *technological:* □ *technocrat* □ *technostructure.*

A second meaning of the word *technical* is "marked by a strict interpretation of law or a set of rules": □ *a technical foul* □ *a technical advantage.*

telephone see **PHONE.**

televise This word is often spelled incorrectly with a *z* instead of an *s*.

• To avoid mistakes, remember that the *s* in *television* remains unchanged. *Televise* is one of the verbs ending in *-ise* that cannot be spelled *-ize:* see **-IZE** OR **-ISE**?

temerity or **timidity?** The word *temerity* is sometimes mistakenly used where *timidity* is intended, though their meanings are completely different. *Temerity* means "audacity or recklessness"; *timidity* means "lacking courage or self-confidence; easily frightened or alarmed."

• The two words are not exact opposites. The opposite of *timidity* is *courage* or *confidence,* each of which has positive connotations, whereas *temerity* has negative ones. It suggests a rash contempt of danger or disapproval, with a lack of reserve that may be interpreted as ill-mannered: □ *He had the temerity to interrupt the meeting.*

temperature *Temperature* can mean "the degree of heat or cold as measured on, for example, a thermometer; "the degree of heat natural to the body"; "abnormally high body heat." To *take someone's temperature* means "to use a thermometer to measure the person's body heat."

• The word is often used as a synonym for *fever:* □ *running a temperature* □ *She's got a temperature,* but this usage is best avoided in writing and formal contexts. A metaphorical use of *temperature* describes the emotional state of a group of people: the *temperature* is high or low according to whether they are agitated or calm.

tense The tense of a verb is used to express distinction of time. Some modern grammarians tend to say that fundamentally there are only two real tenses in English, the *present:* □ *It is hot today,* and the *past:* □ *It was cloudy yesterday.* The *future* is simply formed by the addition of *will* or *shall,* etc.: □ *It will be fine tomorrow,* and all other changes of tense are marked by using *be, have,* or both, with the past or present participle of the verb: □ *She is dancing.* □ *He was talking.* □ *I'll be thinking of you.* □ *They had ridden for three days.* □ *I shall have finished it by then.* □ *They had slept until noon.* □ *He had been praying.* □ *She has been working.* □ *They will have been traveling all day.*

• Tense becomes more complicated when there is more than one verb in a sentence. In such sentences, there is a main clause, containing the most important verb, and a subordinate clause or clauses containing the other verb(s): □ *I thought that I knew him.*

Here the main clause *I thought* is in the past tense, and the subordinate clause *that I knew him* follows the lead of the main clause and is in the same tense. This practce is by no means always the case, for it is quite possible for the clauses to refer to different times: □ *I believe I met him last week.* When the main clause is in the future, the verb of the subordinate clause is usually in the present: □ *I will look him up when I go to London.* When the main clause is in the past but the subordinate clause expresses some permanent fact, then that clause can be in the present: □ *She had learned that Paris is a capital city.* In sentences referring to the future as viewed from the past, the subordinate verb usually changes to the past tense: □ *I hope they will succeed* becomes *I hoped they would succeed.*

The present tense is not used solely in expressions of events in the present. It is frequently used to express the future: □ *I leave on Thursday.* □ *The President speaks to the nation tonight.* The present is also habitually used in newspaper headlines to describe past events: □ *Airliner Lands Safely After Its Fuselage Ruptures* (headline, *The New York Times*, Dec. 27, 1988).

The tense that is generally used for expressing recent events or actions is the *present perfect,* which is formed by adding *have* to the past participle of a verb: □ *You've already told me.* □ *He's just seen his mother.* □ *Has she turned up yet?* In informal English, the simple past tense is used in such sentences: □ *You already told me.* □ *He just saw his mother.* □ *Did she turn up yet?* See also PARTICIPLES; SUBJUNCTIVE; VERBS.

terminal or **terminus?** Used as nouns meaning "end or finishing point," these words are often synonymous. Each can mean the finishing point of a transport line, but *terminal* is more frequent. *Terminal* as an adjective can mean "of or at the end" or "leading to death": □ *a terminal illness.*

• Other meanings of *terminal* as a noun include: "device on a wire or battery for an electrical connection" and "instrument through which a user can communicate with a computer."

terminate *Terminate,* meaning "bring to an end, form the ending of, close," is increasingly used in the context of ending employment. From speaking of *terminating someone's contract,* etc., some people have gone on to use *terminated* as a synonym for dismissed: □ *The workers were terminated when profits fell.*

• *Terminate* is also used of buses and trains to mean "stop at a particular place and go no farther": □ *This train terminates here.*

Another popular use relates to ending pregnancies. A *termination* is synonymous with an *abortion.*

Terminated, with the addition of *with* or *in,* is a fashionable alternative to *resulted in* in sports commentaries: □ *The match terminated in a tie.*

terminus see TERMINAL OR TERMINUS?

terrible or **terrific?** *Terrible* can be used as a general term of disapproval or can mean "very bad" or "causing distress": □ *a terrible accident. Terrific,* on the other hand, expresses approval: □ *Chartres has a terrific cathedral.* Each can mean "unusually great": □ *There's a terrible/terrific amount of paperwork here.*

• Another similar use of *terribly* and *terrifically* is as intensifiers to express either approval or disapproval: □ *a terribly/terrifically dull lecture* □ *a terribly/terrifically good book.*

Both words derive from *terror*, but they are now far removed from any suggestion of fear. Each should be restricted to informal contexts.

than *Than* is used to link two halves of comparisons or contrasts: □ *Jack is taller than Jill.* □ *I am wiser now than I was at that time.*
• Care must be taken with pronouns following *than*. The general rule is to remember the missing verb: □ *You are older than I (am)*, however, the form that is considered correct by careful users sometimes sounds stilted: □ *She runs faster than he* is correct, but *She runs faster than him* is more frequently used. □ *She runs faster than he does* is both correct and natural-sounding.

thankfully As an adverb from *thank*, *thankfully* means "in a thankful, relieved, or grateful way": □ *They received the good news thankfully.* It is also used to mean "it is a matter of relief that": □ *Thankfully, he has survived the operation.*
• Many people dislike the second use of *thankfully*, although it is not as widely objected to as the similar use of *hopefully* (see HOPE-FULLY). It can also occasionally lead to such ambiguous statements as: □ *Thankfully, she went to church on Sunday.*

thank you *Thank you, thanks, many thanks*, etc., are expressions of gratitude: □ *Thank you for a lovely evening.* It is also used in acceptance: □ *"Have a sweet." "Thanks, I will."* or as a polite refusal in conjunction with *no*: □ *"Have a sweet." "No, thanks."* in a firm and less polite refusal: □ *I can manage without your advice, thank you very much* and to show pleasure: □ *Now David's got a new job, we're doing very nicely, thank you very much.*
• *Thanks* can indicate responsibility or blame: □ *Thanks to your coaching, I passed my exam.* □ *She has only herself to thank for her situation. Thank heavens, thank goodness*, and *thank God* are general expressions of relief: □ *Thank heavens you're all right.* □ *"Peace has been declared." "Thank goodness!"*

that *That* is used as a conjunction or relative pronoun to introduce various types of clauses, and in some cases can be omitted. As a conjunction, it can usually be omitted: □ *I'm sure (that) you're lying.* It should not be left out when used with a noun: □ *the fact that grass is green*, or with certain verbs, usually of a formal nature—for example, *assert, contend.* It must not be left out when its omission could lead to ambiguity: □ *I said last week you were wrong* might mean "I said that last week you were wrong" or "I said last week that you were wrong."
• Used as a relative pronoun, *that* can be omitted when it is the object: □ *the man (that) I love*, but not when it is the subject: □ *the thing that upsets me.*

The use of *that* as an adverb: □ *He's not that fat* is best avoided in formal contexts.

that or **which?** Whether to use *that* or *which* depends on whether it appears in a defining or nondefining clause. *That* is used in defining clauses: □ *the school that they go to.* Note that a defining clause is not preceded by a comma. In nondefining clauses, those conveying parenthetical or incidental information, only *which* can be used: □ *The program, which was broadcast on public television, caused much controversy.* Nondefining clauses are always preceded by a comma and, unless at the end of a sentence, followed by one. On the use of *that* or *who/whom*, see **WHO**.

• Careful users dislike the use of *which* in defining clauses, maintaining that only *that* should be used.

the *The* is the most frequently used word in the English language. Its pronunciation is usually a straightforward matter. Before consonants it is pronounced [dhě]; before vowels or an unaspirated *h* it is pronounced [dhee]. The use of [dhee] before consonants has become frequent in recent years, particularly by broadcasters, but it is disliked by many people.

• One use of *the* is to single out one of a class as the best or most significant of a class: □ *Is that the Michael Jackson?* □ *It's the place to go for curry.* In these cases, *the* is emphasized and pronounced [dhee].

theft see **BURGLARIZE, BURGLE, ROB, OR STEAL?**

their or **they're?** These two words are sometimes confused. *Their* means "of them or belonging to them": □ *their house. They're* is a contraction of *they are:* □ *They're/They are always late.*

• Another frequent mistake is the wrong spelling of *theirs* as *their's*. The correct usage is as in: □ *The car was theirs.*

them or **their?** see **-ING FORMS.**

thence *Thence* is a formal and almost archaic word with three meanings: "from there, from that place": □ *We drove to New York and thence to Boston;* "from that premise or for that reason": □ *She proved that x was an even number and thence that it must be 42;* and "from that time": □ *His wife died six years ago, and thence he has become a recluse.*

• As *from* is contained in the meaning of *thence,* it is incorrect to say *from thence* (see **HENCE; WHENCE**).

Thence is sometimes mistakenly used to mean "to there," instead of the even more archaic *thither.*

there are see **THERE IS OR THERE ARE?**

therefore *Therefore* means "for that reason, consequently, as this proves": □ *I dislike worms; therefore I avoid digging in the garden.* □ *Puerto Rico is part of the United States; therefore Puerto Ricans are Americans.*

• *Therefore* normally appears at the beginning of a clause and may be followed by a comma. If it appears parenthetically within a clause, it has a comma before and after: □ *It appears, therefore, that he must be guilty.*

there is or **there are?** Normally, *there is* should precede a singular noun, and *there are* a plural: □ *There is a pine.* □ *There are cedars. There is,* however, is widely used informally in various expressions in which *there are* is formally correct.

• These usages include situations in which the plural noun is regarded as a single unit: □ *There is three tons of coal here;* the first of a list of nouns is singular: □ *There is a rabbit, two gerbils, and some white mice;* two nouns are regarded as a single entity: □ *There is fish and chips for supper;* and one is considering a situation in its entirety: □ *There is my job and career prospects at stake.*

The use of the contraction *there's* followed by a plural is almost universal in informal speech: □ *There's two good films showing,* although unacceptable in formal speech and writing.

they *They, them, their,* etc., are increasingly being used informally to refer to singular entities: □ *Anyone can apply if they have the qualifications.*

• Many careful users object to such phrases as *a person on their own.* The use of *he* and *his* has a male bias unacceptable to many, while *he or she* or *his or her* often sounds stilted. Probably the best solution is to make the noun plural to agree with *they* or *their:* □ *people on their own.* See also HE OR SHE.

they're see THEIR OR THEY'RE?

third or **thirdly?** see FIRST OR FIRSTLY?

this see NEXT OR THIS?

though see ALTHOUGH OR THOUGH?

thrash or **thresh?** The verb *thrash* means "flog or beat with repeated blows" or "defeat": □ *He was thrashed by the principal.* □ *We thrashed the opposition. Thresh* means "separate seeds of cereal from husks by beating."

• *Thrash,* usually with *about,* can also mean "move violently": □ *He thrashed his arms about like a windmill,* and is used in the idiomatic phrasal verb *thrash out* meaning "discuss in detail until a solution is found": □ *Let's thrash out this problem together.*

The two words are occasionally confused, partly because *thresh,* with the meaning given above, is sometimes spelled *thrash.*

threshold Note that there is only one *h* in the spelling of this word, unlike in the word *withhold.*

• *Threshold* may be pronounced either [threshhōld] or [threshōld].

thus The slightly formal adverb *thus* means "in such a manner, in the way indicated, consequently": □ *His rich father died in a accident, and he thus inherited a fortune.*

• *Thus far* means "to this extent, up to now": □ *Thus far we have succeeded.* The word *thusly,* is a colloquial variant.

till or **until?** Each word means "up to the time that, up to as far as": □ *I will work until I drop.* □ *Go on till you reach the traffic lights.*

• They are interchangeable, although *until* is slightly more formal and *till* is more likely to be used in speech. *Until* is usually more appropriate as the first word of a sentence: □ *Until they go, we shall have no peace.*

Till is not an abbreviation of *until,* so *'til* and *'till* are incorrect.

timidity see TEMERITY OR TIMIDITY?

titillate or **titivate?** Literally, *titillate* means the same as *tickle,* but it is almost always used figuratively in the sense of "stimulate or arouse pleasantly": □ *Her interest titillated his vanity. Titivate* is occasionally confused with *titillate,* but its meaning is "tidy or dress up": □ *I must titivate myself for the party.*

• *Titillate* is sometimes used to mean "excite mild sexual pleasure," and modern usage often has negative connotations of superficiality or self-indulgence: □ *Readers of sensationalist tabloids are titillated by reports of sexual offenses.*

titles Generally the titles of literary works, musical works, works of art, films, etc., are set in italics or, in handwriting and typescript, underlined: □ *I saw King Lear last night.* □ *She sang the title role in Carmen.* □ *Citizen Kane.*

• The Bible and the names of its individual books are not set in italics, and neither are the Talmud, the Torah, or the Koran.

The names of newspapers and magazines are set in italics. The definite article before a paper's name is often not italicized: □ the *Daily News* □ the *New York Times*.

The titles of long poems are usually set in italics, but short ones in quotation marks: □ Longfellow's *Evangeline* □ Frost's "The Road Not Taken."

tobacco This word, for the plant product used in cigarettes, cigars, etc., is sometimes misspelled. Note the single *b* and the double *c*.

toilet, lavatory, loo, or **bathroom?** These euphemisms are virtually interchangeable: □ *I need the bathroom.* □ *We're out of toilet paper.* □ *Where's the loo?* Lavatory and *loo* are more frequent in Britain, where *bathroom* means a room containing a bath but not necessarily a toilet.

tolerance or **toleration?** These words are nouns from *tolerate,* but *tolerance* is "the capacity to tolerate," while *toleration* is "the act of tolerating": □ *His tolerance is unlimited.* □ *Her toleration of his habits demonstrates her good nature.*

• *Tolerance* is generally used in speaking of respect for the beliefs of others, although in the context of official government policy, *toleration* is often used: □ *religious toleration.*

Tolerance has several technical meanings in mathematics, statistics, physics, and medicine: an accepted deviation from a standard measurement; the ability of substances to endure heat, stress, etc., without being damaged; the capacity of a person's body to withstand harmful substances, etc.

torpor This word, meaning "inactive condition," is sometimes misspelled. Note the final *-or,* as in *stupor,* rather than *-our.*

tortuous or **torturous?** *Tortuous* means "twisting; winding" and, figuratively, "complex, devious, or overelaborate": □ *a tortuous road* □ *a tortuous policy.* *Torturous* comes from *torture* and means "inflicting torture; agonizing or painful:" □ *a torturous illness.*

• *Torturous* is sometimes used to mean "complicated" or "twisted," but careful users restrict it to the use suggesting physical or mental pain. The context often leads to confusion: □ *a tortuous decision* might mean a complex one or might be a mistake for a *torturous* decision—one that is painful to make.

total *Total* is used as a noun: □ *The total was 115,* a verb: □ *Profits this year total one million dollars,* and an intensifying adjective suggesting completeness: □ *a total failure* □ *a total stranger.*

• Some people dislike the use of *total* as an intensifying adjective synonymous with *utter* or *complete,* and maintain that the word should be used only when there is a sense of parts being added to produce a whole as in: □ *the total cost.*

Another disputed use is one in which the noun already suggests totality; some people think *total* is redundant in such phrases as *total annihilation* or *the sum total.*

tourniquet This word, meaning "a tight bandage tied around an arm or leg to stop bleeding," is pronounced [*toor*nikit] or [*tirni*kit].

• In British English, the final *t* is not pronounced.

toward or **towards?** *Towards* is a variant of *toward,* the usual form of the preposition meaning "in the direction of" or "with regard to": □ *They walked toward the hotel.* □ *What are his feelings toward her?*

• See also -WARD OR -WARDS?

town see CITY OR TOWN?

town house A *town house* suggests an urban, terraced house, usually with two or more stories. When one speaks of someone's *town house*, however, one can also mean a house in town belonging to a rich person whose main residence is in the country: □ *They used their town house for Veronica's party.*

track record The phrase *track record*, meaning "record of past performance," is frequently used as an unnecessary extension of the word *record* or synonym for "experience," especially in job advertisements: □ *a sound track record* □ *a successful track record in sales and marketing* □ *We are looking for individuals with a proven track record at a senior level in finance, business, or industrial management* (*The Guardian*, Sept. 17, 1987). Care should be taken to avoid overusing this expression.

trademarks Trademarks are names given to articles by their manufacturers. Some have become generic names for articles of their kind, even when the article does not actually bear the trade name in question: □ *Thermos bottle* □ *Xerox* □ *Kleenex*.
• Nouns that are actually trade names should be spelled with an initial capital letter, although this rule is frequently overlooked, as in: □ *Fill your thermos with coffee.* When the noun has given rise to a verb, it is spelled with a lower-case initial letter: □ *He xeroxed the document.*

trafficker This word is sometimes misspelled. The word *traffic* adds a *k* before the suffixes *-er*, *-ed*, and *-ing*: □ *drug traffickers* □ *illegal arms trafficking*. See also SPELLING 1.

tranquillity This word, meaning "peaceful state": □ *the perfect tranquillity of the lake* □ *The Sea of Tranquillity* is often misspelled. Note the double *l*.

transient or **transitory?** Each word means "short-lived, lasting only a brief time": □ *It is just a transient/transitory phase.*
• The words are virtually interchangeable but have a slightly different feel to them. *Transient* often suggests passing by quickly, perhaps because of rapid movement from place to place: □ *transient summer visitors*. *Transitory* often carries a suggestion of regret about the way desirable things change or disappear: □ *the transitory nature of human love.*
   Transient is sometimes used as a noun to mean "person who stays for only a short time in any one place."
• **transpire** *Transpire* means "become known; come to light": □ *It later transpired that the President had known of the plan all along.* It is also widely used to mean "happen or occur": □ *I will let you know what transpires.* This second use is disliked by many careful users, although it is a well-established usage.
• *Transpire* is sometimes used to mean "turn out or prove to be": □ *He transpired to be her cousin,* or "arrive or turn up": □ *Subsequently dozens of letters transpired.* Such uses are incorrect.

transverse or **traverse?** *Transverse* is an adjective meaning "lying or set across, crosswise, at right angles to": □ *a transverse section.* *Traverse* is a verb meaning "cross or go across" or a noun meaning "something that lies across; way or path across": □ *The river traverses two counties.* □ *The traverse of this mountain is dangerous to inexperienced climbers.*

T

traumatic *Traumatic* is the adjective from *trauma*, which means "a wound or an injury," and it is still used in this sense in medical contexts: □ *traumatic symptons*. Its main use, however, is with the figurative meaning of "causing great and deeply disturbing emotional shock": □ *a traumatic bereavement* □ *the traumatic effects of divorce* □ *the traumatic experience of a concentration camp.*
  • The word has become very much overworked and is often used for cases of mild distress or annoyance: □ *I spent a traumatic evening filling in my tax return.*
  The usual pronunciation is [trawmă]; the pronunciation [trahmă] is used less frequently.

travel This word is sometimes misspelled. The final *l* is not doubled before the suffixes *-ed*, *-ing*, and *-er*: □ *well-traveled* □ *traveling fast* □ *business travelers.*
  • British English doubles the *l*: □ *travelled* □ *traveller* □ *travelling.* See also SPELLING 1.

traverse see TRANSVERSE OR TRAVERSE?

treble or **triple?** These words can be used as noun, verb, and adjective and are virtually interchangeable in meaning. *Treble*, though, is preferred by some users when the meaning is "three times as great": □ *treble damages*, and *triple* when the meaning is "consisting of three parts": □ *a triple jump.*
  • The words have distinctly different meanings in the context of music. *Treble* refers to a high-pitched voice or instrument, or a singer who performs at this pitch, whereas *triple* is used of rhythm: □ *a treble recorder* □ *triple time.*

tremor This word, meaning "shaking or quivering action": □ *earth tremors*, is sometimes misspelled. Note the ending *-or*, not *-our*.

triple see TREBLE OR TRIPLE?

triumphal or **triumphant?** These adjectives are often confused. *Triumphal* is connected with the celebration of a victory, usually of a military nature: □ *A triumphal march was played as the victorious army paraded through the streets. Triumphant* means "victorious, exulting or rejoicing in success": □ *The champion was again triumphant.* □ *Having succeeded in her task, she returned with a triumphant smile.*
  • *Triumphant* is the more frequently used word, *triumphal* being restricted to narrower, more formal contexts.

trivia *Trivia* means "matters of very minor importance": □ *the trivia of village gossip* □ *Why waste hours fussing over the trivia of everyday life?*
  • The word is actually a plural, so a careful user would not say: □ *Such trivia is beneath my notice*; however, *Such trivia are beneath my notice* has a stilted and unnatural sound, so most users would substitute such phrases as: □ *trivial matters* □ *trivial issues* □ *trivial things* for *trivia* in the preceding example.

troop or **troupe?** These words are sometimes confused. A *troop* is a military unit or group of people or things: □ *troops of soldiers* □ *a Boy Scout troop. Troop* is also used as a verb in informal English to mean "move as a large group": □ *Then they all trooped off home.* A *troupe* is a group of actors or performers: □ *a troupe of traveling acrobats.*
  • The words *trooper* and *trouper* are also sometimes confused. A

trooper is a cavalry soldier, especially a private, or more often a policeman: □ *swear like a trooper* means "swear a lot." A *trouper* is a member of a *troupe* of dancers, singers, etc.

trooping the color *Trooping the color* means "parade the flag of a regiment ceremonially along the ranks of soldiers of that regiment." Written with capital letters, *Trooping the Color* refers to the annual parade in London, usually attended by the Queen, the Prime Minister, and other dignitaries.

troupe see TROOP OR TROUPE?

truism The narrower meaning of *truism* suggests a synonym for *tautology*, which is "a statement of self-evident truth, one containing superfluous repetition of an idea": □ *It is a truism to speak of single bachelors.* The word is more widely used to mean "a statement of a fact that is too obvious to be thought worth stating": □ *the truism that stars are only visible at night.*

• *Truism* is sometimes used as though it were a synonym for *fact* or *truth* in such phrases as: □ *the truism that heterosexuals can contract AIDS,* but such use is widely regarded as unacceptable.

try and or **try to?** The two expressions are virtually interchangeable: □ *Try and catch me!* □ *Try to tell the truth.* *Try and,* however, is colloquial; it is unacceptable in formal written English.

• Note that *try to* sounds better in a negative context: □ *She didn't even try to be polite* and only *try to* can be used in the past tense: □ *They tried to break into the house.*

tsar or **czar?** This word, the title of any of the former Russian emperors, is spelled *tsar, czar,* or, rarely, *tzar.* It is pronounced [zahr].

• Many users prefer the spelling *tsar,* because it more accurately reflects the Russian word as written in the Cyrillic script. The more frequent spelling *czar* shows the origin of the word from the Gothic *kaisar,* and ultimately the Latin *Caesar.*

turquoise The name of this greenish-blue mineral is pronounced [*tur*kwoiz], but [*tur*koiz] is also heard.

twelfth Careful users avoid dropping the *f* in the pronunciation of this word [twelfth]. The word is, however, frequently pronounced without the *f.*

type of see KIND OF.

ultimate *Ultimate* is used mainly as an adjective meaning "last, final, eventual": □ *the ultimate goal,* or "fundamental": □ *ultimate truths.* As a noun, it has traditionally simply meant "something ultimate" or "the extreme": □ *the ultimate in wickedness.* This last use is increasingly being extended, particularly in advertising and journalism, to mean "the best possible; the most modern or advanced thing": □ *the ultimate in swimming pools* □ *the ultimate in high technology.*
• This vogue use, disliked by some, has some similarity to the phrase *the last word.*

ultra *Ultra* is an adjective meaning "going beyond" or "extreme" and is also used as a prefix with other words, either with or without a hyphen. In the sense of "extremely," it is used in such words as: □ *ultramodern* □ *ultra-radical.*
• In the sense of "beyond the range of," it is used in: □ *ultrasonic* □ *ultramicroscopic. UHF* stands for *ultrahigh frequency.*

un- see NON-.

unanimous *Unanimous* means "of one mind; in complete agreement": □ *The committee reached a unanimous decision.* It can only be used when several people all agree about something, and cannot be used as a synonym for *wholehearted* or *enthusiastic* as in: □ *Many of the group were prepared to give the project their unanimous backing.*
• When a vote is taken, someone can be said to have been elected *unanimously,* or a motion passed *unanimously,* only if every person present voted in favor. If there are any abstentions, the motion is said to be passed *nem con,* which is an abbreviation of the Latin *nemine contradicente,* "no one contradicting."

unaware or **unawares?** *Unaware* is an adjective meaning "not aware; not knowing about; not having noticed": □ *I was unaware that you were coming.* □ *He seemed unaware of the reaction he was causing.* It is occasionally used as an adverb, but the usual adverb is *unawares,* meaning "unexpectedly, without warning," often in *caught unawares* or *taken unawares:* □ *The landslide caught the villagers unawares.*
• *Unaware* is often followed by *of* or *that,* but *unawares* should precede another word in that way.

unconscious see SUBCONSCIOUS OR UNCONSCIOUS?

under see BELOW, BENEATH, UNDER, OR UNDERNEATH?

under foot or **underfoot?** This term should be spelled as one word, not as two separate words: □ *It was rather wet underfoot.*

underhand or **underhanded?** *Underhand* and *underhanded* are used as adjectives to mean "sly; marked by dishonesty, trickery,

256

and deception": □ *They used the most underhand/underhanded methods in their campaign.*

• These words can be used in the context of some sports, meaning "with the hand below the shoulder or elbow": □ *underhand shooting* □ *aiming underhanded. Underhanded* is also occasionally used to mean "short of the required number of workers."

underneath see BELOW, BENEATH, UNDER, OR UNDERNEATH?

underprivileged *Underprivileged* has become a fashionable adjective to use in connection with those lacking the standard of income and opportunities common to the society in which they live: □ *She started a clinic for underprivileged children.* □ *Many young criminals come from underprivileged backgrounds.* It is used as a noun as well as an adjective: □ *His concern for the underprivileged drew him toward social work as a career.*

• Its real meaning is not "lacking in privileges" but "lacking in rights; disadvantaged" or at least lacking in those social and economic rights considered to be fundamental in Western developed society.

underway or **under way?** Careful users prefer to write this adverb meaning "moving; in progress" as two words: □ *Preparations for the new project are now well under way.* The expression is, however, increasingly being spelled as one word.

• The spelling *under weigh* is wrong. This spelling probably arises from confusion with the nautical expression *weigh anchor,* meaning "raise anchor."

undiscriminating see INDISCRIMINATE OR UNDISCRIMINATING?

undoubtedly *Undoubtedly, no doubt, doubtless,* and *without (a) doubt* express that something is not disputed. *Undoubtedly* and *without a doubt* express that idea much more positively and strongly than the other expressions: □ *She is undoubtedly the best student in her year. No doubt* and *doubtless* are much weaker expressions, often suggesting that the user is in fact not completely certain, or is even harboring doubts: □ *No doubt he is very clever but I still can't understand what he is saying.*

• *Doubtless* is an adverb as well as an adjective; some prefer *doubtlessly* as the adverb form.

Some people mistakenly spell *undoubtedly* as *undoubtably,* perhaps confused with *indubitably,* which is a more formal and even stronger expression, suggesting that something cannot possibly be doubted: □ *It was indubitably evident that he had acted in a manner that was utterly unacceptable.*

unexceptionable or **unexceptional?** *Unexceptionable* means "inoffensive; not liable to be taken exception to, criticized, or objected to": □ *His behavior had been unexceptionable, so he could not understand how he could have offended his hosts. Unexceptional* means "usual, normal, or ordinary": □ *The weather was unexceptional for the time of year.* It is, however, more frequently used to suggest that something is dull or disappointingly commonplace: □ *I had heard enthusiastic reports of his playing, but I found this an unexceptional performance.*

• The words are often confused, partly because it is quite possible for something to be both inoffensive and rather dull.

uninterested see DISINTERESTED OR UNINTERESTED?

unique *Unique* means "being the only one of its kind": □ *Every* *snowflake has a unique pattern.* Either a thing is *unique* or it is not, so careful users dislike such expressions as *so unique, rather unique, very unique,* etc., and something cannot be *more unique* or *less unique* than something else. *Almost* and *nearly* are often modifiers only informally acceptable with *unique.*

• The word is widely used with a weaker meaning of "unrivaled; outstanding," but many people object to such use. Intensifiers are often used with *unique:* □ *It was absolutely unique,* but such expressions should be restricted to informal use.

United Kingdom see BRITAIN.

United States, United States of America see AMERICA.

unpractical see PRACTICAL OR PRACTICABLE?

unprecedented A *precedent* is "an earlier example or occurrence of a similar thing," so *unprecedented* means "never having happened before; completely new or original": □ *His score was unprecedented in the history of golf.*

• It has recently become a popular word, particularly in the media where its meaning has weakened to "extremely great": *The film is enjoying an uprecedented success.*

unreadable see ILLEGIBLE OR UNREADABLE?

until see TILL OR UNTIL?

unwanted or **unwonted?** *Unwanted* means simply "not wanted": □ *She gave her unwanted clothes to the charity. Unwonted* means "out of the ordinary; unusual": □ *The drug gave him an unwonted feeling of euphoria.*

• The two words are confused because people sometimes mistakenly spell *unwonted* as *unwanted.*

upon or **on?** These two words are synonyms and virtually indistinguishable in use: □ *She threw herself upon the sofa.* □ *He walked on the beach. Upon* has a more formal sound and, particularly in spoken English, *on* is more frequently used.

• In some cases, usage is dictated by the word that is normal in a particular idiom: □ *once upon a time* □ *on the contrary.*

Upon is sometimes used between two repeated nouns to suggest large numbers: □ *We walked mile upon mile.*

upward or **upwards?** *Upward* is an adjective and an adverb meaning "to a higher level": □ *an upward trend* □ *to float upward.*

• The adverb *upwards* is more frequently used in British English. See also -WARD OR -WARDS?

The phrase *upward of* or *upwards of,* meaning "more than," is disliked by some users: □ *The newly privatized company is in contention with America's Pratt & Whitney to supply the engines for upwards of 100 Boeing 757s that Texas Air is planning to order (Sunday Times,* June 7, 1987).

upwardly mobile This term is a very fashionable modern expression, used of ambitious, usually young, people who are moving into a higher class, income bracket, etc.: □ *These days the city is thought to be full of upwardly mobile young men and women trying to enhance their status in society.*

urban or **urbane?** *Urban* means "of a town or city": □ *Unemployment is higher in urban areas. Urbane* is used of someone who is sophisticated and polite, with a smooth and easy manner in any social situation: □ *He turned out to be an elegant and urbane man who charmed them all.*

• *Urbane* actually derives from *urban*, in describing a manner that was thought to be characteristic of a person who came from a city.

us see **WE**.

us or our? see **-ING FORMS**.

U.S., U.S.A. see **AMERICA**.

used to *Used to* means either "accustomed to": □ *I have become used to the noise by now*, or refers to a habitual action or situation in the past: □ *She used to play the piano regularly*.
• Difficulties arise over negative and question forms of the word in its second meaning. In negative forms, the more formal *used not to* or the more informal *did not/didn't use to* are acceptable: □ *He used not to be so aggressive*. □ *She did not use to like fish*. *Didn't used to* is heard, but it is avoided by careful users.

In the question form, the formal and rather old-fashioned *used X to?* and the less formal *did X use to?* are correct: □ *Used there to be a lake in that area?* □ *Did Henry use to visit you? Did X used to?* or *didn't X used to?* are frequently used, though disliked by many careful users. As no form sounds completely natural and correct, many people would reconstruct the sentence and say, for example: □ *Was there once a lake in that area?*

user-friendly *User-friendly* is a term used in computing to describe software that is simple to use, being designed to assist the user and prevent any potential problems: □ *a user-friendly program*.
• The term is increasingly found in other fields, meaning "easy to operate or understand," and describing electrical appliances, cars, and even works of reference: □ *the standard aims to help publishers produce "user-friendly" catalogues* (The Bookseller, June 5, 1987). This implied association with advanced technology may impress some people but will alienate others; it is therefore advisable to reserve the term for its original purpose.

A further development is the use of the adjective *friendly* in other combinations, such as: □ *customer-friendly* □ *environment-friendly*, etc.

User-hostile, the opposite of *user-friendly*, is also found in certain contexts: □ *complex, user-hostile systems which require complicated languages to program and are hard to understand* (The Guardian, July 6, 1984).

utilize *Utilize* means "use in a practical and effective, profitable or productive way": □ *They utilized every machine that was available*. It can also mean "make good use of something not intended for the purpose": □ *She utilized her tights when the fan belt broke*; or to "make use of something that might be thought useless": □ *She utilized all the scraps for stuffing cushions*.
• *Utilize* is often used, particularly in business jargon, as though it were merely a synonym for *use*: □ *Successful applicants will be able to utilize their experience and skills in this field*. Careful users, however, restrict the word to the narrower senses described above.

vacation The main meaning of *vacation* is "restful break." □ *They took a vacation in Miami.* It is also used as a verb: □ *We vacationed in Europe last year.*

A rare meaning of the word is "vacating; making vacant or empty": □ *The landlord insisted on immediate vacation of the house.* In British English, the primary meaning of the noun *vacation* is "the period when universities and law courts are not officially working": □ *She went home for the Christmas vacation.*

vaccinate This word is sometimes misspelled. Note the double *c*, single *n*, and single *t*.

variegated This word, meaning "having different colors; varied": □ *variegated leaves,* is sometimes misspelled. Note the *e* between the *i* and the *g*.

venal or **venial?** *Venal* means literally "for sale," and it is used either of individuals who are capable of being "bought" or corrupted or of systems that operate by bribery and corruption: □ *Their legal system is so venal that criminals openly offer bribes in court.* *Venial* means "pardonable; excusable" and is applied to minor faults and offenses: □ *He was inclined to be thoughtless, but that was a venial fault in one so young.*

• In Roman Catholic theology, a *venial sin* is one that does not deprive the soul of divine grace, as opposed to a *mortal sin.*

vengeance see REVENGE OR VENGEANCE?

venial see VENAL OR VENIAL?

venison This word, meaning "the meat of a deer," is usually pronounced [venisŏn] or [venizŏn], although the traditional pronunciation is [venzŏn].

venue In legal usage, *venue* refers to the area in which a crime is committed or a case is tried: □ *Defense lawyers sought a change of venue for the controversial trial.* Another meaning of *venue* is "the place where a meeting, event, or gathering happens": □ *We have not yet decided on the venue for the annual conference.*

• There is a sense of people coming together to a particular place for a purpose. Recent usage, to the dislike of some, makes *venue* virtually synonymous with *place, scene,* or *setting,* as the site of any activity: □ *A valley in South America is the venue for this experiment in self-sufficient communal living.*

verbal or **oral?** *Verbal* means "expressed in words;" *oral* means "having to do with the mouth" or "expressed in speech." Something *verbal* can be expressed in either speech or writing; however, a *verbal agreement* is generally understood to mean one that is spoken not written.

• Some careful users feel that, despite the established use of *ver-*

260

bal in this way, it is always better to use an *oral agreement,* because there is no question of misunderstanding or ambiguity with the word *oral.*

verbal nouns see INFINITIVE; -ING FORMS.

verbs Verbs refer to actions, occurrences, or existence. They vary in form according to the tense or mood used, usually in a predictable way but, with irregular verbs, in various different ways that need to be learned.

• Verbs differ in their functions. One distinction is between *transitive* and *intransitive verbs.* A transitive verb is one that needs a direct object—for example, *like.* One cannot just like; one has to like someone or something. Either it must take a direct object: □ *He likes chocolate,* or it can be used in the passive: □ *She is liked by everyone.* Intransitive verbs do not take a direct object. *Fall,* for example, is an intransitive verb □ *The old oak fell.* Some verbs can be used both transitively and intransitively in different constructions: □ *Can the boat sail?—She sailed the boat.*

Some transitive verbs are *reflexive verbs,* which have the same subject and object □ *perjure oneself.* In this example, the verb is always reflexive; one cannot perjure anyone or anything other than oneself. But some verbs are not always used reflexively: □ *I introduced myself to our hostess.—I introduced Chris to our hostess.*

Auxiliary verbs are those used with other verbs, enabling them to express variations in tense, mood, voice, etc. The most frequently used auxiliaries are *be, have,* and *do:* □ *He is tired.* □ *I have finished.* □ *We did not agree. Be* is used to form the passive: □ *It was discussed.* Other auxiliaries include: *shall, could, will, might, need, dare,* and *must:* □ *I shall accept the offer.* □ *You must stop immediately.*

Phrasal verbs are verbs that include an adverb, preposition, or both: □ *give in* □ *throw away* □ *take to.* Many such verbs have meanings that go beyond the sum of their parts—for example, *came by* as in: □ *I came by* [i.e. obtained or received] *that engraving in Venice.* Some mean no more than the words suggest: □ *keep down* □ *stay away.* The modern trend to extend ordinary verbs so that they become phrasal verbs, while adding nothing to their meaning: □ *I consulted (with) my accountant* is disliked by many.

New verbs are formed in various ways. One way is by converting nouns: □ *He serviced her car* (see NOUNS). A variation of this practice is the formation of compound verbs: □ *to rubber-stamp* □ *blue-pencil* □ *downgrade.* These verbs are often disliked when first introduced, but they have the advantage of economy if not of elegance. □ *I shall word-process the letters* is briefer than *I shall produce the letters on a word processor.* For other ways of forming new verbs, see BACK-FORMATION; -IZE OR ISE?

See also INFINITIVE; -ING FORMS; PARTICIPLES; SUBJUNCTIVE; TENSE.

very *Very* can be used as an intensifier before most adjectives and adverbs: □ *very unpleasant* □ *very efficiently.* Before past participles, however, *much* is often used instead of *very:* □ *It was much improved.* The exception involves any past participle used adjectivally: □ *She was very excited.*

• Some words come into a gray area where either *very* or *much* can be used: □ *She was very/much distressed. Much* usually has a more formal sound. There are other participles that cannot take either *very* or *much* as an intensifier, although they can take *very* if an adverb is interposed: one cannot be *very wounded* but can be *very badly wounded;* one cannot say *very mended* but can say *very neatly mended.*

veterinary This word causes problems with spelling and pronunciation. Note the *-erin-* in the spelling. Careful users insist on the pronunciation with five syllables [vetĕrinĕree].
• The expression *veterinary surgeon* is usually shortened to *vet.*

via *Via* means "by way of" and is used when talking of the route for a journey: □ *They went to Australia via Hong Kong.* □ *Your best route would be via the Beltway.*
• It is also used to mean "by means of": □ *I'll return it via Fred,* or to speak of a means of transport: □ *We crossed the river via the ferry,* but many people dislike these usages, particularly the latter one.
   The pronunciation normally regarded as correct is [vīă], although [veeă] is sometimes heard.

viable *Viable* means "capable of living or surviving independently," as in: □ *a viable fetus.* It can be used figuratively in this sense of new communities: □ *When the colony shows itself to be viable, it will be granted independence.*
• The meaning has been extended to "capable of carrying on without extra (financial) support": □ *The business is expected to be commercially viable within two years.*
   In vogue use, the meaning is even further extended to become a synonym for *workable, practicable, feasible:* □ *a viable partnership* □ *a viable plan.* This loose use of *viable* is objected to by many careful users.

vice versa This expression, meaning "with the order reversed," is usually pronounced [vīsĕ versĕ]. An alternative pronunciation for the first word is [vīs].

victuals This largely dialect word, meaning "supplies of food," is pronounced [vitlz].

vigorous This word, meaning "healthy and strong," is often misspelled. Note that there is no *u* before the suffix *-ous.*

virgule The *virgule* is also known as the *stroke, slant, slash mark, oblique,* or *solidus.* Its main use is in separating alternatives: □ *A doctor must use his/her diagnostic skill in such cases.* □ *You need butter and/or margarine to make pastry.*
• It is also used, as in this book, to indicate that either of two alternatives is correct or appropriate: □ *a terrible/terrific amount of work.* The virgule is used in the percentage sign %, and is sometimes used for writing fractions: □ ⅔. It is used instead of the word *per* in such expressions as □ *$20/hr.* It is used in certain abbreviations: □ *a/c* □ *c/o.* It is also sometimes used to separate successive time units: □ *the financial year 1986/87* □ *July/August* and in dates: □ *1/4/88.*
   A further use of the virgule is to indicate the breaks in lines of verse, when a poem is not set out in its separate lines: □ *We are the hollow men/We are the stuffed men/Leaning together* (T.S. Eliot).

virus The word *virus* is now more likely to be used of a disease caused by a virus than it is of the causative agent of the disease: □ *He's recovering from a very nasty virus.*

• The word is also often used in a metaphorical sense for an influence or ideology that is thought to be corrupting and to poison people's minds: □ *the virus of anti-Semitism that spread throughout Germany in the 1930's.*

vis-à-vis *Vis-à-vis* literally means "face to face" and is most frequently used as a preposition to mean "in relation to": □ *We shall have to change our policy vis-à-vis the law.* It also means "opposite" or "face to face with" and is sometimes used as a noun to mean "someone or something opposite another; a counterpart." It is also occasionally used as a synonym for *tête-à-tête,* meaning "a private conversation between two people."

• It is pronounced [veezahvee].

visible There is a recent fashionable use of *visible* to mean "in the public eye; well known": □ *He's one of the more visible senators.* It can also be more or less synonymous with *having a high profile,* with the meaning of "being in a position where one's actions are liable to become subject to public comment or notice": □ *The role of Presidential adviser is an increasingly visible one.* Some object to these uses of *visible,* and care should be taken to avoid overworking this word.

visit or **visitation?** In its most frequent use, *visit* is a verb meaning "pay a call on, stay with as a guest, stay somewhere temporarily" and a noun meaning "an act of visiting": □ *I will visit Dallas when I am in Texas.* □ *He was on a visit to his daughter.* A visitation is an official or formal act of visiting: □ *The priest's work includes the visitation of parishioners in the hospital,* and is often found in humorous use, referring to an unwelcome visit: □ *I'm awaiting a visitation from the Internal Revenue Service.*

• *Visitation* can also refer to the visit of a supernatural being: □ *a visitation of angels,* and is also used in referring to an act of affliction, either natural or divine: □ *the visitation of the Black Death* □ *the visitation of God's wrath.*

vitamin This word's pronunciation is [vītămin], the first syllable of which rhymes with *bite.* That pronunciation is now acceptable in British English although disliked by some people; the traditional British pronunciation of this word is [vitămin].

voluntarily Careful users stress this word on the first syllable [volĕntĕrilee].

• Such users object to the alternative pronunciation, with stress on the third syllable [volĕnterrilee], though this pronunciation is widely heard.

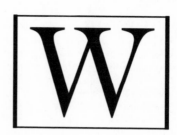

wage, wages see SALARY OR WAGE?

wait see AWAIT OR WAIT?

waive or **wave?** These two words are sometimes confused. The verb *waive* means "relinquish": □ *The judge waived the penalty;* on the other hand, *wave* means "move to and fro": □ *wave good-bye* □ *The corn waved in the wind.* The noun *wave* means "ridge of water."

• The noun *waiver* comes from the verb *waive:* □ *a waiver clause in a contract.* It must not be confused with the verb *waver,* which means "fluctuate or hesitate, become unsteady": □ *Throughout his suffering his faith never wavered.* □ *a wavering voice.*

wake, waken see AWAKE, AWAKEN, WAKE, OR WAKEN?

wander or **wonder?** These spellings are sometimes confused. *Wander* means "roam aimlessly": □ *He wandered through the streets,* whereas *wonder* means "be astonished at" or "think about": □ *I wonder where she is.*

• The pronunciation of *wander* is [wondĕr]; the pronunciation of *wonder* [wundĕr] rhymes with *thunder.*

want The main meanings of *want* as a verb are "to desire": □ *I want a bigger car,* "to need": □ *That door wants mending,* and "to lack": □ *The door wants a handle.* As a noun, *want* means "something desired; a desire for something; a lack" or is used as a synonym for *poverty:* □ *the want experienced by the unemployed. Want to* is sometimes used in informal contexts to mean "ought to": □ *You want to be more careful.*

-ward or **-wards?** The adverbial suffixes *-ward* and *-wards* are used to indicate direction. Each form is correct, although *-ward* is preferred; *-wards* is usually preferred in British English.

• Most of these adverbs have a related adjective ending in *-ward.* The adjectival suffix cannot be replaced by *-wards.*

For further discussion and additional information, see AFTERWARD OR AFTERWARDS?, BACKWARD OR BACKWARDS?, and other individual entries.

was see WERE OR WAS?

wastage or **waste?** *Waste* is used as verb, noun, and adjective. Its main meanings as a noun are "squandering, using carelessly or ungainfully": □ *It was a complete waste of time and money;* and "rubbish; waste material or land": □ *Get rid of all this waste. Wastage* is a noun meaning "loss due to leakage, decay, erosion, evaporation, etc." □ *the wastage of water from a reservoir* □ *Gasoline stored in garages is subject to wastage.*

• *Wastage,* sometimes used as a synonym for *waste,* should instead be confined to the meanings outlined above.

wave, waver see WAIVE OR WAVE?

-ways see -WISE OR -WAYS?

we *We* is used to mean "I and one or more other people": □ *We should get a divorce.* □ *Shall we all go for a walk?*

• It was formerly used to mean "I" by monarchs: □ *We grant by royal decree . . .*, and is sometimes used by writers to give an impression of impersonality: □ *We shall discuss this in a later chapter.* *We* is sometimes used to mean "you," usually in addressing children or invalids in a somewhat patronizing manner: □ *We are in a nasty temper today, aren't we?*

Mistakes are sometimes made in the use of *we* and *us*. *We* is correct with a plural noun as the subject: □ *We children used to play there.* *Us* is correct when the noun is the object: □ *It won't help us workers.*

weather conditions *Weather* means "the condition of the atmosphere, especially in respect of sunshine, rainfall, wind," etc. As the word contains *condition* in its meaning, careful users maintain that it is superfluous to talk of *weather conditions*, as in: □ *The bad weather conditions stopped the game.* □ *The freezing weather conditions in the North will not improve.*

weaved, wove, or **woven?** The usual past tense of *weave* is *wove*: □ *She wove the cloth herself.* □ *The spider wove its web.* *Woven* is the usual past participle of *weave*: □ *It was woven by hand.* □ *They were wearing woven garments.*

• In some tenses of *weave*, *weaved* is used for the past tense or past participle, as when *weave* means "contrive or produce a complicated story": □ *She weaved a sinister plot;* "lurch or stagger": □ *He weaved drunkenly down the street;* and "move around vehicles to avoid hitting them": □ *The car weaved in and out of the traffic.*

Wednesday The name of this day of the week is usually pronounced [wenzday] or, less frequently, [wenzdi]. Some careful users prefer to sound the *d* [wednzdee] or [wednzday].

weird This word, meaning "uncanny or extraordinary," is sometimes misspelled. Note the *-ei-* spelling.

were or **was?** Difficulty is sometimes experienced in the use of the subjunctive form *were* in phrases expressing supposition. The basic rule is that *were* is used when the suggestion is of something hypothetical, unlikely, or not actually the case: □ *If I were you, I'd leave him.* □ *She talks to me as if I were 3 years old.* If the supposition is factual or realistic, then *was* is used: □ *I'm sorry if I was rude.*

• When a supposition might be possible or factual, then *was* may be appropriate: □ *They wondered if he or she was home.* The more doubt there is, the more likely it is that *were* is used.

west, West, or **western?** As an adjective, *west* is always written with a capital *W* when it forms part of a proper name: □ *West Virginia* □ *the West Indies*. The noun *west* is usually written with a capital *W* when it denotes a specific region, such as the noncommunist countries of Europe and America: □ *She defected to the West in 1986.*

• In other contexts, and as an adverb, *west* is usually written with a lowercase *w*: □ *Drive west until you reach the border.* □ *We camped on the west bank of the river.*

W

The adjective *western* is more frequent and usually less specific than the adjective *west:* □ *the western side of the island* □ *in western Pennsylvania.*

Like *west, western* is written with a capital *W* when it forms part of a proper name, such as *Western Hemisphere.* With or without a capital *W,* it also means "of the West": □ *Western/western technology.* A *western* is a film, novel, etc., usually concerning life in the western United States in the 19th century.

wet or **wetted?** The verb *wet* means "make wet": □ *Don't keep wetting your lips,* and "urinate in or on something": □ *Children often wet their beds when they are anxious.* The usual past tense or participle is *wet:* □ *The baby has wet another diaper.* When using the passive form with the verb *to be,* however, *wetted* is used. *The sheets have been wetted* is less ambiguous than *The sheets have been wet.*

wet or **whet?** These two spellings are sometimes confused. *Wet* means "cover with moisture": □ *to wet one's lips; whet* means "stimulate or sharpen": □ *whet someone's appetite.*

• A *whetstone* is a stone used for sharpening knives, etc.; a *wet stone* is simply a stone that is damp.

wetted see WET OR WETTED?

what A difficulty in the use of the pronoun *what* is whether it should be followed by a singular or plural verb. In general the rule is that, when *what* means "that which," it takes a singular verb, even if the complement is plural, and when it means "those which," it takes a plural verb: □ *What we need is a ladder.* □ *I mentioned what I thought were the most important points.*

• *What* cannot follow a noun or pronoun. Constructions such as: □ *the man what I was talking to* are wrong.

what or **which?** In a question form, the use of *what* or *which* affects the interpretation of the meaning. *Which* chooses from a limited range of alternatives; *what* is used in more general inquiries.

• Thus, □ *Which film are you going to see?* suggests that the speaker has several possible films in mind, whereas □ *What film are you going to see?* shows that the speaker is probably unaware of the choice of the various films.

whatever or **what ever?** If *ever* is used to intensify *what,* the expression is written as two words in formal writing: □ *What ever* ["What on earth"] *did he say next?* In less formal writing, one word is sometimes used, but many careful writers object to this usage. If *whatever* means "no matter what," it is written as one word: □ *I'll write whatever I like.* □ *Whatever the weather, he always wears a vest.* □ *There is no chance whatever of him winning.*

• A similar rule applies to the use of *how ever* and *however, when ever* and *whenever, where ever* and *wherever, which ever* and *whichever,* and *who ever* and *whoever:* □ *How ever did you find out?—However carefully I wash my hair, it always looks untidy.* □ *Where ever did you buy such a hat?—Wherever you travel, you'll find businesses that accept our credit card.*

whence *Whence* is a formal, rarely used word meaning "from where; from what place": □ *The monster returned to the swamp whence it had appeared.*

• *From whence* is more frequently used, as in: □ *The country from whence they came,* although the *from* is redundant, being contained in the meaning of *whence,* and many people consider *from whence* to be incorrect. *Whence* is now a word whose use tends to sound either old-fashioned, affected, or jocular, so it is probably better to avoid both *whence* and *from whence* altogether. See also **HENCE; THENCE.**

whenever or **when ever?** see **WHATEVER OR WHAT EVER?**

wherever or **where ever?** see **WHATEVER OR WHAT EVER?**

whet see **WET OR WHET?**

whether *Whether* can be used to introduce an indirect question: □ *He asked whether we were going.* Here it is synonymous with *if* but sounds rather more formal. *Whether* is also used to introduce alternatives or consider possibilities: □ *I wonder whether she'll come.* □ *I don't know whether it is correct.*

• In these cases, there is some confusion concerning the use of *whether or not,* as in: □ *He has not decided whether (or not) to stay.* Here, where the sense is "if he is staying," the *or not* can be considered redundant. It is only necessary when the sense is "regardless of whether or not" as in: □ *He has decided to stay, whether or not he can afford it.*

which see **THAT OR WHICH?; WHAT OR WHICH?**

whichever or **which ever?** see **WHATEVER OR WHAT EVER?**

while or **whilst?** As a conjunction, *while* means "during the time that; as long as," and is also used to mean "although; whereas": □ *I shall be doing his work while he's on vacation.* □ *Elizabeth votes Republican while her husband votes Democrat. Whilst* has the same meanings but is rarely used; it tends to sound formal and old-fashioned.

• Many people dislike *while* or *whilst* in the sense of "although; whereas," because either word can give rise to ambiguity. □ *While she was studying literature, she disliked poetry* could mean "during the time she was studying literature" or "although she was studying literature."

whiskey or **whisky?** The alcoholic drink distilled in the U.S.A. or Ireland is spelled *whiskey* or sometimes *whisky.* The alcohol drink distilled in Scotland is spelled *whisky,* which is the more frequent spelling in British English.

who The pronoun *who* is normally used in reference to human beings (*which* being used for nonhumans): □ *the man who runs the shop.* It is acceptable, however, to use *who* in referring to countries in certain informal contexts and to a group made up of people, especially when taking a plural verb: □ *Iraq, who started the war* □ *the band who plays the loudest.*

• *That* can be used to refer to human beings and things in *defining clauses* (see **THAT OR WHICH?**): □ *the man that* [or *who*] *runs the shop* □ *the band that* [or *who* or *which*] *plays the loudest* □ *the woman that* [or *who,* or the formally correct *whom*] *you just saw.* Care must be taken with the punctuation of phrases containing *who. The boys, who attend public schools, regularly play football* changes its meaning if the commas are omitted. Without the commas, *who* introduces a defining clause, suggesting specific boys: those that attend public school. With commas, the additional clause merely adds extra information about the boys.

who or **whom?** *Who* is used when it is the subject of a verb and *whom* when it is the object of a verb or preposition: □ *the boy* *who delivers the papers* □ *the woman whom you just saw* □ *the people to whom I was talking.* *Whom* is falling into disuse, especially in the interrogative form. □ *Whom did you give it to?* is formally correct, but most people would informally use *who.* As a relative pronoun, *whom* should still be used, when correct, in all but informal speech.

• Although many careful users feel that it is important to use *whom* when it is correct to do so, most would consider that the use of *who* for *whom* is far less of a mistake than the use of *whom* when *who* is correct, as in: □ *The children, whom she thought were dead, had been saved.* The temptation is to use *whom* because it is felt that this pronoun is the object of *she thought,* but it is not. *She thought* is a more or less independent part of the sentence; it could even be moved to another part of the sentence. It is an object of *she thought* that is needed, but a subject (*who*) of the phrase *were dead.*

whodunit This word, used in informal contexts to describe a detective story, may be spelled *whodunit* or, less frequently, *whodunnit.*

• It is, of course, an abbreviation of the grammatically incorrect *who done it?*

whoever or **who ever?** see WHATEVER OR WHAT EVER?

wholly This word, meaning "completely or entirely," is sometimes misspelled. Note the double *l* spelling. See SPELLING 4.

whom see WHO OR WHOM?

whoop This word, meaning "express delight," as in: □ *Sally whooped excitedly,* is sometimes mispronounced. The correct pronunciation is [woop] or [hwoop].

• Note, however, that *whooping* as in *whooping cough* is pronounced [*hooping*].

whose or **who's?** These spellings are sometimes confused. *Whose* means "of whom" or "of which": □ *the children, whose father had left them* □ *political parties whose ideas are radical* □ *Whose book is that?*

• *Who's* is a shortened form of *who is* or *who has:* □ *Who's coming to dinner tonight?*

will see SHALL OR WILL?

window *Window* has various well-established metaphorical uses. It can mean "something that allows people to see something they might otherwise not see": □ *The program is a window on the closed world of the monastery;* or "something in which things are displayed": □ *The exhibition is the annual window of domestic design.*

• A more recent use is "an interval during which conditions are suitable, or an opportunity exists," though care should be taken to avoid overworking this expression: □ *window of opportunity* □ *The calm weather gave them a window when they could take off.*

-wise or **-ways?** The suffix *-ways* combines with certain abstract nouns to form an adverb meaning "in (such) a way, direction, or manner": □ *sideways* □ *lengthways.* It has a more limited use than *-wise,* which can combine with various nouns to mean either "in the position or direction of": □ *clockwise* □ *lengthwise* or "in the manner of": □ *to walk crabwise.* The use of *-wise* to mean

W

"in respect of" in such expressions as: □ *moneywise* □ *weatherwise* □ *careerwise* □ *taxwise* □ *energywise* is becoming increasingly popular but disliked by many people.

with When a singular subject is linked to something else by *with*, it should take a singular verb: □ *The President with members of the Cabinet has been considering the problem.*

withhold This word, meaning "keep back," is sometimes misspelled. Note the double *h* in the spelling of this word, unlike the word *threshold.*

• The correct pronunciation [widh*hōld*] should make certain that the word is spelled correctly.

woman As a general term for an adult female human being, *woman* is more acceptable than *female, girl,* or *lady:* □ *The prize was won by a woman from Denver.*

• The noun *female* is best reserved for animals and plants. It may be applied to human beings when the question of age makes *woman* or *women* inappropriate: □ *He shares the house with five females: his wife and their four young daughters.* In other cases, it may be considered inelegant, contemptuous, or offensive. As an adjective, however, *female* is more acceptable than *woman* or *lady:* □ *There are two female doctors and one male doctor at the local clinic.* □ *Female drivers do not have more road accidents than male drivers.*

A *girl* is a female child or adolescent. The term is often used as a synonym for "woman" but is considered patronizing or disrespectful by some people in some contexts, especially when used by men.

The word *lady* has connotations of nobility, dignity, and good manners: □ *the Lady of the Lake.* □ *She may be wealthy, but she's no lady!* It is used in polite address, as in formal or official contexts: □ *This lady would like to speak to the manager.* □ *Ladies and gentlemen. . . .* It is sometimes regarded, however, as a term of condescension, especially in such phrases as *the cleaning lady,* which may be replaced by *the cleaning woman* or, more simply, *the cleaner.*

As a general rule, *female, girl,* and *lady* are best restricted to contexts in which *male, boy,* or *gentleman* would be used of the opposite sex. See also SEXISM.

wonder see WANDER OR WONDER?

wont This old-fashioned word is used to mean "inclined or accustomed": □ *They were wont to have coffee every morning* and in the expression *as is one's wont.* Its pronunciation is the same as that of the word *want* [wahnt].

woolly Note the spelling of this word: double *o* and double *l*. A single *l* is sometimes used.

worship The single final *p* is not doubled before an ending: □ *worshiped* □ *worshiper* □ *worshiping* □ *worshipful.* See also SPELLING 1.

worthwhile or **worth while?** The traditional rule is that this expression is written as two words after a pronoun or noun and verb and as one word in front of a noun. Increasingly, however, the tendency is to write this expression as one word in all contexts: □ *It is worthwhile spending a little more money.* □ *a project that is worthwhile—a worthwhile project.*

would see SHOULD OR WOULD?
wove, woven see WEAVED, WOVE, OR WOVEN?
wrack see RACK OR WRACK?
wrapped see RAPT OR WRAPPED?

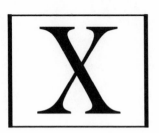

Xerox This word should be spelled *Xerox* if it is referring to the trademarked noun for a type of photographic copier or process. The verb, meaning "copy on a Xerox machine," is spelled with a lowercase *x*. See also **TRADEMARKS**.

• *Xerox* is pronounced [*zeer*roks].

Xmas *Xmas*, an abbreviation for *Christmas*, is used particularly in commercial contexts and newspaper headlines. The *X* derives from the Greek *chi*, the initial letter of *Christos*, the Greek for *Christ*.

• Some people, particularly Christians, find the word offensive, and it is generally considered suitable only for informal writing. When reading the word aloud, one should pronounce it as *Christmas*, and only say [*eskmas*] when this spelling is emphasized.

X-ray or **x-ray?** The noun is nearly always written with a capital *X*; as a verb, this expression is written with a capital letter or sometimes a lowercase letter: □ *He had an X-ray/He was X-rayed* [or *x-rayed*] *after the accident.* Rarely *X ray* or *x ray* is used, without a hyphen.

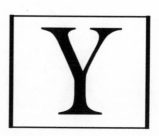

Y

yes and **no** In discussing affirmative or negative expressions, one has the option of writing, for example, either: □ *She said yes to the offer* or: *She said, "Yes," to the offer.* The latter carries more of an implication that the person actually used the word *yes* or *no.*
• In phrases that have no suggestion of someone actually using the word, it is better not to have *yes* or *no* in quotation marks: □ *He says yes to life.* □ *She won't take no for an answer.*
  Phrases such as: □ *He said (that), yes, he agreed* are acceptable. The *yes* is dispensable but adds emphasis.

yet *Yet* has various meanings: "up till now; so far": □ *It has not yet been decided,* "even": □ *a yet greater problem,* "in addition": □ *yet more presents,* "at some future time": □ *We'll do it yet,* and "nevertheless": □ *slow, yet sure.*
• In several of its meanings, *yet* is more or less interchangeable with *still,* but in the sense of "as before": □ *It is yet raining, yet* is now archaic, and *still* is required.
  When the meaning is "so far," *yet* should not be used with the emphatic past tense, except in informal English: □ *Did she go yet?*

yogurt The most frequent spelling of this word is *yogurt.* Acceptable alternatives are *yoghurt* and the less frequent *yoghourt.* The usual pronunciation is [yōgĕrt], [yogŭt] in British English.

yoke or **yolk?** These words are sometimes confused. *Yoke* means "connecting bar or bond": □ *yoked oxen* □ *under the yoke of slavery.* A *yolk* is the yellow part of an egg: □ *Would you like your yolk hard?*

you *You* is often used to mean "people in general" in place of the slightly more formal *one:* □ *You certainly get a good meal at that restaurant.* □ *You hold a hammer like this.* □ *They* [i.e., "The authorities"] *fine you on the spot if you don't have a license.* □ *It's really embarrassing when you forget someone's name.* □ *Dentists say you should clean your teeth at least twice a day.* Although *one* is less frequently used than *you,* it is sometimes better to use *one* to avoid possible confusion as to whether the speaker is talking personally or generally. It is also important to be consistent in the use of either *you* or *one* throughout a single piece of writing.
• The personal pronoun *you* is either singular or plural. Attempts to indicate that more than one person is being addressed: *you all, you lot, you guys,* etc., are informal.
  See also **-ING FORMS**.

you know The expression *you know* is used by speakers who are not sure about what they have just said or who are not sure what to say next: □ *I just wondered . . . you know . . . if you might like to* *come with me to the theater.* The expression is frequently used with this function but is very widely disliked.

your or **you're?** These two words may be confused. *Your* means "belonging to you": □ *your house* □ *your rights. You're* is an abbreviation of *you are:* □ *Hurry up, or you're going to be late!*
• Note also the spelling of *yours:* □ *That's mine, not yours;* the spelling with an apostrophe, *your's,* is wrong.

yuppie *Yuppie,* sometimes spelled *yuppy* stands for "young urban professional" and is used to designate any of the well-educated young adults of the 1980's, living in cities, working in well-paid occupations, and enjoying a fashionable way of life.
• Similar, though less popular, terms are *yumpie,* "young upwardly mobile professional," and *dink,* "double income, no kids." See also **UPWARDLY MOBILE**.

zoology This word, referring to the biological study of animals, has two pronunciations. The more frequent pronunciation is [zoo*ol*-ŏjee], though careful users prefer [zōo*l*ŏjee].